RICH . . . AND FAMOUS

ALAN
Alan Alda . . . portrayed wisecracking Hawkeye in "M*A*S*H"

JEAN-CLAUDE
Jean-Claude Van Damme . . . action hero in films "Bloodsport" and "Kickboxer"

WHITNEY
Whitney Houston . . . chart-topping pop singer turned actress in "Bodyguard," niece of Dionne Warwick

TORI
Tori Spelling . . . actress in TV's "Beverly Hills 90210," daughter of producer Aaron Spelling

The RICH & FAMOUS BABY NAME BOOK

ROBERT DAVENPORT

ST. MARTIN'S PAPERBACKS

THE RICH AND FAMOUS BABY NAME BOOK

Copyright © 1994 by Robert Davenport.

Cover photographs by Vincent Eckersley.

ISBN: 0-312-95407-7

Printed in the United States of America

St. Martin's Paperbacks edition/ December 1994

10 9 8 7 6 5 4 3 2 1

ACKNOWLEDGEMENTS

I would like to thank Roger Cooper, Jennifer Weis, and Todd Keithley of St. Martin's Paperbacks for their faith in this book and their hard work in bringing it to a successful conclusion.

A big thanks is also due my agent, Jim Pinkston, of the Sherry Robb Literary Agency, and agency head Sherry Robb for their support.

In addition, I would like to acknowledge the photography of Vincent Eckersley of Los Angeles on the cover of the book. I learned that photographing babies isn't easy!

Lastly, I would like to acknowledge that I was inspired to write this book after I prepared a list of baby names for my brother, Michael John Davenport, only to discover that he picked the name out of a baby name book!

If anyone believes that a famous person should be included in the next edition of *The Rich & Famous Baby Name Book,* they should send the name of that person, along with a one-line biography, to:

> Robert R. Davenport
> *The Rich & Famous Baby Name Book*
> Post Office Box 1989
> Beverly Hills CA 90213–1989

If the famous person is used in the next edition, and they are the first to submit the name, they will receive a free *Rich & Famous Baby Name Book* t-shirt.

THE RICH & FAMOUS
BABY NAME BOOK

BOYS' NAMES

AARON ◆Aaron Burr — US Vice President who shot Alexander Hamilton in a duel ◆Aaron Neville — country and pop singer, hits include "Tell It Like It is" ◆ Aaron Spelling — producer of "Charlie's Angels," "Dynasty," "Hotel," and "The Love Boat"

ABBIE ◆Abbie Hoffman — 1960's radical who went on the run from the FBI

ABBOTT ◆Abbott Tayer — artist who specialized in landscapes, portraits, and figure paintings ◆ James Abbott McNeill Whistler — artist best known for painting "Whistler's Mother"

ABBY ◆Abby Mann — Oscar nominee for writing "Judgment at Nuremberg"

ABDUL ◆Abdul Fakir — member of The Four Tops, hits include "Reach Out I'll Be There"

ABDULLAH ◆Abdullah Hussein — pro-British former King of Jordan

ABE ◆Abe Burrows — Pulitzer Prize winner for "How to Succeed in Business Without Really Trying" ◆ Abe Saperstein — founder of the Harlem Globetrotters ◆ Abe Vigoda — actor who played Detective Fish on "Barney Miller" and its spinoff "Fish"

ABEL ◆Abel Tasman — explorer who discovered Tasmania and named it after himself

ABNER ◆Abner Doubleday — inventor of baseball at Doubleday Field in Cooperstown, New York

ABRAHAM ◆Abraham Lincoln — US President who freed the slaves during the Civil War ◆Abraham Minsky — burlesque house owner, basis for film "The Night They Raided Minsky's"

ABRAM ◆Abram Chasins — pianist and composer ◆ James Abram Garfield — twentieth President of the United States, one of four assassinated

ABU ◆Abu Bakr — successor to Mohammed who helped make Islam a world religion ◆ Abu Salma — poet voice of exiled Palestinians who wrote "The Homeless"

ACE ◆Ace Frehley — member of the outrageous rock group Kiss which used extensive makeup

ADAM ◆Adam — in the Bible, the first man created by God ◆ Adam Ant — leader of Adam Ant and the Ants, hits include "Goody Two Shoes" ◆Adam Baldwin — actor whose films include "My Bodyguard" and "D.C. Cab" ◆ Adam West — portrayed the Caped Crusader on the television series "Batman"

ADARYLL ◆Toriano Adaryll Jackson — nickname "Tito," with The Jackson Five, number one single "ABC"

ADDISON ◆Addison Powell — actor whose roles included US Admiral Chester Nimitz in "MacArthur"

ADI ◆Adi Berber — portrayed Malluch in Charlton Heston's biblical epic "Ben-Hur"

ADLAI ◆Adlai Stevenson — presidential candidate who lost twice to Eisenhower

ADOLFO ◆Adolfo — Coty winning fashion designer who creates custom and ready-to-wear clothes ◆ Adolfo Sardina — fashion designer who founded the firm of Adolfo

ADOLPH ◆Adolph Caesar — nominated for an Oscar for "A Soldier's Story" ◆ Adolph Coors — German brewer whose company makes Coors Beer

ADOLPHE ◆Adolphe Menjou — well-dressed character actor, "Paths of Glory," "A Star is Born"

ADOLPHUS ◆Adolphus Busch — founder of Anheuser-Busch

ADRIAN ◆Adrian — Hollywood designer who clothed stars like Garbo and Harlow ◆ Adrian Cronauer — disc-jockey played to perfection by Robin Williams in "Good Morning, Vietnam" ◆ Adrian Zmed — star of "Grease II," later in TV series "T. J. Hooker"

AFRICA ◆Africa Bambaataa Aasim — godfather of hip-hop who helped create rap

AGOSTINO ◆Agostino Borgato — actor who played the medicine man in Dolores Del Rio's "Bird of Paradise"

AHMAD ◆Ahmad Jamal — jazz pianist who was in the Top 10 with "But Not for Me" for 108 weeks ◆Ahmad Rashad — host of the TV sports magazine "Insport," husband of "Cosby's" Phylicia Rashad

AHMED ◆Salman Ahmed Rushdie — author of "The Satanic Verses," sentenced to death by the Ayatollah Khomeini

AHMET ◆Ahmet Ertegun — co-founder of Atlantic Records ◆ Ahmet Emuukha Rodan Zappa — son of rock musician Frank Zappa

AIDAN ◆Aidan Quinn — actor whose roles included the title role in the 1989 film "Crusoe"

AIDEN ◆Aiden McNulty — actor whose roles included Jamie Frame on the soap "Another World"

AKEEM ◆Akeem Abdul Olajuwon — seven-foot forward for the Houston Rockets

AKIRA ◆Akira Kurosawa — Japanese director of "The Seven Samurai," model for "The Magnificent Seven"

AL ◆Al Molinaro — actor who played Murray the Cop on TV's "The Odd Couple," Al on "Happy Days" ◆ Al Pacino — actor in "The Godfather," "Serpico," and Oscar winner for "Scent of a Woman" ◆Weird Al Yankovic — satirizes rock hits, wrote "Like a Surgeon" and "I'm Fat"

ALAIN ◆Alain Delon — handsome international French film actor, star of "The Concorde — Airport '79" ◆ Alain Locke — first African-American Rhodes scholar

ALAN ◆Alan Alda — portrayed wisecracking Hawkeye Pierce in TV's long running hit "M*A*S*H" ◆ Alan Hale — character actor, sidekick of Errol Flynn in many of his adventures ◆ Alan Hale, Jr. — actor who played the Skipper on TV's long running sitcom "Gilligan's Island" ◆Alan King — comedian, films include "Author, Author!" ◆ Alan Ladd — pint-sized star of movies, "Shane," "This Gun for Hire," and many, many others ◆ Alan Shepard — first American astronaut to travel in space

ALASTAIR ◆Alastair Sim — actor whose roles included Scrooge in Dickens' "A Christmas Carol"

ALBAN ◆Alban Berg — composer who wrote "Wozzeck"

ALBEN ◆Alben Barkley — Vice President of the United States under Harry Truman

ALBERT ◆Albert Brooks — comic actor whose films include "Broadcast News" and "Lost in America" ◆Albert Einstein — he discovered that everything is relative ◆ Albert Finney — his films include "Under the Volcano," "Annie" ◆ Albert Schweitzer —

French medical missionary who treated leprosy in French Equatorial Africa

ALBERTO ◆Alberto Anastasia — Mafia boss, biopic "My Brother Anastasia" ◆ Alberto Morin — actor whose roles included Armando Sidoni on TV's "Dallas"

ALBION ◆John Albion Andrew — organized the first African-American regiment in the Civil War, biopic "Glory" ◆ Albion Small — first US professor of sociology ◆ Albion Tourgee — author of the novel "Bricks Without Straw"

ALBRECHT ◆Albrecht Altdorfer — fifteenth-century German artist and architect ◆ Albrecht Durer — leading German Renaissance artist

ALDEN ◆Neil Alden Armstrong — first astronaut to walk on the moon ◆ Alden McWilliams — creator of comic strips "Twin Earths" and "Dateline: Danger!"

ALDO ◆Aldo Cipullo — designer for Cartier whose designs are celebrity status symbols ◆ Aldo Gucci — maker of "Gucci" high quality luggage ◆ Aldo Maccione — actor whose roles included the monster in "Frankenstein — Italian Style" ◆ Aldo Ray — actor whose roles included Sergeant Muldoon in John Wayne's "The Green Berets"

ALDOUS ◆Aldous Huxley — author of "Brave New World"

ALEC ◆Alec Baldwin — heartthrob on TV's "Knots Landing," later did "Beetlejuice," "The Marrying Man" ◆ Alec Guinness — actor who played the ancient Jedi warrior in the classic film "Star Wars"

ALEISTER ◆Aleister Crowley — magician and author of "Diary of a Drug Fiend"

ALEJANDRO ◆Alejandro Acuna — member of the group Weather Report, instrumental hits include "Birdland" ◆ Alejandro Rey — portrayed Luis Rueda on TV's "Dallas," Carlos Ramirez on "The Flying Nun"

ALEKSANDR ◆Aleksandr Blok — Russian symbolist who wrote "The Twelve" ◆ Aleksandr Solzhenitsyn — Nobel Prize-winning author who wrote "The Gułag Archipelago"

ALESSANDRO ◆Alessandro Volta — physicist after whom the electrical measurement the "volt" is named

ALEX ◆Alex Haley — author of the best selling "Roots," his own genealogy, and the novel "Queenie" ◆ Alex Karras — former pro football player, later played the father on TV's "Webster" ◆ Alex Trebec — game show host of "Jeopardy" and "Classic Concentration"

ALEXANDER ◆Alexander Hamilton — first US secretary of the treasury in the 1700's ◆ Alexander Nevsky — legendary Russian prince, Sergei Eisenstein biopic "Alexander Nevsky" ◆Alexander the Great — 4th century king who conquered the largest empire of its time

ALEXANDRE ◆Alexandre — hairstylist who developed the short cut called the "artichoke" ◆ Alexandre Dumas — creator of the swashbuckling "Three Musketeers" and "The Count of Monte Cristo" ◆Alexandre Eiffel — designer of the Eiffel Tower in Paris

ALEXEY ◆Alexey Brodovitch — artist and designer, art director for "Harper's Bazaar" ◆ Alexey Tolstoy — author of "Peter the Great"

ALEXIS ◆Alexis Carrel — inventor of the artificial heart ◆Alexis de Tocqueville — author so impressed with the US he wrote "Democracy in America"

ALF ◆Alf Landon — Republican presidential candidate who lost to FDR during the Depression

ALFIE ◆Alfie Bass — character comedian whose works include "Help!" ◆Alfie Wise — actor whose roles included Sidney Pacelli on the medical series "Trauma Center"

ALFONSO ◆Alfonso Bedoya — smiling Mexican bandit in "The Treasure of the Sierra Madre" ◆ Alfonso Ribeiro — started in Michael Jackson commercial, regular on "Fresh Prince of Bel Air"

ALFRED ◆Alfred Hitchcock — director of "Psycho," "North by Northwest," "Rear Window," fond of birds ◆ Alfred, Lord Tennyson — poet laureate of England, author of "The Charge of the Light Brigade"

ALFREDO ◆Alfredo Pacino — nickname Al, starred in "The Godfather," Oscar for "Scent of a Woman"

ALGERNON ◆Algernon Blackwood — English supernatural author ◆ Algernon Sidney — British politician, opposed Cromwell, wrote "God helps those who help themselves"

ALGIS ◆Algis Budrys — authored "To Kill a Clown," which became an Alan Alda film about hunting humans for sport

ALI ◆ Ali Pasha — "The Lion of Yannina," Turkish military governor of Yannina in 1787 ◆ Ali Shaheed Muhammed — member of the rap group A Tribe Called Quest

ALISON ◆ William Alison Anders — astronaut on the first lunar flight of Apollo 8

ALISTAIR ◆ Alistair MacLean — author of war novels, "The Guns of Navarone" was filmed with Gregory Peck ◆ Alistair Mackenzie — actor whose roles included Dickens' boy hero in "David Copperfield"

ALIX ◆ Alix Fres — fashion designer known for Grecian-styled, draped jersey gowns

ALLAN ◆ Allan Clarke — founded The Hollies with Graham Nash ◆ Allan Pinkerton — founder of Pinkerton's Detective Agency, and the US Secret Service ◆ Allan Sherman — known for comedy song "Hello, Muddah, Hello, Faddah"

ALLARD ◆ Allard Lowenstein — former chairman of Americans for Democratic Action

ALLELON ◆ Allelon Ruggiero — actor in Robin Williams film "The Dead Poets Society"

ALLEN ◆ John Allen Astin — actor whose roles included Gomez Addams on TV's "The Addams Family" ◆ Allen Funt — producer, creator, and host of TV's "Candid Camera" ◆ Allen Stewart Konigsberg — real name of actor/comedian/director Woody Allen ◆ Allen Ludden — host of TV's "Password," husband of actress Betty White

ALLYN ◆ Allyn Jones — character comedian whose crumpled features admirably portray bewilderment ◆ Allyn Joslyn — actor whose roles included Jonathan on the sitcom "The Ray Bolger Show"

ALMANZO ◆ Almanzo Wilder — husband of Laura Ingalls of "Little House on the Prairie"

ALMROTH ◆ Almroth Wright — founder of modern immunology, bioplay is Shaw's "The Doctor's Dilemma"

ALOIS ◆ Arnold Alois Schwarzenegger — actor whose films include "The Terminator," "Twins" and "The Last Action Hero"

ALOISE ◆ Aloise — Swiss artist, biopic "Aloise"

ALONZO ◆Alonzo Brown — actor who played Miller in the Oscar-winning "One Flew Over the Cuckoo's Nest" ◆ Alonzo Chaney — real name of actor Lon Chaney

ALOYS ◆Aloys Senefelder — inventor of lithography

ALOYSIUS ◆Alfred Aloysius Horn — adventurer who wrote the best seller "Trader Horn" ◆ Joseph Aloysius Wambaugh — policeman turned author, filmed novels "The Blue Knight" and "The Choir Boys"

ALPHEUS ◆Alpheus Hyatt — founder of the Marine Biological Laboratory at Woods Hole ◆Alpheus Hyatt Verrill — inventor of the autochrome natural color photo process

ALPHONSE ◆Alphonse Ethier — actor whose roles included Cragg in Barbara Stanwyck's "Baby Face"

ALPHONSO ◆Alphonso Johnson — member of the rock group Weather Report, instrumental hits include "Birdland"

ALTON ◆Alton Delmore — one of country western's Brown's Ferry Four ◆Alton Ellis — rock singer, hits include "Willow Tree"

ALVA ◆Thomas Alva Edison — invented just about everything

ALVAH ◆Alvah Bessie — screenwriter, one of the Hollywood Ten who was blacklisted ◆ Alvah Roebuck — watchmaker who partnered with Richard W. Sears to form Sears Roebuck

ALVAN ◆Alvan Adams — 1976 NBA Rookie of the Year ◆Alvan Ashby — hymn singer on the music series "The Lawrence Welk Show"

ALVAR ◆Alvar Aalto — architect who redesigned cities damaged during World War II

ALVAREZ ◆Pedro Alvarez Cabral — Portuguese explorer who discovered Brazil

ALVIN ◆Alvin Karpis — member of the Ma Barker gang during the Depression ◆Alvin "Junior" Samples — regular on the long-running hayseed variety show "Hee Haw" ◆ Alvin C. York — biggest hero of World War I, Gary Cooper's Oscar-winning biopic "Sergeant York"

ALVINO ◆Alvino Rey — pioneer in developing the electric guitar, featured on TV's "The King Family"

ALVIS ◆Alvis "Buck" Owens — host of the popular hayseed variety show "Hee Haw"

7

ALVY ◆Alvy Moore — played Hank Kimball on the successful hayseed comedy series "Green Acres"

ALWIN ◆Alwin Neuss — portrayed Sherlock Holmes in the silent "The Hound of the Baskervilles"

ALY ◆Prince Aly Khan — wealthy ruler who married actress Rita Hayworth

ALYN ◆Alyn F. Warren — played Stephen Douglas in the Walter Huston version of "Abraham Lincoln"

AMADEUS ◆Wolfgang Amadeus Mozart — Austrian composer of over 600 works, including "The Marriage of Figaro"

AMASA ◆Amasa Leland Stanford — railroad baron who founded Stanford University in memory of his son

AMBROSE ◆Ambrose Burnside — Union army general, "sideburns" were named for him ◆Ambrose Bierce — writer who disappeared in Mexico, biopic is "The Old Gringo" with Gregory Peck

AMEDEO ◆Luigi Amedeo Abruzzi — Italian prince who explored the North Pole and climbed the Himalayas ◆ Amedeo Nazzari — Italian leading man in films

AMERIGO ◆Amerigo Bevilacqua — actor who played Herod the Great in "The Gospel According to St. Matthew" ◆ Amerigo Vespucci — navigator for whom America was named

AMID ◆Amid Taftazani — played Karaga Pasha in the classic story of redemption, "The Four Feathers"

AMIN ◆Kemal Amin Kasem — real name of radio personality Casey Kasem

AMIR ◆Amir Williams — portrayed J. T. Rallen on TV's "A Different World"

AMORY ◆Amory Gill — nickname "Slats," coach for Oregon State, career record 599–392, Hall of Fame

AMOS ◆Famous Amos — creator of Famous Amos cookies

AMRISH ◆Amrish Puri — played Mola Ram in Harrison Ford's "Indiana Jones and the Temple of Doom"

AN ◆An Wang — pioneer in computer research, founder of Boston-based Wang Labs

ANATOL ◆Anatol Winogradoff — star of the Harlem Globetrotters' biopic "Go, Man, Go!"

ANATOLE ◆Anatole De Brunwald — British writer-producer, produced "The Yellow Rolls-Royce" ◆Anatole Litvak — director whose films include "The Snake Pit"

ANCEL ◆Ancel Keys — nutrition expert who developed World War II K-rations

ANDERS ◆Anders Angstrom — Swedish astronomer who studied light, especially spectrum analysis ◆ Anders Celsius — invented the centigrade temperature scale, hence, "Celsius"

ANDRAE ◆Andrae Crouch — gospel artist with six Grammys

ANDRE ◆Andre Agassi — 1990's teen heartthrob and tennis star ◆ Andre Courreges — French fashion designer who introduced the miniskirt ◆ Andre Michelin — first to make rubber tires for cars, founder Michelin Tires ◆Andre Previn — composer with two Oscars and seven Grammys, married Mia Farrow

ANDREA ◆Andrea — son of Monaco's Princess Caroline ◆ Andrea Doria — Italian hero after whom the luxury liner that sank in 1956 was named

ANDREI ◆Andrei Amalrik — Russian author and human rights advocate who was sent to a labor camp ◆ Andrei Popov — actor whose roles included the evil Iago in the film version of "Othello"

ANDRES ◆Andres Serrano — artist involved in the debate on federal funding for the arts

ANDREW ◆Prince Andrew — "Randy Andy," Duke of York and Prince of England ◆ Andrew Carnegie — steel magnate and founder of the Carnegie Institute ◆Andrew Dice Clay — stand-up comedian who bashes women, gays and practically everyone in his act

ANDY ◆Andy Garcia — young Latino hunk actor in "The Untouchables" and "Hero" ◆ Andy Gibb — solo singing act whose brothers were The Bee Gees, died of a drug overdose ◆ Andy Griffith — slow-talking Sheriff Taylor on TV's "The Andy Griffith Show," later starred on "Matlock" ◆ Andy Kaufman — comedy actor, played Latka Gravas on the classic sitcom "Taxi" ◆ Andy Rooney — comedy relief on TV's investigative news show "60 Minutes"

ANGEL ◆Miguel Angel Asturias — Guatemalan diplomat who won the Nobel Prize in literature ◆ Angel Cordero — first jockey to win over ten million dollars in one year

ANGELO ◆Angelo Siciliano — real name of Charles Atlas, who developed dynamic tension bodybuilding

ANGUS ◆Angus Young — member of Australian heavy metal band AC/DC, album "For Those About to Rock" ◆ Alan Angus Young — starred in the TV series "Mr. Ed"

ANHEUSER ◆August Anheuser Busch — brewer and president of the St. Louis Cardinals baseball team

ANNUNZIO ◆Annunzio Mantovani — conductor known for the "Mantovani sound," hits include "Donkey Serenade"

ANSEL ◆Ansel Adams — photographer of the scenic splendor of the western United States

ANSELM ◆Anselm — Italian who became Archbishop of Canterbury in 1093, founder of scholasticism ◆ Paul Johann Anselm Feuerbach — painter known for "Judgment of Paris"

ANSELME ◆Anselme Payen — chemist who discovered cellulose

ANSON ◆Egbert Anson Van Alstyne — composer of over 700 songs, including "In the Shade of the Old Apple Tree" ◆ Anson Williams — actor who played the dopey character Potsie on TV's long-running "Happy Days"

ANTHONY ◆Anthony Hopkins — Oscar winner as psycho killer Hannibal Lecter in "The Silence of the Lambs" ◆ Anthony Newley — Brtish actor, composer, singer, and comedian, films include "Doctor Dolittle" ◆ Anthony Perkins — cross-dressing killer Norman Bates in Alfred Hitchcock's "Psycho" ◆ Anthony Quinn — he played every ethnic role in Hollywood, from Indian to Arab to Zorba the Greek

ANTOINE ◆Antoine Cadillac — French explorer who discovered Detroit, they returned the favor with the car ◆Antoine Domino — real name of singer "Fats" Domino, hits include "Blueberry Hill"

ANTOINE-JOSEPH ◆Antoine-Joseph Sax — inventor of the saxophone, which he named after himself

ANTON ◆Anton Chekhov — Russian dramatist whose works include "Three Sisters" ◆Anton Furst — production designer who won an Oscar for "Batman"

ANTONE ◆Antone Tavares — member of the group Tavares, debut hit single "Check It Out"

ANTONIO ◆Antonio Moreno — played Carl Maia in the classic monster movie "Creature From the Black Lagoon" ◆ Antonio

Salieri — composer who envied Mozart, depicted in the Oscar-winning "Amadeus" ◆ Antonio Stradivari — world's most famous violin maker

ANTONY ◆ Antony of Padua — thirteenth century saint who is invoked as the finder of lost articles

ANTRIM ◆ Antrim Short — actor whose roles included Tommy in Marion Davies' "Beauty's Worth"

ANWAR ◆ Anwar Sadat — Nobel Peace Prize winner for treaty with Israel reached at Camp David

APSLEY ◆ Apsley Garrard — polar explorer who died trying, biopic "Scott of the Antarctic"

ARAMIS ◆ Aramis (c) — most elegant of Alexandre Dumas' Three Musketeers

ARATA ◆ Arata Isozaki — architect of Team Disney building on Disney lot, which features mouse-ear shapes

ARCHER ◆ Archer Martin — Nobel Prize winner for the invention of partition chromatography

ARCHIBALD ◆ Archibald Cox — Watergate Special Prosecutor during the Nixon scandal ◆ Archibald Leach — real name of actor Cary Grant ◆ Archibald MacLeish — three-time Pulitzer Prize-winning writer and uncle of actor Bruce Dern

ARCHIE ◆ Archie (c) — comic book hero torn between Betty and Veronica ◆ Archie Bell — with Archie Bell and the Drells, number one gold record debut "Tighten Up" ◆ Archie Campbell — country western comedian, hits include "Trouble in the Amen Corner"

ARD ◆ Ard Schenk — three–time Olympic gold medal winner in speed skating

ARGUS ◆ Argus Hamilton — regular on the comedy variety series "The Richard Pryor Show"

ARI ◆ Ari Zeltner — actor whose roles included Rich Wabach on the sitcom "Joe's World"

ARIEL ◆ Ariel Bender — English hard rock guitarist

ARIK ◆ Arik Lavi — played the leader of the rescue party in "Entebbe: Operation Thunderbolt"

ARISTOTLE ◆ Aristotle — ancient Greek philosopher who created logic, the science of reasoning ◆ Aristotle Onassis —

billionaire Greek shipping tycoon, second husband of First Lady Jackie Kennedy ◆ Aristotle Savalas — real name of "who loves you, baby" actor Telly Savalas

ARLEIGH ◆Arleigh Burke — chief of staff, Atlantic fleet at the end of World War II, the CNO ◆ Arleigh Scott — former governor-general of Barbados

ARLEN ◆Arlen Snyder — actor who played Dr. Charles Sternhauser on the medical series "Trauma Center" ◆ Arlen Specter — senator from Pennsylvania

ARLINGTON ◆Spangler Arlington Brugh — real name of actor Robert Taylor ◆James Arlington Wright — poet, writings include "Shall We Gather at the River?"

ARLISS ◆Arliss Howard — actor who played Cowboy in Matthew Modine's Vietnam tribute "Full Metal Jacket"

ARLO ◆Arlo Guthrie — sixties folk singer best known for "Alice's Restaurant"

ARMAND ◆Armand Assante — actor who played the boyfriend of Goldie Hawn in the film "Private Benjamin" ◆ Armand Hammer — one of the world's most powerful men ◆ Cardinal Armand Richelieu — chief minister to Louis XIII, played as the villain in the "Three Musketeers"

ARMANDO ◆Armando Pereza — member of the rock group Santana, hits include "Evil Ways" and "Hold On"

ARMSTRONG ◆George Armstrong Custer — general who made his last stand at the Little Bighorn ◆Lindley Armstrong Jones — real name of satirical bandleader Spike Jones

ARMY ◆Army Archerd — columnist with entertainment trade rag "Daily Variety"

ARNAUD ◆Arnaud Cazenave — well known restaurant owner in New Orleans

ARNE ◆Arne Carlson — elected Republican governor of New Mexico in 1991 ◆Arne Ross — child of former Supreme and solo singing artist Diana Ross

ARNELL ◆Arnell Carmichael — member of Raydio, debut gold record hit "Jack and Jill"

ARNIE ◆Arnie Satin — member of The Dovells, debut gold record "The Bristol Stomp"

ARNO ◆Arno Penzias — physicist who received the Nobel Prize for the "big bang" theory of creation

ARNOLD ◆Arnold Palmer — golfer who has won the Masters, the US Open, and the British Open ◆ Arnold Schwarzenegger — Austrian bodybuilder dubbed "Conan the Republican" by President Bush

ARNON ◆Arnon Milchan — producer of the very eccentric and bizarre film "Brazil"

ARON ◆Elvis Aron Presley — King of Rock and Roll

ARSENIO ◆Arsenio Hall — talk show host ◆ sidekick to Eddie Murphy in the film "Coming to America"

ART ◆Art Buchwald — syndicated comedy columnist, author of "The Buchwald Stops Here" ◆Art Carney — actor who played Ed Norton in Jackie Gleason's TV series "The Honeymooners" ◆Art Garfunkel — of "Simon and Garfunkel," hits include "Mrs. Robinson," "Scarborough Fair" ◆ Art Linkletter — notorious for saying "Kids say the darnedest things" on his TV show

ARTE ◆Arte Johnson — comic, line as German soldier was "very interesting" on TV's "Laugh-In"

ARTEMUS ◆Artemus Ward — moral lecturer in nineteenth century, humorous comments influenced Mark Twain

ARTHUR ◆Arthur Fiedler — conductor of The Boston Pops Orchestra, he made it a national institution ◆ Arthur Murray — dance teacher, founder of the Arthur Murray Studios ◆ Arthur Treacher — film butler, sidekick to Merv, then founder of Arthur Treacher's Fish and Chips

ARTIE ◆Artie Shaw — clarinetist, prominent swing bandleader, hits include "Begin the Beguine"

ARTIS ◆Artis Gilmore — all time American Basketball Association leader in field goal percentage

ARTUR ◆Artur Balsam — pianist who recorded all of Mozart and Haydn ◆ Artur Bodanzky — former conductor of the NYC Metropolitan Opera ◆ Artur Schnabel — pianist who is an interpreter of Beethoven and Bach

ARTURO ◆Arturo Barea — Spanish author who wrote "Forging of a Rebel" ◆ Arturo de Cordova — actor whose roles included the great lover in "The Adventures of Casanova"

ARYE ◆Arye Gross — actor whose roles included Buddy in Patrick Dempsey's "Coupe de Ville"

ASA ◆Asa Candler — bought the Coca-Cola formula in 1887, the rest is history

ASHER ◆Asher Durand — co-founder of the Hudson River school of landscape painting with Thomas Cole

ASHLEY ◆Ashley Hamilton — acting heartthrob, son of George Hamilton and Alana Hamilton Stewart ◆ Ashley Wilkes (c) — Scarlett's true love played by Leslie Howard in "Gone With the Wind"

ASSAF ◆Assaf Dayan — actor son of Israeli leader Moshe Dayan

ATHOL ◆Athol Fleming — played the gallant English adventurer Bulldog Drummond in "Bulldog Jack"

ATHOLE ◆Athole Stewart — actor whose roles included Sherlock Holmes' Dr. Watson in "The Speckled Band"

ATHOS ◆Athos (c) — most introspective of Dumas' Three Musketeers

ATLEE ◆W. Atlee Burpee — started the world's largest mail-order seed house

ATTILA ◆Attila Jozef — author whose poems include "Medvetanc"

AUBREY ◆Aubrey Beardsley — English illustrator known for macabre black and white illustrations ◆ Reginald Aubrey Fessenden — inventor who made the first radio broadcast ◆ C. Aubrey Smith — actor who played Wellington, the victor of Waterloo in "The Iron Duke"

AUDIE ◆Audie Murphy — most decorated hero of World War II, starred in own biopic "To Hell and Back"

AUGIE ◆Augie Rios — hit the charts with the song "Donde Esta Santa Claus?"

AUGUST ◆Svante August Arrhenius — Nobel Prize winner who founded modern physical chemistry ◆ August Duesenberg — builder of the Duesenberg automobile ◆Carl August Sandburg — three-time Pulitzer Prize winner in poetry

AUGUSTE ◆Auguste Bartholdi — sculptor who designed the Statue of Liberty ◆ Auguste Renoir — impressionist painter ◆ Auguste Rodin — sculptor most famous for "The Thinker" seen on TV's "Dobie Gillis"

AUGUSTIN◆Augustin Anievas — musician ◆ James Leroy Augustin Jagger — son of singer Mick Jagger and Jerry Hall

AUGUSTINE◆Saint Augustine — canonized philosopher whose writings laid foundations for Protestantism ◆ Thomas Augustine Arne — composed "Rule Britannia" in 1740

AUGUSTUS◆Augustus Juilliard — founded the Juilliard School of Music ◆ John Augustus Sutter — discovery of gold at his mill started the California Gold Rush ◆ Augustus Toplady — clergyman who wrote the hymn "Rock of Ages"

AUREL◆Aurel Joliat — Hall of Fame hockey player, left wing with Montreal

AURIC◆Auric Goldfinger (c) — gold-loving criminal out to rob Fort Knox in the James Bond film

AUSTEN◆Austen Layard — archeologist who uncovered the remains of ancient cities in Mesopotamia

AUSTIN◆Austin Trevor — portrayed Agatha Christie's famous detective Hercule Poirot in three films ◆ Austin Willis — actor whose roles included Simmons in the James Bond adventure "Goldfinger"

AUTREY◆Autrey DeWalt, Jr. — alias of Junior Walker of Junior Walker and the All Stars, debut hit "Shotgun"

AVERILL◆Averill Liebow — physician known for research on the pathology of the lung

AVERY◆Avery Schreiber — comedian, starred with Jack Burns in "The Burns and Schreiber Comedy Hour"

AVON◆Avon Long — danced at the Cotton Club, appeared in "Porgy and Bess"

AXEL◆Axel Springer — creator of Europe's largest newspaper chain

AXL◆Axl Rose — bad boy of hard rock, Guns 'n' Roses front man

AYNSLEY◆Aynsley Dunbar — member of the rock group Jefferson Airplane, hits include "White Rabbit"

BABE◆Babe Ruth — greatest hitter of home runs in the history of baseball

BACCHUS◆John Bacchus Dykes — clergyman composer of hymns "Nearer, My God, to Thee" and "Lead, Kindly Light"

BAILEY ◆Thomas Bailey Aldrich — editor "Atlantic Monthly," semi-autobiographical novel "The Story of a Bad Boy" ◆ Bailey Howell — forward who won four National Basketball Association championships

BALLARD ◆Lenwood Ballard Abbott — Oscar and Emmy winner for special effects cinematography ◆Sanford Ballard Dole — first governor of Hawaiian territory, son canned pineapples

BALLINGTON ◆Ballington Booth — social reformer who founded the Volunteers of America

BALTHAZAR ◆Balthazar Getty — portrayed Jud Meadows in "My Heroes Have Always Been Cowboys"

BAPTISTA ◆Jan Baptista van Helmont — inventor of the word "gas"

BAPTISTE ◆Jean Baptiste Rochambeau — arrived with the French forces to help defeat Cornwallis at Yorktown

BARC ◆Barc Doyle — actor who played Joe Bob Blanton in Peter Bogdanovich's "The Last Picture Show"

BARCLAY ◆Samuel Barclay Beckett — two-time Obie winning Irish author

BARNABAS ◆Barnabas — in the Bible, preached the Gospel of Jesus with Paul

BARNARD ◆Barnard Hughes — starred as Joe Bogert on TV's "Doc"

BARNES ◆Barnes Wallis — invented a revolutionary bouncing bomb in WW II, biopic "The Dam Busters"

BARNETT ◆Barnett Parke — actor in Gary Cooper's "The General Died at Dawn" ◆ Arthur Barnett Spingarn — former president of the NAACP

BARNEY ◆Barney Rubble (c) — short next-door neighbor on TV's stone-age classic "The Flintstones" ◆ Barney Oldfield — auto racer, first to travel a mile in a minute

BARRE ◆Barre Lyndon — British playwright and screenwriter

BARRET ◆Barret Oliver (c) — robot turned child in his role in the film "D.A.R.Y.L." ◆ William Barret Travis — died as commander of the Alamo

BARRIE ◆Barrie Ingham — actor whose roles included the legendary outlaw in "A Challenge for Robin Hood"

BARRIEMORE ◆Barriemore Barlow — member of the heavy metal group Jethro Tull, Grammy for "The Crest of a Knave"

BARRINGTON ◆Barrington Levy — soul singer, hits include "It's Not Easy"

BARRY ◆Barry Gibb — member of English group The Bee Gees, hit album "Saturday Night Fever" ◆ Barry Goldwater — Republican presidential candidate who ran against Lyndon Johnson ◆ Barry Manilow — he writes the songs that makes the young girls cry, including "Mandy" ◆ Barry Sadler — composer and performer of "The Ballad of the Green Berets" ◆ Barry Williams — actor whose roles included Greg Brady on ABC's "The Brady Bunch"

BART ◆Bart Connor — gymnast ◆Bart Simpson (c) — obnoxious kid on TV's intelligent animated series "The Simpsons"

BARTHOLOMEW ◆Bartholomew — one of Jesus' twelve disciples ◆ Bartholomew Bottoms — child of actor Timothy Bottoms ◆ Bartholomew Dias — Portuguese navigator who was the first to sail around the Cape of Good Hope

BARTLETT ◆Bartlett Robinson — actor whose roles included Frank Caldwell on the sitcom "Mona McCluskey"

BARTOLOMEO ◆Bartolomeo Cristofori — invented the piano ◆ Bartolomeo Vanzetti — protested he was innocent of robbery, biopic "Sacco and Vanzetti"

BARTON ◆Barton MacLane — played General Martin Peterson on the popular genie sitcom "I Dream of Jeannie"

BARUCH ◆Baruch Lumet — actor whose roles included Mendel in Rod Steiger's "The Pawnbroker" ◆ Baruch Spinoza — philosopher, author of "Ethics Demonstrated With Geometrical Order"

BASIL ◆Saint Basil — founder of Eastern communal monasticism ◆ Basil Davenport — regular panelist on TV's quiz show "Down You Go" ◆ Basil Rathbone — expert swordsman who played Sheriff of Nottingham to Errol Flynn's Robin Hood

BAT ◆Bat Masterson — real-life western lawman, played by Gene Barry in the TV series of the same name

BAYARD ◆John Bayard Anderson — 1980 Independent Party presidential candidate ◆ Bayard Rustin — adviser to Martin Luther King, organized the first Freedom Ride

BAYNARD ◆Calder Baynard Willingham — screenwriter of "The Graduate" with Buck Henry

BAZOOKA ◆Bazooka Burns — inventor of the Bazooka wind instrument ◆ Sam Bazooka Gould — son of actor Elliot Gould ("M*A*S*H")

BEAM ◆H. Beam Piper — wrote the science fiction stories "Little Fuzzy" and "Space Viking"

BEARDSLEY ◆Beardsley Ruml — chair of the Federal Reserve in NYC who devised the modern income tax

BEAU ◆Beau Bridges — actor son of Lloyd Bridges, films include "The Fabulous Baker Boys" ◆ Beau Brummell — nineteenth century English dandy, biopic with John Barrymore and Stewart Granger ◆ Beau Geste (c) — he flees to the Foreign Legion, where he deals with a despotic sergeant

BEAUMONT ◆Beaumont Newhall — pioneer in writing books on the history of photography

BEBE ◆Bebe Rebozo — real estate and banker friend of Richard Nixon

BEEB ◆Beeb Birtles — member of The Little River Band, debut hit single "It's a Long Way There"

BEESON ◆Beeson Carroll — actor who played W. D. Hall on the Alex Haley drama series "Palmerstown"

BELA ◆Bela Fleck — bluegrass banjo player, group Bela Fleck and the Fleckstones ◆ Bela Lugosi — master of horror films who was actually born in Transylvania

BELLAMY ◆Bellamy Patridge — author whose books include "Country Lawyer"

BEN ◆Ben Cartwright (c) — leader of the Cartwright clan on TV's long-running "Bonanza" ◆ Ben Johnson — long time sidekick to John Wayne, Oscar for "The Last Picture Show" ◆Ben Kingsley — won Academy Award as Indian pacifist "Gandhi" ◆ Ben Vereen — actor who played the conniving Chicken George in the TV miniseries "Roots"

BENEDICT ◆Saint Benedict — founder of the Benedictine order of monks ◆ Benedict Arnold — as a Major General, the highest-ranking traitor in the American Revolution

BENITO ◆Benito Juarez — became President of Mexico and defeated Maximilian, biopic "Juarez" ◆ Benito Mussolini — "Il

Duce," Italian dictator during World War II ◆ Benito Santiago — with the Florida Marlins, earns the highest salary ever for a catcher in baseball

BENJAMIN ◆ Benjamin Franklin — politician, inventor, statesman, and kite flyer ◆ Benjamin Spock — baby doctor for the Baby Boomers

BENJI ◆ Benji Gregory — actor whose roles included son Brian Tanner on the hit sitcom "Alf"

BENMONT ◆ Benmont Tench — member of Tom Petty and the Heartbreakers, hit debut record "Breakdown"

BENNETT ◆ Bennett Cohen — "Ben" of Ben and Jerry's Homemade ice cream ◆ Abraham Bennett Minsky — burlesque house owner, basis for film "The Night They Raided Minsky's"

BENNY ◆ Benny Goodman — legendary "King of Swing" and important to the history of jazz ◆ Benny Hill — a pudgy, lecherous British comedy star of his very own "Benny Hill Show"

BENOIT ◆ Benoit Coquelin — French actor known for playing Cyrano de Bergerac

BENSON ◆ Benson DuBois (c) — intelligent butler on ABC's long running "Benson"

BENTON ◆ Nicholas Benton Alexander — Jack Webb's partner on TV's "Dragnet" ◆ Pinckney Benton Stewart — African-American governor of Louisiana after the Civil War

BENVENUTO ◆ Ferruccio Benvenuto Busoni — twentieth-century Italian pianist and composer ◆ Benvenuto Cellini — sixteenth-century Italian sculptor

BERENICE ◆ Berenice Abbott — photographer of black-and-white architectural images of 1930's New York City

BERKE ◆ Berke Lawrence — actor whose roles included Alex Noble on the adventure series "Urban Angel"

BERKELEY ◆ Berkeley Harris — actor whose roles included Phil Roberts on the soap "Texas"

BERMAN ◆ Berman Patterson — member of The Cleftones, debut hit single "You Baby You"

BERNARD ◆ Bernard Lee — actor whose roles included "M" in the James Bond film "Goldfinger" ◆ Bernard Montgomery — Britain's most celebrated commander of World War II ◆ George

Bernard Shaw — Nobel Prize winning dramatist, play "Pygmalion" became film "My Fair Lady"

BERNARDO ◆Bernardo Bertolucci — Italian director of "Last Tango in Paris"

BERNHARD ◆Bernhard — prince consort to Queen Juliana of the Netherlands ◆ Alfred Bernhard Nobel — inventor of dynamite, founded the Nobel Prizes

BERNI ◆Berni Wrightson — co-creator of DC Comics superhero "The Swamp Thing"

BERNIE ◆Bernie Kopell — actor whose roles included the ship's doctor on TV's "The Love Boat"

BERRY ◆Berry Gordy, Jr. — founder of Motown Records ◆Berry Oakley — member of the Allman Brothers Band

BERT ◆Bert Bacharach — father of Burt Bacharach, syndicated column "Now See Here!" ◆ Bert Convy — game show host of TV's "Tattletales," and inventor of "Win, Lose, or Draw" ◆ Bert Parks — host of TV's "Miss America Pageant" for twenty years

BERTIE ◆Bertie Forbes — founder of "Forbes" magazine ◆ Bertie Higgins — singer/songwriter, hit single "Key Largo"

BERTOLT ◆Bertolt Brecht — German poet and dramatist, author of "The Threepenny Opera"

BERTON ◆Berton Averre — member of The Knack, debut number one gold record "My Sharona" ◆ Berton Churchill — actor in Tyrone Power's story of the great fire "In Old Chicago"

BEV ◆Bev Bevan — member of The Electric Light Orchestra, debut hit single "Roll Over Beethoven"

BIFF ◆Biff Elliot — first to play private eye Mike Hammer in "I, the Jury"

BIL ◆Bil Baird — founders of the Bil and Cora Baird Puppet Theatre in Greenwich Village ◆Bil Keane — creator of the comic strip "The Family Circus"

BILL ◆Bill Blass — fashion designer known for apparel, home furnishings, and cars ◆ Bill Clinton — youngest governor of Arkansas, and President of the United States ◆ Bill Cosby — comic star of TV series "I Spy" and "The Cosby Show," loves Jell-O Pudding Pops ◆ Bill Haley — star of Bill Haley and the Comets, megahits include "Rock Around the Clock" ◆ Wild Bill Hickok — legendary marshal of the old West ◆ Bill Murray —

TV's "Saturday Night Live," films "Ghostbusters," "Stripes," "What About Bob?"

BILLY ◆Billy Carter — developed "Billy Beer" to go with his brother President Jimmy Carter's peanuts ◆Billy Crystal — comic who looked marvelous in "City Slickers" and "When Harry Met Sally" ◆Billy Graham — evangelical preacher who leads the Billy Graham Crusades ◆Billy Joel — five number one songs on album "An Innocent Man," platinum "52nd Street"

BILLY DEE ◆Billy Dee Williams — movie hunk featured in "Lady Sings the Blues" and "The Empire Strikes Back"

BILLY JOE ◆Billy Joe Royal — rock singer, debut hit record "Down in the Boondocks"

BILLY RAY ◆Billy Ray Cyrus — country music singer, hits include "Achy Breaky Heart"

BING ◆Bing Crosby — legendary crooner and co-star with Bob Hope in the "Road" films

BIRCH ◆Birch Bayh — Democratic senator from Indiana for twenty years

BIRT ◆Birt Acres — British cinematography pioneer and projector manufacturer

BIX ◆Bix Beiderbecke — one of the greatest jazz musicians, composed "In a Mist"

BJORN ◆Bjorn Borg — Scandinavian professional tennis player ◆ Bjorn Ulvacus — member of the Swedish rock group "Abba" whose hits include "Dancing Queen"

BLAIR ◆Blair Thornton — member of the Canadian heavy metal group Bachman-Turner Overdrive ◆ Blair Underwood — actor whose roles included a hot young attorney on TV's "L.A. Law"

BLAISE ◆Blaise — patron saint of throat ailments, Bishop of Armenia in the fourth century ◆ Blaise Pascal — created Pascal's law, i.e., fluids transmit equal pressure in all directions

BLAKE ◆Blake Edwards — director of "The Pink Panther," "Ten," "Victor/Victoria"

BLAKESLEY ◆Blakesley Fisher — founder of India's Literary Village, autobiography "To Light a Candle"

BLANE ◆Blane Savage — played Don, one of the hopeful dancers in the film version of "A Chorus Line"

BLISS ◆Chester Bliss Bowles — liberal Democrat who was presidential adviser, governor, and congressman ◆ Bliss Perry — nineteenth-century editor of the "Atlantic Monthly"

BLOOD ◆Sage Moon Blood Stallone — son of Sylvester Stallone, played his son Rocky, Jr., in "Rocky V"

BLUE ◆Elijah Blue Allman — son of Cher and Greg Allman of the Allman Brothers Band ◆ Blue Barron — popular bandleader from the 1930's to the 1960's

BLYTHE ◆John Blythe Barrymore — box office draw because of his "great profile"

BO ◆Bo Diddley — not only his stage name, but his biggest hit, "Bo Diddley" ◆ Bo Hopkins — actor in Sam Peckinpah's "The Wild Bunch," Matthew Blaisdel on TV's "Dynasty" ◆Bo Jackson — professional athlete and product spokesperson, "Bo does know diddley" ◆ Bo Svenson — star of the sequels to "Walking Tall"

BOB ◆Bob Denver — played Maynard G. Krebs on "Dobie Gillis" and Gilligan on "Gilligan's Island" ◆ Bob Hope — he's been on the road with Bing Crosby to just about everywhere ◆Bob Hoskins — detective in "Who Framed Roger Rabbit," Cher's boyfriend in "Mermaids" ◆ Bob Newhart — actor in TV's "Bob Newhart," "Newhart," and "Bob," he's now out of titles ◆ Bob Saget — host of the comedy show "America's Funniest Home Videos"

BOBBIE ◆Bobbie Peel — organized London's police force, called "Bobbies" after him

BOBBY ◆Bobby Darin — hubby of Sandra Dee; singer whose hits include "Mack the Knife" ◆ Bobby Goldsboro — country music star, hits "Honey," "The Straight Life" ◆Bobby Rydell — singer, hits include "Forget Him," namesake for high school in "Grease" ◆Bobby Sherman — gold record with "Little Woman," starred in TV series "Here Come the Brides" ◆Bobby Vee — teen idol, hits include "Take Good Care of My Baby" ◆ Bobby Vinton — pop singer, hits include "Blue Velvet"

BOBCAT ◆Bobcat Goldthwait — played Eliot Loudermilk in Bill Murray's Dickens Christmas tale "Scrooged"

BOBS ◆Bobs Watson — actor in Tyrone Power's story of the great fire "In Old Chicago"

BON ◆Bon Scott — member of Australian heavy metal band, album "For Those About to Rock"

BONAR ◆Bonar Colleano — wisecracking actor from a family of acrobats

BONARO ◆Bonaro Overstreet — author of "Search for a Self" and "The Iron Curtain"

BONAVENTURE ◆Spencer Bonaventure Tracy — Oscar winner for "Captains Courageous" and "Boys Town"

BONO ◆Bono Vox — member of the rock group U2, debut hit single "New Year's Day"

BONZO ◆Bonzo Bonham — Led Zeppelin's drummer whose death by asphyxiation led to group disbanding

BOOG ◆Boog Powell — outfielder for the Baltimore Orioles who did Miller Lite commercials

BOOKER ◆Booker T. Jones — leader of the rock group Booker T. and the MG's, hits include "Green Onions" ◆ Booker T. Washington — founded the Tuskegee Institute

BOOTH ◆Booth Conway — actor who played Sherlock Holmes' nemesis Moriarty in "The Valley of Fear" ◆Booth Savage — actor who played crime reporter Jason West on the magazine drama "Hot Shots" ◆Booth Tarkington — Pulitzer Prize-winning author for "The Magnificent Ambersons" and "Alice Adams"

BOOTS ◆Boots Randolph — country western sax player, hits include "Yakety-Sax"

BORDEN ◆Borden Chase — screenwriter of "Red River," "Winchester '73," and "Vera Cruz"

BORIS ◆Boris Karloff — quintessential "Frankenstein," plus many sequels, remakes, and ripoffs ◆ Boris Yeltsin — first popularly elected president of Russia in one thousand years

BOSTON ◆Boston Russell — child of actor Kurt Russell and actress Season Hubley

BOUDLEAUX ◆Boudleaux Bryant — composer, "Bye Bye Love," "Wake Up Little Susie," and "All I Have to Do Is Dream"

BOWIE ◆Bowie Kuhn — baseball commissioner for fifteen years

BOYD ◆John Boyd Dunlop — inventor of the pneumatic tire and the namesake for Dunlop Tire

BOZ ◆Boz Burrell — member of English group Bad Company, hit album "Bad Company" ◆ Boz Scaggs — rock singer, massive acclaim with his album "Silk Degrees"

BRACE ◆Brace Beemer — original radio voice of the Lone Ranger

BRAD ◆Brad Hall — member of The Not Ready for Prime Time Players on "Saturday Night Live" ◆Brad Pitt — actor whose roles included the cocky roadside hustler in "Thelma and Louise"

BRADBURY ◆Bradbury Thompson — designer of the Time-Life "Library of Art" series

BRADFORD ◆Peter Bradford Benchley — writer of "Jaws," "The Deep," and "The Island" ◆ Bradford Dillman — actor in "The Way We Were," "Escape from the Planet of the Apes"

BRADLEY ◆Bradley Kincaid — early country music performer ◆ Bradley Page — actor whose roles included Ferguson in the W. C. Fields film "Six of a Kind" ◆ Bradley Tomlin — abstract painter, mainly of poetic Cubist still lifes

BRAM ◆Bram Nossen — actor who played Harlem Globetrotter James Willoughby in "Go, Man, Go!" ◆Bram Stoker — creator of the vampire Count Dracula

BRAMWELL ◆Bramwell Fletcher — actor whose films include "Raffles," "The Mummy," and "The Scarlet Pimpernel"

BRANCH ◆James Branch Cabell — author whose works include "These Restless Years" ◆ Branch McCracken — Hall of Fame Indiana University coach who won two NCAA titles ◆ Branch Rickey — manager of Brooklyn Dodgers who broke color barrier by signing Jackie Robinson

BRAND ◆Brand Whitlock — author of the novels "Thirteenth District" and "Uprooted"

BRANDIS ◆Brandis Kemp — regular on the comedy variety show "Fridays"

BRANDON ◆Brandon Cruz — actor who played son Eddie in TV's "The Courtship of Eddie's Father" ◆ Brandon De Wilde — nominated for an Oscar as the kid in Alan Ladd's "Shane" ◆ Brandon Lee — martial arts expert and son of the legendary Bruce Lee ◆ Brandon Tartikoff — head of NBC who purchased "The Cosby Show" and "Cheers"

BRANFORD ◆Branford Marsalis — musical director on Jay Leno's "The Tonight Show"

BRANSBY ◆Bransby Williams — distinguished British stage actor who appeared in early films

BRANSCOMBE ◆Branscombe Richmond — actor who played Sgt. Luke Halui on the police drama "Heart of the City"

BRANT ◆Brant Parker — cartoonist who created the strips "The Wizard of Id," "Crock," and "Goosemeyer" ◆Brant Von Hoffman — actor who played Deputy Bottendott on the adventure series "240 Robert"

BRAWLEY ◆Brawley King Nolte — son of actor Nick Nolte

BRAXTON ◆Braxton Bragg — commander-in-chief of the Confederate army, namesake for Fort Bragg

BRAY ◆Bray Hammond — Pulitzer Prize-winning author

BREFNI ◆Brefni O'Rourke — Irish stage actor who made some British films, usually as testy types

BRENDAN ◆Brendan Behan — Irish dramatist, "The Hostage," "Richard's Cork Leg" ◆ Brendan Fay — pool player in Paul Newman's "The Hustler" ◆Brendan Fraser — 1990's teen hunk, film credits include "Encino Man"

BRENDEN ◆Brenden Harkin — in rock group Starz, debut hit single "(She's Just A) Fallen Angel" ◆Brenden Jefferson — actor whose roles included the youngest son on TV's sitcom "Thea" ◆ John Brenden Kelly — Olympic gold medal winner, father of Princess Grace of Monaco

BRENDON ◆Brendon Kasper — actor whose roles included Kevin Channing on TV's "Falcon Crest"

BRENT ◆Brent Spiner — actor who played Lt. Cmdr. Data on the series "Star Trek: The Next Generation"

BRET ◆Bret Hart — author of "The Outcasts of Poker Flat," "Tennessee's Partner," "Miggles" ◆ Bret Maverick (c) — James Garner's TV role as a gambler in search of poker and fun in the Old West

BRETT ◆Brett Halliday — creator of private detective Michael Shayne who appeared in 67 novels ◆Brett Hudson — member of the Hudson Brothers, own TV show "The Razzle Dazzle Comedy Hour"

BRIAN ◆Brian Dennehy — lawman in "Gorky Park," "Silverado," and "Presumed Innocent" ◆Brian Henson — creator of The Teenage Mutant Ninja Turtles, son of muppet master Jim Henson ◆ Brian Keith — father figure in both TV's "Family Affair" and Disney's film "The Parent Trap" ◆ Brian Wilson —

creative force behind The Beach Boys, wrote "California Girls," "Surfin' USA."

BRIAN-ROBERT ◆Brian-Robert Taylor — actor whose roles included Dr. Thomas McCandless on the soap "Capitol"

BRICE ◆Brice Marden — artist whose paintings combine abstract and minimalist influences

BRIGHAM ◆Brigham Young — Mormon who led his people to the valley of the Great Salt Lake

BRINSLEY ◆Brinsley Schwarz — member of the group Graham Parker and the Rumour ◆Brinsley Trench — flying saucer expert, wrote "The Sky People"

BRINTON ◆Brinton Turkle — children's author and illustrator, works include "The Adventures of Obadiah"

BRION ◆Brion James — actor whose roles included Ben Kehoe in Eddie Murphy's "Another 48 Hours"

BRIT ◆Brit Hume — White House correspondent for ABC News

BRITON ◆Briton Hadden — founder of "Time" magazine

BROCK ◆Brock Peters — actor whose roles included Rodriguez in the Rod Steiger film "The Pawnbroker"

BRODERICK ◆Broderick Crawford — rotund star of TV's "Highway Patrol," Oscar winner for "Born Yesterday"

BRONISLAU ◆Bronislau Kaper — Oscar winning composer for the score of the film "Lili"

BRONISLAVA ◆Bronislava Nijinska — went from the Russian Imperial Ballet to his own studio in Hollywood

BRONISLAW ◆Bronislaw "Bronko" Nagurski — Hall of Fame fullback with Chicago Bears

BRONSON ◆Bronson Pinchot — actor who played cousin Balki from Mepos on the sitcom "Perfect Strangers"

BROOK ◆Brook Benton — singer and composer of his own hit "The Boll Weevil Song"

BROOKLYN ◆Brooklyn Demme — son of Jonathan Demme, director of "The Silence of the Lambs," "Philadelphia"

BROOKS ◆Brooks Adams — Pulitzer Prize-winning grandson of President John Quincy Adams ◆ Brooks Atkinson — Pulitzer

Prize-winning drama critic ◆ Brooks Hays — congressman who tried to mediate Little Rock's integration crisis

BRUCE ◆Bruce Dern — first actor to kill John Wayne in "The Cowboys" ◆ Bruce Lee — karate-kicking actor in "Enter the Dragon," biopic is "Dragon" ◆ Bruce Springsteen — The Boss; "Born in the USA," actually New Jersey ◆ Bruce Willis — action star of "Die Hard" and quipping private eye on TV's "Moonlighting"

BRUMSIC ◆Brumsic Brandon — known for the syndicated comic strip "Luther"

BRUNO ◆Bruno Bernard — photographer of film stars, shot Marilyn Monroe in wind-blown skirt ◆ Bruno Kirby — comic co-star of "City Slickers" and "When Harry Met Sally"

BRUTUS ◆Junius Brutus Booth — stage actor for 30 years, father of assassin John Wilkes Booth

BRYAN ◆Bryan Adams — Canadian singer whose songs included "Lonely Nights" and "Heaven" ◆ Bryan Chandler — member of the rock group The Animals, number one hit "House of the Rising Sun" ◆Bryan Ferry — main songwriter for Roxy Music, hit album "Let's Stick Together"

BRYANT ◆Edsel Bryant Ford — son of Henry Ford after whom they named the Edsel ◆ Bryant Gumbel — host of TV's "NBC Sports" and "The Today Show"

BRYTON ◆Bryton McClure — actor whose roles included Richie on Urkel's TV show "Family Matters"

BUBBA ◆Bubba Smith — actor whose roles included Beau on the Joe Pesci sitcom "Half Nelson"

BUCK ◆Buck Henry — frequent guest host on "Saturday Night Live," wrote "The Graduate" ◆ Buck Jones — western hero in "Rough Rider" serials, horse is named Silver ◆ Buck Owens — country western singer, was a co-host of TV's "Hee Haw"

BUCKMINSTER ◆Buckminster Fuller — architect who invented the geodesic dome

BUCKWHEAT ◆Buckwheat Zydeco — Cajun musician whose hit albums include "On a Night Like This"

BUCKY ◆Bucky Walters — pitcher who led the National League in wins three times

BUD ◆Bud Abbott — straight half of the comedy team of Abbott and Costello ◆ Bud Collyer — host of TV's game show "To Tell the Truth" ◆Bud Cort — boy star of the feature film "Harold and Maude"

BUDD ◆Budd Schulberg — author of "What Makes Sammy Run?" and "On the Waterfront"

BUDDY ◆Buddy Ebsen — vittles-loving millionaire Jed Clampett on TV's "The Beverly Hillbillies" ◆Buddy Hackett — comedian, appeared in "It's a Mad, Mad, Mad, Mad World" ◆ Buddy Holly — lead singer of The Crickets, hit songs of the 50's include "Peggy Sue" ◆ Buddy Knox — hit the charts with the number one gold record "Party Doll" ◆Buddy Rich — one of the all-time greatest drummers ◆ Buddy Rogers — starred in first Oscar-winning picture, "Wings," husband of Mary Pickford

BUELL ◆Buell Kazee — country music singer and Baptist minister

BUFFALO ◆John Buffalo Mailer — son of Pulitzer Prize-winning author Norman Mailer

BUFORD ◆Buford Pusser — real-life crime-busting Tennessee sheriff, biopic "Walking Tall"

BUGS ◆Bugs Moran — gangster who took over Chicago's North Side Mob in the 1920's

BUGSY ◆Bugsy Siegel — gangster who built the "Flamingo" casino and invented Las Vegas

BUMPER ◆Bumper Robinson — actor whose roles included Clarence on the Sherman Hemsley hit sitcom "Amen"

BUN ◆Bun Carlos — member of the group Cheap Trick, debut hit single "Surrender"

BUNK ◆Bunk Gardner — member of The Mothers of Invention, backup group for Frank Zappa

BUNNY ◆Bunny Berigan — bandleader and Broadway trumpeter

BURGESS ◆Burgess Meredith — actor whose roles included Sly Stallone's manager in the "Rocky" movies

BURKE ◆Burke Byrnes — actor whose roles included Pete Adams on TV's "Dallas" ◆ J. Burke Wilkinson — author of "By Sea and By Stealth" and "Night of the Short Knives"

BURL ◆Burl Ives — composer and narrator of the classic animated "Rudolph the Red-Nosed Reindeer"

BURLEIGH ◆Burleigh Drummond — member of the group Ambrosia, debut hit single "Holdin' On to Yesterday"

BURNE ◆Burne Hogarth — cartoonist of the "Tarzan" comic strip

BURNETT ◆Burnett Guffey — filmmaker with Oscars for "From Here to Eternity" and "Bonnie and Clyde"

BURNS ◆Burns Singer — author whose best known work is "Living Silver"

BURR ◆Burr DeBenning — actor whose roles included Dr. Nick Hunter on the soap "Search for Tomorrow" ◆ Burr Tillstrom — creator and puppeteer for TV's "Kukla, Fran, & Ollie"

BURT ◆Burt Bacharach — composer, best song Oscar for "Raindrops Keep Falling on My Head" ◆ Burt Lancaster — gymnastic tough-guy actor, Oscar winner for "Elmer Gantry" ◆ Burt Reynolds — just a good old boy in "Smokey and the Bandit" ◆ Burt Ward — played Robin the Boy Wonder in the TV series "Batman"

BURTON ◆Burton Baskin — co-founder of Baskin-Robbins ice cream stores ◆ Burton Cummings — member of The Guess Who, debut hit record "Shakin' All Over" ◆Burton Holmes — producer of travelogues, tag line "sun sinks slowly in the West"

BUSBY ◆Busby Berkeley — film choreographer of 1930's kaleidoscope musicals

BUSHNELL ◆Robert Bushnell Ryan — leading man, films include "Crossfire" and "The Dirty Dozen"

BUSTER ◆Buster Crabbe — original Flash Gordon and an early Tarzan ◆ Buster Keaton — silent film star who specialized in physical comedy

BUTCH ◆Butch Cassidy — western outlaw who couldn't get Hollywood to buy his story

BUTLER ◆William Butler Hickok — real name of western hero Wild Bill Hickok

BUZZ ◆Buzz Aldrin — original astronaut and the second man to walk on the moon

BUZZY ◆Buzzy Feiten — member of the pop group The Rascals, hits "Good Lovin'" and "Groovin'"

BYRON ◆Byron Allen — co-host of TV's "Real People" who later had his own show ◆James Byron Dean — teen idol star of "Rebel

Without a Cause" and "East of Eden" ◆ Byron White — US Supreme Court justice

BYRUM ◆Byrum Saam — commentator on TV's "Gillette Summer Sports Reel"

CAB ◆Cab Calloway — bandleader who was called "King of the Hi De Ho"

CABOT ◆Cabot Forbes — Cary Elwes, one of Matthew Broderick's officers in the film "Glory" ◆ Henry Cabot Lodge — ran for vice president with Nixon against Kennedy

CADE ◆Cade Carradine — son of actor Keith Carradine

CADWALLADER ◆Cadwallader Colden — introduced Linnaeus systems to US botany

CAESAR ◆Caesar Rodney — rode through gloom of a stormy night to ratify the Declaration of Independence ◆ Jules Caesar Stein — founder of MCA, which now controls Universal Pictures

CAIN ◆Cain Devore — actor whose roles included Phil Taylor on TV's "Dreams"

CAL ◆Cal Bolder — actor who played the monster in "Jesse James Meets Frankenstein's Daughter" ◆ Cal Hubbard — only man elected to football and baseball Halls of Fame

CALBRAITH ◆Matthew Calbraith Butler — major general in the Confederate army, later US senator ◆Matthew Calbraith Perry — Commodore who opened Japan to the West, brother of Oliver Hazard Perry

CALDER ◆Calder Willingham — screenwriter of "The Graduate"

CALEB ◆Caleb Bradham — inventor of Pepsi-Cola

CALLEN ◆Callen Tjader — Grammy winning jazz musician with Brubeck Octet and George Shearing

CALVERT ◆Calvert DeForest — portrayed Larry "Bud" Melman on "Late Night with David Letterman" ◆ Calvert Vaux — architect whose landscapes include Central Park in NYC and South Park in Chicago

CALVIN ◆Calvin Coolidge — "Silent Cal," President of the United States during the Roaring Twenties ◆ Calvin Klein — clothing designer with sexually teasing jean ads

CAMERON ◆Cameron Morrell Douglas — son of actor Michael Douglas and grandson of Kirk Douglas ◆ Cameron Mitchell — good-looking actor in the western adventure series "The High Chapparal" ◆John Cameron Swayze — NBC news commentator, did commercials for Timex watches

CAMILLO ◆Camillo Olivetti — founder of the Olivetti typewriter company

CAMILO ◆Camilo Cela — Nobel Prize-winner for literature in 1989

CAMPBELL ◆Campbell Scott — actor son of actor George C. Scott ◆ Campbell Singer — actor who played Sherlock Holmes' Dr. Watson in "The Man With the Twisted Lip"

CANADA ◆Canada Lee — African-American actor in Alfred Hitchcock's "Lifeboat"

CANDIDO ◆Candido Jacuzzi — inventor of the bubbling Jacuzzi

CANDY ◆Candy Dulfer — jazz saxophonist, gold album "Saxuality" with hit single "Lily Was Here"

CANUT ◆Canut Reyes — member of the flamenco band The Gipsy Kings, 15 gold and platinum records

CARBINE ◆Carbine Williams — inventor of the Carbine rifle, Jimmy Stewart biopic "Carbine Williams"

CARL ◆Carl Bernstein — broke Watergate with Bob Woodward, co-author "All the President's Men" ◆ Carl Betz — actor whose roles included Donna's doctor husband on TV's "The Donna Reed Show" ◆Carl Reiner — creator of the "The Dick Van Dyke Show," father of Rob Reiner

CARLE ◆Carle Vickers — member of the rock group L.T.D., debut hit single "Love Ballad"

CARLETON ◆Carleton Carpenter — scored a gold record with Debbie Reynolds singing "Aba Daba Honeymoon" ◆ Carleton Young — character actor, credits include "The Horse Soldiers" and "Sergeant Rutledge"

CARLISLE ◆Carlisle Floyd — composer of operas "Wuthering Heights" and "Of Mice and Men"

CARLO ◆Carlo Imperato — actor whose roles included Danny Amatullo on TV's "Fame" ◆Carlo Ponti — producer and director, discovered and married Sophia Loren

CARLOS ◆Carlos Montoya — internationally renowned flamenco guitarist ◆ Carlos Ray Norris — real name of action superstar Chuck Norris ◆ Carlos Santana — leader of the rock group Santana, debut hit single "Jingo"

CARLTON ◆Carlton Fisk — famous catcher, played for the Red Sox and the White Sox

CARLYLE ◆Carlyle Blackwell — actor who played the gallant English adventurer in the silent "Bulldog Drummond" ◆ Robert Carlyle Byrd — senator who was both majority and minority leader ◆ Carlyle Moore — actor whose roles included western hero Buffalo Bill in "Outlaw Express"

CARMEN ◆Carmen Basilio — world welterweight and middleweight champion ◆ Carmen Cavallaro — big band leader who played the soundtrack for "The Eddy Duchin Story" ◆ Carmen Orrico — real name of actor John Saxon

CARMINE ◆Carmine Appice — member of Vanilla Fudge, debut hit "You Keep Me Hanging On" ◆Carmine Coppola — father of Francis Ford Coppola, won an Oscar for music in "The Godfather II"

CAROL ◆Carol Reed — Oscar-winning director for "Oliver!"

CAROLUS ◆Carolus Linnaeus — created the modern biological system of classifying life forms

CARROL ◆J. Carrol Naish — character actor in over 200 films, Oscar nominee for "Sahara"

CARROLL ◆Carroll Nye — portrayed Frank Kennedy in "Gone With the Wind" ◆ Carroll O'Connor — actor who played bigot Archie Bunker on the sitcom "All in the Family"

CARSON ◆Carson Robison — country music singer called the "granddaddy of the hillbillies"

CARSWELL ◆Carswell Adams — reporter on the news show "Your Sports Special"

CARTER ◆Daniel Carter Beard — founder of the Boy Scouts of America

CARVER ◆Carver Andrews — real name of actor Dana Andrews

CARY ◆Cary Elwes — actor whose roles included Robin Hood for laughs in "Men in Tights" ◆Cary Grant — suave actor in "Gunga Din," "His Girl Friday," "North by Northwest"

CARYL ◆Caryl Chessman — prisoner who studied law and delayed execution, biopic "Cell 2455, Death Row"

CASANOVA ◆Casanova — 18th century profligate and ardent amorist who seduced the flower of Europe

CASEY ◆Casey Jones — died in the crash of the Cannon Ball Express, biosong "Casey Jones" ◆ Casey Kasem — radio and television personality who does "rock countdowns" ◆ Casey Stengel — manager of the New York Yankees when they won ten pennants

CASH ◆James Cash Penney — founder of the J. C. Penney department stores

CASIMIR ◆Casimir — fifteenth-century Polish saint imprisoned for refusing to obey his father the king ◆ Casimir Funk — biochemist who named the vitamins

CASPAR ◆Caspar Weinberger — Secretary of Defense under Reagan and Bush

CASPER ◆Casper — friendly ghost of cartoon fame

CASS ◆Cass Canfield — publisher at Harper and Row, wrote bios of Pierpont Morgan and Jefferson Davis ◆ Cass Gilbert — architect who designed the Supreme Court building in Washington, D.C.

CASSIUS ◆Cassius Clay — heavyweight champion of the world later known as Muhammad Ali

CASSON ◆Casson Ferguson — actor whose roles included the scribe in "The King of Kings"

CASTLETON ◆Castleton Knight — British newsreel producer and film director

CAT ◆Cat Stevens — pop singer of the 1960's and 1970's

CEC ◆Cec Linder — actor who played Felix Leiter in the James Bond adventure "Goldfinger"

CECIL ◆Cecil B. DeMille — legendary director of epic films, Oscar for "The Greatest Show on Earth" ◆ Cecil S. Forester — filmed novels include "Horatio Hornblower" and "The African Queen" ◆ Cecil Rhodes — made a fortune in South African diamonds, Rhodesia named after him

CEDRIC ◆Cedric Hardwicke — actor who played Professor Crayton on the sitcom "The Gertrude Berg Show"

CESAR ◆Cesar Chavez — organized the National Farm Workers Association ◆ Cesar Romero — original screen Joker on the "Batman" TV series

CESARE ◆Cesare Beccaria — eighteenth-century Italian explorer, argued against capital punishment

CHAD ◆Chad Everett — actor whose roles included Dr. Joe Gannon on TV's "Medical Center" ◆ Chad Lowe — younger brother of Rob Lowe, 1990's teen heartthrob, film "Highway to Hell" ◆Chad Mitchell — singer, hit song "Lizzie Borden" ◆Chad Stuart — half of group Chad and Jeremy, hits "Yesterday's Gone" and "A Summer Song"

CHAIM ◆Chaim Arluck — real name of Harold Arlen, who composed "Over the Rainbow" ◆ Chaim Bialik — greatest modern Hebrew poet

CHAKA ◆Chaka — founder of the Zulu Empire, biopic "Shaka Zulu"

CHANDLER ◆Howard Chandler Christy — artist who created "The Christy Girl" ◆ Joel Chandler Harris — creator of "Uncle Remus"

CHANG ◆Chang — half of the original Siamese Twins, with his brother Eng

CHANNING ◆Channing Phillips — first African-American nominated for President ◆Channing Pollock — composer, Fannie Brice made famous his song "My Man" ◆ Channing Tobias — minister active with the NAACP during the beginning of the civil rights movement ◆ Russell Channing Westover — cartoonist who founded the working-girl comic strip "Tillie the Toiler"

CHAPMAN ◆Roy Chapman Andrews — zoologist who discovered fossil fields with unknown animal and plant life ◆ Robert Chapman Sprague — founder of the Sprague Electric Company, radio and TV pioneer

CHARD ◆Chard Smith — author whose works include the verse "Along the Wind" and novel "Ladies Day"

CHARLES ◆Prince Charles — Prince of Wales, heir to the British throne if he outlives his mother ◆ Charles Atlas — developer of the dynamic tension method of bodybuilding ◆ Charles Bronson — tough guy in "Death Wish," "The Great Escape," and "Telefon" ◆Charles Kuralt — CBS news correspondent known for his "On the Road" segments ◆ Charles Laughton — "The

Hunchback of Notre Dame," Oscar for "The Private Lives of Henry VIII"

CHARLEY ◆Charley Pride — country music singer, hits include "Kiss an Angel Good Morning"

CHARLIE ◆Charlie Brown — boyhood friend of Charles Schulz, who named the character after him in "Peanuts" ◆ Charlie Chaplin — silent film star affectionately called "the Little Tramp" ◆ Charlie Rich — country singer, hits include "Behind Closed Doors" ◆ Charlie Sheen — heartthrob actor in "Wall Street," "Hot Shots," "The Three Musketeers"

CHARLTON ◆Charlton Heston — star of biblical epics like "The Ten Commandments" and "Ben-Hur"

CHASE ◆Chase Randolph — series regular on the long-running hayseed series "Hee Haw"

CHAUNCEY ◆Walter Chauncey Camp — father of American football ◆ Chauncey Olcott — wrote "When Irish Eyes Are Smiling," biopic "My Wild Irish Rose"

CHAY ◆Chay Blyth — British adventurer who circumnavigated the world in his yacht in 1970

CHE ◆Che Guevara — Argentine-born guerilla leader in South America, killed in Bolivia

CHEECH ◆Cheech Marin — part of Cheech & Chong, starred in a number of drug-induced films

CHELCIE ◆Chelcie Ross — actor in Gene Hackman's film "Hoosiers"

CHERRY ◆Apsley Cherry Garrard — polar explorer who died trying, biopic "Scott of the Antarctic" ◆ Cherry Kearton — pioneer British travel film producer

CHESARE ◆Chesare Bono — child of rock star and mayor of Palm Springs Sonny Bono

CHESLEY ◆Chesley Bonestell — outer space illustrator best known for mural "A Trip to the Moon"

CHESNEY ◆Chesney Allen — British light comedian, teamed with Bud Flanagan and the Crazy Gang

CHESTER ◆Chester A. Arthur — President of the United States who was a general during the Civil War ◆ Chester Gould — creator of comic strip hero Dick Tracy ◆Chester Morris — Oscar nominee for "Alibi," played Boston Blackie in 13 films

CHET ◆Chet Atkins — guitarist at the Grand Ole Opry ◆ Chet Huntley — network nightly newscaster with David Brinkley

CHEVALIER ◆Chevalier Jackson — American scientist who developed the method for viewing the stomach

CHEVY ◆Chevy Chase — film and TV star who coined the phrase "I'm Chevy Chase, and you're not"

CHEZ ◆Chez Lister — actor whose roles included Eli on TV's "Father Murphy"

CHIC ◆Chic Johnson — vaudeville star with Ole Olsen, film "Hellzapoppin" ◆ Chic Young — creator of the comic strip, films, and TV show "Blondie"

CHICK ◆Chick Chandler — wiry hero of many a 40's second feature ◆ Chick Hearn — TV football announcer

CHICO ◆Chico Marx — Marx Brother who made puns with an even worse accent

CHILL ◆Chill Wills — star of the dramatic TV series "Frontier Circus"

CHRIS ◆Chris Columbus — director of "Home Alone" ◆ Chris Lemmon — star of TV's "Duet" and son of actor Jack Lemmon ◆ Chris Sarandon — starred in "Dog Day Afternoon" and "Protocol" ◆ Chris Columbus Smith — speedboat builder, founder of Chris-Craft boats ◆ Chris Wallace — White House correspondent for NBC News, son of Mike Wallace

CHRISTIAN ◆Christian Dior — designer with brands of clothing, perfume, and cosmetics ◆Christian Slater — actor who played the brother of Kevin Costner's "Robin Hood: Prince of Thieves"

CHRISTO ◆Christo — Bulgarian artist who created 24-mile fabric fence in California

CHRISTOPH ◆Johann Christoph Denner — inventor of the clarinet ◆ Johann Christoph Pepusch — composer of "The Beggar's Opera"

CHRISTOPHER ◆Christopher Columbus — he discovered America for Spain, but the Indians already knew it was there ◆ Christopher Lee — horror actor, roles "Corridor of Mirrors," "Dracula" and "An Eye for an Eye" ◆ Christopher Lloyd — played the crazy Jim Ignatowski on TV's "Taxi," was in "Back to the Future" ◆ Christopher Plummer — starred opposite Julie Andrews in "The Sound of Music" ◆ Christopher Reeve —

definitive "Superman" ◆ Christopher Walken — Oscar winner as best supporting actor in "The Deer Hunter"

CHRISTY ◆Christy Brown — Irish poet, Daniel Day Lewis biopic "My Left Foot" ◆Christy Cabanne — director, films include "The Mummy's Hand" and "The Last Outlaw"

CHUBBY ◆Chubby Checker — inventor of "The Twist" dance craze

CHUCK ◆Chuck Barris — creator of TV's "Dating Game" and "Newlywed Game" ◆ Chuck Berry — original rock and roller whose hits include "Johnny B. Goode" ◆ Chuck Conners — baseball player turned star of the TV series "The Rifleman" ◆ Chuck Mangione — trumpet player, received a Grammy for the title track of "Bellavia" album ◆ Chuck Norris — Indian action hero whose films include "Missing in Action" ◆Chuck Yeager — first test pilot to break the sound barrier, biopic "The Right Stuff"

CICERO ◆Cicero — statesman and orator who tried to save the dying Roman Republic

CISCO ◆Cisco Kid (c) — Mexican hero created by O. Henry, in films and TV, hit song by War

CLAES ◆Claes Oldenburg — sculptor known for soft sculptures of ice cream cones, hamburgers, etc.

CLAIBORNE ◆Claiborne Pell — Democratic senator from Rhode Island

CLAIR ◆Clair Bee — collegiate coach with highest winning percentage

CLAIRE ◆Claire Chennault — created the "Flying Tigers," commanded US Air Force in China during WWII

CLANCY ◆Clancy Brown — actor who played the hard but vulnerable boss of the prisoners in "Bad Boys"

CLARE ◆Forest Clare Allen — basketball coach who helped organize the first NCAA tournament ◆Clare Briggs — creator of the cartoon character "Skin-nay"

CLARENCE ◆Clarence Darrow — lawyer with two of his cases on screen, "Compulsion" and "Inherit the Wind" ◆Clarence Day — authored "Life With Father" on which was based the movie of the same name ◆Clarence "Ducky" Nash — voice of Donald Duck ◆ Clarence Williams III — member of the undercover trio on TV's popular "The Mod Squad"

CLARK ◆Clark Gable — most well-known role is Rhett Butler in "Gone With the Wind" ◆Clark Kent (c) — secret identity of the man from Krypton, Superman

CLARKE ◆Clement Clarke Moore — wrote "The Night Before Christmas"

CLAUD ◆Claud Allister — actor whose roles included Lord Fabian in Cary Grant's "The Awful Truth"

CLAUDE ◆Claude Akins — actor whose roles included Sheriff Lobo on the drama series "BJ and the Bear" ◆Claude Rains — actor who played the police inspector in "Casablanca," was "The Invisible Man"

CLAUDE-OSCAR ◆Claude-Oscar Monet — his painting "Impression Sunrise" gave Impressionists their name

CLAUDIO ◆Claudio Abbado — conductor of La Scala in Milan

CLAUS ◆Claus Spreckels — owner of the largest sugar refinery on the West Coast, invented "spreckels"

CLAXTON ◆Dick Claxton Gregory — first African-American comedian to perform for white audiences

CLAY ◆Clay Blair — author of "Beyond Courage" and "Survive!" ◆ Clay Clement — actor whose roles included Quinn in the original William Powell "Thin Man" film

CLAYDES ◆Claydes Smith — member of Kool and the Gang, hit debut single "Kool and the Gang"

CLAYTON ◆Clayton Moore — man behind the mask in TV's "The Lone Ranger"

CLEAVANT ◆Cleavant Derricks — supporting cast member on TV's "Thea"

CLEAVON ◆Cleavon Little — African-American sheriff who whipped it out in "Blazing Saddles"

CLEM ◆Clem Burke — member of the rock group Blondie, hits include "Rapture" ◆ Clem McCarthy — commentator on TV's "Gillette Summer Sports Reel"

CLEMENCE ◆Clemence Dane — author whose works include "Regiment of Women" and "Bill of Divorcement"

CLEMENT ◆Clement Attlee — Labour Party leader and prime minister of England ◆ Clement Clarke Moore — wrote "The Night Before Christmas"

CLEON ◆Cleon Throckmorton — pioneer stage designer who began his career working with Eugene O'Neill

CLEROW ◆Clerow Wilson — real name of comedian Flip Wilson

CLETUS ◆Cletus Johnson — artist known for shadowbox constructions of imaginary facades

CLEVE ◆Cleve Duncan — lead singer of The Penguins, hits include "Earth Angel" ◆ Cleve Moore — portrayed Captain Russell in Gary Cooper's "Lilac Time"

CLEVELAND ◆Cleveland Abbe — first official meteorologist of the US government ◆ Cleveland Amory — author, historian, and conservationist

CLIFF ◆Cliff Arquette — appeared for years on "Hollywood Squares" as humorist Charley Weaver ◆ Cliff Robertson — best known for playing John F. Kennedy in "PT 109," Oscar for "Charly"

CLIFFIE ◆Cliffie Stone — singer who hated the word "hillbilly," so he coined the term "country music"

CLIFFORD ◆Clifford Berryman — cartoonist who created the teddy bear modeled on Teddy Roosevelt ◆ Clifford Odets — author of plays of social protest; films include "The General Died at Dawn" ◆ Clifford Olin — son of actors Ken Olin and Patricia Wettig

CLIFTON ◆Clifton Davis — actor who played the Rev. Reuben Gregory on NBC's religious comedy "Amen" ◆ Clifton James — Field Marshal Montgomery's stand-in, biopic "I Was Monty's Double" ◆Clifton Webb — actor who was nominated for an Oscar for "Laura"

CLINT ◆Clint Black — top-selling country singer ◆ Clint Eastwood — tough-guy star of "Dirty Harry," best director Oscar for "Unforgiven" ◆ Clint Howard — brother of director Ron Howard; child star of TV's "Gentle Ben" ◆Clint Walker — actor whose roles included Cheyenne Bodie, the star of ABC's "Cheyenne"

CLINTON ◆Clinton Eastwood, Jr. — real name of film actor and Oscar winning director of "Unforgiven" ◆ Clinton Wilder — producer of the plays "The Little Foxes" and "Visit to a Small Planet"

CLIVE ◆Clive Brook — distinguished British leading gentleman of films in silent and sound eras ◆ Clive Burr — member of Iron

Maiden, hit album "Piece of Mind" ◆ Clive Davis — head of Arista records, hits include the soundtrack of "The Bodyguard"

CLOVIS ◆Clovis Ruffin — youngest designer to win the Coty

CLU ◆Clu Gulager — played one of the assassins in the film version of Hemingway's "The Killers"

CLYDE ◆Clyde Barrow — real life gangster portrayed by Warren Beatty in "Bonnie and Clyde" ◆ Clyde Cessna — founder of the Cessna Aircraft Company ◆ Clyde Tombaugh — astronomer who discovered the planet Pluto

CLYFFORD ◆Clyfford Still — artist who is a pioneer in the use of mural sized canvas

CLYVE ◆Robert Clyve Maynard — first African-American to own a newspaper

COBY ◆Coby Denton — actor who played Bull Puckey in the Peter Fonda film "The Wild Angels"

COCHISE ◆Cochise — Apache chief who fought a long war with the US, but finally made peace

CODY ◆Cody Loggins — son of singer Kenny Loggins

COE ◆Coe Norton — actor whose roles included John Dennis on the soap "Love of Life"

COKE ◆Coke Stevenson — former governor of Texas

COKIE ◆Cokie Roberts — special correspondent for ABC

COLBY ◆Colby Chandler — president of Eastman Kodak ◆Colby Chester — actor whose roles included Buckner on the adventure series "Sword of Justice"

COLE ◆Cole Porter — composer whose songs include "High Society," "Kiss Me Kate," "Night and Day" ◆ Cole Younger — leader of the Younger Gang, Confederate guerillas turned bandits in the West

COLGATE ◆Colgate Salisbury — actor whose roles included Cal Foster on the soap "Search for Tomorrow"

COLIN ◆Colin Blakely — actor whose roles included Dr. Watson in "The Private Life of Sherlock Holmes" ◆Colin Hanks — son of comedy film star Tom Hanks of "Big," "Philadelphia" ◆ Colin Powell — chairman of the Joint Chiefs of Staff during the Gulf War

COLLIN ◆Collin Turnbull — anthropologist best known for studies on Pygmies

COLLIS ◆Collis Huntington — builder of the Central Pacific Railroad

COLM ◆Colm Meaney — actor who played Transporter Chief Miles O'Brien on the series "Star Trek: TNG"

COMER ◆Comer Cottrell — founder of Pro-Line, an international ethnic hair care products manufacturer ◆ Comer Vann Woodward — historian who writes primarily on the South

COMPTON ◆Compton Bennett — British director whose films include "King Solomon's Mines"

CON ◆Con Cluskey — one of The Bachelors, debut gold record "Diane" ◆Con MacSunday — played the emperor in the Maurice Chevalier film "The Smiling Lieutenant"

CONAN ◆Arthur Conan Doyle — author and creator of "Sherlock Holmes" ◆ Conan O'Brien — talk show host who succeeded David Letterman on NBC's Late Night

CONARD ◆Conard Fowkes — actor whose roles included Donald Hughes on the soap "As The World Turns"

CONLAN ◆Conlan Carter — played law clerk C. E. Carruthers on the drama series "The Law and Mr. Jones"

CONN ◆Conn Smythe — the Conn Smythe Trophy and the NHL Smythe Division are named after him

CONNIE ◆Connie Codarini — one of The Four Lads, hits "Moments to Remember" and "No Not Much" ◆ Connie Hawkins — nicknamed The Hawk, banned from NBA for fixing games, Hall of Fame 1992

CONOR ◆Conor Clapton — son of rock star Eric Clapton ◆ Conor O'Brien — author and diplomat whose works include "States of Ireland"

CONRAD ◆Conrad Bain — actor whose roles included Philip Drummond on TV's "Diff'rent Strokes" ◆ Conrad Hilton — founder of the Hilton hotel chain ◆ Conrad Janis — Mindy's father on TV's "Mork and Mindy" ◆ Conrad Nagel — matinee idol of the 1920's and the 1930's

CONSTANTIN ◆Constantin Alajalov — Russian-born American artist ◆ Constantin Brancusi — twentieth century Romanian sculptor

CONSTANTINE ◆Constantine Bulgari — founded Rome's deluxe jewelry house with his brother Giorgio

CONSTANTINO ◆Constantino Brumidi — artist who painted the frescoes in the Capitol building

CONWAY ◆Conway Twitty — country music singer, hits include "Lost Her Love" and "To See an Angel Cry"

CORBETT ◆Corbett Monica — actor whose roles included Larry Corbett on the sitcom "The Joey Bishop Show"

CORBIN ◆Corbin Bernsen — good-looking actor whose roles included lecherous Arnie Becker on TV's "L.A. Law"

COREY ◆Corey Feldman — teenage actor whose credits include "The 'burbs" ◆ Corey Haim — portrayed Sam in the vampire film "The Lost Boys" ◆ Corey Hart — rock singer, debut hit single "Sunglasses at Night"

CORIN ◆Corin Nemec — played the lead of Parker Lewis on the sitcom "Parker Lewis Can't Lose" ◆Corin Redgrave — actor son of Sir Michael, credits include "A Man for All Seasons"

CORINTHIAN ◆Corinthian Johnson — member of The Del Vikings, debut gold record "Come Go With Me"

CORKY ◆Corky Laing — member of the heavy-metal group Mountain, albums include "Twin Peaks"

CORMAC ◆Cormac McCarthy — author of "All the Pretty Horses

CORNEL ◆Cornel Wilde — actor nominated for an Oscar in "A Song to Remember"

CORNELIUS ◆Cornelius (c) — Roddy McDowall's role as a scientist chimpanzee in "Planet of the Apes" ◆ Cornelius Vanderbilt — nineteenth-century robber baron who created Vanderbilt University

CORNELL ◆Cornell Capa — documentary photographer

CORY ◆Cory Wells — member of Three Dog Night, hit debut single "Try a Little Tenderness"

COSMO ◆Adam Cosmo Max — son of artist and designer Peter Max

COTTER ◆Cotter Smith — actor whose roles included deputy D. A. Eugene Rogan on TV's "Equal Justice"

COTTON ◆Cotton Mather — hellfire and brimstone Puritan preacher, stirred up Salem Witch Trials ◆ Cotton Wilson — portrayed by Frank Faylen in Burt Lancaster's "Gunfight at the O.K. Corral"

COUGAR ◆John Cougar Mellencamp — rock singer, debut hit single "I Need a Lover"

COURTLANDT ◆Courtlandt Gross — founder of the Lockheed Aircraft Company

COURTNEY ◆Courtney Gains — actor whose roles included Hans Klopek in Tom Hanks' comedy film "The 'burbs"

CRAIG ◆Craig Breedlove — auto racer who set the world land speed record ◆ Craig T. Nelson — plays Coach Hayden Fox on TV's "Coach"

CRANE ◆Clarence Crane Brinton — author, educator, and historian ◆ Cornelius Crane Chase — real name of comic actor Chevy Chase

CRASH ◆Crash Craddock — country western singer, hits include "Knock Three Times"

CRAWFORD ◆Crawford Long — first physician to use ether as an anesthetic

CREADEL ◆Creadel Jones — member of The Chi-Lites, hit debut single "Give It Away"

CREED ◆Creed Bratton — member of The Grass Roots, debut hit "Where Were You When I Needed You"

CREIGHTON ◆Creighton Abrams — commanding general in Vietnam after whom the Abrams tank was named ◆ Creighton Chaney — actor son of Lon Chaney who later went under the name Lon Chaney, Jr. ◆ Creighton Hale — actor who played the gambler in the classic Oscar winning film "Casablanca"

CRISPIN ◆Crispin Glover — actor who played Marty McFly's father George McFly in "Back to the Future"

CRISPUS ◆Crispus Attucks — first colonist killed at the Boston Massacre

CRISTOBAL ◆Cristobal Balenciaga — elegant Spanish fashion designer

CROCKETT ◆Crockett Johnson — creator of the comic strip "Barnaby"

CROSBY ◆Crosby Loggins — son of singer Kenny Loggins

CRUISE ◆Thomas Cruise Mapother IV — real name of superstar Tom Cruise ◆ Conor Cruise O'Brien — author and diplomat whose works include "States of Ireland"

CUBA ◆Cuba Gooding, Jr. — 1990's teen hunk, film credits include "Boyz N the Hood"

CUBBY ◆Cubby Broccoli — producer of the James Bond films

CULLEN ◆William Cullen Bryant — best known poem "Thanatopsis," 19th century editor of the "NY Evening Post" ◆ Cullen Landis — played the male lead in the first all-talking picture, "Lights of New York"

CULLY ◆Cully Richards — actor whose roles included First Sgt. Wozniak on TV's "Don't Call Me Charlie"

CURNAL ◆Curnal Aulisio — actor whose roles included George Dubcek, Jr., on the Phil Lewis sitcom "Teech"

CURT ◆Curt Gowdy — four-time Emmy winner as host of TV's "American Sportsman" ◆Curt Jurgens — German actor in "The Enemy Below" and "The Spy Who Loved Me"

CURTIS ◆Curtis Armstrong — played Herbert Viola on the detective comedy/drama series "Moonlighting" ◆Curtis Mayfield — rock singer, debut hit single "If There's a Hell Below We're All Going to Go"

CUYLER ◆Henry Cuyler Bunner — editor of the comedy magazine "Puck" in the nineteenth century ◆E. Cuyler Hammond — first medical researcher to link cigarette smoking and lung cancer

CY ◆Cy Coleman — songwriter, hits include "If My Friends Could See Me Now" ◆ Cy Curnin — member of Duran Duran, debut hit single "Hungry Like the Wolf" ◆Cy Denneny — Hall of Fame hockey player ◆Cy Endfield — film director, credits include "Zulu" and "Sands of the Kalahari" ◆Cy Young — Hall of Fame pitcher

CYCLONE ◆Cyclone Covey — author whose works include "The Gentle Radical"

CYRANO ◆Cyrano de Bergerac (c) — owner of the longest nose in literature, a soulful poet-swordsman

CYRIL ♦Cyril Cusack — actor whose roles included the evil Chauvelin in "The Elusive Pimpernel" ♦Cyril Magnin — founder of the specialty store I. Magnin

CYRUS ♦Cyrus Zachariah — one of the twin sons of actress Cybill Shepherd ♦ Cyrus McCormick — inventor of the McCormick reaper which opened up the Western plains to wheat ♦ Cyrus Vance — former secretary of state

CZESLAW ♦Czeslaw Milosz — American founder of the catastrophist school of Polish poetry ♦Czeslaw Wollejko — actor who played Polish composer Frederic Chopin in "The Young Chopin"

D'ARCY ♦D'Arcy Corrigan — actor whose roles included the blind man in Victor McLaglen's "The Informer"

DABBS ♦Dabbs Greer — played the Rev. Robert Alden on the drama series "Little House on the Prairie"

DABNEY ♦Dabney Coleman — sardonic feature film actor and star of TV's "Buffalo Bill"

DACK ♦Dack Rambo — portrayed Jack Ewing on TV's "Dallas"

DAG ♦Dag Hammarskjold — Nobel Peace Prize winning secretary general of the United Nations

DAGWOOD ♦Dagwood Bumstead (c) — comic strip and feature film character married to Blondie

DAIN ♦Erwin Dain Canham — post WWII editor of "The Christian Science Monitor" for thirty years ♦Dain Turner — actor who played Richard Allen Harris on the family drama "Harris and Company"

DAKIN ♦Dakin Matthews — played Dr. Harold Stratford on TV's "Doctor, Doctor," also on "Down Home"

DAKOTA ♦Dakota Johnson — son of "Working Girl" actress Melanie Griffith and "Miami Vice"actor Don Johnson

DALE ♦Dale Carnegie — author of "How to Win Friends and Influence People" ♦Dale Robertson — series actor who was also a host of TV's "Death Valley Days"

DALEY ♦Daley Thompson — two-time Olympic gold medal winner in the decathlon

DALLAS ♦Dallas Bower — British head of BBC and producer of "Sir Lancelot" TV series ♦ Dallas Frederick Burroughs — real name of actor Orson Bean

DALTON ◆Dalton Trumbo — one of the maligned "Hollywood Ten," wrote "Thirty Seconds Over Tokyo"

DAMIAN ◆Damian Cagnolatti — actor whose roles included Kenny Sanders on TV's "Drexell's Class"

DAMIEN ◆Father Damien — Belgian missionary to the lepers in Hawaii made famous by Robert Louis Stevenson

DAMION ◆Damion Scheller — actor whose roles included Josh Moreno on the soap "Search for Tomorrow"

DAMON ◆Damon Runyon — author of the stories that formed the basis for the musical "Guys and Dolls" ◆ Damon Wayans — actor on TV's "In Living Color" and Willis' "The Last Boy Scout"

DAN ◆Dan Aykroyd — original cast of "Saturday Night Live," films like "Dragnet" ◆ Dan Blocker — actor who played Hoss Cartwright on TV's long running western hit "Bonanza" ◆ Dan Castellaneta — actor on "The Tracy Ullman Show," also the voice of Homer on "The Simpsons" ◆ Dan Dailey — popular song and dance man in the movies ◆ Dan Rather — anchor for the "CBS Evening News" ◆ Dan Rowan — co-star of the TV comedy series "Laugh-In"

DANA ◆Dana Andrews — major movie star whose films included "The Best Years of Our Lives" ◆ Dana Carvey — played the Church Lady on "Saturday Night Live," starred in "Wayne's World" ◆ Charles Dana Gibson — creator of the trend setting "Gibson Girl"

DANDY ◆Dandy Livingstone — rock singer, hits include "Suzanne Beware" and "Of the Devil" ◆Jim Dandy Mangrum — member Black Oak Arkansas, hits include "Jim Dandy to the Rescue"

DANE ◆Dane Clark — portrayed Harlem Globetrotters manager Abe Saperstein in "Go, Man, Go!" ◆ Dane Coolidge — author who specializes in western novels

DANFORTH ◆J. Danforth Quayle — Vice President of the United States under George Bush

DANIEL ◆Daniel Boone — frontiersman and founder of Boonesboro, Kentucky ◆ Daniel Defoe — author of the classic castaway story before Gilligan, "Robinson Crusoe" ◆ Daniel Day Lewis — actor whose roles included the great white scout in "The Last of the Mohicans" ◆ Daniel Webster — nineteenth century senator known for his brilliant constitutional speeches

DANIELE ◆Daniele Amfiteatrof — composer of over 79 film scores, including Disney's "Song of the South"

DANILO ◆Danilo Donati — Oscar winner for designs in "Romeo and Juliet" and "Fellini's Casanova"

DANN ◆Dann Florek — actor whose roles included David Meyer on the legal drama series "L.A. Law"

DANNIE ◆Dannie Abse — Welsh author whose works include the award winning play "House of Cowards"

DANNY ◆Danny Aiello — actor in "Moonstruck" and "Do the Right Thing" ◆ Danny DeVito — actor whose roles included the ruthless dispatcher Louie DePalma on TV's "Taxi" ◆ Danny Glover — became a superstar in "Lethal Weapon" parts 1, 2, and 3 ◆ Danny Kaye — versatile comedic actor in films like "The Court Jester"

DANTE ◆Dante Alighieri — author of the celebrated "The Divine Comedy" ◆Dante Lavelli — Hall of Fame two-time all-pro end with Cleveland Browns ◆Edmund Dante Lowe — actor who played opposite Victor McLaglen in the "Flagg and Quirt" comedies

DANTES ◆Edmund Dantes Ames — singer with The Ames Brothers, played Mingo on TV's "Daniel Boone"

DANTON ◆Danton Walker — Broadway columnist with the New York Daily News, author of "Danton's Inferno"

DARBY ◆Darby Hinton — actor who played Israel Boone on the Fess Parker western series "Daniel Boone"

DARCEL ◆Wesley Darcel Walker — wide receiver with the NY Jets who led the NFL in receiving

DARCY ◆Darcy Conyers — British director and actor

DARIUS ◆Darius — in the Bible, the Babylonian king who cast Daniel into the lions' den ◆Darius McCrary — actor whose roles included Eddie Winslow on Urkel's TV show "Family Matters" ◆ Darius Mills — founder of the Bank of California

DARLING ◆Darling Legitimus — actor who played the concierge in Marlon Brando's "Last Tango in Paris"

DARLINGTON ◆Darlington Hoopes — ran for Vice President on the Socialist ticket during the Depression ◆ Christopher Darlington Morley — author of the best seller "Kitty Foyle," filmed with Ginger Rogers

DARNELL ◆Darnell Williams — actor whose roles included Jesse Hubbard on the soap "All My Children"

DARRELL ◆Darrell Royal — coach for the University of Texas who won three national championships ◆ Darrell Sweet — member of the hard rock group Nazareth ◆ Darrell Zwerling — portrayed Hollis Mulwray in Jack Nicholson's classic "Chinatown"

DARREN ◆Darren Burrows — actor whose roles included Ed on the drama series "Northern Exposure" ◆Darren McGavin — star of TV's "Kolchak: The Night Stalker"

DARRON ◆Darron Flagg — actor whose roles included Sal, Jr., in the quirky desert film "Bagdad Cafe"

DARROW ◆Darrow Igus — regular on the comedy variety show "Fridays"

DARRYL ◆Darryl Strawberry — troubled professional baseball player, now with the L.A. Dodgers ◆ Darryl F. Zanuck — film producer and mastermind behind Twentieth Century-Fox studios

D'ARTAGNAN ◆D'Artagnan (c) — youthful friend of the Three Musketeers

DARYL ◆Daryl Anderson — actor whose roles included Animal on TV's "Lou Grant" ◆ Daryl Dragon — singer/songwriter "Captain" in The Captain and Tennille ◆Daryl Hall — half of the recording duo Hall and Oates, hits include "She's Gone"

DASH ◆Dash Crofts — one half of Seals and Crofts, debut gold record "Summer Breeze"

DASHIELL ◆Dashiell Anderson — son of actor Harry Anderson from TV's "Night Court" ◆ Dashiell Hammett — author who created Sam Spade in "The Maltese Falcon"

DAULTON ◆Daulton Lee — Soviet spy, Sean Penn's role in the biopic "The Falcon and the Snowman"

DAVE ◆Dave Clark — founder of The Dave Clark Five rock group ◆ Dave Thomas — comedy partner with Rick Moranis, TV's "Grace Under Fire" ◆Dave Thomas — founder of Wendy's hamburger chain, named after his daughter Wendy

DAVID ◆David Bowie — rock star turned actor in "The Man Who Fell to Earth" ◆ David Carradine — star of the TV series "Kung Fu" originally created for Bruce Lee ◆David Cassidy — became a teenage heartthrob as a result of TV's "The Partridge Family" ◆ David Copperfield — magician who made the Statue of Liberty disappear ◆David Letterman — late night off-beat talk show host ◆ David Niven — Oscar winning English gentleman actor in "Separate Tables"

DAVIS ◆Davis Dresser — mystery writer, novels include "Framed in Blood"

DAVISON ◆Stephen Davison Bechtel — founder of the Bechtel Corporation ◆ John Davison Rockefeller — founder of Standard Oil, used the money to fund the Rockefeller Foundation

DAVY ◆Davy Crockett — King of the Wild Frontier, died at the Alamo, his ballad became a 1955 hit song ◆ Davy Jones — only British member of The Monkees rock group

DAWAN ◆Dawan Scott — actor who played Bigfoot Harry on the sitcom "Harry and the Hendersons"

DAWS ◆Daws Butler — voice of Elroy Jetson on the cartoon series "The Jetsons"

DAWSON ◆Dawson Mays — actor whose roles included Mel Wilson on the soap "General Hospital"

DAY ◆Daniel Day Lewis — actor whose roles included the great white scout in "The Last of the Mohicans"

DAYTON ◆Dayton Lummis — played flamboyant Gen. MacArthur in "The Court-Martial of Billy Mitchell"

DAZZY ◆Dazzy Vance — Hall of Fame pitcher who led the NL in strikeouts for eight straight years

DE VOREAUX ◆De Voreaux White — played brainy kid Aristotle on the successful sitcom "Head of the Class"

DEFORD ◆DeFord Bailey — first star of the Grand Ole Opry, known as The Harmonica Wizard

DEFOREST ◆DeForest Covan — actor whose roles included Josh on the Clifton Davis sitcom "That's My Mama" ◆ DeForest Kelley — actor who played the emotional Dr. McCoy on "Star Trek" both on TV and in features

DEWITT ◆DeWitt Carey — real name of actor Harry Carey ◆ DeWitt Clinton — New York governor who built the Erie Canal ◆ DeWitt Wallace — founder of Reader's Digest with his wife Lila

DEAN ◆Richard Dean Anderson — star of the action adventure series "MacGyver" ◆Dean Jagger — won an Oscar for the World War II epic "Twelve O'Clock High" ◆ Dean Jones — comic actor in Disney fare "The Love Bug," "Blackbeard's Ghost," "That

Darn Cat" ◆Dean Martin — former comic partner of Jerry Lewis, later became a leading man ◆Dean Stockwell — hologram star of TV's "Quantum Leap" ◆ Dean Torrence — member of Jan and Dean, sold over ten million albums, hit "Dead Man's Curve"

DECLAN ◆Declan McManus — real name of singer Elvis Costello ◆ Declan Mulligan — member of the group The Beau Brummels, debut hit "Laugh, Laugh" ◆Declan Stokes — member of The Bachelors, debut gold record rock hit "Diane"

DEE ◆Dee Brown — author of "Bury My Heart at Wounded Knee" ◆ Dee Clark — singer whose hits include "Raindrops" ◆ Dee Snider — lead singer of Twisted Sister who composes most of the group's songs

DEEMS ◆Deems Taylor — journalist and musician who was the narrator for Disney's "Fantasia"

DEION ◆Deion Sanders — football and baseball player, with both Atlanta Falcons and Atlanta Braves

DEL ◆Del Shannon — rocker, hits "Runaway" and "Hats Off to Larry"

DELANEY ◆Delaney Bramlett — member of Delaney and Bonnie, hit album "Down Home" ◆Kevin Delaney Kline — Oscar winner for "A Fish Called Wanda"

DELANO ◆Franklin Delano Roosevelt — President during the Depression and World War II

DELBERT ◆Delbert Mann — director of "Marty" and "That Touch of Mink"

DELIGHT ◆Quincy Delight Jones — legendary Hollywood composer and producer, film scores include "The Wiz"

DELL ◆Dell Andrews — nominated for an Oscar for co-writing "All Quiet on the Western Front" ◆ Dell Henderson — actor whose roles included the theater manager in the George Raft film "Bolero"

DELMER ◆Delmer Daves — director whose films include Humphrey Bogart's "Dark Passage"

DELROY ◆Delroy Wilson — rock singer, hits include "What's Going On" and "Sharing the Night Together"

DEMETRIC ◆Eric Demetric Dickerson — running back for the LA Rams who broke O. J. Simpson's record for rushing

DEMIAN ◆Demian Slade — played the smart-alec kid of Frankie and Annette in "Back to the Beach"

DEMOND ◆Demond Wilson — played the son frustrated with his devilish father on TV's "Sanford and Son"

DEMPSEY ◆Dempsey Travis — founder of Travis Realty

DENHOLM ◆Denholm Elliott — played Marcus Brody in Harrison Ford's "Indiana Jones and the Last Crusade"

DENIS ◆Denis D'Ines — actor whose roles included the evil Cardinal Richelieu in "Mistress Barry" ◆Denis Leary — actor in "Gunmen," "Sandlot" and "Judgment Night" ◆Denis Payton — member of The Dave Clark Five, debut hit gold record was "Glad All Over"

DENNIS ◆Dennis Hopper — actor who captured the counterculture of the 1960's with "Easy Rider" ◆Dennis Miller — comic anchorman for "Saturday Night Live" weekend updates ◆ Dennis Quaid — actor in lead role of Jerry Lee Lewis in "Great Balls of Fire!" ◆Dennis Weaver — lanky marshal from Taos, New Mexico in TV's "McCloud"

DENNY ◆Denny Carmassi — member of the group Heart, hit album "Dreamboat Annie" ◆ Denny Crum — basketball coach who won NCAA championship in 1980 ◆ Denny Tufano — member of The Buckinghams, hits include "Kind of a Drag"

DENVER ◆Denver Pyle — long time character actor who played Uncle Jessie on TV's "The Dukes of Hazzard"

DENVIL ◆Denvil Liptrot — with KC and the Sunshine Band, debut number one gold record "Get Down Tonight"

DENYS ◆Denys Cook — British cameraman, films include "Bunny Lake Is Missing" ◆Denys Wortman — cartoonist with the New York World and the New York World-Telegram

DENZEL ◆Denzel Washington — best supporting actor Oscar winner for "Glory," the star of "Malcolm X"

DENZIL ◆Denzil Foster — member of Club Nouveau, hits include "Lean on Me" which sold six million copies

DEODAT ◆Deodat Dolomieu — volcanic geologist after whom "dolomite" is named

DEREK ◆Derek Delevan Harris — real name of actor John Derek ◆ Derek Longmuir — member of the Scottish Bay City

Rollers, hits include "Saturday Night" ◆ Derek McGrath — actor whose roles included Ozwald Valentine on TV's "Dallas"

DERMOT ◆Dermot Mulroney — actor in Sean Astin's "Staying Together" ◆ Dermot Walsh — actor in the British TV series "Richard the Lionheart"

DERREN ◆Derren Nesbitt — actor who played real 19th century graverobber Burke in biopic "Burke and Hare"

DERRICK ◆Derrick de Marney — played British statesman Benjamin Disraeli in the film "Victoria the Great"

DES ◆Des Roberts — played the blood-sucking Count in "Guess What Happened to Count Dracula"

DESI ◆Desi Arnaz — Lucy's real life husband, played Ricky Ricardo on TV's "I Love Lucy"

DESIDERIO ◆Desiderio Arnaz IV — member of Dino, Desi, and Billy, debut hit "I'm a Fool"

DESIRE ◆Desire Defauw — leader of the Chicago Symphony in the 1940's ◆ Henri Desire Landru — French "Bluebeard" guillotined for murdering ten women

DESMOND ◆Desmond Howard — 1991 Heisman Trophy winner ◆ Desmond Llewelyn — actor whose roles included "Q" in the classic James Bond adventure "Goldfinger" ◆Desmond Morris — author of the best selling book "The Naked Ape"

DEVADIP ◆Devadip Carlos Santana — leader of the rock group Santana, debut hit single "Jingo"

DEVEREUX ◆Austin Devereux — son of singer and actress Michelle Phillips

DEVIN ◆Devin Ratray — actor whose roles included Gus Stafford on the sitcom "Heartland"

DEWEY ◆Dewey Bunnell — member of the rock group America, hits include "A Horse With No Name" ◆ Dewey "Pigmeat" Markham — known for his "here comes de judge" skit on "Laugh-In" ◆ Dewey Martin — member of the group Buffalo Springfield, hits include "For What It's Worth"

DEXTER ◆Dexter Means Bullard — his hospital was the setting for "I Never Promised You a Rose Garden"

DIAN ◆Dian Edmonson — one of The Greenbriar Boys

DICK ◆Dick Cavett — television interviewer on various versions of his "Dick Cavett Show" ◆ Dick Clark — host of the long running teen beat show "American Bandstand" ◆Dick Van Dyke — actor whose roles included Rob Petrie on his own "Dick Van Dyke Show"

DICKEY ◆Dickey Lee — country music singer, number one hits "Patches" and "I Saw the Light"

DICKIE ◆Dickie Moore — actor whose roles included Dickens workhouse orphan boy in "Oliver Twist" ◆ Dickie Owen — actor who played the mummified Egyptian in "The Curse of the Mummy's Tomb"

DICKINSON ◆Dickinson Richards — Nobel Prize winner for discoveries in the circulatory system

DICKY ◆Dicky Betts — member of the Allman Brothers Band

DIDIER ◆Didier Pitre — Hockey Hall of Fame defenseman with Montreal

DIEGO ◆Diego Asencio — American ambassador to Colombia held hostage by terrorists in 1980 ◆ Diego Colon — eldest son of Christopher Columbus who became governor of the Indies

DIETRICH ◆Dietrich Bonhoeffer — twentieth century German theologian ◆ Dietrich Buxtehude — organist whom Bach walked 200 miles to hear play

DIGBY ◆Digby Wolfe — Emmy winning writer whose credits include "Laugh-In"

DIK ◆Dik Browne — creator of the cartoons "Hi and Lois" and "Hagar the Horrible"

DIMITRI ◆Stephen Dimitri Georgiou — real name of singer Cat Stevens ◆ Dimitri Hamlin — son of sexy actress Ursula Andress and Harry Hamlin from TV's "L.A. Law" ◆ Dimitri Tiomkin — Oscar winning composer for Gary Cooper's "High Noon"

DINK ◆Dink Templeton — actor who played the reporter in the original Dick Powell "Thin Man" film

DINO ◆Dino De Laurentiis — producer, credits include "Barabbas," "The Bible," "Barbarella," and "Waterloo" ◆ Dino Martin — son of Dean Martin, formed a rock group with Desi Arnaz, Jr.

DION ◆Dion DiMucci — leader of the group Dion and the Belmonts, hits include "Runaround Sue"

DIONYSIUS ◆Dionysius Lardner — author of the 133 volume "Cabinet Cyclopaedia"

DIRK ◆Dirk Benedict — TV actor in the series "Battlestar Galactica" and "The A-Team" ◆ Dirk Blocker — brother of Dan Blocker, played Lt. Bragg on the series "Black Sheep Squadron" ◆ Dirk Bogarde — British actor whose credits include "The Servant" and "Death in Venice"

DITA ◆Dita Davis Beard — lobbyist involved in ITT attempt to subsidize the Republican National Convention

DIXIE ◆Dixie Walker — outfielder who led the National League in RBI's

DIZZY ◆Dizzy Dean — National League's Most Valuable Player for 1934 ◆ Dizzy Gillespie — jazz trumpeter who created "Be-Bop"

DMITRI ◆Dmitri Mendeleev — inventor of the periodic table

DOAK ◆Doak Walker — 1948 Heisman Trophy winner who lead the league in scoring twice

DOBIE ◆Dobie Gray — husky-voiced musician whose hits include "Drift Away"

DOC ◆Doc Holliday — poker player and dentist sidekick to Wyatt Earp ◆ Doc Severinsen — band leader for "The Tonight Show Starring Johnny Carson"

DOCK ◆Dock Boggs — country western banjo picker extraordinaire ◆ Dock Ellis — pitcher who threw a no-hitter in 1970

DOLF ◆Dolf Camilli — first baseman, 1941 Most Valuable Player in the National League

DOLPH ◆Dolph Lundgren — Stallone's opposition in "Rocky IV," a Russian fighting machine named Drago ◆ Dolph Sweet — actor whose roles included Chief Carl Kanisky on the sitcom "Gimme a Break"

DOM ◆Dom Deluise — sidekick to Burt Reynolds in his sillier movies ◆ Dom Raomao — member of Sergio Mendes and Brasil '66, hit song "Mas Que Nada"

DOMENIC ◆Domenic Troiano — member of The Guess Who, debut hit record "Shakin' All Over"

DOMENICO ◆Domenico Modugno — Emmy winner for best record with "Volare"

DOMINGO ◆Domingo Samudio — "Sam" in Sam the Sham and the Pharaohs, debut gold record "Wooly Bully" ◆Domingo Soler — actor whose roles included escaped convict Jean Valjean in "Les Miserables"

DOMINIC ◆Dominic Hoffman — actor whose roles included Julian on TV's "A Different World"

DOMINICK ◆Dominick Dunne — author of "The Two Mrs. Grenvilles," later made as a miniseries

DOMINIQUE ◆Dominique Wilkins — forward with Atlanta who led the NBA in scoring

DON ◆Don Adams — actor whose roles included Maxwell Smart on TV's "Get Smart" ◆ Don Ameche — actor whose roles included the title role in the film "Alexander Graham Bell" ◆Don Johnson — good-looking star of TV's "Miami Vice" ◆ Don Kirshner — host of TV's "Don Kirshner's Rock Concert" ◆Don Knotts — launched to stardom as the bumbling Deputy Barney Fife on "The Andy Griffith Show" ◆ Don Rickles — comedian whose style depends on insulting the audience

DONAL ◆Donal Donnely — Irish stage actor who occasionally worked in films ◆ Donal McCann — actor whose roles included Gabriel in John Huston's "The Dead"

DONALD ◆Donald O'Connor — dancing actor in "Singin' in the Rain," Francis the Talking Mule series ◆ Donald Pleasence — British character actor in "The Great Escape," "Oh, God!," "Halloween" ◆ Donald Sutherland — played the wisecracking Hawkeye Pierce in the film version of "M*A*S*H"

DONALL ◆E. Donall Thomas — Nobel Prize winner for work in transplanting bone marrow

DONATELLO ◆Donatello — finest sculptor of the fifteenth century

DONATIEN ◆Marquis Donatien de Sade — infamous French sex writer responsible for the word "sadism"

DONATO ◆Donato Rico — editor at Marvel Comics, whose magazines include "Captain America"

DONN ◆Donn Eisele — astronaut in command of the module on the first Apollo flight ◆ Donn Tatum — chairman of Disney who developed Disney World and Tokyo Disneyland

DONNELLY ◆Donnelly Rhodes — actor whose roles included Art Foster on TV's "Double Trouble"

DONNIE ◆Donnie Dacus — member of Chicago, hits include "Saturday in the Park" ◆ Donnie Van Zandt — member of the rock group 38 Special, debut hit "Rockin' Into the Night" ◆ Donnie Wahlberg — member of The New Kids on the Block, albums "Hangin' Tough" and "Step by Step"

DONNY ◆Donny Hathaway — best known for duets with Roberta Flack, hits include "The Closer I Get to You" ◆Donny Most — he was the only one who thought he was funny as Ralph Malph on TV's "Happy Days" ◆ Donny Osmond — pop singer for the teenybopper set of the 1970's with songs like "Puppy Love"

DONOVAN ◆Donovan Leitch — folk/rock star, hits "Sunshine Superman" and "Mellow Yellow" ◆ Donovan Scott — actor who played Leonard Stoner on the Lucille Ball sitcom "Life With Lucy"

DOOLEY ◆Dooley Wilson — actor who played Sam, the piano player in Humphrey Bogart's "Casablanca"

DORE ◆Dore Schary — screenwriter of Bing Crosby's "Boys Town"

DORIAN ◆Dorian Henry — son of actress Lindsay Wagner, TV's "Bionic Woman" ◆ Dorian Gray (c) — sells his soul for eternal youth, while his portrait grows old ◆Dorian Harewood — actor in the film "The Jesse Owens Story" and "Full Metal Jacket"

DOROTEO ◆Doroteo Arango — real name of Mexican bandit and revolutionary Pancho Villa

DORSEY ◆Dorsey Wright — actor who played Hud in Treat Williams' homage to the 60's counterculture "Hair"

DOTSON ◆Dotson Rader — author whose novels include "Miracle" and "Beau Monde"

DOUG ◆Doug Henning — magician who hosts TV specials, musical "The Magic Show" ◆ Doug McClure — square-jawed actor in "The Land That Time Forgot," TV's "Out of This World"

DOUGLAS ◆Douglas Fairbanks — original movie swashbuckler, one of the founders of United Artists studios ◆ Douglas MacArthur — flamboyant general who ran the war in the Pacific in World War II

DOUGLASS ◆Harold Douglass Baines — outfielder with the Chicago White Sox ◆ Douglass Montgomery — actor who played the lead in the biopic of Stephen Foster "Harmony Lane" ◆

Douglass Wallop — author of "The Year the Yankees Lost the Pennant," basis for "Damn Yankees"

DOW ◆Dow Finsterwald — championship golfer ◆ Frank Dow Merrill — commander of the WWII guerilla unit, Jeff Chandler biopic "Merrill's Marauders"

DOYLE ◆Doyle Blackwood — member of the country western singing group The Blackwood Brothers ◆ Doyle Wilburn — country western singer, hits "Hurt Her Once for Me," "Which One Is to Blame"

DRAKE ◆Drake Hogestyn — played Frain McFadden on the adventure series "Seven Brides for Seven Brothers" ◆ Drake Levin — member of Paul Revere and the Raiders, debut hit single "Like Long Hair"

DRED ◆Dred Scott — Supreme Court denied his suit for freedom, became a cause of the Civil War

DREW ◆Drew Pearson — wrote syndicated daily column "Washington Merry-Go-Round" ◆ Drew Thatcher (c) — Bill Smitrovich's role on the series "Life Goes On"

DRYDEN ◆Sydney Dryden Chaplin — actor and manager of his half-brother Charlie Chaplin

DUBOSE ◆DuBose Heyward — author of "Porgy" which was adapted as opera "Porgy and Bess"

DUANE ◆Duane Allen — member of the Oak Ridge Boys, whose hits include "Bobby Sue" ◆ Duane Allman — brother in Allman Brothers Band who died in a motorcycle accident ◆ Duane Eddy — rock singer, hits "Movin' 'n' Groovin'," "Rebel Rouser"

DUB ◆Dub Taylor — series regular on the long running hayseed series "Hee Haw"

DUDLEY ◆Dudley Moore — pianist-comedian who starred as the intoxicated but loveable "Arthur"

DUFF ◆Duff McKagan — member of Guns 'n' Roses, hits include platinum "Appetite for Destruction"

DUGGIE ◆Duggie Wakefield — British music hall comedian, in character as a simpleton who always triumphed

DUKE ◆Duke Ellington — bandleader and composer of "Take the 'A' Train" and "Sophisticated Lady"

DUMAS ◆Dumas Malone — Pulitzer Prize winning author for his biography of Thomas Jefferson

DUNCAN ◆Duncan Black — produced first electric drill, company became Black and Decker ◆Duncan Hines — author of "Adventures in Good Eating" ◆Duncan Regehr — played Prince Dirk Blackpool on the adventure series "Wizards and Warriors" ◆ Duncan Renaldo — actor whose roles included the original Cisco Kid on TV

DURWARD ◆Durward Kirby — co-host of the comedy series "Candid Camera"

DUSKO ◆Dusko Popov — British agent during World War II, Ian Fleming's model for James Bond

DUSTIN ◆Dustin Farnum — cowboy silent film star, films include "The Squaw Man" and "The Virginian" ◆ Dustin Hoffman — Oscar winning actor in films like "Tootsie" and "Rain Man" ◆ Dustin Nguyen — played Officer Harry Truman Ioki on the hit teen police drama "21 Jump Street"

DUTCH ◆Dutch Schultz — New York bootlegger during Prohibition who killed Legs Diamond

DWAYNE ◆Dwayne Hickman — portrayed lovesick teenager Dobie Gillis in the TV series of the same name

DWEEZIL ◆Dweezil Zappa — MTV veejay and son of Frank Zappa, solo album "Havin' a Bad Day"

DWIER ◆Dwier Brown — actor whose roles included John Kinsella in Kevin Costner's "Field of Dreams"

DWIGHT ◆Dwight D. Eisenhower — planned the Normandy invasion, which led him to the White House ◆ Dwight Schultz — actor whose roles included the brain-dead whacko on TV's "The A-Team" ◆ Dwight Yoakam — country music's best new male vocalist in 1987, hits include "Honky Tonk Man"

DYLAN ◆Dylan Thomas — Welsh author who wrote "Under Milk Wood" ◆Dylan Walsh — actor who played Louis Klein on James Earl Jones' drama series "Gabriel's Fire"

EADES ◆Eades Hogue — actor whose roles included the town marshal in Karl Malden's "Baby Doll"

EAMONN ◆Eamonn Andrews — Irish TV personality who hosted "This Is Your Life" for Ralph Edwards

EARL ◆Earl of Cardigan — led the Charge of the Light Brigade, cardigan sweater named for him ◆Earl Holliman — actor in "The Sons of Katie Elder," then second banana to TV's "Policewoman" ◆James Earl Jones — voice of Darth Vader in "Star Wars" ◆Earl

Scruggs — country western master of the banjo, hits include "The Ballad of Jed Clampett" ◆Earl Tupper — former DuPont chemist, founder of Tupperware Home Parties ◆ Earl Warren — liberal Supreme Court Chief Justice and head of the JFK Warren Commission

EARLE ◆Earle Dickson — inventor of the "Band-Aid" for those scrapes and cuts ◆Jackie Earle Haley — child actor whose films include "Breaking Away," and the Bad News Bears movies ◆ Clarence Earle Lovejoy — creator of "Lovejoy's College Guide"

EARVIN ◆Earvin Johnson, Jr. — real name of basketball superstar "Magic" Johnson struck down with AIDS

EBENEZER ◆Ebenezer Butterick — inventor of standardized paper patterns for clothes ◆Ebenezer Scrooge (c) — villain in the classic Dickens tale "A Christmas Carol"

ED ◆Ed Asner — actor whose roles included Lou Grant on TV's "The Mary Tyler Moore Show" ◆ Ed Begley — Oscar winning actor for "The Unsinkable Molly Brown" ◆ Ed McMahon — Johnny Carson's chuckling sidekick on "The Tonight Show" for over 20 years ◆ Ed Sullivan — kingpin of TV's long running "Ed Sullivan Show"

EDAN ◆Edan Gross — actor whose roles included Gene Harper on TV's "Free Spirit"

EDD ◆Edd Byrnes — actor whose roles included Kookie on TV's "77 Sunset Strip" ◆Edd Hall — announcer on TV's "The Tonight Show" since 1992

EDDIE ◆Eddie Albert — actor who played Oliver Wendell Douglas on CBS's rural hit "Green Acres" ◆ Eddie Murphy — went from "Saturday Night Live" to film superstardom in "Beverly Hills Cop" ◆Eddie Rabbit — country music singer, hits include "Drinkin' My Baby Off My Mind" ◆Eddie Van Halen — rock singer, musician, and leader of the rock group Van Halen

EDDY ◆Eddy Arnold — country singer called "The Tennessee Plowboy" ◆Eddy Duchin — Boston pianist-bandleader, portrayed by Tyrone Power in "The Eddy Duchin Story"

EDGAR ◆Edgar Bergen — ventriloquist creator of dummy film star Charlie McCarthy, father of Candice ◆Edgar Rice Burroughs — creator of "Tarzan" ◆J. Edgar Hoover — for 50 years, if you'd seen this director of the FBI, you'd seen them all ◆ Edgar Allan Poe — originator of the horror short story, also poet and novelist

EDMON ◆Edmon Ryan — actor whose roles included Harlem Globetrotter Zack Leader in "Go, Man, Go!"

EDMOND ◆Edmond Hoyle — codified card game rules, "according to Hoyle" now means the "highest authority" ◆ Edmond O'Brien — won an Oscar for "The Barefoot Contessa"

EDMUND ◆Edmund Ames — singer with The Ames Brothers, played Mingo on TV's "Daniel Boone" ◆Edmund Gwenn — won an Oscar for playing Santa Claus in "Miracle on 34th Street" ◆ Edmund Halley — discovered that the same comet kept coming to Earth, called it Halley's Comet

EDOUARD ◆Edouard Manet — Impressionist artist, works "Olympia" and "A Bar at the Folies-Bergere" ◆ Edouard Michelin — first to make rubber tires for cars, founder Michelin Tires

EDRIC ◆Edric Connor — British West Indian actor and singer, was in Gregory Peck's "Moby Dick"

EDSEL ◆Edsel Ford — son of Henry Ford after whom the Edsel automobile was named

EDUARDO ◆Eduardo Ciannelli — actor who played the guru in the classic of the Indian frontier, "Gunga Din"

EDVARD ◆Edvard Greig — nineteenth century Norwegian composer, biopic "Song of Norway" ◆ Edvard Munch — melancholic Norwegian artist of portraits and landscapes

EDWARD ◆Edward R. Murrow — broadcast journalist known for his TV show "See It Now" ◆Edward James Olmos — played Lt. Martin Castillo on TV's "Miami Vice," star of "Stand and Deliver" ◆ Edward G. Robinson — perfect heavy for the 1930's gangster movies

EDWIN ◆Edwin Budding — inventor of the lawnmower ◆Edwin Land — founder of the Polaroid Company, invented the Polaroid-Land Camera ◆Edwin Link — founder of Link Aviation, designed the Link Trainers used during World War II

EERO ◆Eero Saarinen — architect who designed the Jefferson Memorial Arch in St. Louis

EFFRON ◆Ermes Effron Borgnino — real name of Italian count and legendary screen actor Ernest Borgnine

EFRAIN ◆Efrain Figuerroa — actor who played Sgt. Estaban Gutierrez on the police drama "Houston Knights"

EFREM ◆Efrem Zimbalist, Jr. — actor whose roles included Lewis Erskine on "The FBI" TV series

EGBERT ◆Egbert R. Murrow — real name of newscaster Edward R. Murrow ◆ Egbert Van Alstyne — composer of over 700 songs, including "In the Shade of the Old Apple Tree"

EGON ◆Egon von Furstenberg — fashion designer who created "The Power Look"

EINAR ◆Einar Scott — actor whose roles included Nels Andersson on the soap "As the World Turns"

ELBERT ◆Elbert Baker — president and publisher of the Tribune Publishing Company ◆ Elbert Hubbard — author of "A Message to Garcia," died on the Lusitania ◆ Elbert Wilkins — member of The Dramatics, debut gold record "Whatcha See Is Whatcha Get"

ELBRIDGE ◆Elbridge Gerry — signer of the Declaration of Independence, name gave rise to term "gerrymander"

ELDEE ◆Eldee Young — member of The Ramsey Lewis Trio, debut hit "Something You Got"

ELDRIDGE ◆Eldridge Bryant — original member of The Temptations ◆ Eldridge Cleaver — civil rights radical during the 1960's

ELEAZAR ◆Eleazar Wheelock — founder of Dartmouth College, married to Abigail Davenport

ELFORD ◆Elford Kingman — real name of dancer Kelly Brown, films include "Daddy Long Legs" with Fred Astaire

ELGIN ◆Elgin Baylor — ten-time All-Star who scored 71 points in one basketball game ◆Horace Elgin Dodge — manufacturer of the Dodge cars

ELI ◆Berna Eli Oldfield — auto racer who was the first to travel a mile a minute ◆ Eli Wallach — portrayed the bad guy in "The Magnificent Seven" ◆ Eli Whitney — inventor of the cotton gin, laid the groundwork for the Civil War

ELIA ◆Elia Kazan — director of "Gentleman's Agreement" and "On the Waterfront"

ELIAS ◆Elias Howe — inventor of the sewing machine

ELIE ◆Elie Abel — Canadian broadcast journalist ◆ Elie Wiesel — Nobel Prize winning concentration camp survivor

ELIHU ◆Elihu Root — Nobel Peace Prize winning secretary of war ◆ Elihu Yale — benefactor after whom Yale University was named

ELIJAH ◆Elijah Blue Allman — son of actress/singer Cher and Greg Allman of the Allman Brothers Band ◆ Elijah Lovejoy — newspaper editor whose presses were destroyed because he was anti-slavery ◆Elijah Muhammad — founder of the Black Muslims

ELIO ◆Elio Petri — Oscar winning director for "Investigation of a Citizen Above Suspicion"

ELIOT ◆Samuel Eliot Morison — Pulitzer Prize winning naval historian ◆ Eliot Ness — 1930's FBI racketbuster, biopic is Kevin Costner's "The Untouchables"

ELIPHALET ◆Eliphalet Remington — manufacturer of the Remington rifle

ELISHA ◆Elisha Cook — slightly built actor, adept at neurotics, played Wilmer in "The Maltese Falcon" ◆Elisha Otis — inventor of the elevator, founded Otis Elevator Company

ELLAS ◆Ellas Bates McDaniel — real name of rock star Bo Diddley

ELLERY ◆Ellery Queen — pseudonym for writing duo Fredric Dannan and Manford B. Lee

ELLIOT ◆Elliot Handler — inventor of the Barbie and Ken dolls named after his children

ELLIOTT ◆Elliott Gould — actor in films "M*A*S*H," "Bugsy" and "Capricorn One" ◆ Elliott Humphrey — trained the first guide dogs for the blind

ELLIS ◆Ellis Briggs — US Ambassador, wrote "Shots Heard Around the World" ◆ Ellis Peters — winner of the Edgar award for "Death and the Joyful Woman"

ELLISON ◆Ellison Onizuka — astronaut who died in the crash of the Challenger space shuttle ◆ Ellison Smith — South Carolina senator critical of the New Deal

ELLSWORTH ◆Ellsworth Fredericks — cinematographer, works "Invasion of the Body Snatchers," "Seven Days in May" ◆ Ellsworth Huntington — explored the Euphrates River, author "Earth and Sun" ◆ Allen Ellsworth Ludden — host of TV's "Password," husband of actress Betty White

ELMER ◆Elmer Bernstein — composer who won an Oscar for score of "Thoroughly Modern Millie"

ELMO ◆Elmo Lincoln — three-time player of the ape-man Tarzan ◆Elmo Zumwalt — youngest four-star admiral in US naval history, chief of naval operations

ELMORE ◆Elmore James — Rock and Roll Hall of Fame blues musician, hits include "Dust My Broom" ◆ Elmore Torn, Jr. — real name of comic actor Rip Torn

ELOY ◆Eloy Casados — actor whose roles included Tsiskwa on the adventure series "Young Dan'l Boone"

ELROY ◆John Elroy Sanford — real name of comedian Redd Foxx, who used his last name for his most famous role

ELSTON ◆Elston Howard — first African-American to win Most Valuable Player

ELTON ◆Elton Britt — one of country music's first superstars ◆ Elton John — pop singer with expansive eyewear collection, started Crocodile Rockin' in 70's ◆Douglas Elton Ulman — real name of legendary screen swashbuckler Douglas Fairbanks

ELVIN ◆Elvin Jellinek — promoted the scientific study of alcoholism ◆ Elvin Jones — highly influential jazz drummer

ELVIS ◆Elvis Costello — performer, hits include the album "Good Year for Roses" ◆ Elvis Perkins — son of "Psycho" actor Anthony Perkins ◆ Elvis Presley — The King of Rock and Roll

ELWOOD ◆Elwood Blues (c) — Dan Aykroyd's character in "The Blues Brothers" on a mission from God ◆Elwood P. Dowd (c) — Jimmy Stewart's character who had an invisible rabbit friend in "Harvey"

ELWYN ◆Elwyn Brook-Jones — thick-set British actor usually seen in villainous roles ◆ Elwyn Brooks White — author of the children's classic "Charlotte's Web"

ELY ◆Ely Culbertson — inventor of contract bridge

ELZIE ◆Elzie Segar — cartoonist who created "Popeye"

EMANUEL ◆Emanuel Goldenberg — real name of actor Edward G. Robinson ◆ Emanuel Noah Hutton — son of actors Debra Winger and Timothy Hutton, grandson of actor Jim Hutton ◆ Emanuel Leutze — artist who painted "Washington Crossing the Delaware"

EMERIC ◆Emeric Pressburger — journalist whose filmed novels include "Behold a Pale Horse"

EMERSON ◆Emerson Fittipaldi — winner of two Formula One world championships and the Indy 500 ◆Curtis Emerson LeMay — air force chief of staff at the end of WW II and during the Berlin Airlift

EMIL ◆James Emil Coco — actor nominated for an Oscar for "Only When I Laugh" ◆Emil Jannings — Oscar winner for "The Last Command"

EMILE ◆Emile Coue — psychologist who said "Day by day in every way, I am getting better and better" ◆ Emile Zola — novelist, biopic "The Life of Emile Zola"

EMILIANO ◆Emiliano Zapata — Mexican revolutionary who joined with Pancho Villa, biopic "Viva Zapata!"

EMILIO ◆Emilio Estefan, Jr. — member of The Miami Sound Machine, debut hit single "Conga" ◆Emilio Estevez — Brat Pack actor of "The Breakfast Club," "Stakeout," "St. Elmo's Fire"

EMLEN ◆Emlen Tunnell — first African-American in the football Hall of Fame

EMLYN ◆Emlyn Williams — portrayed nineteenth century novelist Emile Zola in "I Accuse!"

EMMANUEL ◆Victor Emmanuel II — first King of Italy, who freed his country from Austrian domination ◆Emmanuel Lewis — actor whose roles included the title role in TV's sitcom "Webster"

EMMET ◆Emmet Heflin, Jr. — real name of actor Van Heflin

EMMETT ◆Emmett Dalton — outlaw with the Dalton Gang, wrote "When the Daltons Rode" ◆ Emmett Kelly — legendary sad-eyed circus clown, appeared in "The Greatest Show on Earth"

EMMITT ◆Emmitt Smith — running back for the Dallas Cowboys, 1993 and 1994 Superbowl champions

EMORY ◆Emory Parnell — actor who has played villain, prison warden, weakling and kindly father

EMRYS ◆Hugh Emrys Griffith — won an Oscar for Ben-Hur ◆ Emrys Johnson — British stage actor

EMUUKHA ◆Ahmet Emuukha Rodan Zappa — son of rock singer Frank Zappa

ENDICOTT ◆Endicott Peabody — founder of the Groton prep school

ENG ◆Eng — half of the original Siamese Twins, with his brother Chang

ENGELBERT ◆Engelbert Humperdinck — male vocalist with career spanning three decades

ENGLAND ◆England Dan — music partner of John Ford Coley, hit song "I'd Really Love to See You Tonight"

ENOCH ◆Enoch — in the Bible, Cain's oldest son ◆ Enoch Crosby — patriot spy during the American Revolution

ENOS ◆Enos Slaughter — outfielder with St. Louis Cardinals, led National League in RBI's

ENRICO ◆Enrico Caruso — Italian tenor opera singer

ENRIQUE ◆Henry Enrique Estrada — real name of actor Erik Estrada, played Ponch on TV's "CHiPs" ◆ Enrique Garcia — member of The Miami Sound Machine, debut hit single "Conga"

ENZO ◆Enzo Cerusico — actor who played the lead Tony Novello on the detective drama "My Friend Tony" ◆Enzo Ferrari — developer of the Ferrari automobile

EPHRAIM ◆Ephraim — in the Bible, Joseph's second son ◆ Ephraim McDowell — surgeon who performed the first ovarian operation in the United States

EPPA ◆Eppa Rixey — Cincinnati Hall of Fame pitcher with 266 career wins

ERASMUS ◆Erasmus Darwin — poet grandfather of Charles Darwin, works include "The Botanic Garden"

ERASTUS ◆Erastus Beadle — invented the dime novel with "Malaeska" in 1860 ◆ Erastus Corning — town in New York named after him

ERIC ◆Eric Burdon — lead singer for The Animals ◆ Eric Clapton — in rock groups Cream, The Yardbirds, and Blind Faith ◆ Eric Idle — a member of Monty Python's Flying Circus ◆ Eric Roberts — actor in "Final Analysis" and brother of Julia Roberts ◆ Eric Sevareid — part of the original CBS news team in 1939

ERICH ◆Erich Anderson — actor who played Billy Sidel on the comedy/drama series "thirtysomething" ◆ Erich Segal — author of "Love Story," became a megahit with Ryan O'Neal and Ali

McGraw ◆ Erich von Stroheim — film director of the 1920's, whose great silent film was "Greed"

ERIK ◆Erik Erikson — psychoanalyst who coined the term "identity crisis" ◆ Erik Estrada — portrayed Officer Frank "Ponch" Poncherello on TV's "CHiPs"

ERLAND ◆Erland Josephson — actor who played Henrik Vogler in Ingmar Bergman's "After the Rehearsal"

ERLE ◆Erle Stanley Gardner — author of the "Perry Mason" books on which the TVseries was based

ERMES ◆Ermes Effron Borgnino — real name of Italian count and legendary screen actor Ernest Borgnine

ERN ◆Ern Westmore — dean of Hollywood makeup artists, gave beauty advice on "Hollywood Backstage"

ERNEST ◆Ernest Borgnine — played Quentin McHale on TV's "McHale's Navy," Oscar-winner for "Marty" ◆ Ernest Hemingway — many of his books have been made into films; won Nobel Prize for literature

ERNESTO ◆Ernesto Maserati — Italian auto racer and founder of the Maserati luxury car company ◆ Ernesto Miranda — his Supreme Court case led to the "Miranda" warnings given by police officers

ERNIE ◆Ernie Kovacs — comedy actor and producer of 1950's television ◆Ernie Pyle — World War II newspaper correspondent, biopic "The Story of G.I. Joe"

ERNO ◆Erno Crisa — actor whose roles included the legendary rake in "Don Juan" ◆Erno Rubik — creator of the Rubik's Cube

ERNST ◆Ernst Lubitsch — legendary Oscar nominated Hollywood director ◆ John Ernst Steinbeck — Nobel Prize winning author, wrote "The Grapes of Wrath," "Of Mice and Men"

ERROL ◆Errol Flynn — actor who inherited the swashbuckler mantle of Douglas Fairbanks

ERSEL ◆Ersel Hickey — rock singer, hits include "Bluebirds Over the Mountain"

ERSKINE ◆Erskine Preston Caldwell — novels turned into films include "Tobacco Road" and "God's Little Acre" ◆ Erskine Hamilton Childers — Protestant elected president of Ireland after 30 years of Catholics

ERTE ◆Erte — fashion designer of "Harper's Bazaar" covers for over thirty years

ERVILLE ◆Erville Alderson — actor whose roles included Benedict in John Wayne's "Haunted Gold"

ERVIN ◆Ronald Ervin McNair — astronaut who died in the explosion of the Challenger space shuttle

ERWIN ◆Erwin Canham — post WWII editor of "The Christian Science Monitor" for thirty years ◆ Erwin Fuller — actor whose roles included FBI director J. Edgar Hoover in "Lepke" ◆ Erwin Rommel — "Desert Fox" who led the legendary Afrika Corps in World War II

ESAI ◆Esai Morales — actor whose roles included Latino hood Paco Moreno in Sean Penn's "Bad Boys"

ESME ◆Esme Percy — actor whose roles included French conqueror Napoleon in "Invitation to a Waltz"

ESMOND ◆Esmond Knight — actor who played Austrian composer Johann Strauss in "Waltzes From Vienna"

ESTES ◆Estes Kefauver — Adlai Stevenson's vice presidential running mate

ETHAN ◆Ethan Allen — patriot leader of the Green Mountain Boys during the American Revolution ◆Ethan Coen — one of the producing Coen Brothers, films include "Raising Arizona" ◆ Ethan Hawke — young actor in "The Dead Poets Society" and "Dad"

ETIENNE ◆Etienne Brule — first European to explore the Canadian province of Ontario ◆ Etienne Girardot — dapper French character actor, played Mr. Abernathie in the film "Mandalay"

ETTORE ◆Ettore Bugatti — Italian auto manufacturer noted for racing and luxury cars

EUBIE ◆Eubie Blake — ragtime pianist, hits include "I'm Just Wild About Harry"

EUGENE ◆Henry Eugene Abbey — manager who introduced Sarah Bernhardt to America ◆ Eugene O'Neill — Nobel Prize winning playwright ◆ Eugene Orowitz — real name of actor Michael Landon

EVAN ◆Joe Evan Brown — comedy actor, films include "Some Like It Hot" ◆Evan Cohen — actor whose roles included Johnny

Long on the sitcom "It's Not Easy" ◆Evan Mirand — actor whose roles included Dominic Fopiano on the TV drama "Glory Days"

EVANDER ◆Evander Holyfield — 1990 heavyweight boxing champion

EVANS ◆Evans Carlson — commander of WW II Carlson's Raiders whose battle cry was "Gung Ho!"

EVARTS ◆Evarts Graham — discovered the correlation between smoking and lung cancer

EVEL ◆Evel Knievel — spectacular motorcycle stuntman, played by George Hamilton in his biopic

EVELYN ◆Richard Evelyn Byrd — explorer who was the first man to fly over both the North and South Poles

EVERETT ◆Everett Dirksen — Republican senator who played a major role in passing civil rights laws ◆Edward Everett Horton — often Fred Astaire's sidekick, later a narrator on TV's "Rocky and Bullwinkle" ◆ C. Everett Koop — surgeon general of the United States who campaigned against AIDS

EWAN ◆Ewan Maccoll — singer who wrote the Grammy winning "The First Time Ever I Saw Your Face"

EWEN ◆Ewen Solon — actor whose roles included the serial killer in "Jack the Ripper"

EWING ◆Ewing Brown — played legendary frontier marshal Wild Bill Hickok in "Son of the Renegade"

EZEKIEL ◆Ezekiel — in the Bible, a major prophet of the coming of the Messiah

EZIO ◆Ezio Pinza — host of "The RCA Victor Show"

EZRA ◆Ezra Cornell — founded Western Union Telegraph Company, and then Cornell University ◆ Ezra Pound — established the modernist movement in poetry

FABIAN ◆Fabian — teenage idol, singer, and guitarist, films include "Ten Little Indians" ◆ Fabian Bellinghausen — Russian naval officer who was the first to see Antarctica in 1820

FABIO ◆Fabio — on the cover of over 350 romance novels, known for long blond hair and muscles

FABRICE ◆Fabrice Morvan — with Milli Vanilli, lost their Grammy when it was learned they lip-synched songs

FABRIZIO ◆Fabrizio Mioni — portrayed Jason in muscleman Steve Reeves' film classic "Hercules"

FAIRFAX ◆Fairfax Cone — founder of the advertising agency of Foote, Cone and Belding

FAIRFIELD ◆John Fairfield Dryden — founder of the Prudential Insurance Company ◆ Henry Fairfield Osborn — paleontologist who made the word "dinosaur" a household word ◆ Fairfield Porter — post World War II representative artist

FAISAL ◆Faisal — prince trying to bring about Arab unity, biopic Alec Guinness' "Lawrence of Arabia"

FALCO ◆Falco — musician who hit the charts with "Rock Me, Amadeus"

FALCON ◆Robert Falcon Scott — barely second to reach the South Pole, biopic "Scott of the Antarctic"

FARCIOT ◆Farciot Edouart — special effects man at Paramount whose films include "Alice in Wonderland"

FARLEY ◆Farley Granger — actor whose roles included thrill murderer Nathan Leopold in Hitchcock's "Rope" ◆Farley Mowat — author of books about northern Canada's Eskimos

FARON ◆Faron Young — country music singer called "The Singing Sheriff"

FARRELL ◆A. Farrell MacDonald — minstrel singer turned character actor, films "The Maltese Falcon," "Meet John Doe"

FATS ◆Fats Domino — singer who recorded "Blueberry Hill" and "Ain't That a Shame" ◆ Fats Navarro — bop trumpeter who recorded with Benny Goodman ◆ Fats Waller — pianist, wrote "Ain't Misbehavin'" and "Honeysuckle Rose"

FAUSTO ◆Fausto Cleva — conductor at the New York Metropolitan Opera ◆ Fausto Tozzi — actor who played sheriff Pat Garrett in "The Man Who Killed Billy the Kid"

FAYARD ◆Fayard Nicholas — regular dancer at the Cotton Club

FAZLUR ◆Fazlur Khan — architect who designed Chicago's Sears Tower which was world's tallest building

FEDERICO ◆Federico DeLaurentiis — son of Dino, producer of "King of the Gypsies" ◆ Federico Fellini — Italian film director with four Oscars, including one for "La Dolce Vita"

FEE ◆Fee Waybill — member of The Tubes, debut hit single "Don't Touch Me There"

FELICIANO ◆Feliciano Tavares — member of the rock group Tavares, debut hit single "Check It Out"

FELIPE ◆Felipe Alou — manager of the Montreal Expos ◆Felipe Rose — member of The Village People, debut gold record "Macho Man"

FELIX ◆Felix Frankfurter — Supreme Court justice ◆ Felix Mendelssohn — composer, hits include "A Midsummer Night's Dream"

FELTON ◆Andrew Felton Brimmer — economist and government official ◆ Richard Felton Outcault — cartoonist who created the "Yellow Kid" and "Buster Brown" ◆ Felton Perry — played Inspector McNeil on John Ritter's comedy police series "Hooperman"

FENDALL ◆Fendall Yerxa — host of TV's "Editor's Choice"

FENIMORE ◆James Fenimore Cooper — author of the great adventure story "The Last of the Mohicans"

FERDE ◆Ferde Grofe — composer whose works include "The Grand Canyon Suite"

FERDINAND ◆Ferdinand Magellan — Portuguese explorer who was the first to sail around the world ◆ Ferdinand Porsche — inventor of the Volkswagen, Porsche sportscar named after him ◆ Ferdinand de Lesseps — chief engineer for the Suez Canal, Tyrone Power biopic "Suez"

FERLIN ◆Ferlin Husky — country western singer, hits include "Rosie Cries a Lot"

FERMIN ◆Fermin Goytisolo — member of K.C. and the Sunshine Band, number one debut single "Get Down Tonight"

FERNAND ◆Fernand Gravet — actor who played Austrian composer Johann Strauss in MGM's "The Great Waltz" ◆ Fernand Lamaze — invented the Lamaze Method of natural childbirth

FERNANDEL ◆Fernandel — actor whose roles included the swindling schoolteacher in "Topaz" ◆ Fernandel — eccentric priest in the "Don Camillo" series of comedies

FERNANDO ◆Fernando Lamas — romantic 1950's lead, parodied by Billy Crystal, who said "You look marvelous" ◆

Fernando Rey — actor who played Alain Charnier in Gene Hackman's "The French Connection"

FERRIS ◆Ferris Bueller (c) — luckiest kid in the world in "Ferris Bueller's Day Off" ◆ Ferris Fain — led the American League in batting

FERRUCCIO ◆Ferruccio Busoni — twentieth century Italian pianist and composer ◆Ferruccio Lamborghini — founder of the Lamborghini automobile company

FESS ◆Fess Parker — actor who played both Daniel Boone and Davy Crockett on TV and in films

FIDEL ◆Fidel Castro — baseball player and dictator of Cuba ◆ Fidel La Barba — flyweight and featherweight champ, Olympic gold medalist

FIELDING ◆Fielding Yost — coach at the University of Michigan who won the first Rose Bowl

FIFE ◆J. Fife Symington III — governor of Arkansas elected in 1991

FILIPPO ◆Filippo Brunelleschi — fifteenth century architect of the Florence cathedral ◆ Filippo Del Giudice — Italian producer in England, credits include "In Which We Serve"

FINLAY ◆Finlay Currie — actor whose roles included an aging St. Peter in MGM's "Quo Vadis?"

FINLEY ◆Finley Dunne — creator of Mr. Dooley, a commentator on political issues ◆ Samuel Finley Morse — inventor of the Morse code

FINN ◆Finn Ronne — explorer and geographer who covered over 3600 miles by dog sled

FIORELLO ◆Fiorello La Guardia — flamboyant mayor of New York City during the Depression

FISKE ◆Fiske Kimball — architect behind the restoration of colonial Williamsburg ◆Harlan Fiske Stone — chief justice of the US Supreme Court

FITZ ◆Fitz Ludlow — author whose works include "The Hasheesh Eater"

FITZGERALD ◆David Fitzgerald Doyle — actor whose roles included Bosley on TV's titillating "Charlie's Angels" ◆ John Fitzgerald Kennedy — assassinated US President, biopic "PT 109"

FITZHUGH ◆Fitzhugh Lee — Confederate major general who covered his cousin Lee's retreat to Appomattox

FITZROY ◆Fitzroy Raglan — general who lost his arm in the Crimean war, raglan sleeves named for him

FLASH ◆Flash Gordon (c) — comic book character who has adventures in space ◆ Larry Flash Jenkins — actor whose roles included Lyman Whittaker on TV's "Finder of Lost Loves"

FLAVOR ◆Flavor Flav — member of the group Public Enemy, hits include "Fight the Power"

FLEETWOOD ◆Fleetwood Starr Robbins — son of author Tom Robbins

FLEMING ◆Fleming Williams — member of The Hues Corporation, hit single "Rock the Boat"

FLETCHER ◆Fletcher Christian — leader of the mutineers on the HMS Bounty against the cruel Captain Bligh ◆ Fletcher Harper — founder of "Harper's Weekly" and "Harper's Bazaar"

FLIP ◆Flip Wilson — comedian whose catch line was "Don't fight the feeling"

FLORENZ ◆Florenz Ames — played Inspector Richard Queen on the series "The Adventures of Ellery Queen" ◆ Florenz Ziegfeld — creator of the "Ziegfeld Follies" who discovered Fannie Brice

FLORIAN ◆Florian Zabach — violinist who whistled while performing in concert

FLOYD ◆Floyd Bennett — national hero who flew over the North Pole with Richard Byrd in 1926 ◆ Floyd Patterson — world heavyweight champion and Olympic gold medal boxer

FONTAINE ◆Fontaine Fox, Jr. — created the syndicated comic strip "Toonerville Folks"

FORBES ◆John Forbes Robertson — played the bloody Count Dracula in "The Legend of the Seven Golden Vampires" ◆Forbes Robinson — bass opera singer and actor

FORD ◆John Ford Coley — sang with England Dan, gold debut hit "I'd Really Love to See You Tonight" ◆ Francis Ford Coppola — director of the "Godfather" movies

FOREST ◆Forest Ackerman — his massive collection makes him "the World's Number One Science Fiction Fan" ◆ Forest

Whitaker — actor whose roles included jazz great Charlie Parker in Clint Eastwood's "Bird"

FORREST ◆ Forrest Allen — basketball coach who helped organize the first NCAA tournament ◆ Forrest Mars — maker of the candy covered Mars Bar ◆ Forrest Tucker — actor whose roles included the scheming Sergeant O'Rourke on TV's "F Troop"

FORRESTER ◆ Forrester Harvey — actor whose films include Claudette Colbert's "The Gilded Lily"

FORTUNIO ◆ Fortunio Bonanova — actor whose roles included the temperamental singing teacher in "Citizen Kane"

FOSTER ◆ Foster Brooks — comedian and actor known for playing a drunk

FRAN ◆ Fran Tarkenton — football player turned host of TV's "That's Incredible!"

FRANC ◆ Franc Luz — actor whose roles included Thomas J. Harper on TV's "Free Spirit"

FRANCESCO ◆ Francesco Clemente — avant-garde artist known for collages

FRANCHOT ◆ Franchot Tone — handsome co-star of "Lives of a Bengal Lancer" and "Mutiny on the Bounty"

FRANCIS ◆ Francis X. Bushman — silent film hero, played Messala in the silent epic "Ben-Hur" ◆ Sir Francis Drake — Sea Hawk looter of the Spanish Main, and a favorite of Queen Elizabeth ◆ Francis Scott Key — composed the national anthem "The Star-Spangled Banner" ◆ Francis Marion — "Swamp Fox" of the American Revolution, subject of a Disney TV series

FRANCISCO ◆ Francisco Madero — reformer ruler of Mexico who succeeded Diaz ◆ Francisco de Coronado — Spanish explorer who looked for the Seven Cities of Cibola

FRANCO ◆ Franco Fabrizi — actor who played ruthless Cesare Borgia in "The Nights of Lucrezia Borgia" ◆ Franco Fantasia — actor whose roles included Athos in "Revenge of the Musketeers" ◆ Franco Zeffirelli — director of "The Taming of the Shrew" and "Romeo and Juliet"

FRANCOIS ◆ Francois Truffaut — Oscar winning New Wave French film director ◆ Francois Villon — fifteenth century French poet and rogue depicted in "If I Were King"

FRANCOIS-ERIC ◆Francois-Eric Gendron — actor who played Alexandre in Eric Rohmer's film "Boyfriends and Girlfriends"

FRANK ◆Frank Oz — comedy director of Bill Murray's "What About Bob?" ◆ Frank Sinatra — Chairman of the Board ◆ Frank Lloyd Wright — architect of the American school and creator of modern skyscrapers ◆ Frank Zappa — rock star of the 1960's, backup group The Mothers of Invention

FRANKIE ◆Frankie Avalon — king of the beach movies, like "Beach Blanket Bingo" ◆ Frankie Laine — pop singer, hits "I Believe" and "Jezebel" ◆ Frankie Lymon — singer, hits include the top ten "Why Do Fools Fall in Love?" ◆Frankie Valli — lead singer of The Four Seasons, superhit was "Sherry"

FRANKLIN ◆Benjamin Franklin Goodrich — founded the B.F. Goodrich tire company ◆ Franklin Pierce — tried to settle the slavery question peacefully as President

FRANKLYN ◆Franklyn Ajaye — actor whose roles included T.C. in the comedy film "Car Wash" ◆ Franklyn Branley — educator and author

FRANS ◆Frans Stelling — one of three actors to play Dutch painter Rembrandt

FRANZ ◆Franz Liszt — Hungarian child prodigy composer and virtuoso pianist ◆ Franz Mesmer — used hypnotism to treat diseases, word "mesmerize" coined from name

FRASIER ◆Frasier Crane (c) — Kelsey Grammer took his character from "Cheers" to his own TV show

FRAZIER ◆Frazier Hunt — author whose works include "The Long Trail from Texas"

FRED ◆Fred Astaire — performer who danced his way through his movies of the 1930's into the 1980's ◆ Fred Flintstone (c) — head of our favorite stone age family ◆Fred Gwynne — actor who played Frankenstein character of Herman Munster on TV's "The Munsters" ◆ Fred MacMurray — actor whose talent ranged from "Double Indemnity" to "The Absent Minded Professor" ◆ Fred Savage — actor whose roles included Kevin Arnold on the sitcom "The Wonder Years"

FREDDIE ◆Freddie Bartholomew — child star of 1930's films, including "Little Lord Fauntleroy" ◆ Freddie Jackson — balladeer, platinum albums "Rock Me Tonight" and "Just Like the First Time"

FREDDY ◆Freddy Fender — country western singer, hits include "Before the Next Teardrop Falls"

FREDERIC ◆Frederic Chopin — Polish composer and master pianist, biopic "A Song to Remember" ◆ Frederic Miller — brewery is second largest in US, it's "Miller time" ◆ Frederic Remington — sculptor of western themes who influenced director John Ford

FREDERICK ◆William Frederick Cody — real name of buffalo hunter and entertainer Buffalo Bill ◆ Frederick Mellinger — founder Frederick's of Hollywood ◆Frederick Royce — founded Rolls-Royce with C. S. Rolls ◆Frederick Stanley — founder of the Stanley Cup presented in hockey

FREDERIK ◆Ernst Frederik Alexanderson — co-inventor of the vocal radio broadcast and color TV

FREDRIC ◆Fredric March — actor in "The Best Years of Our Lives," "A Star is Born," "A Tale of Two Cities"

FREELAN ◆Freelan Stanley — founder of the steam powered Stanley Steamer automobile company

FREEMAN ◆Freeman Crofts — mystery author whose tales include "French Strikes Oil" ◆ Freeman Gosden — Amos of the "Amos 'n' Andy" radio show

FRIEDRICH ◆Friedrich Nietzsche — philosopher and poet who glorified the "superman" ◆ Friedrich von Trapp — one of the singing von Trapp children portrayed in "The Sound of Music"

FRITZ ◆Fritz Lang — director of "The Big Heat" ◆Fritz Weaver — received a Tony for the stage production of "Child's Play" ◆ Fritz Wepper — actor whose roles included Fritz Wendel in the film "Cabaret"

FRIZ ◆Friz Freleng — Emmy winning producer of "The Grinch Grinches the Cat in the Hat"

FULTON ◆Fulton Lewis, Jr. — popular right wing radio commentator who attacked the New Deal ◆ Fulton Oursler — author of the filmed "Greatest Story Ever Told" ◆Bishop Fulton Sheen — spokesman for the Catholic church through radio, TV, and books

FUZZY ◆Fuzzy Knight — actor whose roles included Ragtime Kelly in Mae West's "She Done Him Wrong"

FYODOR ◆Fyodor Dostoyevsky — author whose works include "Crime and Punishment" and "The Brothers Karamazov"

GABE ◆Gabe Kaplan — actor who played the teacher to the Sweat Hogs in TV's "Welcome Back, Kotter" ◆ Gabe Mirkin — author of "The Sportsmedicine Book"

GABRIEL ◆Gabriel Byrne — actor, films include "Cool World" ◆ Gabriel Fahrenheit — invented the mercury thermometer and the Fahrenheit scale

GAGE ◆Gage Clark — actor whose roles included the man next door on the sitcom "The Hartmans"

GAHAN ◆Gahan Wilson — artist known for macabre cartoons, collections include "Is Nothing Sacred?"

GAIL ◆Gail Borden — inventor of evaporated milk, founded the Borden Milk Company

GAILARD ◆Gailard Sartain — actor whose roles included LaGrange in the Paul Newman film "Blaze"

GAIUS ◆Gaius Catullus — Roman poet who wrote over 100 poems ◆ Gaius Coriolanus — Plutarch's story of him is the basis for Shakespeare's play "Coriolanus" ◆ James Gaius Watt — outspoken secretary of the interior who banned The Beach Boys from performing

GALE ◆Gale Gordon — actor whose roles included Mr. Mooney on TV's "The Lucy Show" ◆ Gale Sayers — Billy Dee Williams' role in the Brian Piccolo biopic "Brian's Song"

GALEN ◆Galen — ancient Greek physician who proved that arteries carry blood

GALILEO ◆Galileo Galilei — Italian astronomer who believed the Earth revolved around the sun

GALLAGHER ◆Gallagher — messy performer whose stage show includes throwing food on his audience

GALT ◆Galt MacDermot — Grammy winner for the score of "Hair"

GALWAY ◆Galway Kinnell — Pulitzer Prize winning poet for "Selected Poems"

GAMALIEL ◆Gamaliel Bradford — author known for psychological biographies, "Damaged Souls" in 1923 ◆ Warren Gamaliel Harding — US President in the twenties

GAP ◆Gap Mangione — brother of Chuck, his solo album was "Diana in the Autumn Wind"

76

GAR ◆Gar Wood — champion powerboat racer with his boat "Miss America"

GARDNER ◆Gardner Colton — inventor of laughing gas ◆ Gardner Cowles — founded "Look" magazine ◆ Gardner Fox — creator of the comic book "The Flash"

GARETH ◆Gareth Hunt — actor who played Mike Gambit on the hit spy drama series "The Avengers"

GARFIELD ◆Garfield (c) — cool feline of comic strip and TV cartoon fame ◆ Lester Garfield Maddox — segregationist Democratic governor of Georgia ◆ Garfield Oxnam — religious leader, author of "A Testament of Faith"

GARLAND ◆Garland Bunting — actor whose roles included Doc Ferriday in the Paul Newman film "Blaze" ◆ Garland Jeffreys — soul singer, rock/reggae hits include "Ghostwriter"

GARNER ◆Garner Ted Armstrong — evangelist who founded the Church of God International

GARNET ◆John Garnet Carter — inventor of miniature golf

GARNETT ◆Garnett Mimms — rock singer, hits include "Cry Baby" and "A Little Bit of Soap"

GARRET ◆Garret Fitzgerald — prime minister of Ireland who signed historic Anglo-Irish agreement in 1985

GARRETSON ◆Garretson Trudeau — real name of "Doonesbury" cartoonist Garry Trudeau

GARRETT ◆Garrett Morris — an original cast member of "Saturday Night Live" and a regular on Hunter

GARRICK ◆Garrick Utley — foreign correspondent for NBC

GARRISON ◆Daniel Garrison Brinton — anthropologist and author, "Myths of the New World," "The American Race" ◆ Schuyler Garrison Chapin — manager of the Metropolitan Opera, autobiography "Musical Chairs" ◆ Garrison Keillor — creator of "A Prairie Home Companion" about the inhabitants of Lake Wobegon

GARRY ◆Garry Marshall — creator of TV's "Happy Days," "Mork and Mindy," and film "Pretty Woman" ◆ Garry Shandling — played Garry Shandling on "It's Garry Shandling's Show starring Garry Shandling" ◆ Garry Trudeau — creator of "Doonesbury" comic strip

GARSON ◆Garson Kanin — director and author of screenplays with wife Ruth Gordon

GARTH ◆Garth Brooks — top country music artist, "Friends in Low Places," The Dance"

GARY ◆Gary Burghoff — actor whose roles included Radar O'Reilly on TV's long running sitcom "M*A*S*H" ◆ Gary Busey — actor in "The Buddy Holly Story," "Under Siege" ◆ Gary Coleman — child cast member of "Diff'rent Strokes" ◆ Gary Cooper — actor in "High Noon," and "Sergeant York," won an Oscar for both ◆ Gary Puckett — group Gary Puckett and the Union Gap, debut gold record "Woman, Woman"

GASPARD ◆Gaspard Manesse — actor who played Julien Quentin in the French film "Au Revoir les Enfants"

GASTON ◆Gaston Richmond — son of actress Jaclyn Smith ◆ Gaston Rebuffat — mountaineer who ascended Mt. Blanc, author "Men and the Matterhorn"

GAVAN ◆Gavan O'Herlihy — you had to look fast to see his character of Chuck Cunningham on "Happy Days"

GAVIN ◆Gavin Astor — British publisher and head of the Astor dynasty, president of Times Newspapers ◆ Gavin MacLeod — played Murray on "The Mary Tyler Moore Show," the captain of the "Love Boat"

GAY ◆Gay Talese — author whose works include "Honor Thy Father" and "Thy Neighbor's Wife"

GAYELORD ◆Gayelord Hauser — pioneer in the health food industry, author of "Look Younger, Live Longer"

GAYLORD ◆Gaylord Nelson — senator from Wisconsin who originated Earth Day ◆ Gaylord Perry — pitcher known for his spitball

GEDDY ◆Geddy Lee — member of the rock group Rush, debut hit single "Fly By Night/In the Mood"

GEIR ◆Geir Westby — actor who played the melancholic Norwegian artist in the biopic "Edvard Munch"

GELETT ◆Gelett Burgess — comedy author who penned the poem "The Purple Cow"

GEN ◆Gen Alden — member of The Champs, debut gold number one record "Tequila"

GENE ◆Gene Autry — king of the singing cowboys ◆ Gene Hackman — Oscar winning actor in "The French Connection" and "Unforgiven" ◆ Gene Kelly — singer, dancer, and actor in films like "Singin' in the Rain" ◆Gene Pitney — rock singer, hits include number one "Only Love Can Break a Heart" ◆ Gene Roddenberry — creator of "Star Trek" ◆ Gene Wilder — comedian in "The Producers," "Young Frankenstein," "Stir Crazy"

GENEROSO ◆Generoso Pope — owner of "The National Enquirer"

GEOFF ◆Geoff Edwards — actor whose roles included Jeff Powers on the rural sitcom "Petticoat Junction" ◆Geoff Smith — two-time winner of the Boston Marathon

GEOFFREY ◆Geoffrey Chaucer — author of "The Canterbury Tales" ◆Geoffrey Owens — actor who played Elvin, one of Cliff's sons-in-law, on TV's "The Cosby Show"

GEORG ◆Georg Stanford Brown — played the lead of Officer Terry Webster on the drama series "The Rookies" ◆ Georg Solti — winner of 22 Grammys, music director of the Chicago Symphony for 22 years ◆ Georg Wadenius — member of Blood, Sweat, and Tears, hits include "And When I Die"

GEORGE ◆George Burns — went from comedy team of Burns and Allen to playing God ◆ George Harrison — one of The Beatles ◆ George Kennedy — Oscar winner for "Cool Hand Luke" ◆George Lucas — creator of the "Star Wars" and "Indiana Jones" film series ◆George Patton — "Old Blood and Guts," tank commander World War II, biopic won Best Picture Oscar ◆ George Peppard — star of TV's "Banacek" and "The A-Team"

GEORGES ◆Georges Lemaitre — astronomer who conceived the "big bang" theory of creation ◆ Prince Georges Matchabelli — head of the internationally famous perfume Prince Matchabelli ◆ Georges Vezina — hockey player who is namesake for the Vezina Trophy awarded to goalies

GEORGIY ◆Georgiy Millyar — actor whose roles included the Devil in the film "A Night Before Christmas"

GERAINT ◆Geraint Davies — actor who played Major Mike Rivers on the hit adventure series "Airwolf"

GERALD ◆Gerald Ford — only US President who was appointed to the job ◆ Gerald McRaney — star of TV's "Major Dad," also starred on "Simon and Simon"

GERALDO ◆Geraldo Rivera — reporter and host of the TV talk show "Geraldo"

GERANO ◆Gerano Vitaliamo — real name of singer Jerry Vale

GERARD ◆Gerard Christopher — actor who played Clark Kent and his alter ego in the adventure series "Superboy" ◆ Gerard Depardieu — French actor nominated for Best Actor in "Cyrano de Bergerac" ◆ Robert Gerard Goulet — singer who won a Tony for "The Happy Time"

GERARDO ◆Gerardo — rapper, top ten single "Rico Suave"

GERD ◆Gerd Vespermann — actor who appeared as Bobby in the film "Cabaret"

GERHARD ◆Gerhard Riedmann — actor whose roles included Ludwig, the mad king of Bavaria in "Magic Fire"

GERHARDUS ◆Gerhardus Mercator — cartographer who invented the Mercator Projection still used for maps today

GERHART ◆Gerhart Thrasher — member of The Drifters, hits include "Under the Boardwalk"

GEROLAMO ◆Gerolamo Fracastoro — poet

GEROLD ◆Gerold Frabj — author whose works include "Beloved Infidel" and "Judy"

GERONIMO ◆Geronimo — Apache leader who led the US Cavalry on a merry chase around Arizona

GERRIT ◆Gerrit Graham — actor who played Leonard Scribner on the sitcom "Stockard Channing in Just Friends" ◆Gerrit Smith — philanthropist who financed John Brown in his crusade to free the slaves

GERRY ◆Gerry Beckley — member of the rock group America, hits include "A Horse with No Name" ◆ Gerry Conney — heavyweight contender called "The Great White Hope" ◆Gerry Marsden — Gerry in Gerry and the Pacemakers, hit "Don't Let the Sun Catch You Crying"

GERT ◆Gert Frobe — played the super-villain Auric Goldfinger in the third James Bond movie

GIACOMO ◆Giacomo Balla — artist of Italian Futurist group ◆ Giacomo Stuart — actor whose roles included Musketeer Aramis in "Zorro and the Three Musketeers"

GIAN ◆Gian Volonte — actor whose roles included the gangster in the film "Lucky Luciano"

GIANNI ◆Gianni Rizzo — actor whose roles included Athos in "Zorro and the Three Musketeers" ◆Gianni Russo — actor who played Carol Rizzi in the Academy Award winning film "The Godfather"

GIBB ◆Gibb McLaughlin — actor, master of disguise, used his splendidly emaciated features to advantage

GIBSON ◆Gibson Gowland — English actor in American films whose credits include "Birth of a Nation" ◆John Gibson Lockhart — biographer of his father-in-law "Life of Sir Walter Scott"

GID ◆Gid Tanner — country western fiddle player, member of The Skillet Lickers

GIDEON ◆Gideon — in the Bible, chosen by God to free Israel from the Midianites

GIFFORD ◆Gifford Pinchot — reform governor of Pennsylvania during the Roaring Twenties

GIG ◆Gig Young — sidekick to Rock Hudson in many of his Doris Day movies

GIL ◆Gil Gerard — starred in the title role on TV's "Buck Rogers in the 25th Century" ◆ Gil Hodges — managed the NY Mets to victory in the World Series

GILBERT ◆Gilbert Gottfried — comic actor with a voice which can be incredibly grating ◆ Gilbert Roland — Latin lover whose films include "Camille" ◆ Gilbert Stuart — painter known for his three portraits of George Washington

GILL ◆Stephen Gill Spottswood — African Methodist Episcopal bishop who became chairman of the NAACP

GILLIGAN ◆Gilligan (c) — castaways' fumbling first mate on TV's "Gilligan's Island"

GINGER ◆Ginger Baker — singer and drummer with rock groups Blind Faith and Cream

GINO ◆Gino Cappeletti — led the American Football League in scoring ◆Gino Corrado — actor whose roles included Musketeer Aramis in "The Iron Mask" ◆Gino Vannelli — rock singer, debut hit single "People Gotta Move"

GIOACCHINO ◆Gioacchino Rossini — composer whose operas include "The Barber of Seville" and "William Tell"

GIORGIO ◆Giorgio Armani — fashion designer who developed the unconstructed blazer ◆ Giorgio Bulgari — founded Rome's deluxe jewelry house with his brother Constantine ◆ Giorgio DiSant'Angelo — fashion designer known for avant-garde accessories

GIOVANNI ◆Giovanni da Verrazano — discovered Hudson River, namesake for New York City's Verrazano Bridge ◆ Giovanni Casanova — eighteenth century Italian known as a great lover

GIULIO ◆Giulio Andreotti — former Italian prime minister ◆ Giulio Boseti — actor whose roles included the great lover Casanova in "The Return of Casanova" ◆ Giulio Maestro — illustrator of picture books, children's readers, author "Who's Said Meow?"

GIUSEPPE ◆Giuseppe Amato — Italian film producer, credits include "La Dolce Vita" ◆ Giuseppe Bellanca — founder of Italian Bellanca Aircraft, invented convertible landing gear ◆ Giuseppe Garibaldi — major figure in the unification of Italy in the 1800's

GLEN ◆Glen Campbell — actor and country music singer who had his own TV show in the 70's

GLENDON ◆Glendon Swarthout — author whose works included "Where the Boys Are" and "Skeletons"

GLENN ◆Glenn Ford — actor whose films included "Teahouse of the August Moon" ◆ Glenn Miller — bandleader, hits included "Moonlight Serenade," "In the Mood" ◆ Glenn Yarbrough — singer, hits included the top ten "Baby, the Rain Must Fall"

GLENWAY ◆Glenway Wescott — author whose works included "The Grandmothers" and "The Pilgrim Hawk"

GLOVER ◆Glover Corey — member of group Living Colour, Grammy winning hit "Cult of Personality"

GLYN ◆Glyn Houston — Welsh character actor, brother of Donald Houston ◆ Glyn Jones — author of "The Learning Lark"

GLYNN ◆Glynn Edwards — actor who played real 19th century graverobber Hare in biopic "Burke and Hare" ◆Glynn Turman — portrayed Col. Clayton Taylor on TV's "A Different World"

GODFREY ◆Godfrey Cambridge — actor whose films included "Cotton Comes to Harlem" ◆ Godfrey Quigley — actor who played the prison chaplain in Kubrick's violent "A Clockwork Orange"

GOLDWIN ◆Goldwin Smith — author who wrote extensively on Canada becoming part of the United States

GOLDY ◆Goldy McJohn — member of Steppenwolf, hit debut gold record "Born to Be Wild"

GOMER ◆James Gomer Berry — largest newspaper proprietor in Britain

GOMEZ ◆Gomez Addams (c) — patriarch of TV's quirky "The Addams Family"

GONVILLE ◆Gonville Bromhead — Michael Caine played him winning the Victoria Cross in the biopic "Zulu"

GONZALO ◆Gonzalo Madurga — actor whose roles included Dr. Moreno on the soap "The Guiding Light"

GOOBER ◆Stan Goober Knight — member Black Oak Arkansas, hits include "Jim Dandy to the Rescue"

GORDIE ◆Gordie Howe — holder of several National Hockey League records including most career goals ◆ Gordie Tapp — series regular on the long running hayseed variety show "Hee Haw"

GORDON ◆Gordon Cooper — one of the original astronauts ◆ G. Gordon Liddy — original Watergate break-in defendant, twenty year sentence commuted by Carter ◆Gordon Lightfoot — vocalist whose songs include "Sundown," "If You Could Read My Mind" ◆Gordon Waller — half of Peter and Gordon, hit single "A World Without Love"

GORE ◆Gore Vidal — author of historical novels such as "Burr," plays include "The Best Man"

GORHAM ◆Gorham Munson — author whose works include "Twelve Decisive Battles of the Mind"

GOSTA ◆Ingvar Gosta Carlsson — prime minister of Sweden from 1986 to 1991 ◆ Gosta Ekman — actor who played the Spanish cubist painter in "The Adventures of Picasso"

GOTTLIEB ◆Fabian Gottlieb Bellinghausen — Russian naval officer who was the first to see Antarctica in 1820 ◆ Gottlieb Daimler — founder of the Daimler Motor Company which produced the Mercedes

GOULD ◆Myron Gould Beard — first pilot to fly the DC-3, developed Boeing 707 ◆ Robert Gould Shaw — Matthew Broderick as the colonel of the 54th Regiment in "Glory"

GOUVERNEUR ◆Gouverneur Morris — member of the Constitutional Convention, minister to France, senator ◆Horatio Gouverneur Wright — Union general who led the defense of Washington in 1864

GOWER ◆Gower Champion — choreographer with Tonys for "Bye Bye Birdie" and "Hello Dolly"

GRADY ◆Rev. Grady Nutt — series regular on the long running hayseed series "Hee Haw"

GRAEME ◆Graeme Edge — member of The Moody Blues, debut hit gold record "Go Now"

GRAHAM ◆Alexander Graham Bell — invented the telephone, danced with Helen Keller (not on the same day) ◆ Graham Chapman — member of the Monty Python troupe of players, films include "Life of Brian" ◆ Graham Nash — member of Crosby, Stills, Nash, and Young, as well as The Hollies

GRAM ◆Gram Parsons — performer who led the fusion of country, rock, folk, and bluegrass

GRANT ◆Grant Goodeve — actor whose roles included the older brother on TV's "Eight is Enough" ◆ Grant Schaud — portrays the nervous producer Miles Silverberg on "Murphy Brown" ◆ Grant Show — starred in Fox Network's "Melrose Place"

GRANTLAND ◆Grantland Rice — coined the term "the four horsemen" to describe Notre Dame football players

GRANVILLE ◆Granville Owen — Dogpatch's Li'l Abner was his role in the film of the same name ◆ Granville Sharp — philanthropist who founded the English Society for the Abolition of Slaves

GRATTON ◆Gratton Dalton — outlaw with the Dalton Gang, killed during the Coffeyville raid

GRAYSON ◆Grayson Kirk — replaced Dwight Eisenhower as president of Columbia University

GREENLEAF ◆Greenleaf Pickard — pioneer in radio communications, inventor of the crystal detector ◆John Greenleaf Whittier — popular rural poet who devoted his life to social reform, poem "Snow-Bound"

GREG ◆Greg Boyington — top WW II ace in the Pacific, Robert Conrad TV bioseries "Black Sheep Squadron" ◆ Greg Evigan — starred in TV's "BJ and the Bear" and "My Two Dads"

GREGG ◆Gregg Allman — musician with the Allman Brothers Band ◆ Gregg Errico — member of Sly and the Family Stone, hit debut single "Dance to the Music" ◆ Gregg Toland — cinematographer, films include "Citizen Kane"

GREGOIRE ◆Gregoire Aslan — actor whose roles included Herod the Great in "King of Kings"

GREGOR ◆Gregor Mendel — botanist who experimented with garden peas and discovered rules of heredity

GREGORIO ◆Gregorio Allegri — 17th century Italian composer of "Misere" which is sung annually on Good Friday ◆ Gregorio Cortez — Mexican cowhand who killed a Texas sheriff in self defense, biopic "The Ballad of Gregorio Cortez"

GREGORY ◆Gregory Lake — member of Emerson, Lake, and Palmer, hit song "Lucky Man" ◆ Gregory Peck — Oscar winner for "To Kill a Mockingbird" ◆ Gregory Hines — dancer, films include "White Nights" and "A Rage in Harlem"

GRENVILLE ◆Grenville Dodge — engineer responsible for the Union Pacific Railroad ◆Pelham Grenville Wodehouse — creator of Jeeves, manservant and valet to gentleman Bertie Wooster

GRIFFIN ◆Griffin Bell — attorney general in the Carter administration ◆ Griffin Dunne — has a Kafkaesque adventure as Paul Hackett in "After Hours"

GRIFFITH ◆Benjamin Griffith Brawley — clergyman and educator ◆Griffith Jones — British leading man, films include "A Yank at Oxford" ◆ William Griffith Wilson — co-founder of Alcoholics Anonymous

GRIGORI ◆Grigori Alexandrov — Russian film director who worked with Sergei Eisenstein ◆ Grigori Kozintsev — Russian director whose films include "Don Quixote" and "Hamlet"

GROSVENOR ◆Grosvenor Atterbury — architect who designed the earliest practical prefabricated housing ◆Grosvenor Glenn — actor whose roles included chief conspirator Cassius in "Julius Caesar" ◆ Samuel Grosvenor Wood — director of the Marx Brothers film "A Night at the Opera"

GROUCHO ◆Groucho Marx — comedy leader of the Marx Brothers

GROVER ◆Grover Cleveland — only US President to serve two nonconsecutive terms ◆Grover Magnin — founder of the store I. Magnin ◆James Grover Thurber — author of "The Secret Life of Walter Mitty," filmed with Danny Kaye

GUCCIO ◆Guccio Gucci — maker of the high quality "Gucci" loafer

GUICH ◆Guich Koock — actor whose roles included Roscoe Clark on Gabe Kaplan's sitcom "Lewis and Clark"

GUILLAUME ◆Guillaume Apollinaire — French poet who coined the word "surrealism" ◆Count Alfred Guillaume D'Orsay — nineteenth century arbiter of fashion in London and Paris ◆ Guillaume Delisle — founder of modern cartography

GUINN ◆Owen Guinn Smith — Olympic gold medal pole vaulter whose record stood for twenty-five years ◆ Guinn Williams — actor who starred in Claudette Colbert's "Private Worlds"

GUION ◆Guion Bluford — first African-American astronaut to fly in space aboard shuttle "Challenger"

GUNNAR ◆Edda Gunnar Marshall — nickname "E.G.," Emmy winner for the TV courtroom series "The Defenders" ◆ Gunnar Nelson — twin son of Rick Nelson, half of the rock group "Nelson"

GUNNIS ◆Gunnis Davis — actor in Boris Karloff's sequel "The Bride of Frankenstein"

GUNTER ◆Gunter Grass — author, novel "The Tin Drum" ◆ Gunter Krampf — cinematographer whose films include "The Franchise Affair"

GUS ◆Gus Arriola — created the comic strip "Gordo" ◆ Gus Grissom — third astronaut into space, killed in the Apollo I fire

GUSTAF ◆Gustaf Gruendgens — actor whose roles included the Devil in the film version of "Faust" ◆Carl Gustaf XVI — became king of Sweden in 1973

GUSTAV ◆Pierre Gustav Beauregard — Confederate general who ordered bombardment of Ft. Sumter ◆ Gustav Stickley — founded "The Craftsman Magazine," created Mission style furniture

GUSTAVE ◆Alexandre Gustave Eiffel — designer of the Eiffel Tower in Paris ◆Gustave Flaubert — author who was prosecuted for writing "Madame Bovary" ◆ Gustave Mahler — Austrian composer whose biopic with Robert Powell was "Mahler"

GUSTAVO ◆Gustavo Lezcano — member of The Miami Sound Machine, hits include number one "Anything for You"

GUSTAVUS ◆Gustavus Swift — inventor of refrigerated railroad cars

GUTZON ◆Gutzon Borglum — sculptor of the US Presidents on Mt. Rushmore

GUY ◆Guy Fawkes — tried to blow up Parliament, now Guy Fawkes Day is a national holiday in England ◆ Guy Laroche — fashion designer known for chic, sophisticated styles ◆ Guy Lombardo — band leader who made a career out of playing on New Year's Eve ◆ Guy Madison — star of TV's "Wild Bill Hickok" ◆ Guy Williams — played Prof. John Robinson on the science fiction series "Lost in Space"

GWYLLYN ◆Gwyllyn Ford — real name of action actor Glenn Ford

GYULA ◆Gyula Andrassy — prime minister of German and Hungarian dual monarchy ◆ Gyula Bodrogi — portrayed French conqueror Napoleon in "Hary Janos"

HAKEEM ◆Hakeem — actor whose roles included Brandon Russo on TV's "Fathers and Sons"

HAL ◆Hal Holbrook — actor in "Midway," "Magnum Force" and "Wall Street" ◆ Hal Linden — star of the TV series "Barney Miller" ◆ Hal Needham — stuntman who directed "Smokey and the Bandit" and four other Burt Reynolds films ◆ Hal Roach — producer of Hollywood comedies such as the Laurel and Hardy series ◆ Hal Wallis — producer of 32 films with Oscars, including "Casablanca" and "The Maltese Falcon"

HALCYON ◆Halcyon Skinner — inventor of the power loom for weaving carpets

HALE ◆Hale Boggs — congressman lost in Alaskan plane crash ◆ Heywood Hale Broun — stage actor in "I Remember Mama," CBS sports commentator ◆ Hale Irwin — oldest player to win the US Open

HALFORD ◆Halford Mackinder — promoter of geography as an academic subject

HALL ◆Hall Bartlett — producer whose credits include "All the Young Men" ◆Hall Caine — British author of popular novels with a religious basis, wrote "Prodigal Son" ◆ Hall Johnson — organized the Hall Johnson Choir, heard in film "Lost Horizon"

HALLAM ◆Hallam Cooley — actor whose roles included Henry Garrison in Marion Davies' "Beauty's Worth"

HALLIWELL ◆Halliwell Hobbes — actor who played Brig. Gen. Carew in Fredric March's "Dr. Jekyll and Mr. Hyde"

HALSTON ◆Halston — fashion designer who designed the Jackie Kennedy pillbox hat

HALVOR ◆Halvor Bjork — actor whose roles included Viktor in Ingrid Bergman's "Autumn Sonata"

HAM ◆Ham Fisher — creator of the "Joe Palooka" comic strip

HAMILTON ◆Hamilton Fish — Ulysses S. Grant's secretary of state who saved him from corruption scandal ◆ Hamilton Jordan — presidential aide to Jimmy Carter

HAMISH ◆Hamish Maxwell — chairman of Phillip Morris ◆ Hamish Stuart — with English rock group The Average White Band, best selling album "Cut the Cake"

HAMMOND ◆Hugh Hammond Bennett — first chief of the soil conservation service ◆ Glenn Hammond Curtiss — inventor and aircraft manufacturer

HAN ◆Han Solo (c) — mercenary pilot of the Millenium Falcon in the "Star Wars" trilogy

HANIF ◆Hanif Kureishi — British author whose films include "My Beautiful Laundrette"

HANK ◆Hank Aaron — baseball player who set records for home runs ◆ Hank Williams — father of country western music, hits include "Your Cheatin' Heart"

HANNES ◆Hannes Bok — fantasy illustrator who drew woodcut-like scenes for "Weird Tales" ◆Hannes Kolehmainen — four time Olympic gold medal runner

HANNIBAL ◆Hannibal — Carthaginian general who fought the Romans, crossed the Alps with elephants ◆ Hannibal Hamlin — US Vice President under Lincoln

HANNS ◆Hanns Eisler — German composer who scored Hollywood films in the 1940's

HANS ◆Hans Christian Andersen — nineteenth century Danish writer of fairy tales ◆Hans Conried — tall, weedy comic actor with precise diction and a richly variable voice

HANSON ◆Hanson Baldwin — Pulitzer Prize winning journalist

HARCOURT ◆Harcourt Williams — distinguished British stage actor, roles include "Around the World in 80 Days"

HARDIE ◆Hardie Albright — leading man of 1930's films, including "Song of Songs" ◆Hardie Gramatky — illustrator of the favorite book of children "Little Tot"

HARDING ◆Harding Lemay — controversial writer of the soap "Another World"

HARDY ◆Hardy Amies — English fashion designer who specialized in ready-to-wear clothes ◆ Kenneth Hardy Cooper — invented the word aerobics with his book "Aerobics" ◆ Hardy Kruger — actor, films include "The One That Got Away" and "Wild Geese"

HARI ◆Hari Rhodes — starred in TV's "Daktari" and "The Bold Ones"

HARLAN ◆Harlan Day — one of the sons of Clarence Day in the film, book, and TV "Life With Father" ◆Harlan Ellison — author, works include "Shatterday" and "An Edge in My Voice"

HARLAND ◆Col. Harland Sanders — used his secret recipe to found Kentucky Fried Chicken

HARLEN ◆Harlen Carraher — actor who played son Jonathan Muir on the sitcom "The Ghost and Mrs. Muir"

HARLEY ◆Henry Harley Arnold — nicknamed "Hap," first general of the Air Force ◆Harley Cross — actor in the Jane Fonda and Robert De Niro film "Stanley and Iris"

HARLOW ◆Harlow Gage — manager of General Motors' overseas division ◆ Harlow Shapley — Harvard astronomer who studies the Milky Way, author of "Galaxies"

HARMON ◆Harmon Jones — Canadian Hollywood director ◆ Horace Harmon Lurton — conservative Supreme Court justice appointed by President Taft

HARNETT ◆Harnett Kane — author of the South whose works include "New Orleans Woman"

HAROLD ◆Harold Lloyd — silent film comedy star ◆ Harold Ramis — comedy writer whose credits include "Stripes," "Animal House," "Ghostbusters" ◆Harold Robbins — best selling author, novels include "The Carpetbaggers" ◆ Harold Russell — Oscar winning actor with no hands in "The Best Years of Our Lives"

HARPER ◆Harper Lee — Pulitzer Prize winner for "To Kill a Mockingbird" ◆ Harper Simon — son of performer Paul Simon

HARRISON ◆Harrison Fisher — illustrator who created the "Fisher Girl" ◆ Harrison Ford — portrayed adventurer Indiana Jones in "Raiders of the Lost Ark" and two sequels ◆ Harrison Schmitt — astronaut and pilot of the Apollo lunar module, became a US senator

HARRY ◆Harry Anderson — actor whose roles included Judge Harry Stone on the sitcom "Night Court" ◆ Harry Belafonte — Caribbean calypso singer and film star ◆ Harry Connick, Jr. — musician/singer and modern crooner for the 90's ◆Harry Morgan — actor whose roles included Colonel Potter on TV's "M*A*S*H"

HART ◆Hart Bochner — Canadian in "Breaking Away," "Rich and Famous," miniseries "War and Remembrance" ◆ Raymond Hart Massey — distinguished film actor, starred as Dr. Gillespie on TV's "Dr. Kildare"

HARTFORD ◆Hartford Gunn — founder of the Public Broadcasting System (PBS)

HARTLAND ◆Hartland Molson — Hall of Fame owner of the Montreal Canadiens hockey team

HARTLEY ◆Edward Hartley Angle — founder of modern orthodontics ◆ Hartley Power — character actor usually seen as hard-headed agent, general or con man

HARVARD ◆A. Harvard Aranason — author of "The History of Modern Art"

HARVE ◆Harve Bennett — producer who won an Emmy for "A Woman Called Golda" ◆ Harve Presnell — opera singer, films include "The Unsinkable Molly Brown" and "Paint Your Wagon"

HARVEY ◆Harvey (c) — playwright Mary Chase's six foot invisible rabbit who is a pal to Elwood P. Dowd ◆ Harvey Firestone — founder of the Firestone Tire and Rubber Company ◆ Harvey Keitel — actor in films like "Thelma and Louise" and "Bugsy" ◆Harvey Korman — Carol Burnett's foil on her TV show

HARWELL ◆Harwell Harris — leading exponent of the California style of architecture

HASKELL ◆Charles Haskell Revson — founder of Revlon cosmetics ◆ Haskell Wexler — Oscar-winning cinematographer for "Who's Afraid of Virginia Woolf?"

HAVELOCK ◆Havelock Ellis — early twentieth century sex researcher

HAWKSHAW ◆Hawkshaw Hawkins — country music singer, big hit was "Slowpoke"

HAY ◆Hay Petrie — played Dickens' fiendish, deformed moneylender in "The Old Curiosity Shop" ◆Hay Plumb — played the swashbuckling Sir Francis Drake in the silent "Drake's Love Story"

HAYDEN ◆Hayden Rorke — played Dr. Alfred Bellows on the popular genie sitcom "I Dream of Jeannie"

HAYES ◆Hayes Alan — Olympic gold medal and four-time world champion figure skater ◆ T. Hayes Hunter — director, films include "The Triumph of the Scarlet Pimpernel" ◆Hayes Jones — Olympic gold medal high hurdler

HAYWARD ◆Hayward Robillard — actor who played the "cat man" in Dennis Hopper's cult classic "Easy Rider"

HAYWOOD ◆Haywood Nelson — actor whose roles included Haywood Marshall on the sitcom spinoff "Grady" ◆ Haywood Sullivan — catcher who appeared in 312 major league games in seven years

HAZARD ◆Oliver Hazard Morton — Republican senator who played a major role in giving blacks the vote ◆Oliver Hazard Perry — naval hero of the War of 1812, quote "We have met the enemy, and they are ours"

HAZEN ◆Hazen Cuyler — outfielder inducted into the Hall of Fame

HEATHCLIFF ◆Heathcliff (c) — role Laurence Olivier brought to the screen in Emily Bronte's "Wuthering Heights" ◆Heathcliff Huxtable (c) — Bill Cosby's hilarious obstetrician and father on "The Cosby Show"

HECTOR ◆Hector Boiardi — Chef Boyardee and president of the company

HEDLEY ◆Hedley Donovan — editor-in-chief of all Time Inc. publications

HEDRICK ◆Hedrick Smith — Pulitzer Prize winning writer of "The Pentagon Papers"

HEINIE ◆Heinie Conklin — actor in Charlie Chaplin's industrial classic "Modern Times"

HEINRICH ◆Heinrich Focke — inventor of the helicopter ◆ Heinrich Schliemann — archeologist who uncovered ancient Troy

HEINZ ◆Heinz Ruhmann — actor whose roles included amateur detective Father Brown on the screen

HELMUT ◆Helmut Berger — actor whose roles included Peter de Vilbis on TV's "Dynasty" ◆Helmut Griem — actor whose roles included Baron Maximilian von Heune in the film "Cabaret"

HENDERSON ◆Henderson Forsythe — actor whose roles included Ben Bradlee in Cybill Shepherd's film "Chances Are"

HENNING ◆Henning Mikkelsen — creator of the comic strip "Ferd'nand"

HENNY ◆Henny Youngman — comedian best known for the line "Take my wife, please!"

HENRI ◆Henri Charriere — real life escapee from Devil's Island, Steve McQueen biopic "Papillon" ◆ Henri Mathieu — real name of designer Yves St. Laurent ◆ Henri Matisse — French painter who led the artistic group of fauves

HENRIK ◆Henrik Ibsen — playwright, known for "A Doll's House"

HENRY ◆Henry Fonda — screen legend with a career spanning six decades, Oscar for "On Golden Pond" ◆ Henry Ford — founder of the Ford car company ◆ Henry Mancini — Oscar winner for "Moon River," "Days of Wine and Roses," "Victor/ Victoria" ◆ Henry Winkler — actor who played the leather clad suburban hero "The Fonz" on TV's "Happy Days"

HENSON ◆Henson Cargill — country singer who went to number one on the charts with "Skip-a-Rope"

HERB ◆Herb Alpert — founder of the Tijuana Brass and A&M Records, hit "This Guy's in Love With You" ◆ Herb Jaffe — horror producer whose films include "Motel Hell" and "The Gate" ◆ Herb Shriner — TV humorist known for his Hoosier stories

HERBERT ◆Herbert Hoover — President whose administration was dominated by the Great Depression ◆Herbert "H.G." Wells — author of "The Time Machine," "The Invisible Man," "The War of the Worlds"

HERBIE ◆Herbie Faye — actor whose roles included Ben Goldman on TV's "Doc" ◆Herbie Hancock — jazz musician, hits include "You Bet Your Love," "Rockit" ◆ Herbie the Love Bug

(c) — Disney's Volkswagen Beetle with a mind of its own, in film and on TV

HERCULE ◆Hercule Poirot (c) — fictional detective created by author Agatha Christie

HERCULES ◆Charles Hercules Ebbets — owner of the Brooklyn Dodgers who built Ebbets Field ◆ Elton Hercules John — rock singer known for wearing hats and large glasses in concert

HERMAN ◆Herman Melville — author of "Moby Dick," which became a movie with Gregory Peck ◆ Herman Wouk — novelist whose filmed works include "The Caine Mutiny" and "The Winds of War"

HERMANN ◆Othmar Hermann Ammann — designer of George Washington Bridge and Golden Gate Bridge ◆ Hermann Rorschach — psychiatrist who developed the Rorschach inkblot tests

HERMES ◆Hermes Pan — choreographer for 17 Fred Astaire and 10 Betty Grable musicals

HERNANDO ◆Hernando Cortez — conquered Mexico and toppled the Aztec Empire ◆ Hernando DeSoto — Spanish explorer who discovered the Mississippi River

HERSCHEL ◆Walter Herschel Beech — founder of Beech Aircraft Company ◆ Herschel Bernardi — actor whose roles included Tevye on Broadway's "Fiddler on the Roof" ◆ John Herschel Glenn, Jr. — first American to orbit the Earth, later became a US senator

HERSHEL ◆Hershel Walker — Heisman Trophy winner for 1982 from the University of Georgia

HERSHY ◆Hershy Kay — composer whose film scores include "Coco" and "Evita"

HERVE ◆Herve Alphand — French economist and UN ambassador ◆ Herve Villechaize — Tattoo on TV's "Fantasy Island," line was "The plane!"

HERVEY ◆Hervey Allen — author whose works include the best seller "Anthony Adverse"

HEYWOOD ◆Heywood Broun — stage actor in "I Remember Mama," CBS sports commentator

HEZEKIAH ◆Hezekiah — in the Bible, King of Judah who helped defeat the Philistines ◆ Hezekiah Keino — only man to hold Olympic track records for two different distances

HITIDE ◆HiTide Harris — sang the songs in the Huddie Ledbetter biopic "Leadbelly"

HICKS ◆Hicks Waldron — president and chairman of Avon

HIERONYMUS ◆Hieronymus Bosch — sixteenth century Dutch artist ◆ Baron Hieronymus Munchausen — name is associated with wild tales, biopic "Adventures of Baron Munchausen"

HILDY ◆Hildy Johnson (c) — newspaperman trying to quit in the many film versions of "The Front Page"

HILLEL ◆Hillel Slovak — original member of the rock group The Red Hot Chili Peppers

HILMER ◆Hilmer Kenty — lightweight boxing champion

HILTON ◆Hilton Valentine — member of the rock group The Animals, number one hit "House of the Rising Sun"

HINTON ◆Hinton Helper — southerner who opposed slavery, author of "Impending Crisis of the South"

HIPPOLYTE ◆Hippolyte Delaroche — French artist, paintings include "Jonas Saved by Josabeth" ◆Armand Hippolyte Fizeau — first physicist to measure the speed of light

HIRAM ◆Hiram Ulysses Grant — real name of President Ulysses Simpson Grant

HIRO ◆Hiro Yamamoto — member of the heavy metal band Soundgarden, album "Louder Than Love"

HIROAKI ◆Hiroaki Aoki — Olympic wrestler who founded the Benihana restaurants

HOAGY ◆Hoagy Carmichael — songwriter famous for "Stardust"

HOBART ◆Hobart Baker — Hall of Fame hockey player ◆ Hobart Bosworth — actor whose roles included the avenging Count of Monte Cristo in the silent era ◆ Hobart Cavanaugh — character actor who played meek, henpecked, nervous little men

HOBE ◆Hobe Morrison — former editor and critic for "Variety"

HOBIE ◆Hobie Alter — designer of the "Hobie Cat" sailing catamaran

HOD ◆Hod Stuart — Hockey Hall of Fame defenseman

HODDING ◆Hodding Carter — PBS anchorman and later State Department spokesman

HOKE ◆Hoke Howell — actor who played Ben Jenkins on the popular series "Here Come the Brides"

HOLBROOK ◆Holbrook Blinn — silent star whose films include "Janice Meredith" and "Zander the Great"

HOLLAND ◆Holland Smith — father of modern amphibious warfare who led the invasion of Iwo Jima

HOLLIS ◆Hollis Alpert — film critic with "American Film"

HOLMAN ◆Holman Hunt — artist and founder of the pre-Raphaelite Brotherhood

HOLMES ◆Holmes Herbert — actor whose roles included Dr. Lanyon in "Dr. Jekyll and Mr. Hyde"

HOMER ◆Homer — ancient blind Greek poet who wrote the "Iliad" and "The Odyssey" ◆ Homer Murray — son of comedy actor Bill Murray ◆Homer Simpson (c) — father of Bart Simpson on TV's cartoon sitcom "The Simpsons"

HONEY ◆Robert Honey Fabian — detective at Scotland Yard, biopic "Fabian of the Yard"

HONOR ◆Honor Arundel — Welsh author whose books deal with adolescent emotional problems

HONORE ◆Honore de Balzac — French dramatist best known for "Comedie Humaine"

HONUS ◆Honus Wagner — original inductee into the Baseball Hall of Fame

HORACE ◆Horace Greeley — founder of New York Tribune who said "Go West, young man" ◆ Horace Mann — father of American public education

HORATIO ◆Horatio Alger — clergyman who wrote books based on the idea that a poor boy could become rich ◆ Horatio Nelson — British naval hero of Trafalgar who had an affair with Lady Hamilton

HORST ◆Horst Antes — German painter of large, strange "gnomes" ◆ Horst Buchholz — one of the gunfighters in the classic western "The Magnificent Seven" ◆ Horst Horst — longtime fashion photographer for "Vogue"

HORTON ◆Horton Foote — Oscar winning writer for "Tender Mercies" and "To Kill a Mockingbird" ◆Horton Smith — winner of 29 PGA tournaments, including the first Masters

HOSEA ◆Hosea Williams — clergyman and civil rights leader

HOUDINI ◆Harry Houdini — world's greatest escape artist

HOUSE ◆House Jameson — actor whose roles included Dr. Lawson on the soap "Search for Tomorrow" ◆ House Peters — actor who played debonair British jewel thief on the silent screen in "Raffles"

HOUSTON ◆Houston McTear — track star who set the US men's sixty meter indoor record

HOWARD ◆Howard Cosell — big mouth of television sports news ◆ Howard Hesseman — played the teacher on "Head of the Class," started on "WKRP in Cincinnati" ◆ Howard Hughes — ultra-rich eccentric industrialist involved in films and aviation ◆ Howard Johnson — founder of Howard Johnson's ◆ Howard Stern — nationally syndicated, New York-based, outrageous radio host

HOWE ◆Alfred Howe Terry — general in charge of the campaign in which Custer died at Little Bighorn

HOWIE ◆Howie Mandel — comic actor whose roles included Dr. Wayne Fiscus on "St. Elsewhere"

HOWLAND ◆Edwin Howland Blashfield — painter of the murals for the congressional library ◆John Howland Wood — nickname "Maximum John," only federal judge assassinated in the 20th century

HOYT ◆Hoyt Axton — country music singer who has sold over 25 million records ◆Hoyt Vandenberg — air force general, namesake for California's Vandenberg Air Force Base ◆ Hoyt Wilhelm — Hall of Fame pitcher known for his knuckleball

HUBERT ◆Walter Hubert Annenberg — super rich publisher, owner of "TV Guide," "Seventeen" ◆Hubert Humphrey — Vice President under Lyndon Johnson ◆Hubert Van Eyck — artist who is the co-founder of the Flemish School

HUBIE ◆Hubie Brown — basketball coach of the NY Knicks ◆ Hubie Green — championship golfer

HUCKLEBERRY ◆Huckleberry Finn (c) — Mark Twain's carefree, pipe-smoking orphan hero of the Mississippi

HUDDIE ◆Huddie Ledbetter — learned the blues breaking rocks on a chain gang, biopic "Leadbelly"

HUDSON ◆Ken Hudson Campbell — actor who played the symbol of lust on the brain-revealing "Herman's Head" ◆ Rush Hudson Limbaugh — ultra-conservative syndicated talk show host of the "Rush Limbaugh Show"

HUEY ◆Huey Lewis — member of Huey Lewis and the News, debut hit single "Do You Believe in Love"

HUGH ◆Hugh Beaumont — actor who played understanding father Ward Cleaver on "Leave It to Beaver" ◆ Hugh Downs — network newscaster featured on "20/20" ◆ Hugh Hefner — founder of "Playboy" ◆ Hugh O'Brian — star of TV's "Life and Legend of Wyatt Earp"

HUGHIE ◆Hughie Green — Canadian actor in Britain turned popular TV quizmaster ◆Hughie Lehman — Hall of Fame hockey player for Chicago ◆ Hughie Thomasson — member of The Outlaws, hit single "(Ghost) Riders in the Sky"

HUGO ◆Hugo Gernsback — publisher of one of the first science fiction magazines "Amazing Stories" ◆ Hugo Winterhalter — bandleader with 11 gold records, songs performed by Perry Como and Doris Day

HUMBERSTONE ◆Humberstone Wright — played British naval hero Horatio Nelson in "The Romance of Lady Hamilton"

HUMBERTO ◆Cardinal Humberto Medeiros — leader of the Catholic Church in Boston ◆ Humberto Richards — actor whose roles included Elvis on the sitcom "Marblehead Manor"

HUME ◆Hume Cronyn — long lived actor, appearing in films from "Lifeboat" to "Cocoon"

HUMPHREY ◆Humphrey Bogart — Academy Award for "The African Queen," but best remembered for "Casablanca"

HUMPHRY ◆Humphry Repton — one of the leading architects of English landscape gardening

HUNT ◆Hunt Powers — actor whose roles included Dr. Ken Martin on the soap "General Hospital" ◆ Hunt Stromberg — producer of the Nelson Eddy-Jeanette MacDonald films, also, the "Thin Man" series

HUNTER ◆Hunter Thompson — author of "Fear and Loathing in Las Vegas," and other works ◆Hunter Von Leer — actor whose roles included Larry Joe Baker on the soap "General Hospital"

HUNTINGTON ◆Huntington Hartford — founder of the A&P Supermarkets

HUNTLEY◆Huntley Gordon — actor whose films include the Katharine Hepburn/Ginger Rogers film "Stage Door"

HUNTZ◆Huntz Hall — Dead End Kid, later one of the Bowery Boys

HURD◆Hurd Hatfield — actor whose roles included the lead in "The Picture of Dorian Gray"

HUSBAND◆Husband Kimmel — commander-in-chief of the Pacific Fleet during Pearl Harbor

HUW◆Huw Langston — member of the group Hawkwind, hits include "Silver Machine"

HY◆Hy Averback — director of "Where Were You When the Lights Went Out?"

HYMAN◆Hyman Rickover — navy admiral who created the atomic submarine fleet

HYWEL◆Hywel Bennett — Welsh TV and film player whose films include Hayley Mills' "The Family Way"

IAIN◆Iain Glen — played John Hanning Speke in his search for the Nile in "Mountains of the Moon"

IAN◆Ian Fleming — created secret agent James Bond in his series of books ◆ Ian Holm — Oscar nominated actor for "Chariots of Fire" ◆ Ian Hunter — King Richard the Lion-Heart in Errol Flynn's "The Adventures of Robin Hood" ◆ Ian MacShane — played the title role as the antique dealer in the drama series "Lovejoy" ◆ Ian Ziering — blond hunk on TV's "Beverly Hills 90210"

IB◆Ib Andersen — Danish ballet dancer with Balanchine's NYC Ballet ◆ Ib Melchior — Danish-born Hollywood director, films include "The Time Travelers"

IBN◆Abdullah Ibn Hussein — pro-British King of Jordan who was assassinated ◆ Ibn Saud — founder of Saudi Arabia, who named it after himself

IBRAHIM◆Ibrahim Hamouda — portrayed Shakespeare's star-crossed lover in "Romeo and Juliet" ◆Ibrahim Hussein — three-time winner of the Boston Marathon

ICE ◆Ice Cube — rapper whose hit albums include "Death Certificate" ◆ Ice T — best known for his controversial rap song "Cop Killer"

ICHABOD ◆Ichabod Crane (c) — hero of Washington Irving's "Legend of Sleepy Hollow"

IDRIS ◆Idris Muhammad — rock drummer whose hits include "Bony Moronie" and "You Talk Too Much"

IEOH ◆Ieoh Ming Pei — international architect whose works include the glass pyramid at the Louvre

IGGY ◆Iggy Pop — actor who played Johnny Depp's grandfather Belvedere in John Waters' "Cry-Baby"

IGNACE ◆Ignace Paderewski — Polish prime minister and classical pianist

IGNATIUS ◆Joseph Ignatius Breen — powerful 1930's–1940's film censor, won a special Oscar in 1953 ◆Saint Ignatius of Loyola — founder of the Jesuits

IGNAZ ◆Ignaz Schwinn — bicycle pioneer and founder of the Schwinn Bicycle Company

IGOR ◆Igor Cassini — host of the celebrity interview show "The Igor Cassini Show" ◆ Igor Sikorsky — inventor of the helicopter, founder Sikorsky helicopter company

IKE ◆Ike Clanton — portrayed by Lyle Bettger in Burt Lancaster's "Gunfight at the O.K. Corral" ◆ Ike Pappas — correspondent with CBS News ◆Ike Turner — from Ike and Tina Turner, hits include "Proud Mary" and "River Deep Mountain High"

ILLINOIS ◆Illinois Jacquet — tenor saxophonist whose hits include "Flying Home"

ILYA ◆Ilya Bolotowsky — painter known for diamond-shaped canvases, co-founder American Abstract Artists ◆ Ilya Salkind — producer of big Hollywood films such as "Superman"

ILYICH ◆Leonid Ilyich Brezhnev — former general secretary of the Soviet Communist Party ◆Peter Ilyich Tchaikovsky — Russian composer of symphonies and ballets, led a life of torment and anguish ◆ Vladimir Ilyich Ulyanov — real name of Russian Marxist leader Lenin

INCREASE ◆Increase Mather — father of Cotton Mather, colonial president of Harvard University

INDIANA ◆Indiana Jones (c) — Harrison Ford's most famous movie character

INGMAR ◆Ingmar Bergman — legendary Swedish director, films include "The Seventh Seal" and "Virgin Spring"

INGO ◆Ingo Mogendorf — portrayed fighter pilot Baron von Richthoven, the Red Baron, in "Darling Lili"

INIGO ◆Inigo Jones — architect who restored St. Paul's Cathedral

INMAN ◆Inman Jackson — Sidney Poitier's role as a Harlem Globetrotter in the biopic "Go, Man, Go!"

IRA ◆Ira Gershwin — lyricist whose films include "An American in Paris" with Gene Kelly ◆ Ira Grossel — real name of actor Jeff Chandler ◆ Ira Levin — author of "Rosemary's Baby" and "The Stepford Wives," both of them filmed

IRV ◆Irv Kupcinet — columnist with the Chicago Sun Times who hosted TV's "Kup's Show"

IRVIN ◆Irvin Kniberg — real name of comedian Alan King ◆ Irvin McDowell — Union general relieved of command after the Battle of Bull Run ◆Irvin Westheimer — founder of Big Brothers

IRVINE ◆Irvine Robbins — founder with Burton Baskin of Baskin-Robbins ice cream

IRVING ◆Irving Berlin — prolific composer and lyricist whose songs included "White Christmas" ◆ Irving Thalberg — boy genius and studio head of Metro-Goldwyn-Mayer ◆Irving Wallace — one of the best read and best selling authors in twentieth century America

IRWIN ◆Irwin Allen — king of the disaster flicks, he won an Oscar for "The Sea Around Us" ◆ Irwin Corey — double-talking comedian of stage and screen, films include "Car Wash" ◆ Irwin Shaw — author of "Rich Man, Poor Man," became miniseries with Nick Nolte

ISAAC ◆Isaac Asimov — popular author and scientist who invented the term "robotics" ◆ Isaac Hayes — rock singer, debut hit single "Walk On By" ◆ Isaac Newton — discovered the law of gravity when an apple fell on his head

ISAACH ◆Isaach De Bankole — actor who played the lead role of Protee in the African-based film "Chocolat"

ISAIAH ◆Isaiah Rogers — architect who designed the first modern hotel in America ◆ Isaiah Thomas — founder of the American Antiquarian Society

ISAO ◆Isao Abe — founder of the Japanese Socialist Party who introduced baseball to Japan ◆ Isao Aoki — first Japanese golfer to win the PGA tournament

ISHAM ◆Isham Jones — bandleader and composer of "It Had to Be You"

ISHMAEL ◆Ishmael Reed — author, works include "Chattanooga" and "Flight to Canada"

ISIAH ◆Isiah Thomas III — holder of the NBA record for the most assists in a single season

ISIDOR ◆Isidor Stone — godfather of new left journalism, founder of "I. F. Stone's Bi-Weekly" ◆Isidor Straus — founder of Abraham and Straus retailers

ISIDORE ◆Isidore Diamond — screenwriter of "Some Like It Hot" and "The Apartment" ◆ Isidore Itzkowitz — real name of comic actor Eddie Cantor

ISRAEL ◆Israel Baline — real name of songster Irving Berlin ◆ Israel Putnam — Revolutionary War hero, Guiterman's biopoem "Death and General Putnam"

ISSUR ◆Issur Danielovitch Demsky — real name of actor Kirk Douglas

ITALO ◆Italo Balbo — Governor of Libya who built up Mussolini's air force, shot down by own men ◆ Italo Calvino — Italian author of "If on a Winter's Night a Traveler" ◆Italo Tajo — actor whose roles included the Devil in the film "Faust and the Devil"

IVAN ◆Ivan Pavlov — discovered "Pavlov's response," conditioned responses in dogs ◆ Ivan Reitman — comedy film director whose hits include "Ghostbusters" and "Stripes"

IVANOVICH ◆Rudolf Ivanovich Abel — Russian master spy sentenced to 30 years, exchanged for Francis Gary Powers ◆ Petr Ivanovich Bagration — Russian general who led campaigns against Napoleon

IVO ◆Ivo Andric — Nobel Prize winning Yugoslavian author ◆ Ivo Garrani — actor whose roles included Julius Caesar in "Son of Spartacus"

IVOR ◆Ivor Dean — actor who played 19th century graverobber Burke in "Dr. Jekyll and Sister Hyde" ◆ Ivor Francis — actor whose roles included Mr. Brookhaven on TV's "Dusty's Trail" ◆ Ivor Novello — actor whose roles included a suspected killer in "The Lodger"

IVORY ◆Ivory Joe Hunter — singer who scored an R&B gold record hit with "I Almost Lost My Mind" ◆ Ivory Tilmon — member of The Detroit Emeralds, debut hit single "Show Time" ◆ Ivory Watson — baritone with The Ink Spots, hits include the ballad "If I Didn't Care"

IZAAK ◆Izaak Walton — author of the "Compleat Angler"

IZZY ◆Izzy Stradlin — member of Guns 'n' Roses, hits include the platinum "Appetite for Destruction"

JABEZ ◆Jabez Gorham — silversmith who founded Gorham Manufacturing

JACK ◆Jack Benny — cheapest man alive, in the movies as well as on his own TV show ◆ Jack Klugman — actor whose roles included sloppy Oscar Madison on TV's "The Odd Couple" ◆ Jack Lemmon — comedy actor in "Some Like It Hot," "The Fortune Cookie," "The Great Race" ◆ Jack Nicholson — Academy Award winner who did an incredible performance as the Joker in "Batman" ◆ Jack Palance — won an Oscar for Best Supporting Actor in "City Slickers" ◆ Jack Webb — deadpan detective star of TV's "Dragnet"

JACKIE ◆Jackie Coogan — actor whose roles included Uncle Fester on TV's "The Addams Family" ◆ Jackie Cooper — star of the TV comedy/drama series "Hennesey" ◆ Jackie Gleason — actor whose roles included Ralph Kramden on the sitcom "The Honeymooners" ◆ Jackie Jackson — oldest of The Jackson Five, solo album "Jackie Jackson" ◆ Jackie Robinson — athlete who broke the color barrier in professional baseball

JACKSON ◆Jackson Browne — musician/singer/songwriter whose gold album was "The Pretender" ◆ Jackson Frederick Smith — son of celebrity Patti Smith ◆ Jackson Pollock — his action painting was done by throwing or dripping paint onto the canvas ◆ Jackson Scholz — Olympic runner, biopic "Chariots of Fire"

JACO ◆Jaco Pastorius — member of the group Weather Report, instrumental hits include "Birdland"

JACOB ◆John Jacob Astor — founder of the Astor family, wealthiest man in America at his death ◆ Jacob Cohen — real name of comedian Rodney Dangerfield ◆ Jacob Schweppe — invented method of carbonating water, founder of Schweppe's

JACQUES ◆Jacques Cousteau — invented the aqualung, host of TV's "Undersea World of Jacques Cousteau"

JADRIEN ◆Jadrien Steele — actor whose roles included Little John Ryan on the soap "Ryan's Hope"

JAIME ◆Jaime Escalante — Edward James Olmos starred as the math teacher in biopic "Stand and Deliver" ◆ Jaime Sanchez — actor whose roles included Carlos in the film "David and Lisa"

JAIMOE ◆Jaimoe Johanson — member of The Allman Brothers Band, debut hit "Revival (Love is Everywhere)"

JAIN ◆Jain Moncreiffe — genealogist for "Burke's Peerage"

JAKE ◆Jake Paltrow — son of actress Blythe Danner ◆Jake Blues (c) — John Belushi's character in "The Blues Brothers" on a mission from God

JAKOB ◆Jakob Grimm — German writer of fairy tales, biopic "The Wonderful World of the Brothers Grimm"

JALEEL ◆Jaleel White — actor who played pesky next door neighbor Steve Urkel on TV's "Family Matters"

JAMAAL ◆Jamaal Wilkes — 1975 NBA rookie of the year

JAMEEL ◆Jameel Farah — real name of "M*A*S*H" actor Jamie Farr

JAMES ◆James Bond — ornithologist whose name Ian Fleming used for his secret agent "007" ◆ James Brown — Soul Brother Number One with 38 gold records ◆James Caan — "The Jewish Cowboy," starred in "The Godfather" ◆ James Cagney — mega film star, roles in "Yankee Doodle Dandy," "White Heat," "Fighting 69th" ◆ James Dean — troubled actor of the 1950's whose definitive film is "Rebel Without a Cause" ◆James Garner — star of TV's "The Rockford Files" and "Maverick"

JAMESON ◆Jameson Parker — played brother A. J. Simon on the drama detective series "Simon and Simon" ◆ Jameson Sampley — actor whose roles included Danny Carrington on TV's "Dynasty"

JAMIE ◆Jamie Farr — portrayed the cross-dressing Corporal Klinger on TV's "M*A*S*H" ◆ Jamie Foxx — regular cast member of TV's "In Living Color" ◆ Jamie Wyeth — most commercially successful artist of the late twentieth century

JAN ◆Jan Berry — group Jan and Dean, hits include "Surf City," brain damaged in car crash ◆ Jan Murray — vaudeville and nightclub entertainer, films include "The Busybody"

JAN-MICHAEL ◆Jan-Michael Vincent — actor whose films include "White Line Fever" and "Tribes," TV's "Airwolf"

JANCE ◆Jance Garfat — member of Dr. Hook and the Medicine Show, debut gold album "Sylvia's Mother"

JAPE ◆Jape Richardson — nickname the "Big Bopper," number one hit "Chantilly Lace," died with Buddy Holly

JARED ◆Jared Martin — actor whose roles included Dusty Farlow on TV's nighttime soap "Dallas" ◆ Jared Sparks — president of Harvard and editor of the "North American Review"

JARL ◆Jarl Kulle — actor who played the legendary rake Don Juan in Bergman's "The Devil's Eye"

JARROD ◆Jarrod Johnson — actor whose roles included Randy Summerfield on TV's "Friends"

JARVIS ◆Henry Jarvis Raymond — founder of the New York Times and the Republican Party

JASCHA ◆Jascha Heifetz — child prodigy violinist

JASON ◆Jason Alexander — actor whose roles included George on the sitcom series "Seinfeld" ◆ Jason Bateman — played oldest son on TV's "Valerie" which later became "The Hogan Family" ◆ Jason Patric — actor whose films include "The Lost Boys" ◆ Jason Priestley — MTV Veejay and teen idol on TV's "Beverly Hills 90210" ◆ Jason Robards — Oscars for "All the President's Men" and "Julia"

JASPER ◆Jasper Cropsey — painter known for autumn scenes of the Catskill Mountains

JAY ◆Jay Leno — newest host of NBC's "Tonight Show" ◆ Jay North — actor whose roles included Dennis the Menace in the TV series of the same name ◆Jay Silverheels — actor whose roles included Tonto on TV and in films with the "Lone Ranger" ◆Jay Ward — creator of Rocky the Flying Squirrel and Bullwinkle Moose

JAZZY ◆Jazzy Townes — actor whose roles included friend Jazz on TV's "Fresh Prince of Bel Air"

JEAN◆Jean Hersholt — special Oscar Jean Hersholt Humanitarian Award named after him ◆Jean Houdin — father of modern magic, Harry Houdini named himself after him ◆ Jean Lafitte — French-born pirate whose band saved the day at the Battle of New Orleans ◆Jean Renoir — famous film director, son of the artist Auguste Renoir

JEAN-CLAUDE◆Jean-Claude Killy — Olympic gold medal winner in all three men's Alpine skiing events ◆Jean-Claude Van Damme — action hero in films like "Bloodsport" and "Kickboxer"

JEAN-JACQUES◆Jean-Jacques Annaud — director whose films include "Quest for Fire"

JEAN-LOUIS◆Jean-Louis Barrault — director of the French theater ◆ Jean-Louis Trintignant — man in the film classic "A Man and a Woman"

JEAN-LUC◆Jean-Luc Godard — semi-surrealist French writer-director of the "New Wave," directed "Breathless"

JEAN-MARIE◆Jean-Marie Amato — actor who played the legendary rake Don Juan in "Men Think Only of That"

JEAN-PAUL◆Jean-Paul Belmondo — antihero actor, first feature film "Breathless" ◆ Jean-Paul Sartre — French existentialist, wrote "Being and Nothingness," refused Nobel Prize

JEAN-PHILIPPE◆Jean-Philippe Lafont — actor whose roles included Dancairo in the musical film "Carmen"

JEAN-PIERRE◆Jean-Pierre Aumont — French actor and author, autobiography "Sun and Shadow" ◆Jean-Pierre Leaud — actor whose roles included the same character in five of Truffaut's films

JEB◆Jeb Stuart — screenwriter of Eddie Murphy's "Another 48 Hours"

JED◆Jed Prouty — character actor in over 100 films, credits include the "Jones Family" comedies

JEDEDIAH◆Jedediah Smith — fur trader and advocate of western expansion who helped open the West

JEFF◆Jeff Bridges — actor son of Lloyd Bridges, films include "Starman" and "The Last Picture Show" ◆Jeff Chandler — actor in films like "Away All Boats" ◆ Jeff Conaway — actor whose roles included the unemployed actor Bobby Wheeler on TV's

"Taxi" ◆ Jeff Daniels — actor whose roles included the Colonel in "Gettysburg" ◆ Jeff Goldblum — actor in "The Fly," "Jurassic Park" and "The Big Chill" ◆ Jeff Smith — chef and host of TV's "The Frugal Gourmet"

JEFFERSON ◆ William Jefferson Blythe IV — real name of President Bill Clinton ◆ Jefferson Davis — president of the Confederacy ◆ Jefferson MacDonnel — son of actress Britt Ekland and Slim Jim Phantom McDonnel

JEFFREY ◆ Jeffrey Hunter — actor whose roles included Jesus Christ in the film "King of Kings" ◆ Jeffrey Jones — actor whose roles included Ferris Bueller's nemesis, the principal ◆ Jeffrey Osborne — singer, hit single "On the Wings of Love"

JENNINGS ◆ William Jennings Bryan — three-time Democratic presidential candidate ◆ Jennings Randolph — senator from West Virginia for almost thirty years

JENO ◆ Jeno Paulucci — founder of Chun King chinese food, Jeno's pizzas, and Pizza Kwik

JENS ◆ Jens Kuphal — actor who played Axel in the teenage drug addiction film "Christiane F."

JERALD ◆ Jerald TerHorst — White House press secretary under Ford

JEREMIAH ◆ Jeremiah — in the Bible, prophet who foretold destruction of the temple in Jerusalem ◆ Jeremiah Johnson — frontier mountain man portrayed by Robert Redford in the film of the same name

JEREMY ◆ Jeremy Clyde — member of Chad and Jeremy, debut hit record was "Yesterday's Gone" ◆ Jeremy Irons — best actor Oscar for "Reversal of Fortune"; "The French Lieutenant's Woman"

JERMAIN ◆ Jermain Johnson — actor who played Booker T. Freeman on the Alex Haley drama series "Palmerstown"

JERMAINE ◆ Jermaine Jackson — member of The Jackson Five

JEROEN ◆ Jeroen Krabbe — actor whose roles included Anton Maes in Amy Irving's "Crossing Delancey"

JEROME ◆ Jerome Kern — father of modern musical theater ◆ Jerome Lawrence — author of "Inherit the Wind" ◆ Jerome Robbins — choreographer and co-director of Natalie Wood's "West Side Story"

JERRY ◆Jerry Lewis — comedy actor in "The Nutty Professor," "Geisha Boy," and "The Patsy" ◆ Jerry Lee Lewis — country western superstar ◆ Jerry Mathers — played the always-getting-into-trouble Beaver on TV's "Leave It to Beaver" ◆Jerry Seinfeld — stand-up comic and star of NBC's quirky hit "Seinfeld" ◆Jerry Vale — singer, hits include "Innamorata" and "Dommage, Dommage" ◆Jerry Van Dyke — earned Emmy as co-star on TV's "Coach," brother of Dick Van Dyke

JERZY ◆Jerzy Kawalerowicz — Polish director whose films include "The Pharaoh"

JESS ◆Jess Barker — lightweight leading man of the 40's whose films include "Cover Girl"

JESSE ◆Jesse Helms — conservative Republican senator from North Carolina ◆Jesse Jackson — evangelist and political activist ◆ Jesse James — outlaw of the west who is sometimes perceived as a "Robin Hood" ◆ Jesse Owens — superstar athlete of the Berlin Olympics

JESUS ◆Jesus Alou — Dominican baseball player who played for the San Francisco Giants ◆ Jesus Christ — Messiah predicted by the Old Testament prophets

JETHRO ◆Jethro — half of the country music combo Homer and Jethro ◆ Jethro Tull — agrarian inventor, name adopted by rock group, debut hit single "Hymn 43"

JHERYL ◆Jheryl Busby — president and chief executive officer of Motown Records

JIHMI ◆Jihmi Kennedy — actor who played Sharts, one of the soldiers in Matthew Broderick's "Glory"

JIM ◆Jim Belushi — actor brother of John Belushi, "Red Heat," "K-9," "Curly Sue" and "Real Men" ◆ Jim Bowie — inventor of the Bowie knife; death at the Alamo played by Richard Widmark ◆ Jim Henson — puppet master, created the Muppets ◆ Jim Morrison — lead singer of The Doors who died at the age of 27 ◆ Jim Varney — creator of Ernest P. Worrell, films include "Ernest Goes to Camp"

JIMI ◆Jimi Hendrix — singer whose rock classics included "Purple Haze"

JIMMIE ◆Jimmie Rodgers — hit the charts with the gold record "Oh-Oh, I'm Falling in Love Again" ◆ Jimmie Walker — self-styled Black Prince on TV's "Good Times"

JIMMY ◆Jimmy Buffet — country singer whose hits include "Margaritaville" ◆ Jimmy Carter — 39th President of the United States ◆Jimmy Dean — singer of "Big Bad John," now a purveyor of pork sausage ◆ Jimmy Olsen (c) — cub reporter on the Daily Planet and friend of Superman ◆ Jimmy Smits — actor whose roles included attorney Victor Sifuentes on TV's "L.A. Law" ◆ Jimmy Stewart — screen legend of "It's a Wonderful Life," Oscar for "The Philadelphia Story"

JO ◆Jo Swerling — screenwriter whose film credits include Alfred Hitchcock's "Lifeboat"

JO JO ◆Jo Jo White — guard with Boston, Most Valuable Player in the 1976 playoffs

JOACHIM ◆Rolf Joachim Benirschke — placekicker with San Diego who overcame disease to return to football ◆ Joachim Murat — brother-in-law of Napoleon, King of Naples

JOAQUIM ◆Joaquim Andujar — Dominican-born major league pitcher

JOCH ◆Joch Pais — played Teenage Mutant Ninja Turtle Raphael in the film version of the comic

JOCK ◆Jock Mahoney — one of the many screen Tarzans, stepfather of Sally Field

JOE ◆Joe Cocker — musician whose credits include "Up Where We Belong" from "An Officer and a Gentleman" ◆ Joe Louis — heavyweight champion of the world, "The Brown Bomber" ◆Joe Namath — quarterback turned model ◆ Joe Pesci — "Goodfellas," "My Cousin Vinny," and "Lethal Weapon II" ◆Joe Piscopo — regular on TV's "Saturday Night Live"

JOEL ◆Joel Grey — Oscar winner for his role in the film "Cabaret" ◆ Joel McCrea — actor in "Foreign Correspondent," "Buffalo Bill" ◆Joel Murray — actor who played Norris Weldon on NBC's "Grand," brother of Bill Murray

JOEY ◆Joey Bishop — TV personality and member of Frank Sinatra's "rat pack" ◆ Joey Lawrence — pop singer, star of TV's "Blossom," and major teen-beat heartthrob

JOHAN ◆Johan Cruyff — soccer player with LA Aztecs, nickname The Flying Dutchman ◆Johan Vaaler — inventor of the paper clip

JOHANN ◆Johann Sebastian Bach — German composer and organist ◆ Johann Strauss — Austrian composer-conductor of beautiful waltzes ◆ Johann Wyss — author of "The Swiss Family Robinson" which Disney brought to the screen

JOHANNES ◆Johannes Brahms — nineteenth century German composer of "Brahms' Lullaby" ◆ Johannes Kepler — father of modern astronomy

JOHN ◆John Belushi — "Saturday Night Live," created "The Blues Brothers," "Samurai Tailor" ◆ John Candy — Second City comedian who made the transition to big feature films ◆ John Cleese — creator of comedy group Monty Python ◆ John Goodman — actor whose roles included Dan Conner, the husband of TV's "Roseanne" ◆ John Malkovich — evil villain in Clint Eastwood's "In the Line of Fire" ◆ John Wayne — "Well, pilgrim, you better know who I am"

JOHNNIE ◆Johnnie Kristofferson — son of actor/singer Kris Kristofferson ◆ Johnnie Ray — singer, number one hit single "Cry"

JOHNNY ◆Johnny Carson — host of TV's late night "Tonight Show" for over twenty years ◆ Johnny Cash — "The Man in Black" country singer, hit songs include "Ring of Fire" ◆ Johnny Depp — actor whose roles included the title role in director John Waters' "Cry-Baby" ◆ Johnny Paycheck — country singer, hits include "Take This Job and Shove It" ◆ Johnny Weissmuller — Olympic swimmer who became the most popular of the screen Tarzans

JOHNS ◆Johns Hopkins — founder of Johns Hopkins Hospital

JOHNSTON ◆Johnston McCulley — creator of short stories about the Robin Hood of California, Zorro ◆ Laurence Johnston Peter — author of the best seller on human foibles, "The Peter Principle"

JOLIET ◆Joliet Jake Blues (c) — John Belushi's character in the film "The Blues Brothers"

JON ◆Jon Bon Jovi — namesake for rock group Bon Jovi, debut single "Runaway" ◆ Jon Lovitz — comedy performer best known as the liar guy from "Saturday Night Live" ◆Jon Voight — actor in "Coming Home," "Deliverance," "Midnight Cowboy"

JON JON ◆Jon Jon Paulos — with The Buckinghams, debut gold record number one hit "Kind of a Drag"

JON-ERIK ◆Jon-Erik Hexum — fashion model who was actually a secret agent on TV's "Cover Up"

JONAH ◆Jonah — prophet swallowed by a big fish in the Bible

JONAS ◆Jonas Salk — developed the anti-polio vaccine

JONATHAN ◆Jonathan Demme — Oscar winning director for "The Silence of the Lambs" ◆ Jonathan Silverman — actor in "Weekend at Bernie's," "Stealing Home," "Brighton Beach Memoirs" ◆Jonathan Winters — "The Russians are Coming, the Russians are Coming," "It's a Mad, Mad, Mad, Mad World"

JORDAN ◆Jordan Alexander Ferrer — son of rock singer Debby Boone, grandson of Pat Boone ◆Jordan Carpenter — actor whose roles included Harry Hunter in the satire film "Network" ◆Jordan Knight — member of The New Kids on the Block, albums "Hangin' Tough" and "Step by Step"

JORGE ◆Jorge Amado — Brazil's greatest living novelist ◆Jorge Casas — member of The Miami Sound Machine, debut hit single "Conga"

JORMA ◆Jorma Kaukonen — member of The Jefferson Airplane, hits include "Somebody to Love"

JORY ◆Jory Husain — played brainy kid Jawaharlal on the successful sitcom "Head of the Class"

JOSE ◆Jose Feliciano — rock singer, debut hit single was "Light My Fire" ◆ Jose Ferrer — portrayed the film role of "Cyrano de Bergerac" and won an Oscar

JOSEF ◆Josef Albers — color theorist and painter of abstract art ◆ Josef Von Sternberg — director who discovered Marlene Dietrich, starred her in "The Blue Angel"

JOSEPH ◆Joseph Cotten — actor who appeared in "Citizen Kane" ◆Joseph Pulitzer — publisher who established the Pulitzer Prizes ◆ Joseph Seagram — founder of the distillery Joseph E. Seagram's and Sons ◆ Joseph Wambaugh — LA cop turned author in "The Blue Knight" ◆Judge Joseph Wapner — presiding justice on TV's "The People's Court"

JOSEY ◆Josey Wales (c) — Clint Eastwood's best role as the unsurrendered rebel "The Outlaw — Josey Wales"

JOSH ◆Josh Logan — director of "South Pacific," "Sayonara," "Bus Stop" and "Paint Your Wagon" ◆ Josh Mostel — reprised John Belushi's role of Blotto Blutarsky on TV's "Delta House"

JOSHUA ◆Joshua — in the Bible, led his people in conquest of Canaan after Moses' death ◆Joshua Reynolds — painter of over two thousand portraits

JOSIAH ◆Josiah Bartlett — signer of the Declaration of Independence ◆ Josiah Wedgwood — founder of the Wedgwood pottery firm ◆ Josiah Whitney — namesake for California's highest peak, Mt. Whitney

JOSIP ◆Josip Elic — actor who played Bancini in the Oscar winning "One Flew Over the Cuckoo's Nest"

JOSS ◆Joss Ackland — English actor who often portrays powerful men such as kings

JOY ◆Alexander Joy Cartwright, Jr. — father of modern baseball

JOYCE ◆Joyce Hall — founder of Hallmark Cards ◆Joyce Kilmer — poet who wrote "Trees"

JUAN ◆Don Juan — John Barrymore played the legendary lover in "Don Juan" ◆ Juan Alvarez — led the revolt which ousted Santa Anna and became President of Mexico ◆Juan de Bermudez — Spanish navigator who discovered Bermuda in 1522

JUANO ◆Juano Hernandez — actor whose roles included Mr. Smith in Rod Steiger's "The Pawnbroker"

JUBAL ◆Jubal Early — Confederate general who led raid on Washington, D.C.

JUD ◆Jud Taylor — actor whose roles included Dr. Thomas Gerson on TV's "Doctor Kildare"

JUDAH ◆Judah Benjamin — Jewish Confederate secretary of war

JUDAS ◆Judas Maccabeus — Jewish resistance leader, death commemorated by Hanukkah holiday

JUDD ◆Judd Hirsch — portrayed Alex Rieger, the only normal cabbie on the hit sitcom "Taxi" ◆ Judd Holdren — actor in "Captain Video," "Zombies of the Stratosphere," "Last Planet" ◆ Judd Nelson — Brat Pack actor featured in "St. Elmo's Fire" and "The Breakfast Club"

JUDE ◆Doug Jude McKeon — actor whose roles included Jane Fonda's son in "On Golden Pond"

JUDGE ◆Judge Reinhold — comic actor from "Beverly Hills Cop" and "Ruthless People"

JUDSON ◆Judson Laire — actor whose roles included "Papa" Lars Hansen on the long running comedy "Mama" ◆Judson Scott — actor who played the lead role on the science fiction series "The Phoenix"

JUG ◆Jug Ammons — tenor saxophonist

JULE ◆Jule Styne — film composer whose scores include "Three Coins in the Fountain"

JULES ◆Jules Bergman — science editor with ABC News ◆Jules Verne — founder of science fiction, author of "20,000 Leagues Under the Sea"

JULIAN ◆Julian Hawthorne — novelist son of author Nathaniel Hawthorne, novels include "Garth" ◆ Julian Lennon — rock singer son of John Lennon, debut hit single "Valotte"

JULIO ◆Julio Gallo — California wine maker with his brother Ernest Gallo ◆Julio Iglesias — Spanish crooner whose love songs are popular worldwide

JULIUS ◆Julius Caesar — Roman emperor assassinated by Brutus and immortalized by Shakespeare ◆Julius Epstein — won Oscar for the screenplay to "Casablanca" ◆ Julius Erving — professional basketball player known as "Dr. J" ◆Julius Marx — real name of Groucho Marx

JUNIOR ◆Junior Durkin — actor whose roles included Huckleberry Finn in "Tom Sawyer"

JUNIUS ◆Junius Bird — authority on pre-Columbian cultures and textiles ◆ Junius Brutus Booth — stage actor for 30 years, father of assassin John Wilkes Booth

JUPITER ◆Jupiter Hammon — first African-American poet published in the United States

JURGEN ◆Jurgen Prochnow — actor whose roles included the boarder in Demi Moore's "The Seventh Sign"

JUSTIN ◆Justin McCarthy — creator of Francois Villon in his novel "If I Were King" (twice filmed) ◆Justin Shenkarow — actor whose roles included Simon Holmes on TV's supernatural "Eerie, Indiana"

KADEEM ◆Kadeem Hardison — actor whose roles included Dwayne Wayne on TV's "A Different World"

KAHLIL ◆Kahlil Gibran — American artist who creates life-sized steel sculptures

KAI ◆Kai Winding — instrumental in creating Be-Bop style of jazz, with the World's Great Jazz Band

KAJ-ERIK ◆Kaj-Erik Eriksen — actor whose roles included David Scali on the police drama series "The Commish"

KAM ◆Kam Fond — actor whose roles included detective Chin Ho Kelly on TV's "Hawaii Five-O" ◆Kam Tong — as Hey Boy, he brought Paladin his assignment in "Have Gun Will Travel"

KAPLAN ◆Kaplan Lazare — one of the world's best known diamond merchants

KAREEM ◆Kareem Abdul-Jabbar — basketball player who was six-time NBA Most Valuable Player

KAREL ◆Karel Capek — Czech author who invented the word "robot" ◆ Karel Hoger — actor who played long-nosed poet-swordsman Cyrano de Bergerac in "Munchausen" ◆ Karel Reisz — director of "The French Lieutenant's Woman"

KARIO ◆Kario Salem — actor who played detective Rick Arno on the police drama "Heart of the City"

KARL ◆Karl Benz — built first internal combustion car, founder of Mercedes-Benz car company ◆Karl Faberge — jeweler known for lavish Easter eggs, lent his name to the cosmetics firm ◆Karl Malden — detective star of TV's "The Streets of San Francisco"; Oscar winner for "A Streetcar Named Desire"

KAVI ◆Kavi Raz — actor who played Dr. V. J. Kochar on the medical series "St. Elsewhere"

KAY ◆Nolan Kay Bushnell — inventor of the video game "Pong" and the founder of Atari ◆Kay Kyser — bandleader of TV's "Kay Kyser's Kollege of Musical Knowledge" ◆Kay Tendeter — played Poe's decaying nobleman Roderick in "The Fall of the House of Usher"

KE HUY ◆Ke Huy Quan — played Short Round in Harrison Ford's "Indiana Jones and the Temple of Doom"

KEANU ◆Keanu Reeves — most excellent actor in "Bill and Ted's Excellent Adventure"

KECALF ◆Kecalf White — son of singer Aretha Franklin

KEEFE ◆Keefe Brasselle — actor best known for playing the title role in "The Eddie Cantor Story"

KEENAN ◆Keenan Wynn — character actor who appeared in over 65 films, such as "Dr. Strangelove" ◆Tracy Keenan Wynn — Emmy winning writer for "Tribes" and "The Autobiography of Miss Jane Pittman"

KEENE ◆Keene Curtis — actor whose roles included Max Pomeroy on the adventure series "The Magician"

KEENEN ♦Keenen Ivory Wayans — star of TV's hit show "In Living Color"

KEIR ♦Keir Dullea — actor who played the lead, David Bowman, in Kubrick's "2001 A Space Odyssey"

KEITH ♦Keith Carradine — one of the acting Carradine brothers, roles in "Long Riders" and "The Duelists" ♦ Keith Emerson — flamboyant performer on keyboards with Emerson, Lake, and Palmer ♦ Keith Moon — member of The Who, debut hit "I Can't Explain" ♦ Keith Richards — composer of "Satisfaction," made the Rolling Stones superstars

KEKE ♦Keke Rosberg — world champion Formula One auto racer

KEL ♦Kel Nagle — professional championship golfer

KELLEN ♦Kellen Winslow — tight end with San Diego who led the NFL in pass receptions for two years

KELLY ♦Kelly Ward — actor whose roles included World War II dogface Johnson in "The Big Red One"

KELSEY ♦Kelsey Grammer — actor whose roles included the shrink Frasier Crane in the bar on "Cheers"

KEM ♦Kem Dibbs — actor who played Buck Rogers in the science fiction series "Buck Rogers"

KEMAL ♦Kemal Ataturk — founder and first president of modern Turkey ♦ Kemal Amin Kasem — real name of radio personality Casey Kasem

KEMMONS ♦Kemmons Wilson — founder of Holiday Inn

KEN ♦Ken Berry — actor whose roles included Captain Parmenter on TV's "F Troop" ♦Ken Osmond — actor who played Eddie Haskell, the wise guy on TV's "Leave It to Beaver" ♦ Ken Wahl — actor who played undercover cop Vinnie Terranova on the drama series "Wiseguy"

KENDALL ♦Kendall Banning — wrote "The Great Adventure" and "Our Army Today" ♦ Kendall Jones — member of funk-rock band Fishbone, hit single "Everyday Sunshine"

KENE ♦Kene Holliday — actor who played a stock market whiz on Andy Griffith's series "Matlock"

KENJI ♦Kenji Brown — member of rock group Rose Royce, debut number one platinum single "Car Wash" ♦Kenji Mizoguchi — former actor turned director in Japan

KENNETH ◆Kenneth — hairstylist, owner of Kenneth Salons ◆ Kenneth Bald — creator of "Captain Marvel" and "Doc Savage" ◆ Kenneth Lackey — one of the original Three Stooges

KENNY ◆Kenny Loggins — singer, movie soundtracks "Danger Zone" and "Footloose" ◆ Kenny Rogers — country western singer, group The First Edition, hits include "The Gambler"

KENT ◆Kent McCord — actor whose roles included police officer Jim Reed on TV's "Adam 12"

KENTON ◆Kenton Boyer — five-time Gold Glove infielder, also NL Most Valuable Player

KENZO ◆Kenzo Tange — architect who integrates his Japanese heritage into American buildings

KEONE ◆Keone Young — actor whose roles included Dr. Michael Kawn on the medical drama "Kay O'Brien"

KERMIT ◆Kermit the Frog (c) — green frog who is the star of many Muppet films ◆ Kermit Bloomgarden — produced "The Diary of Anne Frank" in 1959 ◆ Kermit Roosevelt — one of two sons of Teddy Roosevelt who died in WW I living up to their father's image

KERRY ◆Kerry Livgren — member of rock group Kansas, debut hit single "Carry On Wayward Son" ◆Kerry Rossall — actor in the Marlon Brando anti-war film "Apocalypse Now"

KERWIN ◆Kerwin Mathews — actor whose roles included Austrian composer Johann Strauss in "The Waltz King"

KEVIN ◆Kevin Bacon — actor whose films include "Flatliners," "Footloose" and "JFK" ◆ Kevin Costner — received Oscars for best director and best picture for "Dances With Wolves" ◆Kevin Dillon — brother of Matt Dillon, films include "Platoon" ◆Kevin Kline — earned best supporting actor Oscar in "A Fish Called Wanda"

KEVYN ◆Kevyn Howard — actor who played Kipling in the science fiction cop story "Alien Nation"

KEYE ◆Keye Luke — Charlie Chan's number two son in the films, Master Po on TV's "Kung Fu"

KIEFER ◆Kiefer Sutherland — actor in "Young Guns," "Flatliners," "The Lost Boys" and "The Three Musketeers"

KIEL ◆Kiel Martin — actor who played detective J. D. LaRue on the drama series "Hill Street Blues"

KIERAN ◆Kieran Doherty — hunger striker who starved to death in Belfast's Maze Prison in 1981

KIEREN ◆Kieren Perkins — world record holder of the 800-meter freestyle in swimming

KIERON ◆Kieron Moore — actor whose films include "Custer of the West"

KIN ◆Kin Hubbard — creator of the cartoon character "Abe Martin" ◆ Kin Shriner — actor whose roles included Scott Baldwin on the soap "General Hospital"

KING ◆King Donovan — actor in "The Enforcer" ◆King Gillette — inventor of the safety razor ◆ King Vidor — director of such films as "The Big Parade"

KINGMAN ◆Kingman Brewster — educator and lawyer

KINGSLEY ◆Kingsley Amis — angry young man whose novel "Lucky Jim" was filmed ◆ Norman Kingsley Mailer — Pulitzer Prize winning author, novels include "The Naked and the Dead"

KINKY ◆Kinky Friedman — country western singer with his group The Texas Jewboys

KIP ◆Kip Keino — only man to hold Olympic track records for two different distances

KIPP ◆Kipp Marcus — played Kip Cleaver on Jerry Mathers' sitcom "The New Leave It to Beaver" ◆ Kipp Osborne — actor whose roles included George Joslyn on the soap "Search for Tomorrow"

KIRBY ◆Kirby Grant — star of the TV series "Sky King" ◆Kirby Puckett — outfielder with Minnesota Twins, 1989 American League batting title

KIRK ◆Kirk Cameron — actor who played the always-in-trouble Mike Seaver on TV's "Growing Pains" ◆ Kirk Douglas — legendary film star of "Spartacus" and "Paths of Glory"

KISHORE ◆Kishore Sahu — actor whose roles included Shakespeare's tragic Dane in "Hamlet"

KIT ◆Kit Carson — frontier scout in the old West, namesake for Carson City, Nevada ◆ Kit Williams — author of "Masquerade," which launched treasure hunt in England

KIWI ◆Kiwi Kingston — actor whose roles included the monster in "The Evil of Frankenstein"

KLAUS ◆Klaus Maria Brandauer — actor whose films include "Never Say Never Again" and "Out of Africa" ◆ Klaus Kinski — actor who played the bloody vampire Count Dracula in "Nosferatu, The Vampyre"

KNUT ◆Knut Bjorn-Larsen — inventor of the garterless girdle

KONO ◆Kono Kalakaua — one of McGarrett's detectives on the detective series "Hawaii Five-O"

KONRAD ◆Konrad Adenauer — first Chancellor of West Germany after World War II ◆ Konrad Heiden — expert on Hitler, coined term "Nazi" as derisive nickname

KONSTANTIN ◆Konstantin Shayne — actor whose roles included Gerhardt Eisler in "I Was a Communist for the FBI" ◆ Konstantin Stanislavski — Russian acting teacher who founded "method acting"

KONSTANTINE ◆Uwe Konstantine Blab — basketball player and member of the Olympic team

KOOL ◆Kool Bell — Kool in Kool and the Gang, hit debut single "Kool and the Gang" ◆Kool Moe Dee — rapper, solo hits include the platinum "How Ya Like Me Now?"

KRAIG ◆Kraig Metzinger — actor whose roles included Phillip on the Bea Arthur sitcom "Maude"

KREKOR ◆Krekor Ohanian — real name of actor Mike Connors

KRESKIN ◆Kreskin — flamboyant mind reader

KRIS ◆Kris Kristofferson — singer/actor of "A Star Is Born," "Alice Doesn't Live Here Anymore" ◆ Kris Neville — author known for science fiction, "The Unearth People" and "Invaders on the Moon"

KRISHNA ◆Krishna Bhanji — real name of actor Ben Kingsley

KRISTOFFER ◆Kristoffer Tabori — son of actress Viveca Lindfors, starred in the TV series "Chicago Story"

KUBLAI ◆Kublai Khan — founder of the Chinese ruling dynasties

KUDA ◆Kuda Bux — star of the TV magic series "Kuda Bux, Hindu Mystic"

KUNTA ◆Kunta Kinte — Alex Haley's progenitor in America who was portrayed in the miniseries "Roots"

KURT ◆Kurt Russell — went from child star at Disney to "Escape From New York" and "Backdraft" ◆ Kurt Vonnegut — author of novels such as "Slaughterhouse Five" and "Breakfast of Champions" ◆ Kurt von Trapp — one of the singing von Trapp children portrayed in Julie Andrew's classic "The Sound of Music"

KURTWOOD ◆Kurtwood Smith — actor in the futuristic mechanical police state of "RoboCop"

KYLE ◆Kyle Chandler — actor who played Jeff Metcalf on the post WW II drama series "Homefront" ◆Kyle Eastwood — son of Clint Eastwood, co-starred with him in "Honkytonk Man" ◆ Kyle MacLachlan — actor who played agent Dale Cooper in David Lynch's series "Twin Peaks"

LA JAUNE ◆Jermaine La Jaune Jackson — member of The Jackson Five, solo hits include "Let's Get Serious"

LAFAYETTE ◆James Lafayette Dickey — author of "Deliverance" which was filmed with Burt Reynolds ◆ Lafayette Ron Hubbard — founder of the Church of Scientology, author of "Dianetics"

LAFFIT ◆Laffit Pincay, Jr. — largest money winning jockey in racing for four years straight

LAIRD ◆Laird Cregar — actor whose roles included serial killer Jack the Ripper in "The Lodger"

LAJOS ◆Lajos Biro — nominated for an Oscar in 1928 for writing "The Last Command" ◆ Marcel Lajos Breuer — designer of NYC's Whitney Museum, also designed the tubular chair

LAMAR ◆Lamar Hunt — founder and president of the American Football League ◆ Lamar Williams — member of the Allman Brothers Band

LAMBERT ◆Lambert Hillyer — director of William S. Hart western films

LAMONTE ◆Lamonte McLemore — member of The Fifth Dimension, debut hit single "Go Where You Wanna Go"

LANCE ◆Lance Henriksen — actor in "Aliens" and "Jennifer 8" ◆ Lance Kerwin — child star of the TV series "James at 15"

LANCELOT ◆Lancelot (c) — Knight of the Round Table who loved King Arthur's Queen Guinevere ◆ Lancelot Brown — English architect who founded modern "English style" landscapes

LANDERS ◆Landers Stevens — played Commander McClure in the Edward G. Robinson gangster film "Little Caesar"

LANE ◆James Lane Allen — popularized Kentucky bluegrass life with his novels ◆James Lane Buckley — US senator who wrote "If Men Were Angels"

LANFORD ◆Lanford Wilson — Pulitzer Prize winning writer for "Talley's Folly"

LANGSTON ◆Langston George — one of Gladys Knight's Pips, hits include "Midnight Train to Georgia"

LARKIN ◆Larkin Malloy — actor whose roles included Schuyler Whitney on the soap "The Edge of Night"

LARRY ◆Larry Fine — one of The Three Stooges ◆ Larry Hagman — actor who went from TV's "I Dream of Jeannie" to J.R. on "Dallas" ◆Larry King — commentator and interviewer on his radio show "Larry King Live" ◆Larry Linville — actor whose roles included the nosey Major Burns on the TV version of "M*A*S*H" ◆Larry Manetti — actor whose roles included Rick on TV's drama series "Magnum, P.I." ◆ Larry Storch — actor whose roles included enterprising Corporal Agarn on TV's "F Troop"

LARS ◆Lars Hansen — actor whose roles included tragic police informer Gypo Nolan in "The Informer"

LARUSHKA ◆Larushka Skikne — real name of actor Laurence Harvey

LASH ◆Lash La Rue — actor who played himself on his western series "Lash of the West"

LASLO ◆Laslo Benedek — director whose films include "The Wild One"

LATHROP ◆Lathrop Douglass — inventor of the shopping mall

LATKA ◆Latka Gravas (c) — Andy Kaufman's quirky cabbie mechanic on the classic sitcom "Taxi"

LAUDIR ◆Laudir DeOliveira — member of Chicago, hits include "Saturday in the Park"

LAURENCE ◆Laurence Harvey — Oscar nominated actor for "Room at the Top" ◆ Laurence Olivier — British actor/director known for Shakespearean roles, won Oscar for "Hamlet" ◆ Laurence Peter — author of the best seller on human foibles, "The Peter Principle"

LAURENS ◆Laurens Hammond — inventor and founder of Hammond Organs

LAURENT ◆Laurent Terzieff — leading man whose films include "The Seven Deadly Sins" ◆Laurent de Brunhoff — continued the "Babar" children's books originally written by his father

LAURINDO ◆Laurindo Almeida — winner of numerous Grammys as a modern jazz guitarist

LAVERNE ◆Laverne Drake — member of The Cadillacs, debut single was "Gloria"

LAVON ◆Larry Lavon Linville — actor whose roles included obnoxious Major Frank Burns on the sitcom "M*A*S*H"

LAWRENCE ◆Lawrence Welk — Champagne Music lasted for two decades on the network "Lawrence Welk Show"

LAWRENCE-HILTON ◆Lawrence-Hilton Jacobs — one of the sweathogs on TV's "Welcome Back, Kotter"

LAWSON ◆Lawson Little — only golfer to win the British and US amateurs in two consecutive years ◆Lawson Smith — member of "The Midnighters, 1954 debut gold record "Work With Me Annie"

LAZARE ◆Lazare Carnot — military genius of the French Revolution ◆Lazare Meerson — nominated for an Oscar in 1931 for interior decoration

LAZLO ◆Lazlo Loewenstein — real name of actor Peter Lorre

LEROY ◆LeRoy Hart — inventor of Moon Shoes and plastic catapulting footwear

LEVAR ◆LeVar Burton — actor who played Kunta Kinte in "Roots," Lt. Geordi La Forge on "Star Trek: TNG"

LEAF ◆Leaf Phoenix — actor brother of River Phoenix

LEAM ◆Leam Blackwood — actor who played Lt. Charles Pine on the adventure series "Street Justice"

LEARNED ◆Learned Hand — considered one of the greatest jurists of all time ◆ William Learned Marcy — secretary of state who coined the phrase "spoils system"

LEAVEIL ◆Leaveil Degree — member of The Whispers, debut hit single "Seems Like I Gotta Do Wrong"

LECH ◆Lech Walesa — Nobel Peace Prize winner, first freely elected president of Poland

LECIL ◆Lecil Martin — self-appointed keeper of the hobo and train-song flames Boxcar Willie

LEE ◆F. Lee Bailey — lawyer who defended Patty Hearst ◆Lee J. Cobb — actor whose roles included the judge on TV's "The Virginian" ◆Lee Majors — actor in TV's "The Big Valley," "The Six Million Dollar Man" and "The Fall Guy" ◆ Lee Marvin — actor who received an Oscar for "Cat Ballou" ◆Lee Van Cleef — actor in "The Good, The Bad, and the Ugly," "The Man Who Shot Liberty Valance"

LEIB ◆Leib Lensky — actor whose films include "Hester Street"

LEICESTER ◆Leicester Hemingway — younger brother of Ernest, author of "My Brother, Ernest Hemingway"

LEIF ◆Leif Erickson — tall, blond actor from "Tea and Sympathy" ◆ Leif Ericson — Icelandic navigator who discovered America ◆ Leif Garrett — rock singer, debut hit record was a remake of "Surfin' U.S.A." ◆ Leif Tilden — played Teenage Mutant Ninja Turtle Donatello in the film version of the comic

LEIGH ◆Leigh Dilley — played British prime minister Sir Winston Churchill in "The Eagle Has Landed" ◆Leigh Lawson — films include "Tess," TV miniseries "Lace" ◆ George Leigh Mallory — quoted as wanting to climb Mt. Everest "because it's there"

LEIGHTON ◆Leighton Lucas — British composer and musical director, former ballet dancer

LELAND ◆Leland Stanford — railroad baron who founded Stanford University in memory of his son

LEM ◆Lem Barney — seven-time all-pro defensive back

LEMON ◆Blind Lemon Jefferson — country-blues singer, album "Blind Lemon Jefferson"

LEMUEL ◆David Lemuel Keith — actor in "An Officer and a Gentleman" and "The Lords of Discipline"

LEN ◆Len Barker — pitched a perfect baseball game on May 15, 1981

LENNARD ◆Eric Lennard Berne — psychiatrist who wrote the best-selling "Games People Play"

LENNOX ◆Lennox Robinson — dramatist hired by Yeats as director of the Abbey Theater

LENNY◆Lenny Bruce — first stand up comic with a political agenda, Dustin Hoffman biopic "Lenny"

LENWOOD◆Lenwood Abbott — Oscar and Emmy winner for special effects cinematography

LEO◆Leo Carrillo — comic sidekick to TV's "Cisco Kid" ◆ Leo Gorcey — comedian in the Dead End Kids and Bowery Boys films ◆ Leo Sayer — singer, hits include "Have You Ever Been In Love" ◆ Leo Tolstoy — Russian novelist who wrote "War and Peace" and "Anna Karenina"

LEON◆Leon Redbone — offbeat singer, did "Your Feets Too Big" for TV's "Harry and the Hendersons" ◆ Leon Russell — country-rock star, hits include Willie Nelson duet "One for the Road" ◆ Leon Spinks — Olympic gold medal boxer, took world heavyweight title from Muhammad Ali ◆ Leon Trotsky — top member of Lenin's Bolshevik government, killed in exile in 1940

LEONARD◆Leonard Bernstein — composer, conductor, musician who wrote "West Side Story" ◆ Leonard Maltin — film critic, syndicated TV series "Entertainment Tonight" ◆ Leonard Nimoy — portrayed Mr. Spock on the TV series and feature films of "Star Trek"

LEONARDO◆Leonardo Da Vinci — sculptor and inventor of the Italian Renaissance, painted the "Mona Lisa" ◆ Leonardo DiCaprio — 1990's teen hunk, films include "This Boy's Life"

LEONE◆Leone Osborne — children's author whose works include "Than Hoa of Viet-Nam"

LEONID◆Leonid Brezhnev — general secretary of the Soviet Communist Party ◆ Leonid Kinskey — actor in Gary Cooper's "The General Died at Dawn"

LEONIDAS◆Leonidas I — defended Greece against Persian invasion at Thermopylae, biopic "The 300 Spartans" ◆ Luther Leonidas Terry — surgeon general whose study revealed that smoking was hazardous to your health

LEONIDE◆Leonide Massine — legendary choreographer with the American Ballet Theatre ◆ Leonide Moguy — Russian newsreel producer who became a director in the United States

LEONWOOD◆L. Leonwood Bean — founder of L. L. Bean sporting goods with brother Guy

LEOPOLD ◆Leopold Godowsky — inventor of Kodachrome ◆ Leopold Stokowski — founder of the American Symphony Orchestra, conductor for the film "Fantasia"

LEPKE ◆Lepke Buchalter — founder of Murder, Inc., labor racketeer and hit man, died in the electric chair

LEQUEINT ◆Lequeint Jobe — member of rock group Rose Royce, debut number one platinum single "Car Wash"

LERONE ◆Lerone Bennett — editor of "Ebony" magazine

LEROY ◆Baby Leroy — Hollywood toddler hated by W. C. Fields, retired at age four ◆ Robert Leroy Ripley — cartoonist who created "Ripley's Believe It or Not"

LES ◆Les Aspin — fired as Secretary of Defense under Clinton ◆ Les Brown — bandleader with "Les Brown's Band of Renown"

LESLIE ◆Leslie Townes Hope — real name of comedy star Bob Hope ◆ Leslie Howard — actor who played the ever-proper Ashley Wilkes in "Gone With the Wind" ◆Leslie Lynch King, Jr. — real name of President Gerald R. Ford ◆ Leslie Nielsen — actor who went from Disney's series "The Swamp Fox" to the "Naked Gun" movies

LESTER ◆Lester Bangs — rock critic with "Rolling Stone" and "The Village Voice" ◆Lester Flatt — country western singer, Flatt and Scruggs hits include "The Ballad of Jed Clampett"

LEVERETT ◆Leverett Saltonstall — governor and senator from Massachusetts

LEVI ◆Levi Strauss — inventor of bluejeans ◆ Levi Stubbs — member of The Four Tops, hits include "Reach Out I'll Be There"

LEVON ◆Levon Helm — member of the rock group The Band, filmed by Scorsese in "The Last Waltz" ◆ Levon Webb — actor whose roles included Ted Webb in Sissy Spacek's "Coal Miner's Daughter"

LEW ◆Lew Soloff — member of Blood, Sweat, and Tears, hits include "Spinning Wheel" ◆ Lew Wallace — western governor who chased Billy the Kid, then wrote "Ben-Hur" ◆ Lew Wasserman — chief executive at Universal for six decades

LEWELYN ◆David Lewelyn Griffith — better known as D. W. Griffith, pioneer film maker and director

LEWIS ◆Lewis Carroll — author of the children's classic "Alice's Adventures in Wonderland" ◆ Robert Lewis May — wrote

"Rudolph the Red-Nosed Reindeer" to promote Montgomery Ward ◆ Lewis Offield — real name of comedian and actor Jack Oakie

LEX ◆Lex Barker — tenth actor to play "Tarzan" in films ◆ Lex Luthor (c) — Superman's arch enemy in the comics, film, and on television

LIAM ◆Liam Neeson — actor in "Darkman," "Leap of Faith," "Husbands and Wives," "Schindler's List" ◆ Liam O'Neill — son of actress Faye Dunaway and Terry O'Neill ◆ Liam Redmond — Irish character actor, appeared in "The Ghost and Mr. Chicken," "Tobruk"

LIBERACE ◆Liberace — glitzy pianist-showman of stage, night clubs and TV

LIDO ◆Lido "Lee" Iacocca — chairman of Chrysler whose autobiography is the best non-fiction seller in history

LIGHTFIELD ◆Lightfield Lewis — actor who played Arthur Carlson, Jr., on the sitcom "WKRP in Cincinnati"

LIGHTFOOT ◆Francis Lightfoot Lee — with brother Richard Henry Lee signed the Declaration of Independence

LIMMIE ◆Limmie Snell — rock singer whose hits include "You Can Do Magic"

LINCOLN ◆Lincoln Filene — merchant who established Filene's Department Store in Boston ◆John Lincoln Freund — real name of actor John Forsythe ◆ Lincoln Kilpatrick — actor who played Rev. Deal on TV's critically acclaimed "Frank's Place"

LINDEN ◆Linden Chiles — actor whose roles included Paul Britton on the soap "The Secret Storm"

LINDLEY ◆Lindley Armstrong Jones — real name of satirical bandleader Spike Jones

LINDSAY ◆Lindsay Anderson — co-founder of the British documentary movement ◆ Walter Lindsay Egan — country-rock guitarist, hit album "Hi Fi"

LINDSEY ◆Lindsey Buckingham — musician with Fleetwood Mac, solo LP "Law and Order" ◆Lindsey Mitchell — member of the rock group Prism, debut hit record "Spaceship Superstar"

LINUS ◆Linus Van Pelt (c) — blanket-toting kid from the "Peanuts" comic strip ◆ Linus Yale — founder of Yale locks

LINVAL ◆Linval Thompson — rock singer, hits include "Kung Fu Fighting"

LINWOOD ◆Linwood Boomer — actor who played Adam Kendall on the drama series "Little House on the Prairie" ◆ Roy Linwood Clark — banjo-playing host of the syndicated hayseed show "Hee Haw" ◆ Charles Linwood Williams — basketball forward with Portland Trailblazers

LIONEL ◆Lionel Barrymore — star of films like "Captains Courageous" with Spencer Tracy ◆Lionel Cowen — invented the toy electric train and started Lionel Trains ◆Lionel Richie — with The Commodores, debut solo platinum number one single "Endless Love"

LISLE ◆Lisle Wilson — actor whose roles included Phillip Woode in Margot Kidder's "Sisters"

LIVINGSTON ◆Ogden Livingston Mills — secretary of the treasury under Hoover ◆ Livingston Taylor — singer brother of James Taylor, hit single "I Will Be in Love With You"

LLEWELLYN ◆Sherman Llewellyn Adams — former Republican governor of New Hampshire ◆Llewellyn Thompson — former US ambassador to the Soviet Union

LLOYD ◆Lloyd Bridges — star of the TV series "Sea Hunt," and miniseries like "Roots" ◆Lloyd Cole — lead singer of Lloyd Cole and the Commotions

LOEWY ◆Loewy Malkovich — son of actor John Malkovich, star of "In the Line of Fire"

LOFTON ◆Lofton Kline — member of The Pozo-Seco Singers, debut hit "Time"

LOGAN ◆Logan Wilson — innovator who introduced racial integration into the University of Texas

LOL ◆Lol Creme — in rock group 10cc, debut hit single "Rubber Bullets"

LON ◆Lon Chaney — silent film star and master of makeup called "The Man of a Thousand Faces"

LONDIE ◆Londie Wiggins — member of New Birth, hit debut single "It's Impossible"

LONNIE ◆Lonnie Coleman — author of "Beulah Land" and its sequels ◆ Lonnie Donegan — singer, hits "Lorelei" and "The Party's Over"

LONNY ◆Lonny Chapman — actor who played Jeff Prior on the detective drama series "The Investigator"

LONZO ◆Lonzo — half of the country music comedy group Lonzo and Oscar

LOOMIS ◆Ezra Loomis Pound — poet and critic, author of "Cantos"

LOOSELEAF ◆Looseleaf Harper — pilot who dropped the atomic bomb on Nagasaki

LORADO ◆Lorado Taft — sculptor whose works include Chicago's Ferguson Fountain of the Great Lakes

LORCAN ◆Lorcan O'Toole — son of "Lawrence of Arabia" actor Peter O'Toole

LOREN ◆Loren Eiseley — anthropologist, author of "The Unexpected Universe"

LORENZ ◆Lorenz Hart — lyricist partnered with Richard Rodgers, hits include "Isn't It Romantic"

LORENZO ◆Lorenzo Lamas — played dashing Lance Cumson on TV's "Falcon Crest," son of Fernando Lamas ◆ Lorenzo Langstroth — minister who invented the moveable-frame beehive ◆Lorenzo Music — voice of Carlton the Doorman on the sitcom "Rhoda"

LOREZ ◆Lorez Alexandria — Grammy nominee for best jazz vocal performance with "Harlem Butterfly"

LORING ◆Loring Smith — actor whose roles included the brother-in-law on the sitcom "The Hartmans"

LORNE ◆Lorne Greene — portrayed Ben Cartwright on TV's long running "Bonanza," later sold dog food ◆Lorne Michaels — Emmy award winning producer of TV's "Saturday Night Live"

LOTHAR ◆Alfred Lothar Wegener — developed the theory of continental drift

LOU ◆Lou Costello — roly-poly half of the comedy team of "Abbott and Costello" ◆ Lou Gehrig — beloved baseball player whom Gary Cooper portrayed in "Pride of the Yankees" ◆ Lou Gossett, Jr. — Oscar winning actor in "An Officer and a Gentleman" ◆Lou Diamond Phillips — actor whose roles include "La Bamba" and "Young Guns" ◆Lou Rawls — singer known for love ballads, hits "You'll Never Find" and "Lady Love"

LOUDON ◆Loudon Wainwright III — singer and guitarist whose hit albums include "Fame and Wealth"

LOUIE ◆Louie DePalma (c) — actor Danny DeVito played this obnoxious dispatcher on TV's "Taxi"

LOUIS ◆Louis Armstrong — jazz musician popularly known as "Satchmo" ◆ Louis L'Amour — western writer, first best selling novel was "Hondo" ◆Louis B. Mayer — co-founder and grand old man of the Metro-Goldwyn-Mayer studio ◆ Louis Pasteur — dedicated French chemist who invented pasteurization ◆ Robert Louis Stevenson — author of "Treasure Island" and "Dr. Jekyll and Mr. Hyde"

LOUIS-ANTOINE ◆Louis-Antoine de Bougainville — settled the Falkland Islands, colorful climbing plant named for him

LOV ◆Lov Jacobs — clown face was the emblem of Ringling Brothers, Barnum and Bailey Circus

LOWELL ◆Lowell Fulsom — rock singer, hits include "Funky Broadway" ◆Lowell Mason — composer, hymns include "Nearer, My God, to Thee" ◆Lowell Thomas — author "With Lawrence in Arabia," host of TV's "High Adventure"

LOWMAN ◆Lowman Pauling — member of The Five Royales, hits include "Dedicated to the One I Love"

LOYAL ◆Loyal Davis — brain surgeon stepfather of Nancy Reagan ◆ Loyal Griggs — cinematographer, films include "The Ten Commandments" and "We're No Angels"

LUC ◆Luc Robitaille — Canadian left wing hockey player, winner of the Calder Trophy ◆ Luc Simon — actor who played legendary knight Lancelot in the film "Lancelot du Lac"

LUCA ◆Luca Bercovici — played Muzzin, the evil adversary of Kevin Costner in "American Flyers"

LUCAS ◆Lucas McCain (c) — Chuck Connors' lead role in the western series "The Rifleman"

LUCIANO ◆Luciano Benetton — founder of the Benetton clothing stores ◆ Luciano Berio — Italian composer and conductor of operas ◆ Luciano Pavarotti — best selling classical vocalist, starred in "Yes, Giorgio"

LUCIEN ◆Rene Lucien Belbenoit — his "My Escape from Devil's Island" led to abolition of the penal colony ◆ Lucien Bonaparte — Napoleon's brother who was exiled for opposing his policies ◆ Lucien Prival — actor who played the Baron von Krantz in Jean Harlow's classic "Hell's Angels"

LUCIO ◆ Lucio Pozzi — artist whose works defy categorization

LUCIUS ◆ Lucius Beebe — writings include "People on Parade," "The Trains We Rode" ◆ Lucius Lamar — Supreme Court justice

LUDOVICO ◆ Ludovico Ariosto — sixteenth century Italian romantic poet ◆ Ludovico Arrighi — sixteenth century type designer who invented italic lettering

LUDWIG ◆ Ludwig Stossel — actor who played Mr. Leuchtag in the classic Oscar winning film "Casablanca" ◆ Ludwig van Beethoven — master of classical music who composed his "Ninth Symphony" when deaf

LUIGI ◆ Luigi Arditi — world-renowned Italian conductor and composer ◆ Luigi Galvani — electrical term for "galvanometer" derived from his name

LUIS ◆ Luis Marcus — inventor of the bobby pin

LUKAS ◆ Lukas Heller — screenwriter, credits "What ever Happened to Baby Jane?", "The Dirty Dozen" ◆ Carl Lukas Norden — inventor of World War II's Norden bombsight

LUKE ◆ Luke Murray — son of comedian Bill Murray ◆ Luke Perry — heartthrob on TV's "Beverly Hills 90210" ◆ Luke Skywalker (c) — young Jedi knight who had the force with him in the "Star Wars" trilogy

LUMSDEN ◆ Lumsden Hare — actor in the Cary Grant classic of the Indian frontier, "Gunga Din"

LUPINO ◆ Lupino Lane — diminutive British stage comedian and tumbler who made clever comedies in the 20's

LUTHER ◆ Luther Gulick — founder of the Camp Fire Girls ◆ Martin Luther King — assassinated civil rights leader of the 1960's ◆ Luther Vandross — rock singer, hits include "Never Too Much"

LYLE ◆ Lyle Lovett — country music singer and husband of Julia Roberts ◆ Lyle Waggoner — actor whose roles included Major Steve Trevor, Wonder Woman's boyfriend

LYMAN ◆ Lyman Bostock — promising 70's outfielder shot by estranged husband of friend ◆ Lyman Hall — signer of the Declaration of Independence ◆ Lyman Young — cartoonist who created the comic strip "Tim Tyler"

LYN ◆Lyn Harding — actor whose roles included English King Henry VIII in "The Pearls of the Crown"

LYNDON ◆Lyndon Johnson — 36th President of the United States ◆ Lyndon Larouche — controversial right wing Democrat, founded National Democratic Policy Committee

LYNN ◆Richard Lynn Carpenter — half of the singing group The Carpenters, hits include "We've Only Just Begun"

LYNNE ◆Lynne Overman — memorable in cynical comedy roles for his relaxed manner and sing-song voice

LYONEL ◆Lyonel Feininger — pioneer of modern art and cartoonist ◆ Lyonel Watts — actor who played the Rev. William Duke in the Leslie Howard film "Outward Bound"

LYTTON ◆Lytton Strachey — historian who revolutionized the art of biography

MAC ◆Mac Davis — country music singer, hits include "Stop and Smell the Roses"

MACFARLANE ◆MacFarlane Burnet — Nobel Prize winner for research in immunology

MACLEAN ◆MacLean Stevenson — briefly played Colonel Blake on the TV series "M*A*S*H"

MACAULAY ◆Macaulay Culkin — played the left-behind kid Kevin in "Home Alone" and "Home Alone 2: Lost in New York"

MACDONALD ◆Macdonald Carey — actor whose roles included Dr. Tom Horton on the soap "Days of Our Lives"

MACEO ◆Maceo Parker — solo saxophonist artist, album "Roots Revisited" ◆ A. Maceo Walker — co-founder of the Tri-State Bank of Memphis

MACINTYRE ◆Macintyre Dixon — actor whose roles included Danny Micelli on the soap "The Edge of Night"

MACK ◆Mack Sennett — king of comedy during Hollywood's silent era ◆ Mack Swain — played Big Jim McKay in Charlie Chaplin's silent classic "The Gold Rush"

MACKENZIE ◆Mackenzie Astin — actor son of Patty Duke and John Astin, star of Disney's "Iron Will" ◆ Mackenzie Colt — series regular on the long running hayseed variety series "Hee Haw" ◆ David Mackenzie Ogilvy — founder of the advertising firm of Ogilvy, Benson and Mather

MACKINLAY ◆Mackinlay Kantor — writer, filmed novels include the Oscar winning "The Best Years of Our Lives"

MACLYN ◆Maclyn McCarty — discovered the genetic DNA

MADISON ◆Madison Jones, Jr. — author whose novels include "The Innocent" and "A Cry of Absence"

MADOX ◆Ford Madox Brown — nineteenth century English artist ◆ Ford Madox Ford — author of "The Good Soldier"

MAHDI ◆Mahdi — Sudanese religious leader

MAHER ◆Maher Boutros — actor whose roles included Col. Ahmed Al Hassin on the soap "Texas"

MALACHI ◆Malachi Throne — cohort to cat burglar Robert Wagner on TV's "It Takes a Thief"

MALACHY ◆Malachy McCourt — actor whose roles included Kevin McGuinnes on the soap "Ryan's Hope"

MALCOLM ◆Malcolm Forbes — billionaire publisher of "Forbes" magazine ◆ Malcolm X — civil rights leader; Spike Lee filmed his biopic with Denzel Washington

MALCOLM-JAMAL ◆Malcolm-Jamal Warner — actor who played the always-in-a-jam son Theo Huxtable on TV's "The Cosby Show"

MALDEN ◆Malden Sekulovich — real name of actor Karl Malden

MALICK ◆Malick Bowens — actor whose roles included Simon on the Wolf Larsen TV series "Tarzan"

MALIK ◆Malik Taylor — member of the rap group A Tribe Called Quest

MALU ◆Malu Valentine Byrne — son of David Byrne, leader of the rock group Talking Heads

MALVIN ◆Malvin Albright — twentieth century sculptor ◆ Malvin Whitfield — two-time Olympic gold medal runner

MAN ◆Man Ray — co-founder of Dadaism

MANDY ◆Mandy Patinkin — actor whose roles included the alien cop Sam Francisco in "Alien Nation"

MANFRED ◆Manfred Lee — author of Ellery Queen mysteries with cousin Frederic Dannay ◆ Manfred Mann — rock musician who scored a gold record with "The Mighty Quinn" ◆ Manfred von Richthoven — the Red Baron, the most famous German air ace of World War I

MANNING ◆Manning Coles — author who created Tommy Hambleton, intelligence agent ◆Manning Whiley — British actor, usually in sinister roles

MANNY ◆Manny Charlton — member of the hard rock group Nazareth

MANOLO ◆Manolo Villaverde — actor who played Rafael Santana on the hit police drama series "Wiseguy"

MANTAN ◆Mantan Moreland — long cast as the frightened valet and in Charlie Chan films of the 40's

MANUEL ◆Manuel Lujan, Jr. — first Hispanic elected to the House of Representatives

MANUTE ◆Manute Bol — Sudanese Dinka tribesman drafted by The Washington Bullets in 1985

MARC ◆Marc Antony — Roman general, part of the love triangle between Julius Caesar and Cleopatra ◆Marc Singer — actor who starred in "Beastmaster" and "V"

MARCEL ◆Marcel Dalio — actor who played Emile the Croupier in the classic Oscar winning "Casablanca" ◆Marcel Marceau — a mime, a man with nothing to say, but spoke volumes

MARCELLO ◆Marcello Mastroianni — Italian actor whose films include "La Dolce Vita" and "Marriage Italian-Style"

MARCELLUS ◆Cassius Marcellus Clay — real name of heavyweight champion Muhammad Ali

MARCO ◆Marco Lopez — actor whose roles included Fireman Lopez on TV's "Emergency" ◆Marco Polo — opened China to the West with his explorations

MARCUS ◆Marcus Aurelius — Roman emperor and philosopher ◆Marcus Garvey — leader of the Back to Africa movement after World War I ◆Marcus Gastineau — son of actress Brigitte Nielsen and Mark Gastineau

MARIANO ◆Mariano Azuela — author whose writings depict his native Mexican society

MARIE ◆Andre Marie Ampere — French experimenter in electricity after whom the "Amp" was named ◆Marie Lafayette — French Revolutionary War general

MARINO ◆Marino Mase — actor whose roles included Jean-Gaston Andre on the war drama series "Jericho"

MARIO ◆Mario Andretti — professional race car driver ◆ Mario Cuomo — popular Democratic governor of New York ◆ Mario Lanza — opera singer popular in MGM musicals until overcome by weight problem ◆ Mario Lopez — co-star of TV's "Saved by the Bell" ◆ Mario Puzo — Oscar winner for writing both "Godfather I" and "Godfather II" ◆Mario Van Peebles — actor who played Stitch in Clint Eastwood's Marine Corps film "Heartbreak Ridge"

MARION ◆Marion Michael Morrison — real name of screen legend John Wayne

MARIUS ◆Marius Petipa — founder of the Bolshoi Ballet ◆ Marius Weyers — actor whose roles included Ronald on the sitcom "Good and Evil"

MARK ◆Mark Hamill — actor whose roles included adventurer Luke Skywalker in the "Star Wars" films ◆ Mark Harmon — athlete turned actor, once "People" magazine's "Sexiest Man Alive" ◆Mark Spitz — first athlete to win seven gold medals in a single Olympic games ◆ Mark Twain — greatest comic writer of his day, his works include "Huckleberry Finn"

MARK-PAUL ◆Mark-Paul Gosselaar — 1990's teen hunk whose credits include TV's "Saved by the Bell"

MARKUS ◆Markus Flanagan — actor who played Bradley Coolidge on the police drama series "Sunset Beat" ◆ Markus Redmond — actor whose roles included Raymond Alexander on TV's "Doogie Howser, M.D."

MARKY ◆Marky Mark — rap and rock singer who started trend of showing his underwear ◆Marky Ramone — member of the new wave band The Ramones, starred in "Rock 'n' Roll High School"

MARLIN ◆Nigel Marlin Balchin — author of "Small Back Room" and "Mine Own Executioner" ◆Marlin Perkins — host of TV's "Wild Kingdom"

MARLON ◆Marlon Brando — won Oscars for "On the Waterfront" and "The Godfather" ◆Marlon Hargis — member of the rock group Exile, debut hit record "Try It On" ◆ Marlon Jackson — member of "The Jackson Five" singing clan

MARNE ◆Marne Maitland — Anglo-Indian actor in British films

MARRIOTT ◆Marriott Edgar — British comedy scenarist who wrote vehicles for Will Hays and the Crazy Gang

MARSHALL ◆Marshall Crenshaw — rock singer, hit single "Someday, Somewhere" ◆ Marshall Efron — comedy actor who was a regular on TV's "The Dick Cavett Show" ◆ Marshall Field — founder of the chain of great stores which bear his name

MART ◆Mart Hulswit — actor whose roles included Dr. Ed Bauer on the soap "The Guiding Light"

MARTENE ◆Martene Corum — announcer for "Sports Cavalcade"

MARTIAL ◆Martial Solal — jazz pianist, composed music for more than 30 films, including "Breathless"

MARTIN ◆Martin Luther — German cleric who led the sixteenth century Protestant Reformation in Europe ◆ Martin Mull — host of TV's "Fernwood 2-night," featured on "Roseanne" ◆ Martin Scorsese — director of "Taxi Driver" and "Raging Bull" ◆ Martin Sheen — starred in "Apocalypse Now," Robert E. Lee in "Gettysburg" epic ◆ Martin Short — cast member of "Saturday Night Live," created character Ed Grimley

MARTON ◆Marton Garas — Hungarian director whose films include "Oliver Twist"

MARTY ◆Marty Balin — founder of rock group Jefferson Airplane/Starship ◆ Marty Feldman — bug-eyed actor in "The Last Remake of Beau Geste" and "Young Frankenstein" ◆ Marty Krofft — puppeteer, cartoon shows include "H. R. Pufnstuf" ◆ Marty Robbins — country western star, Grammy winner for "El Paso" ◆ Marty Stuart — country and bluegrass singer, Grammy winner for "The Whiskey Ain't Workin'"

MARTYN ◆Henry Martyn Leland — founder of the Cadillac Motor Company and the Lincoln Motor Company

MARV ◆Marv Ingram — member of The Four Preps, 1956 debut hit single "Dreamy Eyes" ◆ Marv Johnson — rock singer, debut hit single "Come to Me"

MARVIN ◆Marvin Gaye — rock singer, hits "Pride and Joy," "How Sweet It Is (To Be Loved By You)" ◆ Marvin Hagler — middleweight champ ◆ Marvin Hamlisch — Oscar winning composer for "The Way We Were" and "The Sting"

MASON ◆Mason Adams — actor whose roles included Charlie Hume on TV's "Lou Grant" ◆ Mason Reese — little kid who started making commercials at age four ◆ Mason Williams — Grammy winner for "Classical Gas"

MASSIMO ◆Massimo Girotti — actor whose roles included the slave rebel leader in "Spartacus, the Gladiator" ◆Massimo Serato — actor who played the evil Cardinal Richelieu in "The Secret Mark of D'Artagnan"

MATEO ◆Mateo Alou — Dominican baseball player who played for the San Francisco Giants and the Pittsburgh Pirates

MATHESON ◆Matheson Lang — first to play the swashbuckling Sir Francis Drake in "Drake of England"

MATHEW ◆Mathew Brady — Mr. Lincoln's cameraman, did extensive photographic coverage of the Civil War

MATHIAS ◆John Mathias Engler — Republican governor of Michigan elected in 1991

MATT ◆Matt Dillon — heartthrob actor, former Brat Packer, "The Outsiders," "The Flamingo Kid" ◆ Matt Frewer — actor "Max Headroom," "Shakey Ground," and "Doctor, Doctor"

MATTEO ◆Matteo Bandello — priest whose stories were the source for Shakespeare's "Romeo and Juliet"

MATTHEW ◆Matthew Broderick — his films include "Glory," "Ferris Bueller's Day Off," and "Biloxi Blues" ◆ Matthew Laborteaux — actor who played Albert Ingalls on the drama series "Little House on the Prairie" ◆Matthew Modine — actor in "Full Metal Jacket," "Married to the Mob," "Memphis Belle"

MATTHIAS ◆Matthias — in the Bible, the disciple chosen to take the place of traitor Judas ◆ Matthias Baldwin — first to make bookbinders' tools in the United States

MAURICE ◆Maurice Chevalier — French singer and film actor, Hollywood pics included "Gigi" ◆ Maurice Gibb — member of English group The Bee Gees, hits include "Saturday Night Fever" ◆ Maurice McDonald — original owner of McDonald's restaurant ◆Maurice Micklewhite — real name of actor Michael Caine

MAURIE ◆Maurie Stokes — paralyzed NBA Rookie of the Year, biopic "Maurie"

MAURITZ ◆Mauritz Stiller — Swedish director who went to Hollywood with Greta Garbo

MAURIZIO ◆Maurizio Gucci — head of the "Gucci" quality bag shops

MAURY ◆Maury Chaykin — actor whose roles included Tucci in the Burt Reynolds film "Breaking In" ◆ Jim Maury Henson — puppet master, created The Muppets ◆ Maury Povitch — Washington TV anchorman and host of TV's tabloid show "A Current Affair"

MAX ◆Max Baer, Jr. — actor who played Jethro Bodine on TV's cult classic "The Beverly Hillbillies" ◆Max Casella — actor whose roles included Vinnie on the sitcom "Doogie Howser, M.D." ◆ Max Von Sydow — Scandinavian actor in "Three Days of the Condor," "The Virgin Spring"

MAXIM ◆Maxim Gorky — first great writer from the lower classes of Czarist Russia

MAXIMILIAN ◆Maximilian — Austrian whom the French installed for a short time on the Mexican throne ◆ Maximilian Berlitz — founder of the Berlitz School of Languages ◆ Maximilian Schell — received an Oscar for "Judgment at Nuremberg," brother of Maria Schell

MAXIMILIEN ◆Maximilien Robespierre — leader of the French Revolution and the Reign of Terror

MAXWELL ◆Maxwell Caulfield — hunky actor on the prime time soap "The Colbys" ◆ Maxwell Perkins — book editor who discovered Ernest Hemingway and F. Scott Fitzgerald

MAYER ◆Mayer Rothschild — founder of the Rothschild family banking dynasty, biopic "House of Rothschild"

MAYNARD ◆Maynard Ferguson — jazz musician, hit album "Conquistador" ◆ Maynard Jackson — first African-American mayor of Atlanta

MAYO ◆Henry Mayo Bateman — most highly paid British cartoonist of the twentieth century ◆Mayo Smith — manager of the Detroit Tigers when they won the World Series

MAZO ◆Mazo DeLaRoche — Canadian author whose novels include "Jalna"

MCCLELLAND ◆McClelland Barclay — designed recruiting posters for the world wars, created the "Fisher Body Girl"

MCCOY ◆McCoy Tyner — jazz pianist, member of The John Coltrane Quartet

MCGEORGE ◆McGeorge Bundy — special assistant for national security to Presidents Kennedy and Johnson

MCKINLEY ◆Everett McKinley Dirksen — Republican senator who played a major role in passing civil rights laws ◆ McKinley Morganfield — real name of singer Muddy Waters

MCLEAN ◆Charles McLean Andrews — Pulitzer Prize winning historian ◆ McLean Stevenson — portrayed the original Colonel on TV's "M*A*S*H"

MCLIN ◆McLin Crowell — portrayed Phil Higley on the soap "Another World"

MEADE ◆Meade Lewis — jazz musician who popularized boogie-woogie, composed "Honky Tonk Train Blues"

MEADOWLARK ◆Meadowlark Lemon — Harlem Globetrotters basketball star, regular on TV's "Hello, Larry"

MECO ◆Meco — rock singer who hit platinum with his debut number one record " 'Star Wars' Theme"

MEDGAR ◆Medgar Evers — martyr for the civil rights movement

MEENO ◆Meeno Peluce — portrayed Todd Wyman on CBS's "Detective in the House"

MEIR ◆Theodore Meir Bikel — Oscar nominee for "The Defiant Ones" ◆ Meir Kahane — founder of the militant Jewish Defense League

MEL ◆Mel Blanc — voice of Barney Rubble on TV's "Flintstones" ◆ Mel Brooks — creator of comedy films which include "The Producers" and "Blazing Saddles" ◆Mel Gibson — star of the three "Mad Max" and the three "Lethal Weapon" films ◆ Mel Tillis — stuttering country western singer ◆ Mel Torme — mellow vocalist and the idol of Judge Harry Stone on TV's "Night Court"

MELBOURNE ◆Melbourne Brindle — artist and illustrator

MELCHOR ◆Melchor Ferrer — on TV's "Falcon Crest," married to Audrey Hepburn

MELL ◆Mell Lazarus — cartoonist who draws comic strips "Miss Peach" and "Momma"

MELVIL ◆Melvil Dewey — inventor of the library Dewey Decimal System

MELVILLE ◆Melville Cooper — played the evil Sheriff of Nottingham in "The Adventures of Robin Hood" ◆Melville Stone — founder of Chicago's first penny newspaper, "Daily News"

MELVIN ◆Melvin Belli — defense attorney for Lenny Bruce and Jack Ruby ◆ Melvin Dummar — claimed he was left $156 million by Howard Hughes, biopic "Melvin and Howard" ◆Melvin Purvis — FBI chief who shot down John Dillinger in Chicago ◆ Melvin Van Peebles — wrote and directed "Ain't Supposed to Die a Natural Death"

MELVYN ◆Melvyn Bragg — screenwriter for the rock musical film "Jesus Christ Superstar" ◆ Melvyn Douglas — actor with Oscars for both "Hud" and "Being There"

MENACHEM ◆Menachem Begin — former prime minister of Israel

MENAHEM ◆Menahem Golan — Israeli director and Hollywood producer of innumerable low budget films

MENNEN ◆G. Mennen Williams — six-term governor of Michigan

MERALD ◆Merald Knight — relative of Gladys Knight and one of the Pips

MERCE ◆Merce Cunningham — choreographer who developed new forms of abstract dance

MERCER ◆George Mercer Dawson — the Yukon's gold rush town Dawson City is named for him ◆Mercer Ellington — son of Duke Ellington who took over the orchestra

MERCURY ◆Mercury Morris — halfback with the Miami Dolphins

MEREDITH ◆Forrest Meredith Tucker — actor whose roles included wheeler-dealer Sgt. O'Rourke on the sitcom "F Troop" ◆ Meredith Wilson — composer best known for "The Music Man" and "The Unsinkable Molly Brown"

MERIAN ◆Merian C. Cooper — producer of "King Kong," "She Wore a Yellow Ribbon," and "The Quiet Man"

MERIWETHER ◆Meriwether Lewis — commanded the first expedition across America with William Clark

MERLE ◆Merle Haggard — host of TV's anthology series "Death Valley Days" ◆ Merle Johnson, Jr. — real name of actor Troy Donahue ◆ Merle Kilgore — country music singer, wrote

"Ring of Fire" for Johnny Cash ◆ Merle Travis — country music singer, hits "Sixteen Tons" and "Old Mountain Dew"

MERLIN ◆Merlin — court magician and personal advisor to King Arthur of the Round Table ◆ Merlin Olsen — football player turned actor on "Father Murphy," "Little House on the Prairie"

MERLO ◆Merlo Pusey — Pulitzer Prize winner for his biography of Charles Evans Hughes

MERRILL ◆Merrill Osmond — member of the Mormon group The Osmonds, debut number one hit "One Bad Apple"

MERRIMAN ◆Merriman Smith — Pulitzer Prize winner for his coverage of John F. Kennedy's assassination

MERRITT ◆Merritt Butrick — actor who played Johnny Slash on the hip high school sitcom "Square Pegs" ◆Isaac Merritt Singer — inventor of the sewing machine, founder of Singer sewing machines

MERV ◆Merv Griffin — TV talk show host, producer of "Wheel of Fortune" and "Jeopardy"

MERVIN ◆Mervin Shiner — singer who scored a gold record number one hit with "Peter Cottontail"

MERVYN ◆Mervyn Leroy — producer and director whose films include "The Wizard of Oz"

MERWIN ◆Merwin Goldsmith — actor whose roles included George Coolidge on the sitcom "Goodtime Girls"

MERWYN ◆Merwyn Bogue — real name of Ish Kabibble

MESHACH ◆Meshach Taylor — actor whose roles included Anthony Bouvier on TV's "Designing Women"

MESHULAM ◆Meshulam Riklis — owner of Faberge perfumes, husband of Pia Zadora

MEYER ◆Meyer Guggenheim — founder of the Guggenheim fortune in the copper industry ◆ Meyer Lansky — Marky Rydell played this financial genius in Robert Redford's "Havana" ◆ Meyer Levin — author of "Compulsion" about the Leopold-Loeb murders, later filmed in "Rope"

MICAH ◆Micah — a prophet in the Bible

MICHAEL ◆Michael Caine — cockney actor in too many films, best known for "Alfie" ◆ Michael Douglas — star of "Basic Instinct," "Fatal Attraction," Oscar winner for "Wall Street" ◆

Michael J. Fox — memorable as Alex P. Keaton on "Family Ties," Marty McFly in "Back to the Future" ◆ Michael Jackson — from "The Jackson Five," to superstar with hits "Beat It," "Billie Jean," "Thriller" ◆ Michael Jordan — played for the Chicago Bulls, Olympic gold medalist in basketball ◆ Michael Keaton — actor who went a long way from "Night Shift" to "Batman" ◆ Michael Landon — actor in TV's "Bonanza," "Little House on the Prairie," and "Highway to Heaven"

MICHAELE ◆Michaele Vollbracht — Coty winning fashion designer who now has own namesake firm

MICHEL ◆Michel Audiard — French screenwriter of over 40 films

MICHELAN ◆Michelan Sisti — played Teenage Mutant Ninja Turtle Michelangelo in the film version of the comic

MICHELANGELO ◆Michelangelo Buonarotti — painter of the Sistine Chapel, Charlton Heston biopic "The Agony and the Ecstasy" ◆ Michelangelo Antonioni — Italian film director, first hit "L'Aventura"

MICK ◆Mick Fleetwood — drummer with Fleetwood Mac, "Rumours" second biggest selling album of all time ◆Mick Jagger — big lipped leader of the Rolling Stones

MICKEY ◆Mickey Gilley — singer whose club "Gilley's" was the setting for the film "Urban Cowboy" ◆Mickey Mantle — with The New York Yankees, his team won 11 pennants and 7 world championships ◆ Mickey Rooney — made a number of "Andy Hardy" films, as well as musicals with Judy Garland ◆ Mickey Rourke — actor in "Diner," "Rumble Fish," "9½ Weeks," "Angel Heart" ◆ Mickey Spillane — creator of private eye hero Mike Hammer

MICKY ◆Micky Dolenz — member of The Monkees, also the father of actress Ami Dolenz

MIGUEL ◆Miguel Ferrer — actor who played Albert Rosenfield on David Lynch's drama series "Twin Peaks" ◆ Miguel de Cervantes — Spanish author of Don Quixote, biopic "Cervantes," "Man of La Mancha"

MIK ◆Mik Kaminski — member of The Electric Light Orchestra, debut hit "Roll Over Beethoven"

MIKA ◆Mika Waltari — author of "The Egyptian" which was filmed with Victor Mature and Peter Ustinov

MIKAEL ◆Mikael Rikfors — member of The Hollies, hits include "He Ain't Heavy, He's My Brother"

MIKAL ◆Thomas Mikal Ford — played Rafer Freeman on the sitcom version of the hit film "Uncle Buck"

MIKE ◆Mike Douglas — Emmy winning host of "The Mike Douglas Show" ◆ Mike Myers — creator of character Wayne Campbell, which became megahit movie "Wayne's World" ◆Mike Nesmith — guy in the green wool hat in the group and TV series "The Monkees" ◆Mike Wallace — investigative reporter on TV's "60 Minutes"

MIKHAIL ◆Mikhail Baryshnikov — ballet dancer, director, and choreographer ◆ Mikhail Gorbachev — secretary general of the USSR who started glasnost

MIKIS ◆Mikis Theodorakis — composer who wrote the film score for "Zorba the Greek"

MIKLOS ◆Miklos Hajmassy — actor whose roles included Shakespeare's Petruchio in "The Taming of the Shrew" ◆ Miklos Rozsa — Hungarian Hollywood composer, credits include an Oscar for "Ben-Hur"

MILAN ◆Milan Stefanik — astronomer and general who was one of the founders of Czechoslovakia ◆Milan Williams — member of The Commodores, hits include "Machine Gun"

MILBURN ◆Clifford Milburn Holland — engineer and creator of the Holland Tunnel ◆ Milburn Stone — actor whose roles included Doc Adams on TV's long running western "Gunsmoke"

MILES ◆Miles Davis — one of the great jazz trumpet players

MILLARD ◆Millard Fillmore — thirteenth President of the United States ◆ Millard Mitchell — nasal-voiced, rangy character actor, films include "Singin' in the Rain"

MILLS ◆Mills Watson — played Winslow Homer Smith on Barbara Eden's sitcom "Harper Valley P.T.A."

MILO ◆Milo O'Shea — actor whose roles included the concierge in Jane Fonda's film "Barbarella"

MILOS ◆Milos Forman — director of "One Flew Over the Cuckoo's Nest" and "Amadeus"

MILT ◆Milt Gross — created cartoons "Baby" and " Banana Oil"

MILTON ◆Milton Berle — "Mr. Television," he dominated early TV as "Uncle Milty" ◆ Milton Bradley — manufacturer of board games, founded the Milton Bradley Company ◆ Milton Hershey — created the Hershey Bar

MINARD ◆Minard LaFever — author of books on building, including "The Modern Builder's Guide"

MINNESOTA ◆Minnesota Fats — pool player, Jackie Gleason biopic "The Hustler"

MINOR ◆Minor Watson — character actor who often played lawyers or kindly fathers, films include "Trapeze" ◆ Minor White — one of the most important photographers of the post World War II era

MIO ◆Mio Domani — actor whose roles included the Devil in the film "Scratch Harry"

MISCHA ◆Mischa Auer — Oscar nominated actor for "My Man Godfrey" ◆ Larushka Mischa Skikne — real name of actor Laurence Harvey

MISSISSIPPI ◆Mississippi Hurt — musician whose hits include "Candy Man Blues"

MITCH ◆Mitch Miller — host of TV's "Sing Along With Mitch," hits include "The Yellow Rose of Texas" ◆Mitch Ryder — vocalist whose songs include "Devil with the Blue Dress"

MITCHELL ◆Mitchell Ayres — bandleader who backed singer Perry Como on radio and television ◆ Mitchell Margo — member of The Tokens, debut gold record "Tonight I Fell in Love" ◆ Mitchell Pressman — actor whose roles included Dr. Jack McGuire on TV's "Doogie Howser, M.D."

MO ◆Mo Udall — congressman and presidential aspirant in 1976

MOE ◆Moe Bandy — country singer, hits include "Hank Williams, You Wrote My Life" ◆ Moe Howard — one of The Three Stooges

MOHAMMAD ◆Mohammad Abdullah — "Lion of Kashmir" who struggled to free his country from Indian domination

MOHAMMED ◆Mohammed — founder of the Islamic religion ◆ Mohammed Mahdi — religious leader who united the Sudan, Charlton Heston biopic "Khartoum"

MOHANDAS ◆Mohandas Gandhi — pacifist revolutionary who brought India to independence

MOISHE ◆Moishe Rosen — founder of Jews for Jesus

MOJO ◆Jesse Mojo Shepard — son of actor/writer Sam Shepard

MONCURE ◆Moncure Conway — clergyman who wrote biographies of New England authors

MONROE ◆Monroe Rathbone — chairman of Standard Oil who developed the cracking process ◆ Charles Monroe Schulz — cartoonist who created the comic strip "Peanuts"

MONTA ◆Monta Bell — director whose films include "Men in White"

MONTAGU ◆Montagu Love — actor whose roles included Count Donati in John Barrymore's "Don Juan" ◆ Montagu O'Reilly — pen name of author Wayne Andrews

MONTE ◆Monte Blue — played the evil Hamzulia Khan in Gary Cooper's "Lives of a Bengal Lancer" ◆Monte Markham — actor on TV's "Mr. Deeds Goes to Town"

MONTEL ◆Montel Williams — host of his own talk show "The Montel Williams Show"

MONTGOMERY ◆Montgomery Clift — actor who co-starred in John Wayne's film "Red River" ◆ Montgomery Ward — founder of Montgomery Ward department stores

MONTSERRAT ◆Montserrat Caballe — Spanish opera singer noted for Mozart who recorded over 120 roles

MONTY ◆Monty Banks — actor married to Gracie Fields, appeared in "A Bell for Adano" ◆Monty Hall — game show host of TV's long running "Let's Make a Deal"

MOON ◆Moon Carroll — actor whose roles included Briggs in Bela Lugosi's horror classic "Dracula" ◆Moon Mullican — called king of the hillbilly piano players

MOONBLOOD ◆Sage Moonblood Stallone — son of Sylvester Stallone, played his son Rocky, Jr., in "Rocky V"

MOONEY ◆Mooney Lynn — husband of country star Loretta Lynn, played by Tommy Lee Jones in "Coal Miner's Daughter"

MOORE ◆Moore Marriott — beloved as the ancient but resilient old Harbottle of the Will Hays comedies

MORDECAI ◆Mordecai Brown — Hall of Fame pitcher who helped develop the curve ball ◆ Mordecai Lawner — played Alvy Singer's (Woody Allen's) dad in the Oscar winning "Annie Hall"

MOREY ◆Morey Amsterdam — part of Rob's comedy writing team on TV's "The Dick Van Dyke Show" ◆ Morey Carr — member of The Playmates, debut hit "Jo-Ann"

MORGAN ◆Morgan Baylis — son of actress Rae Dawn Chong ◆ Morgan Earp — brother of Wyatt Earp who fought with him at Tombstone's O.K. Corral ◆ Morgan Freeman — actor in "Driving Miss Daisy," "Glory," "Unforgiven," and "Robin Hood"

MORITZ ◆Moritz Bomhard — conductor ◆ Moritz Jagendorf — American folklorist, author "Tyll Ulenspiegel's Merry Pranks"

MORLAND ◆Morland Graham — Scottish character actor whose credits include "The Scarlet Pimpernel"

MORLEY ◆Morley Callaghan — author of "Many-Colored Coat" and "No Man's Meat" ◆ Morley Safer — co-host of the network news magazine "60 Minutes"

MORONI ◆Moroni Olsen — actor whose roles included western hero Buffalo Bill in "Annie Oakley"

MORRIE ◆Morrie Brickman — syndicated cartoonist, author "This Little Pigeon Went to Market" ◆ Morrie Turner — cartoonist, creator of the syndicated strip "Wee Pals"

MORRIS ◆Morris Kline — math teacher, author of "Why Johnny Can't Add" ◆Morris Weinstein — real name of actor Jack Weston

MORRISSEY ◆Morrissey — rock singer whose albums include "Kill Uncle" and "Your Arsenal"

MORT ◆Mort Lindsey — award winning musical director of TV shows, song "Lorna" ◆ Mort Sahl — talk show host with an intellectual leftist slant ◆ Mort Walker — creator of comic strips "Beetle Bailey" and "Hi and Lois"

MORTIMER ◆Mortimer Adler — philosopher who wrote the best selling "How to Read a Book" ◆ George Mortimer Pullman — inventor of the railroad sleeping car, called the Pullman Car

MORTON ◆Morton Da Costa — director of "Auntie Mame" and "The Music Man" ◆Morton Dean — journalist with CBS News ◆ Morton Downey, Jr. — confrontational, controversial talk show host of "The Morton Downey, Jr., Show"

MOSE ◆Mose Allison — Grammy nominated as Best Jazz Vocalist for "Lessons in Living"

MOSES ◆Moses Cleveland — founder of Cleveland, Ohio, cousin of President Grover Cleveland ◆Moses Horowitz — real name of The Three Stooges' Moe

MOSHE ◆Moshe Arens — Israeli ambassador to the United States ◆ Moshe Dayan — hero of Israeli Six-Day War

MOSS ◆Moss Hart — screenwriter of "A Star is Born," biopic "Act One" with George Hamilton

MOULTON ◆Stephen Moulton Babcock — scientist who helped discover vitamin A ◆ William Moulton Marston — creator of comic book and TV hero Wonder Woman

MUDDY ◆Muddy Waters — five-time Grammy winner, hits include "I'm a Man" and "I've Got My Mojo Working"

MUHAMMAD ◆Muhammad Ali — he said "I am the greatest," and he was, three times the heavyweight champion

MUIR ◆Muir Mathieson — composer whose film scores include "The Swiss Family Robinson"

MUNRO ◆Munro Edmonson — anthropologist, author "The Book of Counsel" ◆ Munro Leaf — created the children's classic "The Story of Ferdinand"

MURDOCK ◆Murdock McQuarrie — actor who played a doctor in Fredric March's "Dr. Jekyll and Mr. Hyde"

MURPHY ◆Murphy Dunne — played the piano player in the Belushi/Aykroyd classic "The Blues Brothers"

MURRAY ◆F. Murray Abraham — Oscar winning actor for "Amadeus" ◆ Murray Kaufman — nickname Murray the K, promoter of the Beatles' first US Tour

MURVYN ◆Murvyn Vye — actor whose roles included Blackbeard in "The Boy and the Pirates"

MUTHA ◆Mutha Withem — member of Gary Puckett and the Union Gap whose hits include "Young Girl"

MUZYAD ◆Muzyad Yakhoob — real name of television star and entertainer Danny Thomas

MUZZ ◆Muzz Skillings — with hard rock group Living Colour, Grammy winning hit "Cult of Personality"

MYKEL ◆Mykel Williamson — actor whose roles included Deacon Bridges on the drama series "Midnight Caller"

MYLES ◆Myles Standish — Mayflower Pilgrim in the love triangle poem "The Courtship of Myles Standish"

MYRON ◆Myron McCormick — actor whose roles included Charlie Burns in Paul Newman's "The Hustler" ◆Myron Wallace — real name of TV's "60 Minutes" investigative reporter Mike Wallace

NACIO ◆Nacio Brown — film composer whose credits include "Singin' in the Rain"

NAP ◆Nap Lajoie — Hall of Fame infielder

NAPOLEON ◆Napoleon Bonaparte — Emperor of France and conqueror of Europe defeated at Waterloo ◆ Napoleon Whiting — actor whose roles included Silas on the western series "The Big Valley"

NAPPY ◆Nappy Brown — rock singer whose hits include "Pitter Patter" and "Cried Like a Baby"

NARCISO ◆Narciso Menta — actor whose roles included the bloody Count in "The Dracula Saga"

NARVEL ◆Narvel Felts — country singer whose hits include "Drift Away"

NASH ◆Nash Baldwin — co-founder of the American Civil Liberties Union

NAT ◆Nat Avery — appeared in Robert De Niro's film "Taxi Driver" as the stick-up man ◆ Nat King Cole — singer and jazz pianist whose songs include "Mona Lisa" and "Unforgettable" ◆ Nat Turner — preacher who led a slave revolt in Virginia in 1831

NATE ◆Nate Archibald — basketball guard who played for the Boston Celtics

NATHAN ◆Nathan Hale — spy hung in Revolution who said "I regret I have but one life to give for my country" ◆ Nathan Lithgow — son of actor John Lithgow ◆Nathan Pritikin — creator of the Pritikin Diet

NATHANAEL ◆Nathanael — in the Bible, one of the Twelve Apostles ◆ Nathanael Greene — Revolutionary War general and hero in the southern campaign

NATHANIEL ◆Nathaniel Crosby — youngest son of Bing Crosby, won US Amateur Golf Championship ◆ Nathaniel Hawthorne — author of "The House of the Seven Gables," made into a film with Vincent Price

NAUNTON ◆Naunton Wayne — mild-mannered British light comedy actor

NAVARONE ◆Navarone Anthony Garibaldi — son of actress Priscilla Presley

NAVARRE ◆Navarre Momaday — Pulitzer Prize winning Kiowa Indian whose novels include "The House of Dawn"

NEAIL ◆Neail Holland — actor whose roles included Danny Wolek on the soap "One Life to Live"

NEAL ◆Neal Broten — first American-born hockey player to score 100 points in one NHL season

NED ◆Ned Beatty — film actor whose credits include "Deliverance" and "Superman" ◆ Ned Buntline — dime novelist played by Burt Lancaster in "Buffalo Bill and the Indians"

NEHEMIAH ◆Nehemiah Persoff — actor whose films include "On the Waterfront" and "The Commancheros"

NEIL ◆Neil Armstrong — first astronaut to walk on the moon ◆ Neil Diamond — vocalist, songs include "Cracklin' Rose" and "You Don't Bring Me Flowers" ◆Neil Patrick Harris — star of the sitcom "Doogie Howser, M.D." ◆ Neil Sedaka — singer/songwriter, hits include "Calendar Girl" "Happy Birthday, Sweet Sixteen" ◆ Neil Simon — writer of comedy plays and films, most notably "The Odd Couple" ◆ Neil Young — member of Buffalo Springfield, and Crosby, Stills, Nash, and Young

NELS ◆Nels Oleson — storekeeper in the books and TV series "Little House on the Prairie" ◆Nels Stewart — Hall of Famer who was the first to score 300 goals in hockey

NELSON ◆Nelson Eddy — starred in a string of musical movies with Jeanette MacDonald ◆ Nelson Mandela — South African political activist who was imprisoned but became president ◆ Charles Nelson Reilly — funnyman who was a regular on the sitcom "The Ghost and Mrs. Muir" ◆Nelson Rockefeller — only Vice President appointed to the job who did not become President

NERO ◆Nero Wolfe (c) — detective hero of over 47 novels written by Rex Stout

NESTER ◆Nester Chylak — American League umpire

NESTOR ◆Nestor Paiva — played Lucas in the classic monster movie "Creature from the Black Lagoon" ◆ Nestor Serrano — actor who played Officer Geno Toffenelli on the police drama series "True Blue"

NEVIL ◆Nevil Shute — best selling Australian novelist whose film works include "On the Beach"

NEVILL ◆Barnes Nevill Wallis — invented a revolutionary bouncing bomb in WW II, biopic "The Dam Busters"

NEVILLE ◆Neville Brand — portrayed Al Capone twice, in "The Scarface Mob" and "Spin of a Coin" ◆ Neville Chamberlain — thought he had bought "peace in our time" for England from Hitler ◆ James Neville Mason — actor whose films include "A Star Is Born"

NEWELL ◆Newell Jenkins — founder of New York's Clarion Music Society ◆ Newell Wyeth — illustrator of popular children's novels

NEWTON ◆Newton Arvin — literary critic and author of books on American literature ◆ Cody Newton Gifford — son of Kathie Lee and Frank Gifford ◆ Isaac Newton Lewis — inventor of the air-cooled Lewis machine gun used in World War I

NIALL ◆Niall McGinnis — actor who played plump, jovial Friar Tuck in "The Sword of Sherwood Forest" ◆Niall O'Brien — actor who played Captain Twilley in Sigourney Weaver's "Half Moon Street"

NICCOLO ◆Niccolo Machiavelli — Italian philosopher on government, author of "The Prince"

NICHOLAS ◆Saint Nicholas — patron saint of children, Dutch version of Santa Claus ◆Nicholas Colasanto — died while playing Coach Ernie Pantusso on the sitcom "Cheers" ◆ Nicholas II — last Czar of Russia, who was killed with his whole family by the Bolsheviks

NICK ◆Nick the Greek — gambler who was the fastest craps shooter in the United States ◆ Nick Cravat — Burt Lancaster's pint-sized acrobatic partner in many adventure films ◆Nick Nolte — starred in "48 Hours" and "Down and Out in Beverly Hills"

NICKOLAS ◆Nickolas Ashford — composer of "Ain't No Mountain High Enough," recorded by The Supremes

NICKY ◆Nicky Arnstein — gambler who married Fanny Brice, biopic "Funny Girl"

NICOL ◆Nicol Williamson — actor whose roles included Shakespeare's tragic Dane in "Hamlet"

NICOLA ◆Nicola Sacco — protested he was innocent of robbery, biopic "Sacco and Vanzetti"

NICOLAS ◆Nicolas Boileau — French poet whose chief work is the poem "Art Poetique" ◆Nicolas Cage — off-beat roles include "Moonstruck," "Honeymoon in Vegas," "Raising Arizona" ◆ Nicolas Hammond — actor who played Friedrich, one of the von Trapp kids, in "The Sound of Music"

NICOLAUS ◆Nicolaus Copernicus — Polish astronomer who discovered that the sun was the center of the universe

NICOLO ◆Nicolo Amati — seventeenth century Italian violin maker who taught Antonio Stradivari

NIELS ◆Niels Bohr — Danish physicist who helped develop the atomic bomb at Los Alamos during WW II

NIGEL ◆Nigel Bruce — Dr. Watson to Basil Rathbone's Sherlock Holmes ◆Nigel Davenport — actor whose roles included the evil Count's deadliest foe in "Dracula"

NIKITA ◆Nikita Khrushchev — premier of the USSR during the Cuban missile crisis with John F. Kennedy

NIKKI ◆Nikki Sixx — member of Motley Crue, debut hit single "Looks That Kill"

NIKOLAI ◆Nikolai Cherkassov — actor who played the legendary Russian prince in the epic "Alexander Nevsky" ◆ Nikolai Rimsky-Korsakov — nineteenth century Russian composer, hits "Scheherazade," "Capriccio Espagnol"

NILE ◆Nile Kinnick — 1939 Heisman Trophy winning quarterback ◆ Nile Rodgers — member of Chic, hits include "Dance, Dance, Dance" and "Good Times"

NILES ◆Niles Welch — actor who played William Jennings Bryan in Edward G. Robinson's "Silver Dollar"

NILS ◆Nils Asther — actor whose films include "The Bitter Tea of General Yen" ◆Nils Lofgren — pop-rock singer, guitarist, band Grin, album "Nils Lofgren"

NINO ◆Nino Tempo — singer, debut hit single with April Stevens "Sweet and Lovely"

NIPSEY ◆Nipsey Russell — although a perennial TV personality, he hit feature films in "The Wiz"

NOAH ◆Noah Beery — character actor whose credits include "Red River," "Sergeant York" ◆ Noah Dietrich — chief business adviser to Howard Hughes, author "Howard The Amazing Mr.

Hughes" ◆ Noah Webster — created the first dictionary in the world after the American Revolution

NOAM ◆Noam Pitlik — Emmy winning director for the sitcom "Barney Miller"

NOBLE ◆Noble Johnson — actor whose roles included Bobo in the 1931 film "The Lost Lady" ◆ Noble Sissle — leader of The Sizzling Syncopators, composer "I'm Just Wild About Harry"

NODDY ◆Noddy Holder — member of the rock group Slade, debut single hit "Take Me Bak 'Ome"

NOEL ◆Noel Coward — British dramatist, playwright, composer, and entertainer ◆Noel Langley — screenwriter of "The Wizard of Oz" ◆ Noel Paul Stookey — Paul in Peter, Paul, and Mary, hits include "Blowin' in the Wind"

NOEL-NOEL ◆Noel-Noel — dapper French character comedian

NOKIE ◆Nokie Edwards — member of The Ventures, hits include "Walk, Don't Run" and "Hawaii Five-O"

NOLAN ◆Nolan Bushnell — inventor of the video game "Pong" and the founder of Atari ◆ Nolan Miller — fashion designer for TV series "Dynasty" ◆ Nolan Ryan — record holder for lifetime strikeouts by a pitcher

NORBERT ◆Norbert Brodine — cinematographer, films include Errol Flynn's "The Sea Hawk" ◆ Norbert Pearlroth — only researcher for "Ripley's Believe It or Not"

NORM ◆Norm Peterson (c) — George Wendt never moved from his personal bar stool on TV's "Cheers"

NORMAN ◆Norman Fell — best known as the landlord on TV's "Three's Company" ◆ Norman Mailer — Pulitzer Prize winning author, novels include "The Naked and the Dead" ◆ Norman Rockwell — painter of the American way of life on the covers of the "Saturday Evening Post" ◆ Norman Schwarzkopf — field commander for Operation Desert Storm, won the Gulf War

NORMANN ◆Normann Burton — actor whose roles included Burt Dennis on the sitcom "The Ted Knight Show"

NORRIS ◆James Norris Gamble — founded Proctor and Gamble, developed Ivory Soap ◆ Norris McWhirter — editor of "The Guinness Book of World Records"

NORTHCOTE ◆C. Northcote Parkinson — wrote "Parkinson's Law," humorous essays on bureaucracy and management ◆

Lawrence Northcote Upjohn — president of Upjohn Pharmaceuticals

NORTON ◆Norton Simon — founder of Norton Simon, Inc., which makes Canada Dry

NOSTRADAMUS ◆Nostradamus — astrologer who predicted the rise of Hitler

NUNEZ ◆Alvar Nunez Cabeza de Vaca — Conquistador captured by Indians in Florida after being shipwrecked ◆ Vasco Nunez de Balboa — Spanish explorer who in 1513 discovered the Pacific Ocean

NUNNALLY ◆Nunnally Johnson — screenwriter and director whose films include "The Grapes of Wrath"

O'KELLY ◆O'Kelly Isley — member of The Isley Brothers whose hits include "It's Your Thing"

OBEDIAH ◆Obediah Carter — member of The Five Royales whose hits include "Dedicated to the One I Love"

OCTAVIO ◆Octavio Paz — Nobel Prize winning poet

OCTAVIUS ◆Octavius Caesar — Roman emperor who returned Rome to constitutional rule after Caesar's death ◆ Felix Octavius Darley — illustrated Irving's "Rip Van Winkle" and "The Legend of Sleepy Hollow"

ODELL ◆Odell Shepard — Pulitzer Prize winning founder of the Thoreau Society of America

ODYSSEUS ◆Odysseus Elytis — Nobel Prize winning poet

OGDEN ◆Ogden Nash — poems include "Candy is dandy, But liquor is quicker" ◆Ogden Reid — combined the NY Tribune and NY Herald to create the NY Herald Tribune ◆ David Ogden Stiers — actor whose roles included the staid, back-bay Boston doctor on TV's "M*A*S*H"

OLAN ◆Olan Soule — actor whose films include "The Apple Dumpling Gang" and "St. Ives"

OLE ◆Ole Olsen — comedian in vaudeville partnered with Chic Johnson ◆ Ole Rolvaag — author of "Giants in the Earth"

OLEY ◆Oley Speaks — songwriter whose hits include "On the Road to Mandalay" and "Sylvia"

OLIN ◆Olin Dutra — golfer in the Hall of Fame ◆Olin Howland — actor whose roles included Jensen in the James Whitmore horror film "Them!"

OLIVER ◆Oliver Hardy — fat half of the comedy team of Laurel and Hardy ◆ Oliver Hazard Perry — naval hero of the War of 1812, quote "We have met the enemy, and they are ours" ◆Oliver Reed — at his best as the troubled Musketeer in "The Three Musketeers" ◆Oliver Stone — director of "Platoon," which won the Oscar for best picture

OLLIE ◆Ollie North — Marine colonel who sparked the Iran-Contra scandal

OLOF ◆Robert Olof Blucker — hostage in Iran during the Carter administration

OLOFF ◆Oloff Van Cortlandt — former deputy mayor and namesake for New York City's Van Cortlandt Park

OMAR ◆Omar Bradley — field general in command of the Allied invasion of Europe ◆ Omar Kiam — fashion designer for Hollywood stars ◆ Omar Sharif — dark, exotic leading man in "Doctor Zhivago" and "Funny Girl"

OMRI ◆Omri Katz — actor who played Marshall Teller on TV's supernatural "Eerie, Indiana"

ONNIE ◆Onnie McIntyre — with The Average White Band, debut number one gold single "Pick Up the Pieces"

ONSLOW ◆Onslow Stevens — actor whose roles included Aramis in "The Three Musketeers"

OPAL ◆Opal Courtney, Jr. — member of The Spaniels, debut hit "Goodnight Sweetheart, Goodnight"

ORAL ◆Oral Roberts — TV evangelist and founder of Oklahoma's Oral Roberts University

OREL ◆Orel Hershiser IV — pitcher who broke Don Drysdale's record for consecutive scoreless innings

OREN ◆Oren Arnold — children's author whose works include "Wit of the West"

ORENTHAL ◆Orenthal James Simpson — full name of sports figure O. J. Simpson

ORESTES ◆Orestes Brownson — editor of the nineteenth century "Brownson's Quarterly Review" ◆ Orestes Rallis — portrayed the chief of police in Alan Ladd's "Boy on a Dolphin"

ORLANDO ◆Orlando Cassavitis — real name of singer Tony Orlando ◆Orlando Cepeda — Puerto Rican baseball player, Most Valuable Player

ORNETTE ◆Ornette Coleman — jazz saxophonist whose hit albums include "Song X"

ORPHEUS ◆Orpheus Kerr — humorist who lampooned Civil War politicians

ORRIN ◆Orrin Hatch — conservative Republican senator from Utah elected in 1977 ◆ Orrin Tucker — big band leader, hits include "Oh, Johnny, Oh" with Bonnie Baker

ORRY-KELLY ◆Orry-Kelly — Oscar winning costumer for "An American in Paris" and "Some Like It Hot"

ORSEN ◆Jim Orsen Bakker — television clergyman embroiled in scandal

ORSON ◆Orson Bean — TV game show personality, including "To Tell The Truth" ◆ Orson Welles — director and star of the feature film classic "Citizen Kane"

ORTON ◆Orton Hungerford — real name of Ty Hardin

ORVILLE ◆Robert Orville Cummings — real name of the sitcom star of "Love That Bob" ◆Orville Redenbacher — developed the best selling popcorn in the US ◆ Orville Wright — one of the Wright Brothers, co-inventors of the airplane

OSBERT ◆Osbert Lancaster — cartoonist who created Maudie Littlehampton character ◆ Sir Osbert Sitwell — author, novel "Before the Bombardment"

OSBORN ◆Osborn Elliott — editor of "Newsweek" and dean of the Columbia School of Journalism

OSCAR ◆Oscar DeLaRenta — fashion designer known for lavish evening clothes ◆ Oscar Hammerstein II — wrote the words and libretto for "Oklahoma," "Carousel," and "South Pacific" ◆Oscar Mayer — founder of the baloney which has a first name, it's "O-S-C-A-R" ◆ Oscar Wilde — British poet, novelist, and playwright

OSGOOD ◆Osgood Perkins — actor whose roles included the evil Cardinal Richelieu in "Madame DuBarry" ◆Osgood Perkins II — son of "Psycho" actor Anthony Perkins, named after his actor father

OSKAR ◆ Oskar Barnack — inventor of the first miniature camera, the Leica ◆ Oskar Minkowski — discovered insulin as a cure for diabetes

OSMOND ◆ Osmond Borradaile — Canadian cinematographer whose films include "The Four Feathers"

OSSIE ◆ Ossie Davis — actor who starred opposite Burt Lancaster in "The Scalphunters"

OSWALD ◆ Oswald Jacoby — best card player in the world, syndicated bridge columnist ◆ Oswald Nelson — real name of TV star Ozzie Nelson, of "The Adventures of Ozzie and Harriet"

OTELLO ◆ Otello Sestili — played betrayer Judas Iscariot in "The Gospel According to St. Matthew"

OTHMAR ◆ Othmar Ammann — designer of the George Washington Bridge and the Golden Gate Bridge

OTHO ◆ Otho Gaines — founder of the gospel-blues quartet the Delta Rhythm Boys ◆ Edward Otho Ord — general in the Union army after whom California's Fort Ord is named

OTIS ◆ Otis Redding — singer whose hit songs include "(Sitting on) The Dock of the Bay"

OTTIS ◆ Ottis Anderson — football player who was Rookie of the Year and Player of the Year

OTTO ◆ Otto Preminger — director of "In Harm's Way," "Exodus," and "Anatomy of a Murder" ◆ Otto Ringling — with brothers, founded Ringling Brothers, Barnum and Bailey Circus

OWEN ◆ Owen Madden — gang leader employed by Lindbergh to find his kidnapped son ◆ Owen Wister — author of "The Virginian," basis for play, three movies, and a TV series

OZZIE ◆ Ozzie Nelson — creator and star of the TV series "The Adventures of Ozzie and Harriet" ◆ Ozzie Smith — holder of the major league record for most assists by a shortstop

OZZY ◆ Ozzy Osbourne — lead singer of the heavy-metal band Black Sabbath, hit album "Paranoid"

PABLO ◆ Benito Pablo Juarez — became president of Mexico and defeated1 Maximilian, biopic "Juarez" ◆ Pablo Picasso — dominant figure of twentieth century art

PADDY ◆ Paddy Chayevsky — screenwriter known for "Marty," won an Oscar for "Network"

PADRAIC ◆Padraic Colum — founder of the Irish National Theatre ◆Padraic Pearse — Irish poet shot by the British because of the Easter Week rebellion

PAGE ◆Page Smith — historian, author of "People's History of the United States"

PAIGE ◆Henry Paige Comstock — discovered the Comstock Lode at Virginia City, world's richest silver mine

PANCHO ◆Pancho Gonzales — tennis player who dominated the pro tour from 1953 to 1962 ◆Pancho Villa — Mexican bandit and leader in the 1910 revolution

PANDRO ◆Pandro Berman — MGM producer of Astaire/Rogers films

PAOLO ◆Paolo Bortoluzzi — artistic adviser and choreographer for La Scala ◆Paolo Soleri — architect who designed the planned community of Arcosanti, Arizona ◆Paolo Stoppa — actor whose roles included Pope Alexander III in Richard Burton's film "Becket"

PAPILLON ◆Papillon — falsely accused of murder, survived the horrors of the infamous "Devil's Island"

PARE ◆Pare Lorentz — filmmaker of US government documentaries during the Depression

PARKER ◆Clifford Parker Robertson III — real name of actor Cliff Robertson ◆ Parker Stevenson — played Frank Hardy on TV's "The Hardy Boys," also in the film "Life Guard"

PARLEY ◆Parley Baer — actor whose roles included Mr. Hamble on TV's "The Double Life of Henry Phyfe"

PARNELLI ◆Parnelli Jones — winner of the Indianapolis 500

PASCAL ◆Pascal Covici — publisher who promoted John Steinbeck

PAT ◆Pat Boone — pop singer, milk drinker, and descendant of Daniel Boone ◆Pat Morita — actor who played the original owner of Al's Diner on TV's "Happy Days" ◆ Pat O'Brien — actor in "Angels With Dirty Faces," "Fightin' 69th" ◆ Pat Paulsen — comedian on "The Smothers Brothers Show," ran for President in 1968 ◆Pat Sajak — host of the syndicated TV game show "Wheel of Fortune"

PATRIC ◆Patric Knowles — actor in "The Adventures of Robin Hood" and "The Charge of the Light Brigade"

PATRICK ◆Patrick Duffy — actor whose roles included Bobby Ewing on TV's "Dallas," star of "Step by Step" ◆Patrick Henry — patriot famous for saying "Give me liberty or give me death" ◆ Patrick MacNee — actor whose roles included secret agent John Steed on TV's "The Avengers" ◆ Patrick Stewart — actor who played Captain Jean-Luc Picard on "Star Trek: The Next Generation" ◆ Patrick Swayze — gymnastic actor in "Dirty Dancing" and "Ghost" ◆ Patrick Wayne — actor from "The Searchers" and "The Green Berets," son of John Wayne

PAUL ◆Paul Anka — Canadian singer/songwriter, hits "Diana," "My Way" ◆ Paul Henreid — actor whose roles included Victor Laszlo in Bogart's "Casablanca" ◆Paul Masson — wine merchant who "will sell no wine, before its time" ◆ Paul McCartney — legendary singer and songwriter with musical groups The Beatles and Wings ◆ Paul Newman — actor in "Butch Cassidy and the Sundance Kid," "The Verdict," "Cool Hand Luke" ◆Paul Simon — singer/musician who went solo after "Simon and Garfunkel"

PAVEL ◆Pavel Cherenkov — Nobel Prize in physics for discovering the "Cherenkov Effect" ◆ Pavel Kadotchnikov — actor whose roles included the shipwrecked English squire in "Robinson Crusoe"

PAXTON ◆Terry Paxton Bradshaw — quarterback who led The Pittsburgh Steelers to four Super Bowl victories ◆ Paxton Whitehead — actor who played the lead role of Albert Dudley on the sitcom "Marblehead Manor"

PEABO ◆Peabo Bryson — blues singer whose hits include "Lookin' Like Love"

PEADAR ◆Peadar O'Donnell — IRA member, author "The Big Window"

PEANUTS ◆Peanuts Mann — regular on TV's "The Doodles Weaver Show"

PEDRO ◆Pedro Armendariz — top Mexican actor, films include "From Russia With Love" ◆Pedro Nino — navigator of the Nina, one of Columbus' three ships in 1492

PEE-WEE ◆Pee-wee Herman — off-beat comedian, films "Pee-wee's Big Adventure," "Big Top Pee-wee" ◆ Pee Wee King — scored a hit with his song "Bimbo"

PELE ◆Pele — one of the most famous soccer players in the world

PELHAM ◆Pelham Grenville "P. G." Wodehouse — creator of Jeeves, manservant and valet to gentleman Bertie Wooster

PENDLETON ◆Pendleton Brown — actor whose roles included Ken on the sitcom "Mama Malone"

PENDRANT ◆Pendrant Netherly — actor whose roles included Al Cowley on the school drama series "Room 222"

PENN ◆Penn Jillette — half of comedy act Penn and Teller ◆Will Penn Rogers — comedy star of Ziegfeld Follies who made fun of politicians

PER ◆Per Oscarsson — actor whose roles included the monster in "Victor Frankenstein"

PERC ◆Perc Westmore — Hollywood makeup artist who founded the House of Westmore

PERCIVAL ◆Percival Dalton — husband of bad girl Nellie Oleson on TV's "Little House on the Prairie" ◆Percival Lowell — founder of the Lowell Observatory in Flagstaff, Arizona

PERCY ◆Percy Faith — scored a gold record hit with his rendition of "Delicado" ◆Percy Ross — made a fortune in plastic bags, now gives it away in column "Thanks a Million" ◆Percy Sledge — soul singer, debut number one gold record hit "When A Man Loves a Woman"

PEREGRINE ◆Peregrine White — first child born in America from the Mayflower, ancestor of Vincent Price

PEREZ ◆Perez Prado — rock singer who went gold with "Cherry Pink and Apple Blossom White"

PERICLES ◆Pericles Jacobs, Jr. — member of The Blackbyrds, hit debut single "Do It, Fluid"

PERNELL ◆Pernell Roberts — actor whose roles included oldest son Adam Cartwright on TV's oater "Bonanza"

PERRY ◆Perry Como — laid-back singer and host of TV's "The Perry Como Show" ◆Perry King — actor whose roles include the lead on the drama series "Riptide" ◆ Perry Mason (c) — Raymond Burr was the lawyer who never lost on TV's "Perry Mason"

PERVIS ◆Pervis Jackson — member of The Spinners, debut hit single "That's What Girls Are Made For" ◆ Pervis Staple — member of The Staple Singers, debut hit "Why? (Am I Treated So Bad)

PETE ♦Pete Best — unknown Beatle, replaced by Ringo Starr just before fame hit ♦ Pete Rose — baseball legend, later team manager, hired and fired from Cincinnati Reds ♦ Pete Seeger — guitarist, composer of song "If I Had a Hammer" ♦ Pete Townshend — member of The Who, debut hit "I Can't Explain"

PETER ♦Peter Falk — actor who played "Columbo," TV's quirky detective in a crumpled rain coat ♦ Peter Lorre — character actor with distinctive voice in "Casablanca" and "The Maltese Falcon" ♦ Peter O'Toole — actor who played the title role in the awesome epic "Lawrence of Arabia" ♦ Peter Sellers — played the bumbling Inspector Clouseau in the "The Pink Panther" movies ♦ Peter Ustinov — Oscar nominee for "Quo Vadis"

PETROVICH ♦Mikhail Petrovich Artsybashev — Russian author best known for sensational novel "Sanin" about sex ♦ Ivan Petrovich Pavlov — discovered "Pavlov's response," conditioned responses in dogs

PEVERELL ♦J. Peverell Marley — cinematographer who worked with DeMille, films include "The Ten Commandments"

PEYTON ♦Peyton Randolph — first president of the Continental Congress

PHALON ♦Phalon Jones — member of The Bar-Kays, debut hit single "Soul Finger"

PHANTOM ♦Slim Jim Phantom MacDonnell — member of The Stray Cats, debut hit single "Rock This Town"

PHIL ♦Phil Collins — member of the rock group Genesis, debut hit single "Your Own Special Way" ♦Phil Donahue — host of the talk show "Donahue" ♦ Phil Everly — member of The Everly Brothers, hits "Bye Bye Love" and "Cathy's Clown" ♦ Phil Rizzuto — baseball player and sportscaster, front man for "The Money Store" ♦Phil Silvers — fast talking comedian whose roles included TV's "Sergeant Bilko"

PHILEAS ♦Phileas Fogg (c) — David Niven's role in "Around the World in 80 Days"

PHILIP ♦Prince Philip — married Queen Elizabeth II of England, father of Prince Charles ♦ John Philip Sousa — composer of over 140 marches, including "Stars and Stripes Forever"

PHILIPPE ♦Philippe Aries — French author who described his work as a history of non-events ♦Philippe Petit — stuntman who walked between the two World Trade Center buildings on a tightrope

PHILLIPPE ◆Phillippe Wynn — member of The Spinners, debut hit single "That's What Girls Are Made For"

PHILLIPS ◆Phillips Holmes — portrayed Dickens' Pip in the film "Great Expectations" ◆ Howard Phillips Lovecraft — author of macabre horror stories, often published in "Weird Tales" magazine

PHILO ◆Philo Farnsworth — inventor of the television

PHINEAS ◆Phineas Taylor "P. T." Barnum — showman and creator of "The Greatest Show on Earth"

PICK ◆Pick Withers — member of Dire Straits, debut hit single "Sultans of Swing"

PIE ◆Pie Traynor — infielder with Pittsburgh Pirates, had 100 or more RBI's seven times

PIER ◆Pier Pasolini — Italian director whose films include "The Gospel According to St. Matthew"

PIERCE ◆Pierce Brosnan — played the dashing detective Remington Steele in the TV series of the same name ◆ Huey Pierce Long — "the Kingfish," presidential candidate with "every man a king" campaign

PIERINO ◆Pierino Roland Como — real name of singer Perry Como

PIERPONT ◆J. Pierpont Morgan — nineteenth century robber baron

PIERRE ◆Pierre Balmain — French fashion designer to the stars ◆ Pierre Cardin — founder of the French fashion house which bears his name ◆ Pierre Cartier — founder of Cartier's jewelers, sold the Hope Diamond ◆ Pierre Salinger — JFK's press secretary, foreign correspondent for ABC News ◆Pierre Trudeau — colorful Liberal prime minister of Canada

PIERS ◆Piers Read — author whose works include "Alive!" which was later filmed by Disney

PIETER ◆Pieter Botha — eighth prime minister of South Africa ◆ Pieter Bruegel — sixteenth century Flemish artist

PIETRO ◆Pietro Annigoni — portrait painter to the rich and famous ◆ Pietro Aretino — Italian satirist who wrote the tragedy

"Orazia" ◆Pietro Badoglio — Italian Field Marshal who defeated Austria in World War I

PINCKNEY ◆Roone Pinckney Arledge — President of ABC Sports who introduced slow-action and split-screens ◆ Pinckney Stewart — African-American governor of Louisiana after the Civil War

PINKLON ◆Pinklon Thomas — WBC heavyweight champion who lost his title to Trevor Berbick

PINKY ◆Pinky Tomlin — composer of "The Object of My Affection" used in film "Times Square Lady" ◆ Pinky Lee — vaudeville and burlesque star who had TV's "Pinky Lee Show"

PINO ◆Pino Conti — played Dickens' fiendish, deformed moneylender in "The Old Curiosity Shop"

PIRI ◆Piri Thomas — author whose works include "Down These Mean Streets" and "Seven Long Times"

PITT ◆Pitt Herbert — actor who appeared as Larker in Paul Newman's "Hud"

PITTS ◆Pitts Sanborn — newspaper music editor, author "Metropolitan Book of the Opera"

PLACIDO ◆Placido Domingo — opera singer who played Don Jose in the 1984 version of the musical "Carmen"

PLEASANT ◆Pleasant Hanes — founder of the Hanes Underwear company, feels "good all under"

PLUTO ◆Pluto Felix — actor whose roles included Count Dracula in "The Worst Crime of All!"

PONCE ◆Ponce de Leon — discovered Florida and searched for the legendary fountain of youth

PONCIE ◆Poncie Ponce — played one-man taxi service Kazuo Kim on the detective drama "Hawaiian Eye"

PONTIAC ◆Pontiac — Ottawa chief who attacked the British at Detroit, car named after him

POPEYE ◆Popeye Doyle — fanatical cop played by Gene Hackman in "The French Connection"

PORL ◆Porl Thompson — member of The Cure, hit album "Kiss Me, Kiss Me, Kiss Me"

PORTER ◆Porter Hall — actor who played MacCauley in the original William Powell "Thin Man" film ◆ Porter Wagoner —

country singer, hits "Satisfied Mind," "Skid Row Joe" and "Big Wind"

PORTHOS ◆Porthos (c) — most jovial and good-hearted of Dumas' "Three Musketeers"

POTTER ◆Potter Stewart — youngest person ever to resign from the Supreme Court

POWEL ◆Powel Crosley — inventor of night baseball

POWELL ◆Edwin Powell Hubbell — creator of the Hubbell Telescope ◆ William Powell Lear — founder of the Lear Jet Corporation

POWERS ◆Powers Boothe — played the Rev. Jones in the TV movie "Guyana Tragedy The Story of Jim Jones"

PRAIRIE ◆Prairie Prince — member of The Tubes, debut hit single "Don't Touch Me There"

PRENTISS ◆Prentiss Barnes — member of The Moonglows, hit "Sincerely"

PRESTON ◆Preston Foster — starred in TV's "Sergeant Preston of the Yukon" ◆Preston Sturges — comedy director of "The Palm Beach Story" and "Sullivan's Travels" ◆ Preston Tucker — Jeff Bridges' maverick automobile maker in the biopic "Tucker"

PRIMO ◆Primo Carnera — called the "Ambling Alp," heavyweight champ

PRINCE ◆Prince — pop singer of androgynous appearance whose hits include "Purple Rain"

PROSPER ◆Prosper Merimee — creator of "Carmen," the ultimate femme fatale

PROTEUS ◆Charles Proteus Steinmetz — engineer who invented more than 100 electrical appliances

PRUITT ◆Pruitt Taylor Vince — actor whose films include Jill Clayburgh's "Shy People"

PUGGY ◆Puggy White — actor who played Eddie in the Shirley Temple film "Little Miss Marker"

PUGSLEY ◆Pugsley Addams (c) — son in the film and sitcom "The Addams Family"

PURNELL ◆Purnell Pratt — played Wayne Wayland in the Evelyn Brent vehicle "The Silver Horde"

QUENTIN ◆Quentin Crisp — known for autobiography "The Naked Civil Servant" ◆ Quentin Dean — actor who played Delores Purdy in Sidney Poitier's "In the Heat of the Night" ◆ Quentin Roosevelt — one of two sons of Teddy Roosevelt who died in WW I living up to their father's image

QUINCY ◆John Quincy Adams — only US President to be the son of a President ◆ Quincy Jones — big man in pop music, produced Michael Jackson's "Thriller"

QUINN ◆Quinn Martin — producer of many popular TV shows, including "The Fugitive," and "The Untouchables"

QUINTON ◆Quinton Reynolds — adopted son of Lonnie Anderson and Burt Reynolds

RABBIT ◆Rabbit Bundrick — member of the rock group Free, hits include "All Right Now" and "Free"

RABON ◆Rabon Delmore — one of country western's Brown's Ferry Four

RAD ◆Rad Daly — actor whose roles included Michael Pusser on the drama series "Walking Tall"

RADAMES ◆Radames Pera — played Caine as a boy (grasshopper) on David Carradine's TV show "Kung Fu"

RADCLIFF ◆Radcliff Hall — commentator on TV's "Gillette Summer Sports Reel"

RADCLIFFE ◆Callen Radcliffe Tjader — Grammy winning jazz musician with the Brubeck Octet

RADCLYFFE ◆Radclyffe Hall — author whose works include "The Well of Loneliness"

RAFAEL ◆Rafael Campos — actor whose roles included Ramon Diaz, Jr., on the Valerie Harper sitcom "Rhoda" ◆Rafael Rivelles — actor who played the evil Cardinal Richelieu in "Cyrano and D'Artagnan" ◆ Rafael Sabatini — author of filmed novels, including "The Sea Hawk" and "Captain Blood"

RAFE ◆Rafe Garretson — Ken Meeker's role on the soap "One Life to Live" ◆Rafe Hollister — character on "The Andy Griffith Show"

RAFER ◆Rafer Johnson — former Olympic athlete turned actor, films include "The Lion"

RAFFAELLO ◆Raffaello Santi — Renaissance painter, works include "The School of Athens"

RAFFI ◆Raffi — children's performer whose albums include "Singable Songs for the Very Young"

RAGHIB ◆Raghib Ismail — nicknamed "Rocket," named "Sporting News' " College Football Player of the Year

RAGS ◆Rags Ragland — boxer turned character actor whose films include "Anchors Aweigh"

RAHSAAN ◆Rahsaan Kirk — jazz musician who invented the rokon whistle

RAINER ◆Rainer Fassbinder — films include "Lili Marleen," "Lola" and "The Marriage of Maria Braun"

RAINIER ◆Prince Rainier III — ruler of Monaco and the husband of actress Grace Kelly

RAL ◆Ral Donner — rock singer, debut hit single "Girl of My Best Friend"

RALEIGH ◆Raleigh Bond — actor who played Captain Hooker in Joseph Wambaugh's "The Black Marble" ◆John Raleigh Mott — Nobel Peace Prize winner for founding the World Council of Churches

RALF ◆Ralf Harolde — actor whose roles included Piet Van Saal in the film "The Lost Lady"

RALPH ◆Ralph Bellamy — movie roles include "His Girl Friday," "Trading Places" ◆Ralph Edwards — host of TV's "This is Your Life" ◆ Ralph Lauren — designer with his own brand of clothing ◆ Ralph Macchio — star of "The Karate Kid"

RALSEY ◆Robert Ralsey Davenport — author whose works include "Baby Names of the Rich and Famous"

RAM ◆Ram Holder — actor who played Lindsay Walker in Sigourney Weaver's "Half Moon Street"

RAMON ◆Ramon Estevez — real name of actor Martin Sheen ◆ Ramon Novarro — actor whose roles included the title character in the original film of "Ben-Hur" ◆Ramon Sheen — actor son of Martin Sheen

RAMSAY ◆Frank Ramsay Adams — wrote over 200 songs and 25 film scripts ◆ Titian Ramsay Peale — artist with the first expedition to climb Pike's Peak

RAMSEY ◆Ramsey Clark — attorney general under President Lyndon Johnson ◆Ramsey Lewis — pianist and singer

RANCE ◆Rance Allen — soul singer, hits include "See What You Done" ◆ Rance Howard — actor whose roles included Henry Boomhauer on TV's bear show "Gentle Ben"

RAND ◆Rand Brooks — actor who played Charles Hamilton in Clark Gable's "Gone With the Wind"

RANDALL ◆Randall Deal — actor in Burt Reynolds' hillbilly classic film "Deliverance" ◆Randall Terry — controversial leader of the anti-abortion group Operation Rescue

RANDOLPH ◆William Randolph Hearst — publisher who became the model for Charles Foster Kane in "Citizen Kane" ◆ Randolph Scott — western star in films like "Western Union"

RANDY ◆Randy Bachman — Canadian singer and performer in Bachman-Turner Overdrive, The Guess Who ◆Randy Newman — song writer and performer, hits include "Short People" ◆ Randy Quaid — actor in "The Last Picture Show," "The Long Riders" ◆ Randy Travis — country singer, number one single "Forever and Ever, Amen"

RANSOM ◆Ransom Sherman — actor whose roles included Herbert Dunston on TV's "Father of the Bride" ◆Ransom Wilson — flutist, founder of Solisti New York

RANSON ◆Ranson Olds — founder of the Oldsmobile Motor Company

RAOL ◆Raol Cita — one of The Harptones, recorded "A Sunday Kind of Love," "Life Is But a Dream"

RAOUL ◆Raoul Wallenberg — saved Budapest Jews during World War II, biominiseries "Wallenberg" ◆ Raoul Walsh — directed the silent screen classic "The Thief of Bagdad" with Douglas Fairbanks

RAP ◆H. Rap Brown — civil rights activist who ended up in prison

RAPHAEL ◆Raphael Eugene De Niro — son of actor Robert De Niro

RASHI ◆Rashi — eleventh century French scholar known for religious commentaries

RAUL ◆Raul Julia — actor who played the father in the feature film version of "The Addams Family"

RAVI ◆Ravi Shankar — taught The Beatles and Beach Boys the sitar, composed film score for "Gandhi"

RAVON ◆Rick Ravon Mears — four-time winner of the Indianapolis 500

RAY ◆Ray Bolger — actor best known as the Scarecrow in "The Wizard of Oz" ◆ Ray Charles — songwriter and performer, hits include "What'd I Say,""Georgia on My Mind" ◆ Ray Milland — actor in "Dial M for Murder" and "The Lost Weekend," for which he won an Oscar ◆ Ray Parker, Jr. — singer, number one hit "Ghostbusters" soundtrack of the film of the same name ◆ Ray Price — pop country singer, hits include "For the Good Times" ◆ Ray Stevens — singer and producer of comedy records in a country style, such as "The Streak"

RAYE ◆Raye Birk — actor whose roles included Mr. DiPerna on the hit sitcom "The Wonder Years"

RAYMOND ◆Raymond Burr — played Perry Mason in the TV series of the same name, and later "Ironsides" ◆ Raymond Chandler — created the detective Philip Marlowe in "The Big Sleep" ◆ Raymond Massey — portrayed Dr. Gillespie on TV's "Dr. Kildare"

RE ◆Re Styles — member of The Tubes, debut hit single "Don't Touch Me There"

REA ◆Rea Irvin — artist of the first "New Yorker" cover, created character "Eustace Tilley"

REB ◆Reb Brown — actor whose roles included the TV version of superhero Captain America

RED ◆Red Buttons — credits include "The Poseidon Adventure," Oscar winner for "Sayonara" ◆Red Skelton — movie comic, later star of long running TV variety show

REDD ◆Redd Foxx — actor whose roles included Fred Sanford on TV's "Sanford and Son"

REDMOND ◆Redmond Fawcett O'Neal — son of actress Farrah Fawcett and actor Ryan O'Neal

REED ◆Richmond Reed Carradine — real name of legendary actor John Carradine ◆ Reed Hadley — actor whose roles included legendary Wild Bill Hickok in the film "Dallas"

REESE ◆Rollo Reese May — psychoanalyst who wrote about anxiety, author "Man's Search for Himself"

REG ◆Reg Owen — hit the charts with the song "Manhattan Spiritual" ◆ Reg Presley — member of The Troggs, debut number one gold record "Wild Thing"

REGGIE ◆Reggie Jackson — American League home run champion

REGINALD ◆Reginald Denny — yet another victim of the LA riots whose assualt was captured on videotape ◆ Reginald Smythe — cartoonist who created "Andy Capp" ◆ Reginald VelJohnson — actor who played father Carl Winslow on Urkel's TV show "Family Matters"

REGIS ◆Regis Philbin — co-star of TV's daytime series "Live with Regis and Kathie Lee" ◆ Regis Toomey — actor who played Arvid Abernathy in the Marlon Brando musical "Guys and Dolls"

REINER ◆Reiner Wolk — actor who played Leiche in the teenage drug addiction film "Christiane F."

REINHOLD ◆Reinhold Messner — first mountaineer to climb Mt. Everest without artificial oxygen ◆ Reinhold Schuenzrel — actor who played Czar Nicholas of Russia in "1914 The Last Days Before the War"

REMBRANDT ◆Rembrandt Peale — artist who established the Peale Portrait Gallery in Washington, D.C. ◆Rembrandt van Rijn — 17th century Dutch painter who proved quality could be synonymous with quantity

REMINGTON ◆Remington Steele (c) — suave television private investigator

REMO ◆Remo Williams (c) — hero of the "Destroyer" books, film "Remo Williams The Adventure Continues"

REMY ◆Remy Charlip — dancer, author, and actor

RENALDO ◆Renaldo Benson — singer with The Four Tops, hits include "Reach Out I'll Be There"

RENATO ◆Renato Scarpa — actor who played Inspector Longhi in the Donald Sutherland film "Don't Look Now"

RENE ◆Rene Auberjonois — a foil for Benson on the TV series of the same name ◆ Rene Descartes — father of philosophy, said "I think, therefore I am" ◆ Rene La Salle — traveled Mississippi River, claimed it for France, named it Louisiana

RENI ◆Reni Santoni — played Hobbs in Kathleen Quinlan's "I Never Promised You a Rose Garden"

RENNIE ◆Rennie Davis — one of The Chicago Seven who disrupted the 1968 Democratic Convention

RENNY ◆Renny Harlin — director of "Die Hard 2" and "Cliffhanger"

RENZO ◆Renzo Rossellini — film composer, uncle of actress Isabella Rossellini

REUBEN ◆Reuben Kinkaid (c) — David Madden's role as the manager on the sitcom "The Partridge Family"

REUBIN ◆Reubin Askew — 1984 aspirant for the Democratic presidential nomination

REUEL ◆John Ronald Reuel Tolkien — author of "The Hobbit" and "The Lord of the Rings"

REX ◆Rex Harrison — British actor in the features "My Fair Lady" and "Doctor Dolittle" ◆Rex Humbard — TV evangelist on over 360 TV stations ◆Rex Ingram — silent film director of "The Prisoner of Zenda" and "Scaramouche" ◆Rex Reed — panelist on TV's bizarre talent search "The Gong Show" ◆Rex Smith — singer, hit single "You Take My Breath Away"

REYNOLDS ◆Reynolds Price — author whose best known work is "A Long and Happy Life"

RHETT ◆Rhett Butler (c) — Clark Gable's debonair character in "Gone With the Wind"

RHODES ◆Rhodes Reason — actor in the British TV series "White Hunter"

RHYS ◆Rhys Williams — actor in Joan Crawford's "Johnny Guitar"

RIAN ◆Rian Garrick — actor who played detective Bruce Janna on the police drama series "Manhunt"

RIC ◆Ric Ocasek — skinny rock star who married supermodel Paulina Porizkova ◆Ric Waite — Emmy winning cinematographer for "Captains and Kings"

RICARDO ◆Ricardo Montalban — "Fantasy Island" actor who is also an expert on corinthian leather

RICH ◆Rich Anderson — bass player with The Tubes ◆Rich Hall — comedian and star of TV's "The Rich Hall Show" ◆Rich Little — celebrity voice impersonator

RICHARD ◆Richard Chamberlain — king of the TV miniseries, including "Centennial" and "Shogun" ◆Richard Crenna — co-starred with Sylvester Stallone in the "Rambo" films ◆Richard Dreyfuss — "Close Encounters of the Third Kind," "Jaws," Oscar for "The Goodbye Girl" ◆ Richard Gere — actor who graduated from "American Gigolo" to "Pretty Woman" ◆ Richard Pryor — troubled comic actor in films "Stir Crazy," "Silver Streak," "The Toy" ◆ Richard Simmons — creator of the diet plan "Deal-a-Meal," exercise video "Sweatin' to the Oldies"

RICHIE ◆Richie Allen — controversial baseball infielder, Rookie of the Year, MVP

RICHMOND ◆Richmond Barthe — sculptor known for busts of African-American historical figures and celebrities ◆ Cade Richmond Carradine — son of actor Keith Carradine ◆Richmond Reed Carradine — real name of legendary actor John Carradine

RICK ◆Rick Astley — singer, hit singles "Never Gonna Give You Up" and "She Wants to Dance With Me" ◆ Rick James — funk star, platinum album "Street Songs," hit single "Superfreak" ◆ Rick Schroder — star of the sitcom "Silver Spoons," appeared in the miniseries "Lonesome Dove" ◆ Rick Springfield — star of soap "General Hospital," Grammy winning hit song "Jessie's Girl"

RICKEY ◆Rickey Henderson — outfielder who broke Lou Brock's major league record for stolen bases

RICKIE ◆Rickie Sorensen — actor whose roles included Tommy Banks on TV's "Father of the Bride"

RICKY ◆Ricky Nelson — rock singer son of Ozzie and Harriet, starred on their TV show ◆ Ricky Skaggs — Country Music Association's best male vocalist and newcomer for 1982

RICOU ◆Ricou Browning — stuntman who played the title role in "Creature From the Black Lagoon"

RIDDICK ◆Riddick Bowe — heavyweight champion of the world in 1992

RIDER ◆H. Rider Haggard — author of the often-filmed African adventure novel "King Solomon's Mines"

RIDGELY ◆Ridgely Torrence — award winning poet whose works include "Plays for a Negro Theatre"

RIDLEY ◆Ridley Scott — director of "Alien," "Blade Runner," and "Thelma and Louise"

RIF ◆Rif Hutton — actor whose roles included Dr. Welch on TV's "Doogie Howser, M.D."

RIFF ◆Riff West — member of the group Molly Hatchet, hit gold album "Beating the Odds"

RIK ◆Rik Elswit — member of Dr. Hook and the Medicine Show, gold record debut "Sylvia's Mother" ◆Rik Emmett — member of the rock group Triumph, debut hit single "Hold On"

RILEY ◆Riley Burnett — author of "High Sierra" which was filmed with Humphrey Bogart ◆ Riley B. King — real name of B. B. King ◆Riley Puckett — country music performer and singer

RING ◆Ring Lardner — author of satirical sketches whose works include "Treat 'Em Rough"

RINGGOLD ◆Ringgold Lardner, Jr. — Oscar winning screenwriter for "M*A*S*H"

RINGO ◆Ringo Starr — drum player of the quartet known as The Beatles

RINUS ◆Rinus Gerritsen — member of Golden Earring, debut hit single "Radar Love"

RIP ◆Rip Taylor — comedic actor who appeared in films like "Defending Your Life" ◆ Rip Torn — actor in "Sweet Bird of Youth," "Heartland," "Baby Doll"

RITCHIE ◆Ritchie Blackmore — co-founder of Deep Purple, hits include "Stone Cold" ◆ Ritchie Valens — teenage singer whose biopic was "La Bamba," also his greatest hit

RIVER ◆River Phoenix — Oscar nominee for "Running on Empty," died tragically young

ROALD ◆Roald Amundsen — first man to reach the South Pole, biopic "The Red Tent" ◆ Roald Dahl — author of "Willie Wonka and the Chocolate Factory," filmed by Gene Wilder

ROAME ◆Roame Lowry — member of the jazz-pop group Maze whose albums include "Joy and Pain"

ROARK ◆Roark Bradford — author and dramatist who wrote about blacks and the Bible

ROB ◆Rob Lowe — Brat Pack actor involved in sex scandal at the Democratic National Convention ◆ Rob Reiner — now a great film director, was the "meathead" on "All in the Family"

ROBB ◆Robb Armstrong — creator of the cartoon strip "Jump Start" ◆ Robb Royer — member of the rock group Bread, hits "If," "Diary," and "Make It With You" ◆Robb Weller — regular host on TV's "Entertainment Tonight"

ROBBY ◆Robby Benson — actor in "One on One," "Ice Castles," and "The Chosen"

ROBERT ◆Robert Carradine — actor whose credits include "The Big Red One" ◆ Robert De Niro — supreme actor in "The Godfather II," "Goodfellas," "Taxi Driver," and "Raging Bull" ◆ Robert Duvall — extraordinary performer in "The Godfather," "The Great Santini," "Lonesome Dove" ◆ Robert Mitchum — film actor, known for miniseries "The Winds of War" ◆ Robert Redford — actor in "Butch Cassidy and the Sundance Kid," "The Sting," "The Way We Were" ◆ Robert Wagner — TV's co-star of "Hart to Hart"

ROBERTO ◆Roberto Clemente — Puerto Rican baseball player who won three National League batting titles ◆ Roberto Contreras — actor who played ranch hand Pedro on the western TV series "The High Chaparral" ◆ Roberto Rossellini — Italian director who created a scandal over his affair with Ingrid Bergman

ROBIN ◆Robin Gibb — member of English group The Bee Gees, hits include "Saturday Night Fever" ◆ Robin Hood — nemesis of the Sheriff of Nottingham who lived in Sherwood Forest ◆ Robin Leach — nasal-voiced host of TV's "Lifestyles of the Rich and Famous" ◆ Christopher Robin Milne — original Christopher Robin in his father's "Winnie the Pooh" books ◆ Robin Williams — off-the-wall comedian in "Mork and Mindy," "Good Morning, Vietnam"

ROBINSON ◆Robinson Crusoe (c) — Daniel Defoe's hero castaway on a desert island ◆ Edward Robinson Squibb — founded the E.R. Squibb pharmaceutical firm

ROBYN ◆Robyn Hitchcock — founded punk-rock band Soft Boys, albums include "Globe of Frogs"

ROCCO ◆Rocco Barbella — real name of fighter Rocky Graziano ◆ Rocco Marchegiano — real name of Rocky Marciano

ROCHESTER ◆Rochester Anderson — gravel-voiced assistant to Jack Benny on radio and television

ROCK ◆Rock Hudson — dashing leading man in "Giant," "Pillow Talk," "Send Me No Flowers"

ROCKNE ◆Rockne O'Bannon — screenwriter of the futuristic science fiction cop movie "Alien Nation"

ROCKWELL ◆Rockwell Kent — artist noted for stark lithographs and exotic landscapes

ROCKY ◆Rocky Balboa (c) — Sylvester Stallone's prize-fighting underdog in "Rocky" and its sequels ◆ Rocky Graziano — boxed his way to the middleweight championship of the world ◆ Rocky Marciano — heavyweight champion of the world

ROD ◆Rod McKuen — singer, composed "Jean" for the "The Prime of Miss Jean Brodie" ◆Rod Serling — creator of TV's "The Twilight Zone" ◆ Rod Steiger — "On the Waterfront," "Dr. Zhivago," Oscar for "In the Heat of the Night" ◆Rod Stewart — Scottish rocker sings "Da Ya Think I'm Sexy?" ◆ Rod Taylor — best known as the hero of Hitchcock's "The Birds"

RODAN ◆Ahmet Emuukha Rodan Zappa — son of rock musician Frank Zappa

RODDY ◆Roddy McDowall — films range from "National Velvet" to "Planet of the Apes"

RODERICK ◆Sean Roderick Stewart — son of rock singer Rod Stewart and Alana Hamilton

RODNEY ◆Rodney Dangerfield — stand-up comedian with films like "Back to School" ◆ Rodney Allen Rippy — pint-sized child star of commercials for Jack-in-the Box

RODOLFO ◆Rodolfo Acosta — cold-eyed Mexican-American character actor, usually a villain or henchman ◆Rodolfo Gucci — with his brothers made Gucci a quality name in elegance in fashion ◆ Rodolfo Hoyos — actor whose roles included bandit leader Pancho Villa in "Villa!"

ROEBUCK ◆Roebuck Staples — member of The Staple Singers, debut hit "Why? (Am I Treated So Bad)"

ROGER ◆Roger Daltrey — singer, hit albums "The Kids Are Alright," "Who Are You?" ◆ Roger Moore — went from TV's "The Saint" to a number of James Bond films ◆Roger Mudd — television news commentator ◆ Roger Staubach — Heisman Trophy winner, Most Valuable Player in 1972 Super Bowl

ROGERS ◆George Rogers Clark — soldier and explorer who gained control of Illinois during the Revolution ◆Rogers Hornsby — infielder with highest lifetime batting average for a right-handed hitter ◆ Samuel Rogers Shepard IV — son of actor Sam Shepard and actress Jessica Lange

ROLAND ◆Joseph Roland Barbera — founder of Hanna/ Barbera, creator of "The Flintstones," "Huckleberry Hound" ◆ Roland Gift — lead singer for the rock group Fine Young

Cannibals ◆ Roland Young — played the 'ever so humble' Uriah Heep in the classic "David Copperfield"

ROLF ◆Rolf Benirschke — placekicker with San Diego who overcame disease to return to football ◆ Rolf Stiefel — actor whose roles included Nazi Fuhrer Adolf Hitler in "Battle of Britain"

ROLFE ◆Rolfe Sedan — actor whose films include Miriam Hopkins' "Trouble in Paradise"

ROLLA ◆Rolla Harger — invented the Drunkometer to test driver intoxication

ROLLIE ◆Rollie Fingers — relief pitcher who holds major league record for career saves ◆ Rollie McGill — hit the charts with the song "There Goes That Train" ◆ Rollie Totheroh — Chaplin's cinematographer, credits include "City Lights" and "The Great Dictator"

ROLLIN ◆Rollin Kirby — Pulitzer Prize winning political cartoonist ◆ Rollin Sullivan — original Oscar in the country music comedy team Lonzo and Oscar

ROLLO ◆Rollo Lloyd — actor whose roles included French conqueror Napoleon in "Anthony Adverse"

ROMAINE ◆Romaine Callender — actor in the Merle Oberon version of Emily Bronte's novel "Wuthering Heights"

ROMAN ◆Roman Bohnen — character actor usually found in honest-working-man parts ◆ Roman Gabriel — four-time all-pro quarterback, autobiography "Player of the Year" ◆ Roman Polanski — film director of "Chinatown"

ROMARE ◆Romare Bearden — painter and writer of African-American art history

ROME ◆Rome Johnson — one of country western's Brown's Ferry Four

ROMEO ◆Romeo Montague (c) — immortal star-crossed lover in Shakespeare's "Romeo and Juliet"

ROMER ◆Frank Romer Pierson — Oscar winning screenwriter for "Dog Day Afternoon"

ROMNEY ◆Romney Brent — collaborated with Cole Porter on the musical "Nymph Errant"

ROMO ◆Romo Vincent — emcee of the comedy variety series "You're Invited"

ROMULUS ◆John Romulus Brinkley — alleged charlatan doctor who rejuvenated men with goat gland transplants

RON ◆Ron Ely — looked good in a loincloth as TV's "Tarzan" ◆ Ron Howard — Opie on "Andy Griffith," Ritchie Cunningham on "Happy Days," film director ◆ L. Ron Hubbard — founder of the Church of Scientology, author of "Dianetics" ◆ Ron Kovic — Oscar winning Vietnam vet autobiography "Born on the Fourth of July" with Tom Cruise ◆ Ron Perlman — actor whose roles included Vincent on the TV series "Beauty and the Beast" ◆ Ron Silver — actor in "Reversal of Fortune," "Married to It"

RONALD ◆Ronald Colman — actor in films "Lost Horizon," "The Prisoner of Zenda," and "A Tale of Two Cities" ◆ Ronald McDonald (c) — clown used as the mascot for McDonald's hamburgers ◆ Ronald Reagan — only actor to become President of the United States

RONDO ◆Rondo Hatton — actor in Tyrone Power's story of the great fire "In Old Chicago"

RONI ◆Roni Stoneman — series regular on the long running hayseed variety show "Hee Haw"

RONN ◆Ronn Moss — member of the rock group Player, hit gold with the number one "Baby Come Back"

RONNIE ◆Ronnie Hawkins — rock singer, hits "Forty Days" and "Mary Lou" ◆Ronnie Milsap — blind country western singer, hits include "Too Late to Worry, Too Blue to Cry" ◆ Ronnie Van Zandt — singer

RONNY ◆Ronny Graham — composer whose film scores include "To Be or Not To Be" and "Finders Keepers"

ROONE ◆Roone Arledge — President of ABC Sports, introduced stop-action and split-screens to TV

ROOSEVELT ◆Roosevelt Grier — football player turned actor, author "Rosey Grier Needlepoint Book for Men" ◆ Jack Roosevelt Robinson — real name of baseball great Jackie Robinson

RORY ◆Rory Calhoun — western film actor in films "Ticket to Tomahawk," "Treasure of Pancho Villa" ◆ Rory O'Brien — actor whose roles included Danny Morley on TV's "The Farmer's Daughter"

ROSCO ◆Rosco Gordon — Memphis based singer and pianist, hits include "Just a Little Bit"

ROSCOE ◆Roscoe "Fatty" Arbuckle — fat-boy superstar whose career was ruined by the scandal of a murder trial ◆ Egbert Roscoe Murrow — real name of newscaster Edward R. Murrow

ROSEY ◆Rosey Grier — football player turned actor, author "Rosey Grier Needlepoint Book for Men"

ROSS ◆Ross Martin — actor who played the sidekick Artemus Gordon on TV's "Wild Wild West" ◆ Ross Trudeau — one of the twin sons of newscaster Jane Pauley and cartoonist Garry Trudeau

ROSSANO ◆Rossano Brazzi — actor whose films include "The Barefoot Contessa" and "South Pacific"

ROSWELL ◆Roswell Garst — advised Eastern Europe on US farm methods, author "No Need for Hunger" ◆Roswell Gilpatric — US deputy secretary of defense during the Vietnam buildup

ROUBEN ◆Rouben Mamoulian — director of "Dr. Jekyll and Mr. Hyde" and "The Mark of Zorro"

ROWAN ◆Rowan Atkinson — British comedian best known for the "Black Adder" and HBO's "Mr. Bean"

ROWE ◆Harold Rowe Holbrook, Jr. — real name of actor Hal Holbrook

ROWLAND ◆Rowland Brown — director acclaimed for "Quick Millions" ◆ Rowland Macy — founder of Macy's Department Store that runs annual Thanksgiving Day Parade

ROY ◆Roy Bean — 'law west of the Pecos,' biopic "The Life and Times of Judge Roy Bean" ◆Roy Clark — country western singer and host of TV's "Hee Haw" ◆ Roy Orbison — sang "Pretty Woman" and "Crying," always while wearing sun glasses ◆ Roy Rogers — singing cowboy hero, with Dale Evans, of innumerable westerns ◆ Roy Scheider — actor in "All That Jazz" and "Jaws"

ROYAL ◆Royal Bauer — author ◆Royal Dano — perennial guest star of television westerns

ROYCE ◆Royce Kendall — with daughter Jeannie, the country music group The Kendalls ◆Johnny Royce Mathis — singer with eight gold albums, hits include "Too Much Too Little Too Late" ◆ William Royce Scaggs — real name of Boz Scaggs

RUBE ◆Rube Goldberg — known for drawings of absurd mechanical "Rube Goldberg devices"

RUBEN ◆Ruben Blades — songwriter who revolutionized salsa music

RUBENS ◆Rubens Bassini — member of Sergio Mendes and Brasil '66, debut hit single "Mas Que Nada"

RUBY ◆Ruby Braff — jazz trumpet player

RUDD ◆Rudd Weatherwax — animal trainer for all seven Lassies in film and TV

RUDI ◆Rudi Maugeri — one of The Crew Cuts, debut single was "Crazy 'Bout You, Baby"

RUDOLF ◆Rudolf Nureyev — Russian ballet dancer whose roles included the lead in the film "Valentino"

RUDOLPH ◆Gerald Rudolph Ford — only US President who was appointed to the job ◆ Rudolph Valentino — debonair leading man of the twenties who starred in silent film "The Sheik"

RUDOLPHE ◆Rudolphe Peugeot — founder of the Peugeot automobile company

RUDY ◆Rudy Vallee — first great crooner of the twentieth century, "I'm Just a Vagabond Lover"

RUDYARD ◆Rudyard Kipling — poet of the British Raj, whose works included "Gunga Din"

RUFE ◆Rufe Davis — actor whose roles included Floyd Smoot on the rural sitcom "Petticoat Junction"

RUFUS ◆James Rufus Agee — won a Pulitzer for "A Death in the Family" ◆ Rufus McKahan — real name of actor Alan Hale

RUGGIERO ◆Ruggiero Boscovich — eighteenth century Italian mathematician and physicist ◆ Ruggiero Ricci — child prodigy violinist

RULON ◆Rulon Allred — Mormon religious leader who practices polygamy

RUMER ◆Rumer Godden — author whose novels adapted for film include "In This House of Brede"

RUPERT ◆Rupert Holmes — singer, number one single "Escape (The Pina Colada Song)" ◆ Rupert Murdoch — Australian publisher and owner of Twentieth Century-Fox

RUSH ◆Rush Limbaugh — conservative and controversial radio and TV talk show personality

RUSS ◆Russ Giguere — member of the pop-rock band The Association, hits "Cherish," "Never My Love" ◆Russ Tamblyn — Oscar nominee for "Peyton Place," starred in "West Side Story"

RUSSEL ◆Russel Simpson — actor whose roles included Hamlin in Edward G. Robinson's "Silver Dollar"

RUSSELL ◆Russell Johnson — actor who played The Professor on TV's classic sitcom "Gilligan's Island" ◆ Russell Stover — perfected the Eskimo Pie, founder of Russell Stover Candies

RUSTY ◆Rusty Hamer — actor whose roles included the son on TV's "The Danny Thomas Show" ◆Rusty Stevens — actor whose roles included Larry Mondello on the sitcom "Leave It to Beaver"

RUTGER ◆Rutger Hauer — performer in action films "The Hitcher" and "Blade Runner"

RUTHERFORD ◆Rutherford B. Hayes — post Civil War President of the US

RY ◆Ry Cooder — guitarist whose movie scores included "The Long Riders"

RYAN ◆Ryan O'Neal — said "Love is never having to say you're sorry" in the film "Love Story" ◆ Paul Ryan Rudd — actor on "Beacon Hill," "Beulah Land" and "Knots Landing"

RYNE ◆Ryne Duren — baseball player who led the American League in saves

SABIN ◆Sabin Carr — Olympic gold medal winner in pole vaulting

SABINE ◆Sabine Baring-Gould — clergyman who wrote "Onward Christian Soldiers"

SAGE ◆Sage Moonblood Stallone — Sylvester Stallone's son, who appeared as Rocky, Jr., in "Rocky V"

SAL ◆Sal Mineo — teenage actor in "Rebel Without a Cause," "Cheyenne Autumn" ◆ Sal Valentino — member of The Beau Brummels, debut hit "Laugh, Laugh" ◆Sal Viscuso — actor who played Father Timothy Flotsky on the controversial sitcom "Soap"

SALADIN ◆Saladin — legendary leader of the Saracens in their fight against the Crusaders

SALAH ◆Salah Zulficar — actor whose roles included King Richard the Lionheart in "Saladin"

SALEM ◆Salem Ludwig — actor in the Sean Connery/Dustin Hoffman film "Family Business" ◆ Salem Wales — nineteenth century editor of "Scientific American"

SALMAN ◆Salman Rushdie — author of "The Satanic Verses," sentenced to death by the Ayatollah Khomeini

SALMON ◆Salmon P. Chase — Supreme Court justice whose portrait is on the $10,000 bill

SALOMON ◆Salomon Andree — first to explore Arctic by balloon, his body and diary were later found ◆ Frederick Salomon Perls — founder of the Gestalt school of therapy

SALVADOR ◆Salvador Allende — Chilean president who brought in free elections ◆ Salvador Dali — Spanish surrealist painter influenced by Freud's psychoanalytic theories

SALVATORE ◆Salvatore Bono — "Sonny," hits include "I Got You Babe" recorded with then-wife Cher ◆ Salvatore Capezio — inventor of ballet slippers in 1887

SAM ◆Sam Bottoms — actor whose roles included the draft dodging kid in Eastwood's "Bronco Billy" ◆ Sam Waterston — dramatic actor nominated for an Oscar for "The Killing Fields"

SAMM ◆Samm Baker — wrote "The Complete Scarsdale Medical Diet"

SAMM-ART ◆Samm-Art Williams — actor whose roles included Maurice in the film "Blood Simple"

SAMMEE ◆Sammee Tong — actor whose roles included Sammy Ling on the Mickey Rooney sitcom "Mickey"

SAMMY ◆Sammy Cahn — won four Oscars for film songs, including "Three Coins in the Fountain" ◆ Sammy Davis, Jr. — sang "Mr. Bojangles" and "The Candy Man," member of Sinatra's Rat Pack

SAMSON ◆Samson — strongest man in the Bible who received his strength from his long hair ◆ Samson Raphaelson — screenwriter, wrote the play of "The Jazz Singer," later first talking picture

SAMUEL ◆Samuel Goldwyn — producer of quality films who lent his name to Metro-Goldwyn-Mayer studios ◆Samuel Maverick — founder of Texas, coined word "maverick" to mean unbranded wandering cattle ◆ Samuel Morse — inventor of Morse Code

SANDER ◆Sander Vanocur — anchorman on the TV news magazine "First Tuesday"

SANDOR ◆Sandor Stern — screenwriter of "Fast Break" and "The Amityville Horror"

SANDRO ◆Sandro Botticelli — fifteenth century Italian artist after whom the name game was named

SANDY ◆Sandy Koufax — Los Angeles Dodgers pitcher, youngest player in the Hall of Fame

SANFORD ◆Sanford Jensen — actor who played Assistant D. A. DeVries on the legal sitcom "Foley Square"

SANTIAGO ◆Santiago Ziesmer — actor who played the boy musical genius in "Mozart: A Childhood Chronicle"

SANTO ◆Santo — member of Santo and Johnny, hits include the number one gold record "Sleepwalk"

SANTOS ◆Santos Ortega — actor whose roles included Pa Hughes on the soap "As the World Turns"

SARGENT ◆John Sargent Pillsbury — founder of the Pillsbury flour company ◆ Sargent Shriver — brother-in-law of JFK, first director of the Peace Corps

SASHA ◆Sasha Mitchell — actor whose roles included James Richard Beaumont on TV's "Dallas"

SATCHEL ◆Satchel Allen — son of actor/director Woody Allen and actress Mia Farrow ◆ Satchel Paige — baseball player who said, "Don't look back . . . someone might be gaining on you"

SAUL ◆Saul Bass — revolutionized film credits by animating names, titles include "Vertigo" ◆Saul Bellow — Pulitzer Prize and Nobel Prize winning author, works include "Humboldt's Gift" ◆ Saul Chaplin — songwriter, scored films include "West Side Story"

SAUNDERS ◆Saunders Lewis — founder of the Welsh Nationalist Party

SAX ◆Sax Rohmer — British novelist who created Dr. Fu Manchu

SCATMAN ◆Scatman Crothers — actor who played Turkle in the Oscar winning "One Flew Over the Cuckoo's Nest"

SCHUYLER ◆Schuyler Colfax — Vice President of the United States under Grant ◆Schuyler Wheeler — inventor of the electric fan

SCOTT ◆Scott Baio — teenage heartthrob in TV's "Happy Days," and "Charles in Charge" ◆Scott Bakula — starred as Sam in the time-traveling series "Quantum Leap" ◆Scott Carpenter — one of the seven original astronauts, orbited earth in Mercury spacecraft ◆F. Scott Fitzgerald — novelist of the jazz age ◆Scott

Joplin — ragtime pianist-composer, hit "The Entertainer" soundtrack for "The Sting"

SCOTTIE ◆Scottie Pippen — forward with the Chicago Bulls

SCOTTY ◆Scotty Beckett — child actor who was a member of "Our Gang" ◆ Scotty Bowman — coach of Montreal Canadiens when they won four Stanley Cups

SEAMON ◆Seamon Glass — actor in the Burt Reynolds' hillbilly classic film "Deliverance"

SEAMUS ◆Peter Seamus O'Toole — became a star playing T. E. Lawrence in "Lawrence of Arabia"

SEAN ◆Sean Astin — 1990's teen heartthrob, films include "Encino Man" ◆ Sean Connery — original Bond, James Bond in feature films ◆ Sean Patrick Flanery — 1990's teen hunk, played teenage Indie on "The Young Indiana Jones Chronicles" ◆ Sean Penn — made his mark in goofy surfer role in "Fast Times at Ridgemont High"

SEARGEOH ◆Seargeoh Stallone — son of the first action hero Sylvester Stallone

SEBASTIAN ◆Sebastian Cabot — he played the overweight butler Mr. French on TV's "Family Affair" ◆ Sebastian Kresge — founder of S. S. Kresge's, which became K-Mart

SEBASTIANE ◆Sebastiane — Christian martyr in old Rome, biopic "Sebastiane"

SEBASTIAO ◆Sebastiao Neto — member of Sergio Mendes and Brasil '66, debut hit "Mas Que Nada"

SELDEN ◆Robert Selden Duvall — actor known for "The Great Santini" and the miniseries "Lonesome Dove" ◆ Selden Rodman — writer, known for poem "Lawrence: The Last Crusade" ◆ William Selden Todman — with Mark Goodson, created game shows "What's My Line?" and "Match Game"

SELMAN ◆Selman Waksman — Nobel Prize winner in medicine who coined the term "antibiotic"

SELMER ◆Selmer Jackson — actor who played US Navy Admiral Chester Nimitz in "Hellcats of the Navy"

SELWYN ◆Selwyn Lloyd — British foreign secretary during the Suez crisis ◆Selwyn Raab — reporter for the New York Times and NBC News

SENNIE ◆Sennie Martin III — member of the Jazz Band, Grammy winner for "Let It Whip"

SERGE ◆Serge Baudo — French conductor ◆ Yvan Serge Courneyor — Canadian hockey player nicknamed "The Roadrunner" ◆Serge Semenenko — financier with First National Bank of Boston that bought Warner Brothers

SERGEI ◆Sergei Aksakov — author who described life in his native nineteenth century Russia ◆ Sergei Eisenstein — Russian director of "Battleship Potemkin," "October," and "Alexander Nevsky"

SERGIO ◆Sergio Leone — Italian director of spaghetti westerns starring Clint Eastwood ◆ Sergio Mendes — member of Sergio Mendes and Brasil '66, debut hit "Mas Que Nada"

SESSUE ◆Sessue Hayakawa — actor who played Col. Saito in Alec Guinness' "The Bridge on the River Kwai"

SETH ◆Seth Thomas — founder of the Seth Thomas Clock company ◆ Seth Ward — real name of Jimmy Dean, country singer and sausage king

SETON ◆Seton Miller — Oscar nominated screenwriter for co-writing "The Criminal Code"

SEVE ◆Seve Ballesteros — youngest golfer, at 23, to win the Masters Tournament

SEWELL ◆Sewell Avery — retailer who served on the board of Montgomery Ward ◆ George Sewell Boutwell — politician

SEYMOUR ◆Seymour Hicks — actor whose roles included Dicken's favorite skinflint in "Scrooge" ◆ Arthur Seymour Sullivan — half of Gilbert and Sullivan, composed "Onward Christian Soldiers"

SHADOE ◆Shadoe Stevens — TV personality who frequently appears on "Hollywood Squares"

SHADRACH ◆Shadrach — in the Bible, one of Daniel's companions who survived the fiery furnace

SHAEMAS ◆Shaemas O'Sheel — best known for his poem "They Went Forth to Battle, But They Always Fell"

SHAHRAD ◆Shahrad Vossoughi — actor whose roles included Nick Massoud on TV's "Falcon Crest"

SHAKA ◆Shaka — founder of the Zulu empire, biopic "Shaka Zulu"

SHALOM ◆Shalom Aleichem — author of "Tevye" which was the basis for "Fiddler on the Roof"

SHANE ◆Shane (c) — Jack Schaefer's legendary gunfighter, played in the movies by Alan Ladd ◆ Shane Conrad — starred in the TV series "High Mountain Rangers" with his father Robert Conrad

SHAQUILLE ◆Shaquille O'Neal — 1993 National Basketball League Rookie of the Year

SHAUN ◆Shaun Cassidy — like his brother David, teenage idol and TV star of "The Hardy Boys"

SHAWN ◆Walter Shawn Browne — US grandmaster and champion chess player ◆ Shawn Thompson — actor who played Corny Collins in John Waters' homage to the 50's "Hairspray"

SHEA ◆Shea Farrell — actor who played Steve Lacey on the detective series "The Law and Harry McGraw"

SHEB ◆Sheb Wooley — played cavalry officer George Armstrong Custer in "Bugles in the Afternoon"

SHECKY ◆Shecky Greene — Las Vegas comedian, film credits include "Tony Rome"

SHEL ◆Shel Silverstein — cartoonist whose best sellers include "Where the Sidewalk Ends"

SHELBY ◆Shelby Foote — historian who appeared in the PBS hit miniseries "The Civil War" ◆ Shelby Steele — writer on African-American oppression

SHELDON ◆Sheldon Coleman — president of the Coleman sports equipment company, including Coleman lamps ◆ Sheldon Leonard — creator of TV's "The Dick Van Dyke Show"

SHELTON ◆Shelton Jackson Lee — real name of controversial filmmaker Spike Lee, director of "Malcolm X"

SHEMP ◆Shemp Howard — one of the The Three Stooges, took an early retirement

SHEP ◆Shep Fields — big band leader whose orchestra was noted for its distinctive bubbling sound

SHEPPERD ◆Shepperd Strudwick — actor whose roles included Jim Matthews on the soap "Another World"

SHERLOCK ◆Sherlock Holmes (c) — Conan Doyle's famous sleuth of 221-B Baker Street

SHERMAN ◆Sherman Hemsley — actor who played conniving George Jefferson of the TV series "The Jeffersons"

SHERRILL ◆Sherrill Milnes — Verdi baritone with the NY Metropolitan Opera

SHERWOOD ◆Sherwood Anderson — poet of small town life in America ◆ Sherwood Schwartz — creator of the classic castaway sitcom "Gilligan's Island"

SHIMON ◆Shimon Peres — prime minister of Israel ◆ Shimon Wincelberg — TV writer on "Gunsmoke," "Star Trek," and "Police Woman"

SHMUEL ◆Shmuel Ashkenasi — Israeli musician ◆ Shmuel Rodensky — portrayed Nazi-hunter Simon Wiesenthal in "The Odessa File"

SHOBAL ◆Shobal Clevenger — sculptor whose bust of Daniel Webster is on the fifteen cent stamp

SIB ◆Sib Hashian — member of the rock group Boston, their debut album sold 6.5 million copies

SID ◆Sid Caesar — his TV hits included "Your Show of Shows" and "The Sid Caesar Show" ◆ Sid Krofft — puppeteer, cartoon shows include "H.R. Pufnstuf" ◆Sid Vicious — lead singer of The Sex Pistols, biopic "Sid and Nancy"

SIDNEY ◆Sidney Greenstreet — "fat man" in "The Maltese Falcon" and "Casablanca" ◆ Sidney Lumet — director of "Fail Safe," "The Verdict," "12 Angry Men," and "Network" ◆ Sidney Poitier — distinguished actor in "Guess Who's Coming to Dinner," "They Call Me Mr. Tibbs!" ◆Sidney Sheldon — popular author, works include "The Other Side of Midnight"

SIEGFRIED ◆Siegfried Fischbacher — partner in Siegfried and Roy, world famous Las Vegas entertainers ◆ Siegfried Rauch — actor whose roles included World War II dogface Schroeder in "The Big Red One"

SIG ◆Sig Arno — German comedy actor from the early 30's typecast as a funny foreigner

SIGMUND ◆Sigmund Freud — invented the idea of psychoanalysis, creating a whole new industry of "shrinks" ◆ Sigmund Esco Jackson — oldest of The Jackson Five, nickname "Jackie" ◆ Raul Sigmund Julia — son of actor Raul Julia ◆ Sigmund Romberg — Hungarian-born composer of light operas and Broadway shows

SIL ◆Sil Austin — artist who landed on the charts with the hit song "Slow Walk"

SILAS ◆John Silas Reed — author, political activist, portrayed in Warren Beatty biopic "Reds"

SILVANO ◆Silvano Arieti — psychoanalyst who believed depression could be treated without drugs

SILVIO ◆Silvio Narizzano — Canadian film director in Britain, films include Redgrave's "Georgy Girl"

SIM ◆Sim Iness — Olympic gold medal discus athlete

SIME ◆Sime Silverman — founder of the show business newspaper "Variety"

SIMEON ◆Simeon Bellison — first clarinetist with NY Philharmonic who recorded Hebrew songs

SIMMS ◆E. Simms Campbell — first African-American artist to work for a national publication, "Esquire"

SIMON ◆Simon Farber — created silver- and nickel-plated Farberware ◆Simon Wiesenthal — famed Nazi hunter, portrayed in "The Odessa File" and "The Boys from Brazil"

SINBAD ◆Sinbad — standup comic who portrayed Walter Oakes on TV's "A Different World"

SINCLAIR ◆Samm Sinclair Baker — wrote "The Complete Scarsdale Medical Diet" ◆ Sinclair Lewis — author of filmed novels "Babbitt" and "Elmer Gantry"

SINGLETON ◆John Singleton Copley — greatest American old master, painted portraits of persons like Paul Revere ◆ John Singleton Mosby — leader of Confederate "Mosby's Rangers," bio TV series "The Gray Ghost"

SIXTUS ◆Edmund Sixtus Muskie — secretary of state under Carter

SKEETER ◆Skeeter Willis — one of country music's Willis Brothers, hits include "Drive My Blues Away"

SKIP ◆Skip Battin — member of The Byrds, hits "Mr. Tambourine Man," "Turn! Turn! Turn!" ◆ Skip Stephenson — comedian and co-host of the TV series "Real People" ◆Skip Ward — actor whose roles included Joe Caldwell on the sitcom "The Gertrude Berg Show"

SLADE ◆Slade Gorton — Republican senator from Washington elected in 1981

SLAPPY ◆Slappy White — comedian whose films include "Amazing Grace"

SLASH ◆Slash — member of Guns 'n' Roses, hits include platinum "Appetite for Destruction"

SLIM ◆Slim Pickens — actor whose roles included the B-52 plane commander in "Dr. Strangelove" ◆ Slim Whitman — country western singer, hits include "Beautiful Dreamer"

SLOAN ◆Sloan Hayes — member of Starbuck, debut hit single "Moonlight Feels Right" ◆Sloan Wilson — author, "The Man in the Gray Flannel Suit," filmed with Gregory Peck

SLY ◆Sly Stone — leader of Sly and the Family Stone, hits include "Dance to the Music"

SMILEY ◆Smiley Burnette — Gene Autry's sidekick in 81 films ◆ Smiley Lewis — hit the charts with his song "I Hear You Knocking"

SMITH ◆Gen. George Smith Patton — World War II tank commander, George C. Scott Oscar winning biopic "Patton"

SMOKEY ◆Smokey Robinson — leader of the Motown group The Miracles, hits include "I Second That Emotion"

SMOKY ◆Smoky Burgess — baseball catcher who set a record with 145 pinch hits

SNITZ ◆Snitz Edwards — portrayed Douglas Fairbanks' evil associate in "The Thief of Bagdad"

SNOOKY ◆Snooky Lanson — star of TV's "Your Hit Parade"

SOCRATES ◆Socrates — ancient Greek who viewed philosophy as a necessary pursuit for all men ◆ Aristotle Socrates Onassis — Greek shipping tycoon who married Jackie Kennedy

SOD ◆Sod Voccaro — member of The Four Aces, whose hits include the gold record "Sin"

SOL ◆Sol Taishoff — founder of "Broadcasting" magazine

SOLOMON ◆Solomon — in the Bible, King David's son who became king and built the first Temple

SOLON ◆Solon Borglum — sculptor known for horses, cowboys, and Indians

SOLVEIG ◆Solveig Russell — author of informational children's books whose works include "Johnny Appleseed"

SOMERSET ◆Somerset Maugham — twentieth century English writer, biopic "The Razor's Edge"

SONNY ◆Sonny Bono — male half of "Sonny and Cher" whose hits include "I Got You Babe" ◆ Sonny James — Southern Gentleman, hits include "Young Love" ◆ Sonny Liston — world heavyweight champion defeated by Muhammad Ali

SORRELL ◆Sorrell Booke — actor whose roles included character "Boss" Hogg on TV's "The Dukes of Hazzard"

SOUPY ◆Soupy Sales — known for his pie throwing act on his own "Soupy Sales" TV show

SPADE ◆Spade Cooley — country western big band leader and TV personality

SPALDING ◆Spalding Gray — actor whose roles included Dr. Milstein in Bette Midler's "Beaches"

SPANGLER ◆Spangler Arlington Brugh — real name of actor Robert Taylor

SPANKY ◆Spanky McFarland — fat boy in the "Our Gang" shorts of the 1930's

SPARKY ◆Sparky Anderson — manager of the Cincinnati Reds and Detroit Tigers ◆Sparky Marcus — actor whose roles included Skeeter on the sitcom "Goodtime Girls"

SPENCER ◆Spencer Davis — leader of The Spencer Davis Group, hits include "Gimmie Some Lovin' " ◆ Spencer Tracy — double Oscar winning actor of "Boys Town" and "Captains Courageous"

SPIKE ◆Spike Jones — leader of the City Slickers band, noted for lampooning popular songs ◆Spike Lee — outspoken film director of "Malcolm X" and "Jungle Fever" ◆Spike Milligan — starred in TV's "The Goon Show" with Peter Sellers

SPIRO ◆Spiro T. Agnew — only US Vice President to resign from office

SPIROS ◆Spiros Focas — portrayed Omar in Michael Douglas action sequel "The Jewel of the Nile"

SPOTTISWOODE ◆Spottiswoode Aitken — actor who played the role of Rudolph Valentino's father in "The Eagle"

SPRAGUE ◆Sprague Cleghorn — Canadian hockey player inducted into Hall of Fame in 1958 ◆ L. Sprague DeCamp — author of "Conan" books based on character created by Robert E. Howard

SPYROS ◆Spyros Skouras — president of Twentieth Century-Fox who developed CinemaScope

ST. CLAIR ◆St. Clair Lee — member of The Hues Corporation, hits include "Rock the Boat"

STAATS ◆Staats Cotsworth — actor whose roles included Dr. George Mitchell on the soap "The Doctors"

STACEY ◆William Stacey Burr — real name of big-boned actor Raymond Burr

STACY ◆Stacy Keach, Jr. — TV's detective "Mike Hammer" ◆ Stacy Keach, Sr. — actor whose roles included Clarence Birdseye on TV commercials

STAFFORD ◆Conrad Stafford Bain — played father Philip Drummond on Gary Coleman's show "Diff'rent Strokes" ◆ Stafford Repp — actor whose roles included Chief O'Hara on the TV version of "Batman"

STAN ◆Stan Ivar — actor who played John Carter on the drama series "Little House on the Prairie" ◆ Stan Laurel — thin half of the comedy team of Laurel and Hardy ◆ Stan Lee — legendary comic book writer, co-creator of "Spiderman"

STANFORD ◆Georg Stanford Brown — played the lead of Officer Terry Webster on the drama series "The Rookies" ◆ Stanford White — architect killed by Harry K. Thaw, biopic "The Girl in the Red Velvet Swing"

STANISLAW ◆Major General Stanislaw Sosobowski — Gene Hackman brought this WW II Polish hero to life in "A Bridge Too Far"

STANLEY ◆Stanley Baker — Welsh actor whose films include "The Guns of Navarone" ◆ Stanley Kramer — director, whose 15 Oscar winning films include "High Noon"

STANSFIELD ◆Stansfield Turner — former director of the Central Intelligence Agency

STANTON ◆Stanton Delaplane — Pulitzer Prize winning reporter

STARK ♦Stark Young — author whose best known work is "So Red the Rose"

STARR ♦Fleetwood Starr Robbins — son of author Tom Robbins

STEDE ♦Stede Bonnet — eighteenth century English pirate

STEELE ♦Steele Commager — author best known for works about the classics

STEFAN ♦Stefan Gierasch — actor whose roles included the preacher in Paul Newman's "The Hustler" ♦ Stefan Sileanu — actor who played the bloody Count in the Rumanian "The True Life of Dracula"

STEFANO ♦Stefano Casiraghi — second husband of Princess Caroline of Monaco, killed in a boating accident

STEFEN ♦Stefen Arngrim — played Barry Lockridge on the science fiction series "Land of the Giants"

STEPHAN ♦Stephan Burns — actor who played Deputy Brett Cueva on the adventure series "240-Robert" ♦ Richard Stephan Dreyfuss — "Jaws," "Close Encounters of the Third Kind," Oscar for "The Goodbye Girl"

STEPHANUS ♦Stephanus Van Cortlandt — first American born mayor of New York City

STEPHEN ♦Stephen Austin — colonizer who founded Austin, Texas ♦ Stephen J. Cannell — creator of TV's "The Rockford Files" and "The A-Team" ♦ Stephen King — horror novelist whose books include "Misery," "Pet Sematary," and "Carrie" ♦ Stephen Stills — member of rock group Buffalo Springfield, then Crosby, Stills, Nash, and Young

STERLING ♦Sterling Hayden — played General Jack D. Ripper in the end-of-the-world comedy "Dr. Strangelove" ♦ Sterling Macer, Jr. — actor who played Cpl. Robert Davis on the post WW II era drama series "Homefront"

STEUART ♦Steuart Britt — author of over 200 articles on marketing, wrote "The Spenders"

STEVAN ♦Stevan Dohanos — inducted into Society of Illustrators Hall of Fame

STEVE ♦Steve Allen — TV comedian, early host of "The Tonight Show" ♦Steve Lawrence — singer who has won seven Emmys for TV specials with his wife Eydie Gorme ♦ Steve Martin — a wild and crazy comedy actor in "The Lonely Guy," "The Jerk," and

"Roxanne" ◆ Steve McQueen — action hero in "Bullitt," "The Magnificent Seven," "Nevada Smith," and "The Sand Pebbles"

STEVELAND ◆Steveland Judkins — real name of music superstar Stevie Wonder

STEVEN ◆Steven Biko — killed fighting apartheid in South Africa, biopic "Cry Freedom" ◆ Steven Ford — son of President Ford, starred on the soap "The Young and the Restless" ◆ Steven Seagal — action hero in films like "Above the Law" ◆ Steven Spielberg — director of "E.T. The Extra-Terrestrial," "Jurassic Park"

STEVIE ◆Stevie Winwood — member of the group Blind Faith, hit "Can't Find My Way Home" ◆Stevie Wonder — composer and performer whose songs include "I Just Called to Say I Love You"

STEWART ◆Stewart Copeland — writer of hits for The Police ◆ Stewart Granger — actor in "Wild Geese," "Scaramouche," and "The Prisoner of Zenda" ◆ Charles Stewart Rolls — founder of the Rolls-Royce car company

STIG ◆Stig Jarrel — actor whose roles included the Devil in Bergman's "The Devil's Eye"

STING ◆Sting — English rock star, originally with The Police

STIRLING ◆Stirling Moss — six-time Grand Prix winner ◆ Stirling Silliphant — Oscar winning screenwriter for "In the Heat of the Night" ◆Harold Stirling Vanderbilt — inventor of contract bridge

STIX ◆Stix Hooper — member of The Crusaders, hit single "Uptight, Everything's Alright"

STODDARD ◆Richard Stoddard Aldrich — Broadway producer of "Pygmalion," "The Moon Is Blue" ◆Marriner Stoddard Eccles — chairman of the Federal Reserve Board

STOKELY ◆Stokely Carmichael — responsible for the 1960's concept of Black Power

STOKER ◆Stoker Lashly — polar explorer depicted in the biopic "Scott of the Antarctic"

STONEWALL ◆Stonewall Jackson — Confederate general during the Civil War ◆ Stonewall Jackson — country music singer and descendant of the Confederate general

STONEY ◆Stoney Edwards — African-American country music star ◆ Stoney Jackson — actor whose roles included Travis Filmore on the Marla Gibbs hit sitcom "227"

STORMIE ◆Stormie Jones — world's first combined heart/liver transplant at age six, died age thirteen

STRATTEN ◆Stratten Jack Roeg — son of actress Theresa Russell and director Nicholas Roeg

STRINGER ◆Stringer Davis — gentle-mannered British actor found in the films of his wife Margaret Rutherford

STRINGFELLOW ◆Stringfellow Barr — president of St. John's College who started the great books curriculum

STROM ◆Strom Thurmond — senator from South Carolina in favor of segregation

STROTHER ◆Strother Martin — famous for "What we have here is a failure to communicate" from "Cool Hand Luke"

STRYKER ◆William Stryker Gummere — created the rules and organized the first football game

STU ◆Stu Erwin — actor who played himself on the long running sitcom "The Stu Erwin Show" ◆Stu Gilliam — actor who played Charlie Adams on the family drama series "Harris and Company"

STUART ◆Stuart Margolin — actor whose roles included Angel on James Garner's series "The Rockford Files" ◆Stuart Pankin — fat comic actor whose roles included Jace Sampson on TV's "Falcon Crest" ◆ Stuart Whitman — actor in "The Comancheros," "Rio Conchos"

STUBBY ◆Stubby Kaye — played Nicely-Nicely Johnson in the Marlon Brando musical "Guys and Dolls"

STYMIE ◆Stymie Beard — actor in Bette Davis' Academy award winning "Jezebel"

SUE ◆Sue (c) — Johnny Cash proved in his hit song that you could have "A Boy Named Sue"

SUMNER ◆Sumner Crosby — author of books on medieval art and architecture ◆ Sumner Redstone — inventor of the multiplex movie theater, owner of MTV

SUTTON ◆Sutton Vane — author whose novels include "Outward Bound"

SVEN ◆Sven Nykvist — Ingmar Bergman's cinematographer whose films include "Sawdust and Tinsel"

SWAIN ◆Swain Scharfer — member of the blue-eyed soul band The Box Tops, hits include "The Letter"

SWEENEY ◆Sweeney Todd — demon barber who cut the throats of customers, musical "Sweeney Todd"

SY ◆Sy Bartlett — screenwriter whose credits include "12 O'Clock High"

SYD ◆Syd Barrett — founder of rock group Pink Floyd ◆ Syd Field — screenwriting teacher and author of the book "Screenplay"

SYDNEY ◆Sydney Chaplin — actor and manager of his half-brother Charlie Chaplin ◆Sydney Pollack — director of "Absence of Malice" and "Tootsie"

SYLVAN ◆Sylvan Barnet — author and educator ◆ Sylvan Goldman — inventor of the grocery cart

SYLVANUS ◆General Sylvanus Thayer — father of the military academy at West Point

SYLVESTER ◆Sylvester Graham — inventor of the graham cracker ◆Sylvester Stallone — action hero of "Rocky," "Rambo," and "Demolition Man"

SYLVIO ◆Sylvio Mantha — Hockey Hall of Fame defenseman with Montreal

TAB ◆Tab Hunter — heartthrob from the 50's, actor in "Damn Yankees," "Ride the Wild Surf"

TAD ◆Tad Mosel — Pulitzer Prize winning author for "All the Way Home"

TADEUS ◆Tadeus Reichstein — Nobel Prize winner who was the first to synthesize Vitamin C

TADEWURZ ◆Tadewurz Wladziu Konopka — real name of "The Mary Tyler Moore Show's" Ted Knight

TAGE ◆Tage Aurell — Swedish author whose works include "Skilling Tryck"

TAIDJE ◆Taidje Khan — real name of actor Yul Brynner

TAJ ◆Taj Johnson — actor who played Frank Lemmer on the hit sitcom "Parker Lewis Can't Lose" ◆ Taj Mahal — actor whose roles included Ike in Cicely Tyson's "Sounder"

TALBOT ◆Talbot Hamlin — Pulitzer Prize winner for biography "Benjamin Henry Latrobe" ◆ Talbot Jennings — screenwriter of "The Good Earth" and "Mutiny on the Bounty"

TALIAFERRO ◆John Taliaferro Thompson — inventor of the "Tommy gun" which was named after him ◆ Booker Taliaferro Washington — founder of the Tuskegee Institute

TAMMANY ◆Tammany Young — actor whose roles included Chuck Connors in Mae West's "She Done Him Wrong"

TARAN ◆Taran Smith — played the youngest son Mark Taylor on the tool sitcom "Home Improvement"

TARAS ◆Taras Genet — youngest person, at age 12, to climb Mt. McKinley

TARRY ◆Tarry Green — actor whose roles included Joey Roberts on the soap "The Guiding Light"

TARZAN ◆Tarzan (c) — Edgar Rice Burroughs' English nobleman raised in the jungle by apes ◆ Tarzan Brown — track athlete

TATE ◆Tate Donovan — actor whose roles included Donald Towle in Michael Keaton's "Clean and Sober"

TAUREAN ◆Taurean Blacque — actor whose roles included Neal Washington on TV's "Hill Street Blues"

TAY ◆Tay Garnett — director of the film "The Postman Always Rings Twice"

TAYLOR ◆Phineas Taylor Barnum — creator of "The Greatest Show on Earth" ◆ Taylor Levi Estevez — son of actor Emilio Estevez ◆ Taylor Hackford — director of "An Officer and a Gentleman" ◆Jonathan Taylor Thomas — played the middle son Randy Taylor on the tool sitcom "Home Improvement"

TECUMSEH ◆Tecumseh — Shawnee Indian chief who tried to unite the tribes against westward expansion ◆ William Tecumseh Sherman — Union general who marched from Atlanta to the sea, said "War is hell"

TED ◆Ted Danson — actor whose roles included bar owner Sam Malone on TV's "Cheers" ◆Ted Healy — actor in "Reckless" and "Hollywood Hotel" ◆ Ted Koppel — anchor of ABC News' "Nightline" ◆ Ted Mack — creator and host of "Ted Mack's Original Amateur Hour" ◆Ted Turner — founder of the CNN and TNT cable networks

TEDDY ◆Teddy Gentry — member of country western band Alabama, hits include "The Closer You Get" ◆Teddy Pendergrass — rock singer, hits include "Wake Up Everybody" and "Bad Luck" ◆Teddy Roosevelt — his command of the Rough Riders at San Juan Hill led to the Presidency

TELLY ◆Telly Savalas — gained his greatest fame as the lollipop-loving detective "Kojak"

TEMPLE ◆Temple Fielding — producer of "Fielding's Travel Guide to Europe"

TENEN ◆Tenen Holtz — portrayed Jesse Watson in Jack Pickford's "Exit Smiling"

TENNESSEE ◆Tennessee Ernie Ford — country western singer, best known for "Sixteen Tons" ◆Tennessee Williams — playwright of "A Streetcar Named Desire," "Cat on a Hot Tin Roof"

TEO ◆Teo Tabi — first rookie auto racer in 34 years to win a pole position at the Indy 500

TERENCE ◆Terence Rattigan — British playwright, films include "Goodbye, Mr. Chips," "The Yellow Rolls-Royce" ◆ Terence Stamp — actor whose roles included General Zod in the first "Superman" movie ◆ Terence Young — director of James Bond films "Dr. No," "From Russia With Love," and "Thunderball"

TERRELL ◆Guy Terrell Bush — Mississippi Mudcat, pitcher who gave up Babe Ruth's last home run ◆ Zack Terrell Mosley — creator of the syndicated cartoon "Smilin' Jack" ◆Terrell Woods — with B.T. Express, debut gold record single "Do It ('Till You're Satisfied)"

TERRY ◆Terry Bradshaw — quarterback who led Pittsburgh Steelers to four Super Bowl victories ◆ Terry Fox — athlete who lost his leg to cancer, Robert Duvall biopic "The Terry Fox Story" ◆ Terry Jones — directed "Monty Python's Life of Brian"

TETSU ◆Tetsu Kamauchi — member of the rock group Free, hits include "All Right Now" and "Free"

TEVIN ◆Tevin Campbell — rhythm and blues singer, hits include "Tomorrow (A Better You, Better Me)"

TEX ◆Tex Avery — cartoonist who created Daffy Duck and Bugs Bunny ◆ Tex Ritter — old time hero of film westerns who begat John Ritter ◆ Tex Williams — country western singer, best selling hit single "Smoke! Smoke! Smoke!"

TEXAS ◆T. Texas Tyler — country western singer, wrote "Deck of Cards"

THAAO ◆Thaao Penghis — actor in William Hurt's "Altered States" and on the soap "General Hospital"

THADDEUS ◆Thaddeus Kosciuszko — fought in the American army during the Revolution, namesake of a highway in New Jersey ◆ Thaddeus Stevens — abolitionist who sponsored the Fourteenth Amendment

THALMUS ◆Thalmus Rasulala — actor whose roles included Capt. Boltz on the syndicated revival of "Dragnet"

THAYER ◆Thayer David — actor whose roles included Mordecai Grimes on the vampire soap "Dark Shadows" ◆ Alfred Thayer Mahan — influential naval historian, author of "Influence of Sea Power Upon History"

THELONIOUS ◆Thelonious Monk, Jr. — jazz pianist who invented "bop"

THEO ◆Theo Kojak (c) — Telly Savalas' "Who loves you, baby" role on the drama series "Kojak"

THEOBALD ◆Theobald Smith — pathologist who specialized in infectious diseases in animals ◆ Theobald Tone — founder of the United Irishmen

THEODOPHOLOUS ◆Theodopholous Stiffel — founder of TA Stiffel Company, producers of high quality brass lamps

THEODOR ◆Theodor Seuss Geisel — real name of rhyming children's book author Dr. Seuss ◆ Theodor Herzl — father of modern Zionism who advocated settlement in Palestine

THEODORE ◆Theodore Roosevelt — President famous for his "rough ride" up San Juan Hill

THEONI ◆Theoni Aldredge — designer with Tonys for "Annie," "La Cage Aux Folles," Oscar for "Great Gatsby"

THEOPHILE ◆Zenobe Theophile Gramme — invented the Gramme dynamo electrical generator

THEOPHILUS ◆Theophilus Eaton — co-founder with the Rev. John Davenport of the New Haven colony

THERON ◆Paul Theron Silas — forward with six NBA teams, won three NBA championships, coach for San Diego

THIERRY ◆Thierry Hermes — fashion designer who specialized in luggage, handbags, and jewelry

THOM ◆Thom Bell — classically trained soul singer, hits include "Ain't Nothin' But a House-Party" ◆ Thom Bray — played computer nerd Murray Bozinsky on the detective drama series "Riptide" ◆ Thom Sharp — actor whose roles included Dave Poole on TV's "First Impressions"

THOMAS ◆Thomas Carvel — founded the Carvel ice cream company ◆ Thomas Jefferson — President who wrote the Declaration of Independence ◆ Thomas Nast — political cartoonist whose style created the term "nasty" ◆Thomas Sopwith — designer of the Sopwith Camel, airplane used in WW I and by Snoopy in "Peanuts" ◆ Thomas Welch — prohibitionist who developed an unfermented wine, Welch's Grape Juice

THOR ◆Thor Fields — actor whose roles included Erich Aldrich on the soap "The Doctors" ◆ Thor Heyerdahl — author and explorer who sailed across the Pacific, wrote "Kon-Tiki"

THORLEY ◆Thorley Walters — actor, roles include Dr. Watson in "Sherlock Holmes and the Deadly Necklace"

THORNE ◆Thorne Smith — humorous novelist whose filmed works include the ghost story "Topper"

THORNTON ◆Thornton Wilder — author who won three Pulitzer Prizes, including "The Bridge of San Luis Rey"

THOROLD ◆Thorold Dickinson — British director whose credits include "Gaslight"

THORSTEIN ◆Thorstein Veblen — economist, divided society into classes in his "The Theory of the Leisure Class"

THURGOOD ◆Thurgood Marshall — first African-American Supreme Court justice

THURLOW ◆Thurlow Weed — influential nineteenth century newspaper owner

THURMAN ◆Thurman Wesley Arnold — well-known lawyer ◆ Thurman Thomas — running back for the Buffalo Bills football team in the 1990's ◆Thurman "Teddy" Wilburn — country music performer with his brother Doyle as The Wilburn Brothers

THURSTON ◆Thurston Harris — hit the charts with the song "Do What You Did" ◆Thurston Howell III (c) — Jim Backus as the very, very rich castaway on TV's "Gilligan's Island"

TIBERIUS ◆James Tiberius Kirk (c) — Captain of the Enterprise on TV's "Star Trek"

TICO ◆Tico Torres — member of the group Bon Jovi, debut hit single "Runaway"

TIGE ◆Tige Andrews — actor whose roles include Capt. Adam Greer on TV's "The Mod Squad"

TIGER ◆Tiger Haynes — pianist and singer, very popular cabaret performer in the 1950's and 1960's

TIKI ◆Tiki Fulwood — member of the dance band Funkadelic, hits include "Knee Deep"

TIM ◆Tiny Tim — falsetto singer, hit "Tiptoe Through the Tulips," married on Johnny Carson's TV show ◆Tim Allen — king of power tools, and the star of ABC's superhit "Home Improvement" ◆ Tim Burton — director of "Batman" and "Beetlejuice" ◆Tim Conway — portrayed Ensign Palmer on TV's "McHale's Navy," created "Dorf" ◆ Tim Holt — actor, best known for Bogart's "Treasure of the Sierra Madre" ◆ Tim Matheson — starred in the comedy film classic "Animal House"

TIMMIE ◆Timmie Rogers — hit the charts with the song "Back to School Again"

TIMOTHY ◆Timothy Bottoms — actor whose credits include "The Last Picture Show" and "Paper Chase" ◆Timothy Dalton — another in the line of actors who identify themselves as "Bond, James Bond" ◆Timothy Daly — stars as conservative brother on TV's "Wings," films include "Diner" ◆Timothy Leary — advocate of LSD, recorded "Give Peace a Chance" with John Lennon

TINY ◆Tiny Stowe — actor whose roles included the Sheriff of Nottingham in "Tales of Robin Hood"

TIP ◆Tip O'Neil — Democratic speaker of the house

TIRAN ◆Tiran Porter — with The Doobie Brothers, hit albums "Minute by Minute" and "One Step Closer"

TITIAN ◆Titian — Renaissance artist, works include "Assumption of the Virgin" ◆ Titian Peale — artist with the first expedition to climb Pike's Peak

TITO ◆Tito Jackson — member of "The Jackson Five" brotherly musical group

TITOS ◆Titos Vandis — actor who played Angelo Luigi Perino in Laurence Olivier's "The Betsy"

TITUS ◆Titus — in the Bible, Paul's Greek assistant and companion

TOBIAS ◆Tobias Owen — NASA physicist involved with the "Voyager" probe ◆ Tobias Smollett — author of the novels "Roderick Random" and "Humphrey Clinker"

TOD ◆Tod Andrews — portrayed Confederate hero Major Mosby on the adventure series "The Gray Ghost"

TODD ◆Todd Bridges — actor who played Willis Jackson on TV's "Diff'rent Strokes," later went to jail ◆ Todd Rundgren — rock singer, hit debut single "We Gotta Get You a Woman"

TODHUNTER ◆Rex Todhunter Stout — creator of the fictional detective Nero Wolfe

TOLBERT ◆Tolbert Lanston — inventor of the typesetting machine

TOLLER ◆Toller Cranston — Olympic medal winning innovative figure skater

TOM ◆Tom Arnold — he married comedienne Roseanne Barr and turned her into Roseanne Arnold ◆ Tom Clancy — hot author, first filmed work "The Hunt For Red October" ◆ Tom Cruise — box office draw in films like "Risky Business" and "Top Gun" ◆ Tom Hanks — actor who rose from TV's "Bosom Buddies" to the feature film "Big" ◆ Tom Selleck — actor who played Hawaiian based, Ferrari-driving Thomas Magnum of "Magnum, P.I."

TOMAS ◆Tomas Milian — actor whose roles included Menocal in Robert Redford's "Havana"

TOMMASO ◆Tommaso Albinoni — Italian composer and violinist

TOMMIE ◆Tommie Smith — Olympic gold medalist who raised a clenched fist to protest racism in the US

TOMMY ◆Tommy Lee Jones — compelling actor in "Coal Miner's Daughter," "JFK" and "The Fugitive" ◆ Tommy Lasorda — baseball manager and Ultra Slim-Fast advocate ◆ Tommy Roe — singer, hit singles "Sheila," "Sweet Pea," and "Dizzy" ◆ Tommy Sands — first husband of Nancy Sinatra, hits include "Teenage Crush" ◆ Tommy Tune — only person to win nine Tonys in four different categories

TOMPALL ◆Tompall Glaser — country western singer, hits include "Charlie," was in The Glaser Brothers

TOMPKINS ◆Tompkins Matteson — artist of American history whose most famous work is "The Spirit of '76"

TONEY ◆Toney Anaya — first Hispanic governor in the United States

TONINO ◆Tonino Baliardo — member of the flamenco band Gipsy Kings, fifteen gold and platinum records

TONY ◆Tony Curtis — actor in "The Great Race," "Some Like It Hot," and "Spartacus" ◆Tony Danza — actor who played a cabbie on TV's "Taxi," then star of "Who's the Boss" ◆ Tony Dow — actor who played Wally Cleaver, the big brother in TV's "Leave It to Beaver" ◆Tony Orlando — Tony in the 1970's rock group "Tony Orlando and Dawn" ◆ Tony Randall — actor who played the neatnik, allergy-prone Felix Unger on TV's "The Odd Couple"

TOOLSIE ◆Toolsie Persaud — actor whose roles included the mummified Egyptian in "The Mummy's Shroud"

TOOTS ◆Toots Shor — owner of New York City watering holes for celebrities

TOPO ◆Topo Swope — child of actress Dorothy McGuire

TOPOL ◆Topol — actor whose roles included the famed Italian astronomer in "Galileo"

TOPPER ◆Topper Headon — member of The Clash, 1982 hit album "Combat Rock"

TORBEN ◆Torben Meyer — actor whose films include "Judgment at Nuremberg"

TORIANO ◆Toriano Jackson — nickname "Tito," with The Jackson Five, hits include number one single "ABC"

TORIN ◆Torin Thatcher — played notorious Welsh buccaneer Sir Henry Morgan in "Blackbeard the Pirate"

TORO ◆Toro Iwatani — inventor of the video game "Pac-Man"

TORSTEN ◆Torsten Ralf — tenor at the NY Metropolitan Opera noted for Wagner and Verdi ◆ Torsten Wiesel — Nobel Prize winning scientist for vision research

TORY ◆Tory Tyler — portrayed Terrence Johann Taylor on TV's "A Different World"

TOSHIRO ◆Toshiro Mifune — actor whose roles included a Japanese Macbeth in Kurosawa's "Throne of Blood"

TOULOUSE ◆Toulouse-Lautrec — stunted Parisian artist who found solace among the dancers of Montmartre

TOY ◆Toy Caldwell — member of The Marshall Tucker Band, hit debut single "This Ol' Cowboy"

TRACY ◆Tracy Lord — with Little Anthony and the Imperials, debut gold record "Tears on My Pillow" ◆ Tracy Keenan Wynn — Emmy winning writer for "Tribes" and "The Autobiography of Miss Jane Pittman"

TRAVIS ◆Travis Sedg Bacon — son of actor Kevin Bacon and Kyra Sedgwick ◆ Travis Fine — actor who played Ike McSwain on the hit western series "The Young Riders" ◆ Travis Tritt — country western singer, hits, "Anymore," "Here's a Quarter" ◆ Travis Walton — alleged UFO abductee whose story is told in the film "Fire in the Sky"

TREAT ◆Robert Treat Paine — signer of the Declaration of Independence ◆ Treat Williams — actor whose films include "Hair," "Streets of Fire," "1941"

TRENT ◆Trent Cameron — actor whose roles included Sam on the school based sitcom "Homeroom" ◆ Trent Jones — actor whose roles included Ken George Jones on the soap "Ryan's Hope"

TREVOR ◆Trevor Bullock — actor whose roles included Robbie Davis on TV's "Davis Rules" ◆ Trevor Howard — actor in "The Bridge on the River Kwai," "Von Ryan's Express"

TREY ◆Trey Wilson — actor who played Skip in Kevin Costner's first baseball picture "Bull Durham"

TRIGGER ◆Trigger Lund — regular on TV's "The Ernie Kovacs Show"

TRINI ◆Trini Lopez — actor who played Pedro Jiminez in Lee Marvin's classic "The Dirty Dozen"

TRISTAN ◆Tristan Rogers — actor whose roles included Robert Scorpio on the soap "General Hospital" ◆ Tristan Tzara — poet and leader of the Dadaist movement, editor of the "Dada" magazine

TRISTRAM ◆Tristram Speaker — outfielder who holds the Major League record for doubles in career

TRITIA ◆Tritia Setoguchi — actor who played one of the students in the school based sitcom "Homeroom"

TROY◆Troy Aikman — quarterback for the Dallas Cowboys, 1993 and 1994 Superbowl champions ◆Troy Donahue — actor in TV's "Hawaiian Eye," "Surfside Six"

TROYAL◆Troyal Garth Brooks — first singer to win six Academy of Country Music Awards

TRUE◆William True Stevenson — son of "Cheers" star Kirstie Alley

TRUMAN◆Truman Capote — author who wrote "In Cold Blood" and "Breakfast at Tiffany's"

TUBAL◆Tubal Ryan — builder of Lindbergh's trans-oceanic airplane the "Spirit of St. Louis"

TUCK◆Friar Tuck — plump, jovial friar and swordsman who ministered to Robin Hood's men

TUDOR◆Tudor Sherrard — actor whose roles included Paul Quinie in the film "Heartbreak Hotel"

TULI◆Tuli Kupferberg — member of The Fugs, a group who satirized politics, rock, and sex

TULLIO◆Tullio Carminati — Italian nobleman who became an actor in Hollywood

TULLY◆Tully Marshall — played the villainous old fence who trains pickpockets in "Oliver Twist"

TUNIA◆Lucas Tunia Ross — member of Funkadelic, debut hit "I'll Be You"

TURK◆Turk Broda — Canadian Hockey Hall of Fame goalie

TUTTE◆Tutte Lemkow — actor whose roles included the fiddler in the musical "Fiddler on the Roof"

TWEED◆Tweed Smith — member of the rock group War, hits include "Cisco Kid" and "Low Rider"

TY◆Ty Cobb — Detroit Tigers player in early 1900's, first member of the National Hall of Fame ◆ Ty Hardin — brawny leading man of TV's "Bronco," films include "Battle of the Bulge"

TYLER◆Tyler Ritter — son of actor John Ritter

TYRONE◆Tyrone Power — action star whose films include "Blood and Sand," "The Mark of Zorro"

UB◆Ub Iwerks — double Oscar winning cartoonist who developed Mickey Mouse for Walt Disney

UGO ◆Ugo Sasso — actor who played Czar Nicholas II of Russia in "The Nights of Rasputin" ◆Ugo Tognazzi — actor whose roles included Mark Hand in Jane Fonda's "Barbarella"

ULLRICH ◆Ullrich Haupt — portrayed the Captain in John Barrymore's "Tempest"

ULU ◆Ulu Grosbard — director of "True Confessions," "Falling in Love" and "The Subject Was Roses"

ULYSSES ◆Ulysses Simpson Grant — commander in chief of the Union army during the Civil War

UMBERTO ◆Umberto Eco — mystery writer, novel "The Name of the Rose" was made into a film ◆ Umberto II — last king of Italy whose monarchy was abolished by Mussolini

UPTON ◆Upton Sinclair — author of the muckraking "The Jungle"

URBAN ◆Pope Urban II — Pope who launched the First Crusade

URBIE ◆Urbie Green — Grammy nominee for best jazz solo performance

URI ◆Uri Geller — psychic who can bend metal and stop watches

URIAH ◆Uriah Heep (c) — ever so 'umble clerk to solicitor Wickfield in Dickens' "David Copperfield" ◆ Uriah Levy — first Jewish officer in the US Navy

URICK ◆Urick Ames — member of The Ames Brothers, hits include "You, You, You"

VACHEL ◆Vachel Lindsay — poet whose works include "The Congo" and "Johnny Appleseed"

VACLAY ◆Vaclay Voska — actor whose roles included Dr. Watson in "Sherlock Holmes' Desire"

VADIM ◆Vadim Uraneff — actor in John Barrymore's silent version of "Moby Dick"

VAL ◆Val Doonican — Irish singer with his own musical variety series "The Val Doonican Show" ◆ Val DuFour — actor whose roles included Walter Curtin on the soap "Another World" ◆ Val Kilmer — actor whose films include "The Doors" in which he played Jim Morrison

VALENTIN ◆Johann Valentin Andrae — Lutheran pastor known as the originator of the Rosicrucian legend

VALENTINE ◆Malu Valentine Byrne — son of David Byrne, leader of the rock group Talking Heads ◆ Valentine Dyall — actor whose roles included serial killer Jack the Ripper in "Room to Let"

VALENTINO ◆Valentino — fashion designer known for elegance and simple lines ◆ Valentino Garavani — fashion designer whose clients include Jackie Kennedy and Liz Taylor

VALERY ◆Valery Giscard d'Estaing — former president of France

VAN ◆Van Heflin — actor in film "Shane," won Oscar for "Johnny Eager" ◆ Van Johnson — 1940's teen idol of MGM films ◆ Van McCoy — disco hits include "The Hustle" ◆ Van Morrison — rock singer, debut gold record hit with "Brown Eyed Girl"

VAN WYCK ◆Van Wyck Brooks — literary historian, won a Pulitzer for "The Flowering of New England" ◆ F. Van Wyck Mason — author, creator of army intelligence officer Hugh North

VANCE ◆Vance Colvig — voice of Disney's Pluto, Goofy, wrote "Who's Afraid of the Big Bad Wolf?" ◆Richard Vance Corben — horror illustrator who invented the fantasy strip "Rowlf"

VANGELIS ◆Vangelis — Oscar winner for the film score of "Chariots of Fire"

VANILLA ◆Vanilla Ice — singer whose album is "To the Extreme"

VARDIS ◆Vardis Fisher — author whose writings include his autobiography "In Tragic Life"

VASCO ◆Vasco de Balboa — Spanish explorer who in 1513 discovered the Pacific Ocean

VASILI ◆Vasili Bogazianos — actor whose roles included Benny Sago on the soap "All My Children" ◆ Vasili Smyslov — former world chess champion

VASLAV ◆Vaslav Nijinsky — legendary Russian dancer, biopic "Nijinsky"

VAUGHAN ◆Vaughan Jones — bandleader who unexpectedly appeared as the hero in westerns

VAUGHN ◆Vaughn Bode — underground comic book artist best known for lizards ◆ Vaughn Meader — celebrity impersonator of John F. Kennedy, hit album "The First Family" ◆Vaughn Monroe — noted for songs "Racing With the Moon" and "Ballerina" ◆

Vaughn Taylor — actor whose roles included Marion's boss in Hitchcock's thriller "Psycho"

VEIT ◆ Veit Harlan — German film director whose films include "Youth," "The Ruler"

VERDEN ◆ Verden Allen — hard rock English musician with the group Mott the Hoople

VERDINE ◆ Verdine White — member of Earth, Wind & Fire, debut hit single "Love Is Life"

VERMONT ◆ Vermont Connecticut Royster — Pulitzer Prize winning columnist with the Wall Street Journal

VERN ◆ Vern Gosdin — country western singer, hits include "If You're Gonna Do Me Wrong, Do It Right" ◆ Vern Law — pitcher with Pittsburg, winner of the National League's Cy Young Award

VERNE ◆ Verne Allison — member of The Dells, 1955 debut hit single "Tell the World" ◆ Verne Rowe — actor whose roles included Verne Taylor on TV's "Fernwood 2-Night"

VERNON ◆ Vernon Castle — dancer portrayed by Fred Astaire in "The Story of Vernon and Irene Castle" ◆ Vernon Presley — father of Elvis Presley

VESTO ◆ Vesto Slipher — first astronomer to find evidence of the expanding universe theory

VIC ◆ Vic Bergeron — founder of the worldwide Trader Vic restaurant chain ◆ Vic Damone — won the Arthur Godfrey talent show which launched his singing career ◆ Vic Morrow — star of the TV series "Combat" ◆ Vic Tanny — founder of the chain of stylish Vic Tanny gyms ◆ Vic Tayback — actor whose roles included Mel of Mel's Diner on TV's "Alice"

VICENTE ◆ Vicente Aleixandre — Nobel Prize winning Spanish surrealist poet ◆ Vicente Blasco-Ibanez — wrote novels "Blood and Sand," "Four Horseman of the Apocalypse"

VICTOR ◆ Victor Borge — Danish born pianist-comedian ◆ Victor French — played the sidekick to angel Michael Landon on TV's "Highway to Heaven" ◆ Victor Herbert — composer who dominated Broadway musicals, hits include "March of the Toys" ◆ Victor Hugo — Frenchman who wrote "The Hunchback of Notre Dame" and "Les Miserables" ◆ Victor Mature — beefy actor who went from "The Robe" to parodying himself in "After the Fox"

VIDA ◆ Vida Blue — fifth pitcher to win the Cy Young Award and MVP in the same year

VIDAL ♦Vidal Sassoon — designer, has his own brand of clothing and hair-care products

VIDO ♦Vido Musso — jazz musician who played tenor sax and clarinet with the big bands

VIJAY ♦Vijay Amritraj — actor who played Ali Nadeem on the Yakov Smirnoff sitcom "What a Country"

VINCE ♦Vince Edwards — leading man of the tough, sincere kind, played TV's "Ben Casey" ♦ Vince Gill — country music singer, hits "Turn Me Loose" and "When I Call Your Name" ♦ Vince Lombardi — coach of the Green Bay Packers and Washington Redskins, in Hall of Fame

VINCENT ♦Vincent Gardenia — character actor in such films as "Moonstruck" and "The Little Shop of Horrors" ♦ Vincent Price — master of horror best known for the original "The Fly" ♦ Vincent Sardi — founder of Sardi's restaurant in New York City ♦ Vincent Van Gogh — Impressionist painter who cut off his ear in anguish

VINCENTE ♦Vincente Minnelli — father of Liza Minnelli, director of "Gigi"

VINE ♦Vine Deloria — Indian rights activist and author of "Custer Died for Your Sins"

VINNIE ♦Vinnie Barbarino (c) — John Travolta's role as a sweathog on the sitcom "Welcome Back, Kotter"

VINNY ♦Vinny Leary — member of The Fugs, who satirize politics, rock, and sex ♦Vinny Testaverde — 1986 Heisman Trophy winner, 1987 America's richest draft pick

VINTO ♦Vinto Bogatja — Yugoslav skier who epitomizes "the agony of defeat" for ABC's "Wide World of Sports"

VINTON ♦Vinton Hayworth — played Gen. Winfield Schaeffer on the popular genie sitcom "I Dream of Jeannie"

VIRGIL ♦Virgil Earp — sheriff brother to Wyatt Earp in Tombstone

VIRGINIUS ♦Virginius Dabney — Pulitzer Prize winning editor of the Richmond Times Dispatch

VITAS ♦Vitas Gerulaitis — championship tennis player

VITO ♦Vito Corleone (c) — Marlon Brando's Oscar winning role as a Mafia leader in "The Godfather" ♦ Vito Farinola — real name of singer Vic Damone

VITTORIO ◆Vittorio Alfieri — eighteenth century Italian artist and author of tragedies ◆ Vittorio DeSica — won four Oscars as best director of foreign films

VITUS ◆Vitus Bering — Russian who discovered the Bering Straights

VIVIAN ◆Gilbert Vivian Seldes — author of "The Seven Lively Arts" and "The Wings of the Eagle"

VIVIEN ◆Vivien Kellems — founder of Kellems metal clips

VLADIMIR ◆Vladimir Dracula — real-life prince of Transylvania who became the fictional blood-sucking Count ◆ Vladimir Horowitz — brilliant technical pianist and leading exponent of romantic pianism ◆ Vladimir Lenin — Russian revolutionary leader who helped found the ill-fated USSR

VOLKER ◆Volker Schlondorff — Oscar winning director for "The Tin Drum"

VOLTAIRE ◆Voltaire — French satirist and novelist, pseudonym for Francois Marie Arouet

VON ◆Von Vogel Russell — real name of actor Kurt Russell, star of "Escape From New York" and "Captain Ron"

WADE ◆Wade Barnes — actor and writer whose films include "Annie Hall" and "Diner" ◆ Wade Baskin — author of "The Sorcerer's Handbook" ◆ Wade Hampton — commander-in-chief of the Confederate cavalry

WADSWORTH ◆Henry Wadsworth Longfellow — poet of New England history, including "Paul Revere's Ride"

WALDEN ◆Walden Robert Cassotto — real name of teenage heartthrob Bobby Darin

WALDO ◆Ferdinand Waldo Demara — con man, Tony Curtis biopic "The Great Imposter" ◆ Ralph Waldo Emerson — his essays are landmarks in the development of thought and expression ◆ Waldo Salt — Oscar winner for writing "Midnight Cowboy" and "Coming Home"

WALDORF ◆William Waldorf Astor — head of Astor family in England

WALKER ◆Clarence Walker Barron — founder of the Wall Street Journal and "Barron's Financial Weekly" ◆ George Herbert Walker Bush — President of the United States

WALLACE ◆Wallace Beery — roles included "Dinner at Eight," "Treasure Island," won Oscar for "The Champ" ◆ Wallace Shawn — comedy character actor exclaimed "Inconceivable!" in "The Princess Bride"

WALLIS ◆Wallis Clark — actor who played President Theodore Roosevelt in "Yankee Doodle Dandy" ◆ King Wallis Vidor — legendary Hollywood director, films include "The Big Parade"

WALLY ◆Wally Cox — actor whose roles included Robinson Peepers in the sitcom "Mr. Peepers" ◆Wally Schirra — astronaut, pilot of Gemini 6, commander of Apollo 7

WALT ◆Walt Disney — visionary who created Disney Studios and Disneyland as well as Mickey Mouse ◆ Walt Whitman — nineteenth century American poet

WALTER ◆Walter Brennan — character actor in films like "Red River," "Northwest Passage," "Meet John Doe" ◆ Walter Cronkite — network evening news anchorman respected by millions ◆ Walter Lantz — Oscar winning creator of Woody Woodpecker ◆ Walter Matthau — actor in "The Bad News Bears," "A New Leaf," "The Fortune Cookie," "The Odd Couple" ◆ Sir Walter Raleigh — failed to colonize Virginia, but did get England hooked on smoking tobacco

WALTHER ◆Walther Bauersfeld — co-inventor of the world's first planetarium

WALTON ◆George Walton Lucas — creator of the "Star Wars" and "Indiana Jones" film series

WANYA ◆Wanya Morris — in rock group Boyz II Men, hits include "It's So Hard to Say Goodbye to Yesterday"

WARD ◆Ward Bond — one of John Wayne's and John Ford's troupe of players

WARE ◆Edward Ware Barrett — educator and editor ◆ Henry Ware Lawton — Indian fighter who captured Geronimo

WARNER ◆Warner Anderson — character actor in "The Caine Mutiny" ◆Warner Baxter — Oscar winner for his role as the Cisco Kid "In Old Arizona" ◆ Warner Oland — actor in the Charlie Chan film series

WARREN ◆Warren Beatty — notorious womanizer, films "Bonnie and Clyde," "Dick Tracy," "Heaven Can Wait" ◆Warren G. Harding — US President in the twenties ◆ Warren Oates —

actor who played the drill sergeant in "Stripes," who was "blown up, sir!"

WARWICK ◆Warwick Davis — star of director Ron Howard's fantasy "Willow" ◆ Warwick Sims — actor whose roles included Basil Durban on the soap "General Hospital"

WASHINGTON ◆George Washington Carver — chemist best known for developing uses for the peanut ◆ Washington Irving — author of "The Legend of Sleepy Hollow" and "Rip Van Winkle" ◆ George Washington Trendle — creator of "The Lone Ranger," "The Green Hornet," and "Sergeant Preston of the Yukon"

WAT ◆Wat Bowie — lawyer and spy for the Confederacy ◆ Wat Tyler — English revolutionary who led the Peasant's Revolt against Richard II

WAY ◆Way Bandy — world's best known makeup artist whose clients include Elizabeth Taylor

WAYLAND ◆Francis Wayland Ayer — advertising executive who pioneered use of slogans and trademarks in ads ◆ Wayland Flowers — ventriloquist whose TV show featured his puppet "Madame" ◆ Dan Wayland Seals — England Dan who forms a duo with John Ford Coley, hits include "Bop"

WAYLON ◆Waylon Jennings — legendary country western singer

WAYNE ◆Wayne Gretzky — Canadian born hockey star with the LA Kings ◆ Wayne McLaren — model who played the Marlboro Man ◆ Wayne Newton — actor and musician who spends most of his time playing Las Vegas ◆ Wayne Rogers — Trapper John on TV's "M*A*S*H" but not "Trapper John," the spin-off

WEBB ◆Webb Hollenbeck — real name of actor Clifton Webb, Oscar nominee for "Laura" ◆ Webb Pierce — country western singer, hits include "Why Baby, Why"

WEBSTER ◆Webster Long (c) — Emmanuel Lewis' role on the hit sitcom "Webster"

WELLESLEY ◆Duke Arthur Wellesley Wellington — English hero who defeated Napoleon at Waterloo

WELLINGTON ◆Wellington Mara — owner and president of the New York Giants ◆ Wellington Webb — mayor of Denver, Colorado, elected in 1991

WELLS ◆Wells Kelly — member of the group Orleans, hit singles include "Love Takes Time"

WENDEL ◆Wendel Clark — Canadian hockey player with Toronto

WENDELL ◆Oliver Wendell Holmes — influential Supreme Court Justice ◆ Wendell Scott — first African-American stock-car racer, Richard Pryor biopic "Greased Lightning" ◆ Wendell Wilkie — defeated by Roosevelt for president in 1940

WERNER ◆Werner Hinz — actor who played legendary German Field Marshal Rommel in "The Longest Day" ◆ Werner Klemperer — incredibly inept camp commander Col. Klink on TV's "Hogan's Heroes" ◆Werner Krauss — actor who played the title role in the classic "Cabinet of Dr. Caligari"

WERNHER ◆Wernher von Braun — German designer of rockets for Hitler, biopic "I Aim at the Stars"

WES ◆Wes Forbes — member of The Five Satins, debut gold hit single "In the Still of the Night" ◆ Wes Montgomery — guitarist who recorded one of the best selling jazz albums "A Day in the Life"

WESLEY ◆John Wesley Hardin — Texas gunslinger who killed over twenty men after the Civil War ◆ Wesley Snipes — actor whose films include "Demolition Man" and "Passenger 57"

WESTBROOK ◆Westbrook Pegler — controversial Pulitzer Prize winning reporter on racketeering ◆ Westbrook Van Voorhis — narrator of TV's "Doorway to Danger"

WESTLEY ◆Joseph Westley Newman — inventor of the automobile windshield wiper

WEYMAN ◆Weyman Jones — author whose works include "The Talking Leaf" and "Edge of Two Worlds"

WHIT ◆Whit Bissell — actor who played Bob Ford, who shot Jesse James, in "The Great Missouri Raid" ◆Whit Burnett — co-founder of "Story" magazine

WHITBY ◆Whitby Hertford — actor whose roles included Josh Tobin on TV's "Family Man"

WHITEY ◆Whitey Ford — known to his country music fans as the Duke of Paducah

WHITFIELD ◆Whitfield Connor — actor whose roles included Bart Fenway on the soap "The Secret Storm" ◆George Whitfield Scranton — founder of Scranton, Pennsylvania

WHITLEY ◆Whitley Strieber — alien abductee whose books include "Communion"

WHITMAN ◆Whitman Mayo — played Fred's friend Grady Wilson on "Sanford and Son," then had his own sitcom

WHITNEY ◆Whitney Darrow, Jr. — cartoonist with the "New Yorker" ◆ Whitney Day — one of the sons in the novel, film, and TV show "Life With Father"

WIL ◆Wil Wheaton — played Wesley Crusher on syndicated TV's "Star Trek: The Next Generation"

WILBERT ◆Wilbert Harrison — rock singer, hits include the number one gold record "Kansas City"

WILBUR ◆Wilbur Shaw — three time Indy 500 winner who invented the crash helmet ◆Wilbur Wright — Wright brother who flew the first powered airplane

WILCIL ◆Wilcil McDowell — member of The Irish Rovers, hits include "The Unicorn" and "Wasn't That a Party"

WILEY ◆ Wiley Post — aviator who was killed in a crash in Alaska with Will Rogers

WILF ◆Wilf Carter — Canada's top country entertainer, called the "Cowboy Yodeler" ◆ Wilf Gibson — member of The Electric Light Orchestra, debut hit "Roll Over Beethoven"

WILFORD ◆Wilford Brimley — actor whose roles included Ben in the renewal-of-life film "Cocoon"

WILFRED ◆Wilfred Funk — with Funk & Wagnalls, wrote "Increase Your Word Power" for "Reader's Digest"

WILFRID ◆Wilfrid Brambell — star of British TV's "Steptoe and Son" which became US "Sanford and Son" ◆ Wilfrid Hyde-White — actor who played Colonel Hugh Pickering in Rex Harrison's "My Fair Lady"

WILHELM ◆Wilhelm Grimm — one of the Brothers Grimm who penned Grimm's Fairy Tales ◆Wilhelm Tell — Swiss archer forced to shoot an apple from his son's head

WILKIE ◆Wilkie Cooper — British cinematographer whose credits include "One Million Years B.C."

WILKINS ◆Wilkins Micawber (c) — eternal optimist of Dickens' "David Copperfield" played on film by W.C. Fields

WILL ◆Will Geer — actor whose roles included the grandfather on TV's "The Waltons" ◆ Will Hays — Hollywood censor known for his "Purity Seal" ◆ Will Rogers — vaudeville comedian whose specialty was making fun of politicians ◆ Will Scarlett — one of Robin Hood's Merry Men ◆ Will Smith — rap singer and star of TV's "The Fresh Prince of Bel Air"

WILLARD ◆Willard Scott — weatherman on TV's "Today" show

WILLEM ◆ Willem Barents — sixteenth century Dutch explorer ◆ Willem Dafoe — actor in "Born on the Fourth of July" and "Mississippi Burning"

WILLIAM ◆William Holden — actor in "The Bridge on the River Kwai" and "Stalag 17" for which he won an Oscar ◆ William Hurt — "Body Heat," "Broadcast News," Oscar for "Kiss of the Spider Woman" ◆ William Shakespeare — Bard of Avon, wrote plays like "Romeo and Juliet" ◆ William Shatner — played Captain Kirk of the Enterprise, both on the large screen and small

WILLIE ◆Willie Mays — outfielder with San Francisco Giants and New York Mets, in Hall of Fame ◆ Willie Nelson — country western singer whose songs include "On the Road Again" ◆Willie Sutton — when asked why he robbed banks, he said "Because that's where the money is"

WILLIS ◆Willis Carrier — invented the air conditioner ◆ Willis O'Brien — produced the special effects for "King Kong," Oscar for "Mighty Joe Young"

WILLY ◆Willy Brandt — chancellor of West Germany who won the Nobel Peace Prize

WILSON ◆Wilson Pickett — soul star, hits "In the Midnight Hour" and "Mustang Sally" ◆ Ronald Wilson Reagan — actor, President, coined term "Reaganomics"

WILT ◆Wilt Chamberlain — actor who played Bombaata in Arnold Schwarzenegger's "Conan the Destroyer"

WIN ◆Win Stracke — actor who played town loafer Laif Flaigle on the comedy series "Hawkins Falls"

WINCHESTER ◆Howard Winchester Hawks — legendary film director, films include "The Big Sleep," "Bringing Up Baby"

WINFIELD ◆Julius Winfield Erving — basketball player known as "Doctor J" ◆ Frank Winfield Woolworth — founder of the Woolworth's five and ten cent store

WINFRED ◆Norton Winfred Simon — founder of Norton Simon, Inc., including Canada Dry

WINGS ◆Wings Hauser — actor whose roles included Greg Foster on the soap "The Young and the Restless"

WINK ◆Wink Martindale — host of many game shows, including "Tic Tac Dough"

WINSLOW ◆Winslow Homer — painter of Civil War battlefields and interiors

WINSOR ◆Winsor McCay — artist best known for "Little Nemo" cartoons

WINSTON ◆Winston Churchill — prime minister of England during World War II ◆ John Winston Lennon — one of the four Beatles ◆ Michael Winston Steiger — son of actor Rod Steiger

WINTHOP ◆Winthop Aldrich — banker and financier

WINTHROP ◆Winthrop Ames — author of "Snow White," the first play especially for children ◆ Winthrop Rockefeller — governor of Arkansas, descendant of John D. Rockefeller

WINTON ◆Winton Hoch — cinematographer, films include "She Wore a Yellow Ribbon" and "The Green Berets"

WISMER ◆Wismer Washam — head writer for the soap opera "All My Children"

WITON ◆Witon Felder — member of The Crusaders, hits include "Uptight, Everything's Alright"

WLADZIU ◆Tadewurz Wladziu Konopka — real name of "The Mary Tyler Moore Show's" Ted Knight ◆ Wladziu Valentino Liberace — real name of performer Liberace

WOLF ◆Alan Wolf Arkin — comic actor and director, won a Tony for "Enter Laughing"

WOLFE ◆Willem Wolfe Idol — son of rock singer Billy Idol ◆ Theobald Wolfe Tone — founder of the United Irishmen

WOLFGANG ◆Wolfgang Amadeus Mozart — Austrian composer of over 600 works, including "The Marriage of Figaro" ◆ Wolfgang Peterson — best director Oscar for "Das Boot" ◆ Wolfgang Puck — restauranteur, of particular note Spago and Chinoise on Main

WOODBRIDGE ◆Ethelbert Woodbridge Nevin — composer, piano works "Narcissus," "The Rosary" and "Mighty Like a

Rose" ◆ Woodbridge Van Dyke — director known for only one take, obtained spontaneous performances from actors

WOODROW◆Woodrow Guthrie — folksinger, nickname "Woody," hits include "This Land is Your Land" ◆ Woodrow Wilson — President during World War I, tried to get the US into the League of Nations

WOODWARD◆Woodward Ritter — real name of singing cowboy Tex Ritter

WOODY◆Woody Allen — writer/director of "Annie Hall," "Sleeper," and many, many other films ◆ Woody Harrelson — actor who played the naive bartender Woody on TV's long running "Cheers" ◆ Woody Herman — clarinet playing band leader of the 40's through the 70's ◆ Woody Strode — actor in "Spartacus" and "The Professionals"

WOOLCOTT◆Woolcott Gibbs — critic with the "New Yorker" magazine in the "Talk of the Town" section

WOOLWORTH◆Woolworth Donahue — heir to the F.W. Woolworth chain stores, cousin of Barbara Hutton

WORLD◆World B. Free — basketball guard with a number of NBA teams

WORTHINGTON◆Worthington Miner — creator of TV's "The Ed Sullivan Show"

WRIGHT◆Wright Morris — author whose novels include "Ceremony in Lone Tree"

WYATT◆Wyatt Earp — Marshal of Tombstone, Arizona, where he fought at the O.K. Corral ◆ Wyatt Russell — son of actress Goldie Hawn and actor Kurt Russell

WYLIE◆Wylie Watson — British character actor, usually in "little man" roles

WYLLIS◆Edward Wyllis Scripps — founder of Scripps-Howard Newspapers

WYMAN◆Wyman Pendleton — actor whose roles included Dr. Gus Norwood on the soap "The Edge of Night"

WYNDHAM◆Wyndham Goldie — actor who played British Empire builder Cecil Rhodes in "Victoria the Great" ◆ Wyndham Standing — actor who played the squadron commander in Jean Harlow's classic "Hell's Angels"

WYNN ◆Wynn Irwin — actor whose roles included Arthur Swann on the Dom DeLuise sitcom "Lotsa Luck" ◆ Wynn Stewart — country western singer, hits include "After the Storm"

WYNNE ◆Brian Wynne Garfield — Edgar award winning author for "Hopscotch"

WYNTON ◆Wynton Marsalis — first artist to win Grammys in both classical and jazz

XAVER ◆Franz Xaver Gruber — organist who wrote the music for "Silent Night"

XAVIER ◆Francis Xavier Bushman — silent film hero, played Messala in the silent epic "Ben-Hur" ◆ Xavier Cugat — Spanish bandleader known as the "Rhumba King" ◆ Xavier Roberts — creator of the Cabbage Patch Kids

YAHOO ◆Yahoo Serious — actor whose roles included the starring role in "Young Einstein"

YAKIMA ◆Yakima Canutt — legendary half-Indian stunt man of Hollywood

YAKOV ◆Yakov Smirnoff — comedian whose routine is based on knocking his native Russia

YALE ◆Yale Lary — Hall of Famer who led the NFL in punting three times

YAMIL ◆Yamil Borges — played Morales in the Michael Douglas film of the hit play "A Chorus Line"

YAPHET ◆Yaphet Kotto — actor who played Sgt. China Bell on TV's army soap "For Love and Honor"

YELBERTON ◆Yelberton Tittle — three time all-pro quarterback who led the NFL in passing

YOGI ◆Yogi Berra — baseball player, coined phrase "It ain't over till it's over"

YONNI ◆Yonni Netanyahu — colonel who led the Israeli assault in the rescue raid on the Entebbe airport

YOUNG ◆Young Corbett III — world welterweight champion boxer during the Depression ◆ Young Stribling — known as the Georgia Peach, boxer had 126 knockouts out of 286 fights

YUL ◆Yul Brynner — bald actor most well known for "The King and I" and "The Magnificent Seven"

YURI ◆ Yuri Andropov — became General Secretary of the Communist Party on the death of Brezhnev

YUSEF ◆ Yusef Lateef — jazz musician on the saxophone, flute, oboe, shahnai, argole, and bassoon

YVAN ◆ Yvan Courneyor — Canadian hockey player nicknamed "The Roadrunner"

YVES ◆ Yves Allegret — director of film noir works starring Simone Signoret ◆ Yves Montand — French actor in "A Man and a Woman," "On a Clear Day You Can See Forever" ◆ Yves St. Laurent — French fashion figure who took over the House of Dior, now has his own line

ZABDIEL ◆ Zabdiel Boylston — first doctor to use the smallpox vaccine in the US

ZACHARIAH ◆ Cyrus Zachariah Oppenheim — one of the twin sons of actress Cybill Shepherd ◆ Zachariah — in the Bible, his teachings gave name to an Old Testament book ◆ Zachariah Chandler — founder of the Republican Party

ZACHARY ◆ Zachary Scott — character actor in many 40's programmers, usually in smarmy roles ◆ Zachary Taylor — being the hero of the Mexican War launched him to the Presidency ◆ Zachary Williams — son of comedy actor Robin Williams

ZACHERY ◆ Zachery Bryan — actor who played eldest son Brad Taylor on the tool sitcom "Home Improvement"

ZACK ◆ Zack Norman — actor who played Harry Munchak in Robin Williams' car-selling "Cadillac Man"

ZAK ◆ Zak Starr — son of Beatle drummer Ringo Starr

ZAL ◆ Zal Yanovsky — member of The Lovin' Spoonful, debut hit "Do You Believe in Magic"

ZALMAN ◆ Zalman King — actor whose roles included Jesus the savior in "The Passover Plot"

ZALMON ◆ Zalmon Simmons — founder of Simmons' mattress company

ZAMA ◆ Martin Zama Agronsky — Washington broadcast journalist and commentator

ZANDOR ◆ Zandor Vorkov — actor whose roles included the bloody Count Dracula in "Blood of Frankenstein"

ZANE ◆Zane Grey — author of over 60 western books, including "Riders of the Purple Sage" ◆Edward Zane Judson — originated the dime novel, christened W.F. Cody "Buffalo Bill" ◆Zane Lasky — actor whose roles included Bob Phillips on the nighttime soap "Knots Landing"

ZBIGNIEW ◆Zbigniew Brzezinski — Jimmy Carter's advisor on national security affairs ◆Zbigniew Cybulski — leading actor who appeared in "He, She, or It," "To Love"

ZEBULON ◆Zebulon Pike — discovered Colorado's Pike's Peak

ZEKE ◆Zeke Bratkowski — quarterback for the Los Angeles Rams ◆Zeke Clements — comedian and country western singer of eclectic abilities

ZELL ◆Zell Miller — Democratic governor of Georgia

ZERO ◆Zero Mostel — actor in "A Funny Thing Happened on the Way to the Forum," "The Producers"

ZEV ◆Zev Bufman — producer whose credits include "The Little Foxes," "Your Own Thing" and "Peter Pan"

ZIGGY ◆Ziggy Elman — trumpet star, hit song "And the Angels Sing" ◆ Ziggy Marley — crown prince of reggae, album "Conscious Party"

ZITTO ◆Zitto Kazann — actor whose roles included Crazy Horse on the drama series "Hell Town"

ZOLA ◆Emile Zola Berman — defended Sirhan Sirhan in 1969 ◆ Zola Pearnell — member of Garnet Mimms and the Enchanters, debut hit "Cry Baby"

ZOLTAN ◆Zoltan Fabri — Hungarian director, films include "The Last Goal" and "Twenty Hours" ◆ Zoltan Korda — Hungarian Hollywood director, films include the classic "Four Feathers"

ZOOEY ◆Zooey Hall — actor whose roles included Bob Lee on the drama series "The New People"

ZOOT ◆Zoot Sims — Grammy winning jazz saxophonist

ZOWIE ◆Zowie Bowie — son of rock star David Bowie

ZUBIN ◆Zubin Mehta — one of the great Maestros

ZULU ◆Zulu — actor who played detective Kono Kalakaua on the police drama "Hawaii Five-O"

GIRLS' NAMES

AARIANA ◆Aariana Knowles — regular on Sid Caesar's "Your Show of Shows"

ABBE ◆Abbe Lane — ex-wife of Xavier Cugat who starred with him on "The Xavier Cugat Show"

ABBEY ◆Abbey Lincoln — singer and actress whose films include "For Love of Ivy"

ABBY ◆Abby Dalton — actress who played Wild Bill Hickok's girlfriend Calamity Jane in "The Plainsman"

ABIGAIL ◆Abigail Adams — only woman to be both the wife and the mother of a president ◆ Abigail Van Buren — gives advice to millions of newspaper readers as "Dear Abby"

ADAH ◆Adah Menken — actress and poet

ADDIE ◆Addie Harris — member of The Shirelles, hits include "I Met Him On Sunday" and "Soldier Boy"

ADELA ◆Adela Rogers St. John — nominated for an Oscar in 1931 for writing "What Price Hollywood?"

ADELAIDE ◆Marie Adelaide Lowndes — author of "The Lodger" about Jack the Ripper, became Alfred Hitchcock film

ADELE ◆Adele Astaire — dancing partner of her brother Fred Astaire in the early years ◆ Adele Hugo — her relentless pursuit of her former lover brought about insanity ◆ Adele Jergens — brassy blonde in over 50 B-films, including "The Day the World Ended" ◆ Adele Simpson — one of the highest paid designers, first to go on tour with her collections

ADELLE ◆Adelle Davis — nutritionist who wrote "Let's Cook It Right"

ADELYN ◆Adelyn Breeskin — first woman director of a museum in the US, the Baltimore Museum of Art

ADRIAN ◆Adrian — fashion designer, leading lady in "The Big Parade"

ADRIANA ◆Adriana Kaegi — member of Kid Creole and the Coconuts, hit album "Tropical Gangsters"

ADRIANE ◆Adriane Munker — actress who played Marianne Randolph Halloway on the soap "Another World"

ADRIEN ◆Adrien Stoutenburg — children's author, books include "Fee, Fi, Fo, Fum: Friendly and Funny Giants"

ADRIENNE ◆Adrienne Barbeau — curvy brunette from "Escape From New York" and TV's "Maude" ◆Adrienne Posta — actress specializing in cheeky teenagers, films include "To Sir With Love"

AGATHA ◆Agatha Christie — prolific English novelist, creator of characters Hercule Poirot and Miss Marple

AGETHA ◆Agetha Ulvacus — member of Swedish rock group Abba whose hits include "Dancing Queen"

AGNES ◆Agnes DeMille — choreograher of "Oklahoma," "Carousel," and "Brigadoon" ◆Agnes Moorehead — actress who went from "Citizen Kane's" mother to Endora on TV's "Bewitched"

AGNETHA ◆Agnetha Faltskog — member of Abba, debut gold record "Waterloo"

AILEEN ◆Aileen Quinn — actress who played the ever optimistic Little Orphan Annie in the film "Annie"

AILSA ◆Ailsa Bruce — philanthropist

AIMEE ◆Aimee McPherson — glamorous evangelist, Faye Dunaway biopic "The Disappearance of Aimee"

AISHA ◆Aisha Wonder — child of super rock star Stevie Wonder ◆ Aisha Kahlil — member of Sweet Honey in the Rock

ALAINA ◆Alaina Reed-Hall — actress who played Rose Lee Holloway on the Marla Gibbs hit sitcom "227"

ALANA ◆Alana Hamilton Stewart — model and former wife of both George Hamilton and Rod Stewart

ALANNAH ◆Alannah Currie — member of The Thompson Twins, debut hit single "Lies" ◆ Alannah Myles — singer/ songwriter, hits include the solo number one "Black Velvet"

ALBERTA ◆Alberta King — mother of the Rev. Martin Luther King, Jr. ◆Alberta Watson — actress who played Nina Delaney on the medical drama series "Island Sun"

ALDINE ◆Aldine King — portrayed Jody on the TV detective drama "Hagen"

ALENE ◆Alene Duerk — first woman admiral in the United States Navy

ALEXA ◆Alexa Ray Joel — child of model Christie Brinkley and rock star Billy Joel ◆ Alexa Hamilton — Darlene the spy was her character on the sitcom "Hail to the Chief"

ALEXANDRA ◆Alexandra Feodorovna — last Czarina of Russia, executed by Bolsheviks with entire family ◆ Alexandra Paul — actress who played the virgin Connie Swail in Dan Aykroyd's hilarious "Dragnet" ◆ Alexandra Zuck — real name of singer/actress Sandra Dee

ALEXANDRIA ◆Alexandria Richards — child of celebrities Keith Richards and Patti Hanson

ALEXIS ◆Alexis Danson — child of "Cheers" superstar Ted Danson ◆ Alexis Smith — screen actress of the 40's, success later on Broadway in Sondheim's "Follies"

ALFEA ◆Helen Alfea Bottel — journalist

ALFRE ◆Alfre Woodard — actress who played Grace Cooley in Bill Murray's Dickens story "Scrooged"

ALI ◆Ali MacGraw — actress who died in "Love Story" and got the whole country choked up

ALICE ◆Alice Brock — owner of "Alice's Restaurant" on which Arlo Guthrie based his song ◆ Alice Faye — beautiful blond star, films include "Alexander's Ragtime Band" ◆ Alice B. Toklas — Gertrude Stein's secretary and longtime companion

ALICIA ◆Alicia Foster — real name of actress/director Jodie Foster ◆ Alicia Patterson — founder of "Newsday" magazine

ALIDA ◆Alida Valli — first to play the luxury-craving Manon Lescaut on the screen

ALINE ◆Aline MacMahon — actress who played Sarah Martin in Edward G. Robinson's "Silver Dollar" ◆ Aline Saarinen — critic with the New York Times, author of "The Proud Possessors"

ALISAN ◆Alisan Porter — actress whose roles included Tess Holland on the hit sitcom "Perfect Strangers"

ALISON ◆Alison Arngrim — played Nellie Oleson on the drama series "Little House on the Prairie" ◆ Alison Eastwood — daughter of Clint Eastwood, starred in his film "Tightrope" ◆ Alison Skipworth — actress who specialized in dowagers, film "If I Had a Million"

ALIX ◆Alix Elias — actress whose roles included Rose Kosinski on the spinoff sitcom "Grady"

ALLA ◆Alla Nazimova — actress whose films include "The Bridge of San Luis Rey"

ALLEGRA ◆Allegra Allison — regular on the comedy variety series "The Richard Pryor Show" ◆Allegra Kent — ballerina best known for ballet "The Seven Deadly Sins"

ALLEY ◆Alley Mills — actress who played the mother, Norma, on the sitcom "The Wonder Years"

ALLIE ◆Allie Lowell (c) — Jane Curtin's starring role on the sitcom "Kate and Allie"

ALLISON ◆Allison Smith — played Jane Curtin's daughter Jennie Lowell on the sitcom "Kate and Allie"

ALLY ◆Ally Sheedy — 1980's Brat Pack member, starred in "The Breakfast Club," "War Games" ◆ Ally Walker — actress who played Officer Jessica Haley on the police drama series "True Blue"

ALLYCE ◆Allyce Beasley — played receptionist Agnes Dipesto on Bruce Willis' series "Moonlighting" ◆ Allyce Ghostley — real name of actress who played addle-brained Bernice on TV's "Designing Women"

ALLYN ◆Allyn McLerie — actress who played Florence Bickford on TV's "The Days and Nights of Molly Dodd"

ALMA ◆Alma Gluck — NY Met soprano, wife of Efrem Zimbalist, gold hit "Carry Me Back to Old Virginny" ◆ Alma Kruger — actress whose roles included the head nurse on TV's "Dr. Kildare" ◆ Alma Reville — screenwriter married to Alfred Hitchcock, wrote "The 39 Steps"

ALOHA ◆Aloha Burke — member of The Five Stairsteps, debut hit "You Waited Too Long"

ALOHILANI ◆Sophie Frederica Alohilani von Haselberg — daughter of actress and singer Bette Midler

ALTA ◆Claudia Alta Taylor Johnson — First Lady of President Johnson, nickname "Lady Bird"

ALTHEA ◆Louise Althea Brough — US women's single champion, also won three titles at Wimbledon ◆Althea Gibson — first African-American to win Wimbledon

ALTHEA SUE ◆Althea Sue Flynt — co-publisher of "Hustler" magazine

ALVA ◆Alva Erskine Belmont — militant feminist and suffragette

ALYCE ◆Alyce King — one of the singing King Sisters, musical variety series "The King Family Show"

ALYSON ◆Alyson Hannigan — actress whose roles included Jessie Harper on TV's "Free Spirit" ◆ Alyson Reed — actress whose roles included Alex in John Ritter's "Skin Deep"

ALYSSA ◆Alyssa Milano — actress whose roles included Samantha Micelli on TV's "Who's the Boss"

AMANDA ◆Amanda Bearse — played next-door neighbor Marcy on the sitcom "Married . . . with Children" ◆ Amanda Blake — actress who played bar-girl Miss Kitty on TV's long running western "Gunsmoke" ◆ Amanda Plummer — Emmy award winning actress for "L.A. Law," daughter of Christopher Plummer

AMANDINE ◆Amandine Malkovich — daughter of "In the Line of Fire" actor John Malkovich

AMBER ◆Willow Amber Daltrey — daughter of English singer Roger Daltrey

AMBROSINE ◆Ambrosine Philpotts — British character actress whose roles include "Room at the Top"

AMELIA ◆Amelia Batchler — the woman with the torch who posed for the Columbia Pictures logo ◆ Amelia Earhart — adventurous woman aviator presumably killed by the Japanese during World War II

AMELIE ◆Amelie Rives — author of "Shadows of Flames," an early account of drug addiction

AMI ◆Ami Dolenz — actress whose roles included Sloan Peterson on TV's "Ferris Bueller" ◆ Ami Foster — actress whose roles included Margaux Kramer on the sitcom "Punky Brewster"

AMII ◆Amii Stewart — singer who recorded disco remakes of "Knock on Wood" and "Light My Fire"

AMY ◆Amy Carter — only daughter of President Jimmy Carter ◆ Amy Fisher — Long Island Lolita convicted of attempted murder of Mary Jo Buttafuoco ◆ Amy Grant — "Heart in Motion" album included her smash hit "Every Heartbeat" ◆ Amy Irving — fresh-faced, curly-haired actress in "Crossing Delancey" and "Micki and Maude" ◆ Amy Vanderbilt — etiquette expert, author of "The Complete Book of Etiquette"

AMZIE ◆Amzie Strickland — actress whose roles included Beth Perce on the soap "Full Circle"

ANA ◆Ana Alicia — actress whose roles included Melissa Cumson Gioberti on TV's "Falcon Crest"

ANA-ALICIA ◆Ana-Alicia — actress who played Melissa Agretti on the prime time soap "Falcon Crest"

ANASTASIA ◆Anastasia Romanov — reputed to have survived the Bolsheviks' execution of the Russian royal family

ANDIE ◆Andie MacDowell — portrayed another Jane to Tarzan in "Greystoke"

ANDREA ◆Andrea King — French-American leading lady whose films include "The Lemon Drop Kid" ◆ Andrea Lawrence — Olympic gold medal skier ◆ Andrea McArdle — actress whose roles included Annie on Broadway and in the musical film "Annie"

ANDREE ◆Andree Lafayette — actress who played George du Maurier's tragic heroine Trilby in "Svengali"

ANETA ◆Aneta Corsaut — actress whose roles included Irma Howell on the sitcom "The Gertrude Berg Show"

ANGELA ◆Angela Cartwright — actress who played daughter Linda Williams on TV's "The Danny Thomas Show" ◆ Angela Lansbury — saucy senior citizen detective Jessica Fletcher on TV's "Murder, She Wrote"

ANGELINA ◆Angelina McKeithen — popular Christian instrumentalist and singer with Charity Records

ANGELINE ◆Angeline Brown — real name of actress Angie Dickinson

ANGIE ◆Angie Dickinson — tough blonde with a badge in TV's "Policewoman"

ANISSA ◆Anissa Jones — actress whose roles included Buffy on TV's "Family Affair"

ANITA ◆Anita Baker — Grammy winner, hit gold album "Rapture," hit single "Sweet Love" ◆ Anita Bryant — right wing purveyor of orange juice ◆Anita Ekberg — actress called the "ice maiden," films include "La Dolce Vita" ◆ Anita Hill — accused Supreme Court Justice Clarence Thomas of sexual harassment

ANJANETTE ◆Anjanette Comer — actress whose leading roles have included "Fire Sale"

ANJELICA ◆Anjelica Huston — exotic actress from "The Addams Family," "Prizzi's Honor," and "Lonesome Dove"

ANN ◆Ann B. Davis — actress who played Alice, the housekeeper on the sitcom "The Brady Bunch" ◆Ann Jillian — platinum blond TV star of "It's a Living," and the TV movie "Mae West" ◆Ann Landers — twin sister of Dear Abby, gives advice to the lovelorn in newspapers ◆ Ann Rutherford — actress whose roles included Polly Benedict in the "Andy Hardy" film series ◆Ann Sheridan — actress called the "Oomph Girl" ◆ Ann Sothern — star of "Maisie" film series, TV's "The Ann Sothern Show"

ANN-MARGRET ◆Ann-Margret — actress/dancer in "Bye Bye, Birdie," "Viva Las Vegas," "The Train Robbers"

ANN-MARIE ◆Ann-Marie Johnson — actress who played Nadine Hudson Thomas on the hit sitcom "What's Happening!"

ANNA ◆Anna Maria Alberghetti — opera singer who made films, musicals, won a Tony for "Carnival" ◆Anna Kate Denver — child of "Rocky Mountain High" singer John Denver

ANNA-LOU ◆Anna-Lou Leibovitz — celebrity photographer with "Rolling Stone" and "Vanity Fair"

ANNABEL ◆Annabel — child of actress Lynn Redgrave

ANNABELLA ◆Annabella Charpentier — French actress wife of Tyrone Power ◆Annabella Lwin — member of British New Wave band Bow Wow Wow

ANNABELLE ◆Annabelle Gurwitch — actress whose roles included Billie on TV's "Eddie Dodd"

ANNABETH ◆Annabeth Gish — actress whose roles included Tammy in Patrick Dempsey's "Coupe de Ville"

ANNE ◆Anne Archer — Oscar nominee for "Fatal Attraction," daughter of Marjorie Lord ◆ Anne Bancroft — actress whose roles included Mrs. Robinson to Dustin Hoffman in "The Graduate" ◆ Anne Baxter — actress with credits from DeMille's "The Ten Commandments" to TV's "Hotel" ◆ Anne Klein — fashion designer known for sophisticated sportswear

ANNE-LAURE ◆Anne-Laure Meury — actress who played Adrienne in Eric Rohmer's film "Boyfriends and Girlfriends"

ANNE-MARIE ◆Carole Anne-Marie Gist — first African-American to become Miss USA

ANNEKE ◆Anneke Wills — actress who played Evelyn McLean on the detective drama series "Strange Report"

ANNELISE ◆Annelise Gaboid — portrayed Cordelia in Paul Scofield's "King Lear"

ANNEMARIE ◆Annemarie Moser — Olympic gold medal skier

ANNETTE ◆Annette Bening — wife of Warren Beatty, lead in "Regarding Henry" and "Bugsy" ◆ Annette Funicello — "Mouseketeer" on TV who later graduated to beach movies ◆ Annette O'Toole — actress whose roles included Alice Perrin in the cult film "Cat People"

ANNIE ◆Annie Costner — child of "Dances With Wolves" actor Kevin Costner ◆Annie Guest — child of actress Jamie Lee Curtis and Christopher Guest ◆ Annie Maude — daughter of "Fatal Attraction" actress Glenn Close ◆ Annie Oakley — Buffalo Bill's sharpshootin' gal, whose bio pic was made with Barbara Stanwyck ◆Annie Potts — actress whose roles included Mary Jo Shively on TV's "Designing Women"

ANNIFRID ◆Annifrid Lyngstad-Fredriksson — member of Swedish rock group Abba whose hits include "Dancing Queen"

ANOUK ◆Anouk Aimee — Oscar nominated French actress for "A Man and a Woman"

ANTOINETTE ◆Antoinette Blackwell — first ordained woman minister in the United States ◆ Antoinette Perry — actress after whom the Tony Award is named

ANTONIA ◆Antonia Franceschi — actress whose roles included Hilary in the kids-turned-performers film "Fame" ◆ Antonia Novello — first woman and first Hispanic to be surgeon general ◆ Susan Antonia Stockard — real name of actress Stockard Channing

ANYA ◆Anya Seton — author whose works include "Dragonwyck"

ANZIA ◆Anzia Yezierska — author of New York's Jewish immigrants whose works include "Hungry Hearts"

APHRA ◆Aphra Behn — seventeenth century writer, first woman to support herself by writing

APOLLONIA ◆Apollonia — singer and actress who played Prince's girlfriend in the movie "Purple Rain"

APRIL ◆April Kent — actress who appeared in numerous films, including "Tammy and the Bachelor"

APRILE ◆Aprile Millo — Verdian soprano of the 1980's at the Metropolitan Opera

ARCHERA ◆Laura Archera Huxley — wife of Aldous, author "This Timeless Moment: A Personal View of Aldous Huxley"

ARDELL ◆Ardell Sheridan — actress whose roles included Francesca Gireli on the sitcom "The Super"

ARDIS ◆Ardis Krainik — general manager of the Lyric Opera of Chicago

ARETHA ◆Aretha Franklin — Queen of Soul, hits include "Respect," "Baby I Love," "Freeway of Love"

ARI ◆Ari Meyers — played Susan St. James' daughter Emma McArdle on the sitcom "Kate and Allie"

ARIANA ◆Ariana Richards — actress who played Tess Delaney on the medical drama series "Island Son"

ARIANE ◆Ariane Munker — actress who played Dr. Annie Stewart Ward on the soap "As the World Turns"

ARIEL ◆Molly Ariel — one of the twin daughters of actress Cybill Shepherd

ARIZONA ◆Arizona Barker — nickname "Ma Barker," held up banks with her sons during the Depression

ARLEEN ◆Arleen Auger — opera singer known for Bach and Mozart ◆ Arleen Sorkin — host of the comedy series "America's Funniest People"

ARLENE ◆Arlene Dahl — glamor star of the 1950's, mother of Lorenzo Lamas ◆Arlene Francis — actress known as a panelist on TV's "What's My Line?"

ARLETTE ◆Arlette Marchal — portrayed Celeste in the Clara Bow silent classic "Wings"

ARLETTY ◆Arletty — French actress who appeared in "Children of Paradise," "No Exit"

ARLINE ◆Arline Judge — leading lady whose credits include "The Lady Is Willing"

ARMELIA ◆Armelia McQueen — actress whose roles included Whoopi Goldberg's sister in the tearjerker "Ghost"

ARYNESS ◆Aryness Wickens — researcher critical to the development of the consumer price index

ASHLEIGH ◆Ashleigh Sterling — actress whose roles included little Allison Taylor on TV's "The Family Man"

ASHLEY ◆Ashley Johnson — actress whose roles included new arrival Chrissy Seaver on TV's "Growing Pains" ◆Ashley Olsen — with twin sister played Michelle on the sitcom "Full House"

ASSUMPTA ◆Assumpta Serna — actress whose roles included Anna Cellini on TV's "Falcon Crest"

ASTRID ◆Astrid Allwyn — played Susan Paine in Jimmy Stewart's classic "Mr. Smith Goes to Washington" ◆ Astrid Lindgren — author of the "Pippi Longstocking" stories for children

ATHENA ◆Athena Lorde — actress who played Judith Richardson on the soap "One Man's Family" ◆Athena Onassis — granddaughter and sole heir of Greek shipping tycoon Aristotle Onassis

ATHENE ◆Athene Seyler — actress whose roles included the ruthless Queen Elizabeth in "Drake of England"

ATTALLAH ◆Attallah Shabazz — daughter of Malcolm X, actress who founded the theater troupe Nucleus

AUDRA ◆Audra Lindley — actress who played Mrs. Roper on John Ritter's sitcom "Three's Company"

AUDRE ◆Audre Johnston — actress whose roles included Martha Ann Ashley on the soap "The Secret Storm" ◆ Audre Lorde — poet laureate, won the 1989 American Book Award for "A Burst of Light"

AUDREY ◆Audrey Hepburn — almond-eyed beauty in "Charade," "Wait Until Dark," Oscar for "Roman Holiday" ◆ Audrey Landers — actress whose roles included Afton Cooper on TV's "Dallas" ◆ Audrey Meadows — played Ralph Kramden's wife on TV's "The Honeymooners" ("To the Moon Alice!")

AUDRIE ◆Audrie Neenan — actress whose roles included Nurse Faye Baryiski on TV's "Doctor, Doctor"

AUGUSTA ◆Maria Augusta von Trapp — founder of The Trapp Family Singers, Julie Andrews biopic "The Sound of Music" ◆

Augusta Anderson — actress who played Mrs. Wallaby in Charles Laughton's "Ruggles of Red Gap"

AURORA ◆Aurora Cornu — actress in the French film "Claire's Knee"

AUTANYA ◆Autanya Alda — actress whose roles included Carol Ann in Faye Dunaway's "Mommie Dearest"

AVA ◆Ava Gardner — starred in "Show Boat," married to Mickey Rooney, Artie Shaw, and Frank Sinatra

AVICE ◆Avice Landone — British stage actress, usually in cool, unruffled roles

AVIS ◆Avis McCarther — actress whose roles included Nancy Grant on the soap "All My Children"

AVRIL ◆Avril Angers — British character comedienne, appeared in Hayley Mills' "The Family Way"

AYESHA ◆Ayesha — second wife of Mohammad

AYN ◆Ayn Rand — author whose novels include "The Fountainhead" and "Atlas Shrugged"

AZZEDINE ◆Azzedine Alaia — fashion designer of elegant ready-to-wear fashions that are clingy and sexy

BABE ◆Babe Zacharias — one of the greatest female athletes of all time, Susan Clark biopic "Babe"

BABETTE ◆Babette De Castro — one of The De Castro Sisters, 1954 debut hit single "Teach Me Tonight" ◆Alice Babette Toklas — her "Autobiography" was actually written by her companion Gertrude Stein

BAMBI ◆Bambi Linn — dancer for Shirley Jones in the musical "Oklahoma"

BARBARA ◆Barbara Bach — married Ringo Starr after starring with him in the film "Caveman" ◆ Barbara Eden — made TV magic in "I Dream of Jeannie" ◆Barbara Feldon — actress whose roles included Agent 99 on the sitcom "Get Smart" ◆ Barbara Hershey — actress in such films as "Beaches," "The Entity," "Return to Lonesome Dove" ◆Barbara Mandrell — country pop singer, hits include number one "Sleeping Single in a Double Bed" ◆ Barbara Stanwyck — screen legend of "Double Indemnity," "Meet John Doe," on TV's "Big Valley"

BARBARA ANN ◆Barbara Ann Scott — two-time world figure skating champion and Olympic gold medal winner

BARBI ◆Barbi Benton — nine-year girlfriend of "Playboy" founder Hugh Hefner

BARBRA ◆Barbra Streisand — supreme vocalist and Oscar winner launched to superstar status with "Funny Girl"

BARRIE ◆Barrie Youngfellow — actress who played Linda Barry on TV's "Fernwood 2-Night," also on "It's a Living"

BEA ◆Bea Arthur — comedienne whose TV successes include "Maude" and "The Golden Girls" ◆ Bea Benaderet — actress whose roles included Kate Bradley on TV's "Petticoat Junction"

BEAH ◆Beah Richards — Oscar nominee as Sidney Poitier's mother in "Guess Who's Coming to Dinner"

BEATRICE ◆Beatrice Straight — Oscar winner for her role of Louise Schumacher in "Network"

BEATRIS ◆Alexandra Beatris Brown — child of actress Tyne Daly and Georg Sanford Brown

BEATRIX ◆Beatrix — became Queen of the Netherlands in 1980 ◆ Beatrix Potter — author of "The Tales of Peter Rabbit"

BEBE ◆Bebe Daniels — played Lily Owens in Edward G. Robinson's "Silver Dollar" ◆ Bebe Miller — choreographer, artistic director of the Bebe Miller Company ◆Bebe Neuwirth — actress who played the annoying Lilith, wife of Frasier, on TV's "Cheers"

BECKY ◆Becky Thatcher (c) — girlfriend in "The Adventures of Tom Sawyer"

BEE-BE ◆Bee-be Smith — portrayed Gloria on TV's "A Different World"

BEEBE ◆Margaret Beebe Sutton — children's author best known for the Judy Bolton series

BEIGE ◆Beige Dawn Adams — daughter of secret agent "Maxwell Smart" Don Adams

BEL ◆Barbara Bel Geddes — Emmy winner for role as Miss Ellie on prime-time soap "Dallas" ◆Bel Kaufman — author of "Up the Down Staircase," filmed with Sandy Dennis

BELINDA ◆Belinda Carlisle — lead singer for the Go-Go's, solo hits "Mad About You" and "Circle in the Sand" ◆ Belinda Montgomery — actress whose roles included the mother of TV's "Doogie Howser, M.D."

BELITA ◆Belita Jepson-Turner — British ice skating star, films include "Ice Capades" ◆ Belita Moreno — actress who played Edwina Twinkacetti on the hit sitcom "Perfect Strangers"

BELLA ◆Bella Darvi — actress who played Denise in the Richard Widmark film "Hell and High Water" ◆ Bella Spewack — wrote the Broadway hits "Boy Meets Girl" and "Kiss Me Kate"

BELLE ◆Belle Starr — Wild West heroine who was a rustler and cohort of Cole Younger

BELVA ◆Belva Plain — author of "Evergreen" and "Random Winds"

BENAY ◆Benay Venuta — actress who played Dolly Tate in the Betty Hutton musical "Annie Get Your Gun"

BENITA ◆Benita Hume — actress who played Vicki Hall in Ronald Colman's TV show "Halls of Ivy" ◆Benita Valente — lyric soprano with the New York Metropolitan Opera

BENJAMINE ◆Benjamine Lou Abruzzo — one of the first to make a trans-Atlantic balloon flight

BENNYE ◆Bennye Gatteys — actress who played Susan Hunter Peters on the soap "Days of Our Lives"

BERET ◆Beret Arcaya — actress whose roles included Linda Skerba on the soap "Flame in the Wind"

BERLINDA ◆Berlinda Tolbert — actress who played the girlfriend of Lionel on the sitcom "The Jeffersons"

BERNNADETTE ◆BernNadette Stanis — actress whose roles included daughter Thelma on the hit sitcom "Good Times"

BERNADETTE ◆Bernadette Peters — petite, pouty-lipped performer of "Pink Cadillac" and "The Jerk" ◆ Bernadette of Lourdes — French peasant girl who saw the Virgin Mary, biopic "The Song of Bernadette"

BERNADINE ◆Bernadine Dohrn — leader of the militant Weathermen, fled prosecution for breaking anti-riot laws

BERNADOTTE ◆Bernadotte Schmitt — Pulitzer Prize winning historian whose works include "The Coming of War"

BERNEICE ◆Marilyn Berneice Horne — opera singer who dubbed Dorothy Dandridge's voice in "Carmen Jones"

BERNICE ◆Bernice Clifton (c) — ditzy character played by Alice Ghostley on CBS's "Designing Women"

BERTA ◆Berta Gertsen — leading performer in New York's Yiddish theater

BERTHA ◆Bertha Krupp — daughter of arms manufacturer A. Krupp, cannon named after her was Big Bertha

BERYL ◆Beryl Markham — legendary pilot, Stephanie Powers biopic "Beryl Markham: A Shadow in the Sun" ◆Beryl Mercer — actress who played Mrs. Midget in the Leslie Howard film "Outward Bound"

BESS ◆Bess Armstrong — actress in "Four Seasons" and "High Road to China" ◆ Bess Myerson — first Jewish Miss America ◆ Bess Truman — First Lady to President Harry S Truman

BESSIE ◆Bessie Coleman — first African-American woman to become a pilot ◆ Bessie Love — nominated for an Oscar for "Broadway Melody"

BETH ◆Beth Howland — actress whose roles included Vera on TV's "Alice" ◆ Beth Levine — designer of fashionable shoes

BETHEL ◆Bethel Leslie — actress whose roles included Cornelia Otis skinner on "The Girls"

BETSY ◆Betsy Blair — Oscar nominee for her starring role in "Marty" ◆ Betsy Ross — made the first flag of the United States

BETTA ◆Betta St. John — actress whose films include "The Robe"

BETTE ◆Bette Davis — screen legend, double Oscar winner for "Dangerous" and "Jezebel" ◆ Bette Midler — vocalist and comedienne from "Big Business," "Down and Out in Beverly Hills"

BETTINA ◆Bettina — French model ◆Bettina Brenna — actress who played Gloria Buckles on the hit sitcom "The Beverly Hillbillies" ◆Bettina Gregory — White House correspondent with ABC news

BETTY ◆Betty Ford — founder of the Betty Ford Center, biopic "The Betty Ford Story" ◆ Betty Grable — pin up girl of World War II who had her legs insured for a million dollars ◆ Betty Hutton — actress in film musical "Annie Get Your Gun" ◆Betty White — animal rights activist on TV's "Mary Tyler Moore," ditziest "Golden Girl"

BETTYE ◆Bettye Ackerman — actress who starred in the medical drama series "Ben Casey"

BEULAH ◆Beulah Bondi — Oscar nominee for "Gorgeous Hussy Of Human Hearts," Emmy for TV's "Waltons"

BEVERLEE ◆Beverlee McKinsey — actress whose roles included Emma Ordway on the soap "Another World"

BEVERLY ◆Beverly Andland — actress who caused a scandal with her Errol Flynn romance ◆ Beverly D'Angelo — actress in "Hair" and all of the National Lampoon "Vacation" movies ◆ Beverly Sills — coloratura soprano, director of the New York City opera

BIANCA ◆Bianca DeGarr — played Patty in the Joseph Bologna comedy/drama series "Rags to Riches" ◆Bianca Jagger — ex-wife of rocker Mick Jagger, who didn't "get no satisfaction"

BIBA ◆Biba — English fashion designer

BIBI ◆Bibi Andersson — actress in Ingmar Bergman films, "The Seventh Seal," "Brink of Life" ◆ Bibi Besch — actress who played Adrienne Duncan Mortimer on the drama series "The Hamptons" ◆ Bibi Osterwald — a regular on the musical variety show "Front Row Center"

BIDDY ◆Biddy Mason — nurse who became one of the first African-American women to own property in LA

BIJOUX ◆Bijoux Phillips — child of singer John Phillips and Genevieve Waite

BILLIE ◆Billie Burke — actress who played Glinda, the Good Witch of the North, in "The Wizard of Oz" ◆ Billie Holiday — tragic singer of the Jazz Age, songs included "God Bless the Child"

BILLIE JEAN ◆Billie Jean King — most famous woman tennis player ever, won twenty Wimbledon titles

BILLIE LOU ◆Billie Lou Watt — actress who played Ellie Harper Bergman on the soap "Search for Tomorrow"

BINA ◆Bina Rothschild — actress who played the Queen of Transylvania in Audrey Hepburn's "My Fair Lady"

BINKIE ◆Binkie Stuart — British child actress of the 30's whose films include "Moonlight Sonata"

BINNIE ◆Binnie Barnes — played Catherine Howard in "The Private Life of Henry VIII" with Charles Laughton

BIRGITTA ◆Birgitta Tolksdorf — actress whose roles included Arlene Lovett Slater on the soap "Love of Life"

BITHIAH ◆Bithiah — Nina Foch's role in DeMille's biblical epic "The Ten Commandments"

BLAIR ◆Blair Brown — star of TV's "The Days and Nights of Molly Dodd"

BLAKE ◆Blake Amanda Perlman — daughter of actor Ron Perlman

BLANCHE ◆Blanche Barrow — Estelle Parsons role in Warren Beatty's classic "Bonnie and Clyde" ◆ Blanche Du Bois (c) — Vivien Leigh's role in "A Streetcar Named Desire"

BLAZE ◆Blaze Starr — stripper girlfriend of the governor of Louisiana, Paul Newman biopic "Blaze"

BLONDIE ◆Blondie — rock group of Deborah Harry, forerunner of punk rock, hits include "Rapture"

BLOSSOM ◆Blossom Rock — actress who played Grandmama Addams on the hit sitcom "The Addams Family" ◆ Blossom Seeley — vaudeville performer, biopic "Somebody Loves Me"

BLYTHE ◆Blythe Danner — actress in "The Great Santini," "The Prince of Tides," "Brighton Beach Memoirs"

BO ◆Bo Derek — showed all of her assets in "10" and "Bolero"

BOBBI ◆Bobbi Jordan — actress whose roles included Ada on the comedy western series "The Rounders" ◆Bobbi Trout — early pioneer in woman's aviation

BOBBIE ◆Bobbie Arnstein — Hugh Hefner's secretary, convicted of cocaine dealing, who committed suicide ◆ Bobbie Gentry — composed and sang "Ode to Billy Joe," which became a film

BOND ◆Bond Gideon — actress who played Jill Foster Abbott on the soap "The Young and the Restless"

BONITA ◆Bonita Granville — played the little girl in the store in Edward G. Robinson's "Silver Dollar"

BONNIE ◆Bonnie Bedelia — played the no-nonsense wife of Bruce Willis in "Die Hard" and "Die Harder" ◆Bonnie Parker — girl bandit who terrorized the Depression era midwest, biopic "Bonnie and Clyde" ◆ Bonnie Raitt — Grammy winning blues singer, hits include "Nick of Time" ◆Bonnie Tyler — raspy-voiced singer, hits include number one "Total Eclipse of the Heart"

BOYD ◆Boyd Bennett — scored a hit with the song "My Boy Flat-Top"

BRANDI ◆Brandi Tucker — actress who played Karen Becker on the soap "The Young and the Restless"

BRANDY ◆Brandy Gold — actress whose roles included Lindsay Dutton on TV's "First Impressions" ◆Brandy Norwood — actress whose roles included the daughter on the sitcom "Thea"

BRENDA ◆Brenda Lee — country western singer, hits include "Rockin' Round the Christmas Tree" ◆Brenda Vaccaro — raspy-voiced actress in "Midnight Cowboy," "Once is not Enough," "Airport '77"

BREON ◆Breon Gorman — actress whose roles included Ellen Snow on the soap "One Life to Live"

BRETT ◆Brett Butler — star of the ABC hit sitcom "Grace Under Fire" ◆Brett Somers — actress, ex-wife of Jack Klugman

BRIDEY ◆Bridey Murphy — reincarnated in "The Search for Bridey Murphy"

BRIDGET ◆Bridget Fonda — one of the Fonda acting clan, "Doc Hollywood" and "Single White Female"

BRIGID ◆Brigid Bazlen — actress whose roles included the seductive biblical Salome in "King of Kings" ◆ Angela Brigid Lansbury — longtime film actress on TV as the star of "Murder She Wrote" ◆ Brigid of Kildare — after St. Patrick, the greatest religious figure in Ireland

BRIGITTA ◆Brigitta von Trapp — one of the singing children in Julie Andrews' classic "The Sound of Music"

BRIGITTE ◆Brigitte Michael Sumner — daughter of rock singer Sting ◆ Brigitte Bardot — French sex kitten of the 1960's who made film temperatures rise ◆Brigitte Nielsen — beautiful villain Karla Fry in Eddie Murphy's "Beverly Hills Cop II"

BRITT ◆Britt Ekland — Swedish actress, married Peter Sellers, starred in "The Man with the Golden Gun"

BRITTANY ◆Brittany Craven — actress who played Janey Steadman on the comedy/drama series "thirtysomething" ◆ Brittany Thornton — actress whose roles included Laurie Escobar on the sitcom "Knight and Daye"

BROOKE ◆Brooke Adams — actress in the remake of "Invasion of the Body Snatchers" ◆Brooke Hayward — actress daughter of Leland Hayward and Margaret Sullavan, author of "Haywire" ◆ Brooke Shields — professional good girl trying to live down her "Pretty Baby" image

BROWNIE ◆Brownie McGhee — actress whose roles included Toots Sweet in Mickey Rourke's film "Angel Heart"

BRYNN ◆Brynn Thayer — actress who played Dr. Margaret Judd on the medical drama "Island Son"

BUFFY ◆Buffy Sainte-Marie — singer and composer, Oscar for the song from "An Officer and a Gentleman"

BUNNY ◆Bunny DeBarge — singer with family group DeBarge, hit single "Rhythm of the Night"

BURDETTA ◆Burdetta Beebe — children's author, works include "Run, Light Buck, Run!" and "African Elephants"

BURNITA ◆Burnita Matthews — first female federal district court judge

BUTTERFLY ◆Butterfly McQueen — in "Gone With the Wind" she "didn't know nothing about birthing no babies"

CAITLIN ◆Caitlin Cassidy — daughter of rock singer and teen idol Shaun Cassidy ◆ Caitlin O'Heaney — actress who played Snow White on TV's enchanted sitcom "The Charmings"

CALEY ◆Caley Chase — daughter of comedy actor Chevy Chase

CALLIE ◆Callie Khourie — Oscar winning screenwriter for "Thelma and Louise"

CALPURNIA ◆Calpurnia — third wife of Julius Caesar who dreamed of his assassination

CAMERA ◆Camera Ashe — daughter of tennis player Arthur Ashe

CAMI ◆Cami Copper — actress who played a member of the human insect family in "The Applegates"

CAMILA ◆Camila Ashland — actress whose roles included Alice Grant on the soap "General Hospital"

CAMILLA ◆Camilla Horn — actress whose films include "The Return of Raffles"

CAMILLE ◆Camille Claudel — French sculptress and mistress to Auguste Rodin, biopic "Camille Claudel" ◆ Camille Javal — real name of screen sex goddess Brigitte Bardot

CAMMIE ◆Cammie King — actress who played Rhett's daughter Bonnie Blue Butler in "Gone With the Wind"

CANDACE ◆Candace Cameron — actress whose roles included D. J. Tanner on the sitcom "Full House" ◆ Candace Hutson — actress whose roles included Molly Newton on TV's "Evening Shade"

CANDI ◆Candi Brough — played twin Teri Garrison with her sister Randi on the series "B.J. and the Bear" ◆ Candi Staton — soul singer, hits include "I'd Rather Be an Old Man's Sweetheart"

CANDICE ◆Candice Bergen — Emmy-winner for her tough-tongued TV journalist character "Murphy Brown"

CANDY ◆Candy Clark — gum-chomping curvey blond in "American Graffiti" ◆ Candy Johnson — actress whose roles included Miss Perpetual Motion in the film "Beach Party" ◆ Candy Jones — model and cover girl who founded Candy Jones Career Girls School

CAPUCINE ◆Capucine — played Simone Clouseau, the bored, frustrated wife of Inspector Clouseau

CARA ◆Cara Williams — played the lead role of Gladys Porter on the sitcom "Pete and Gladys"

CAREN ◆Caren Kaye — actress whose roles included Eileen Burton on the sitcom "It's Your Move"

CAREY ◆Carey Lowell — played Pam Bouvier in Timothy Dalton's James Bond film "Licence to Kill"

CARI ◆Cari Warder — actress whose roles included Amy Vining on the soap "General Hospital"

CARIL ◆Caril Fugate — friend of Charles Starkweather allegedly involved in his murders

CARIS ◆Caris Corfman — actress whose roles included Sally Mackeson in the film "Dreamchild"

CARLA ◆Carla Thompson — rock singer, debut hit single "Gee Whiz (Look at His Eyes)" ◆Carla Tortelli (c) — Rhea Perlman's caustic waitress character on TV's "Cheers"

CARLENE ◆Carlene Carter — country music singer, stepdaughter of Johnny Cash ◆Carlene Watkins — actress whose roles included the wife of Bob Newhart on TV's "Bob"

CARLIN ◆Carlin Glynn — played Sylvia in John Belushi's high mountain comedy "Continental Divide"

CARLOTA ◆Carlota — wife of Maximilian and empress of Mexico in the nineteenth century

CARLY ◆Carly Ritter — daughter of comedy actor John Ritter of TV's "Three's Company" ◆ Carly Simon — vocalist whose hits include "You're so Vain" and "Anticipation"

CARMAN ◆Carman Schreider — actress who played Dr. Annie Stewart Ward on the soap "As the World Turns"

CARMEL ◆Carmel Myers — portrayed Zaya in Lon Chaney's "Tell It to the Marines" ◆ Carmel Snow — editor of "Harper's Bazaar" who promoted Parisian designers

CARMELA ◆Carmela Ponselle — mezzo-soprano with the NY Metropolitan Opera

CARMELITA ◆Carmelita Pope — regular on TV's quiz show "Down You Go"

CARMEN ◆Carmen (c) — gypsy tigress of Prosper Merimee who wrecks a Spanish officer's career ◆Carmen McRae — jazz singer ◆ Carmen Miranda — Brazilian rhumba singer whose trademark was wearing fruit on her head

CARMENCITA ◆Carmencita Johnson — actress whose films included Miriam Hopkins' "These Three"

CARNIE ◆Carnie Wilson — singer in female vocal group "Wilson Phillips," daughter of Beach Boy Brian Wilson

CAROL ◆Carol Burnett — multi-talented singer/actress/comedienne extraordinaire of TV and film ◆ Carol Channing — comedienne who was vivacious in "Thoroughly Modern Millie" ◆ Carol Kane — actress who played the immigrant Simka on the classic TV sitcom "Taxi" ◆ Carol Lynley — actress in "Return to Peyton Place" and "The Poseidon Adventure"

CAROL-ANN ◆Carol-Ann Plante — played Sara Henderson on the Sasquatch sitcom "Harry and the Hendersons"

CAROLE ◆Carole King — successful songwriter, album "Tapestry" considered finest of the 1970's ◆ Carole Lombard — star in the 30's, married to Clark Gable when she was killed in a plane crash ◆ Carole Sager — Emmy winner for "That's What Friends Are For"

CAROLINA ◆Carolina Herrera — fashion designer of ready-to-wear elegant clothing ◆ Carolina Kava — played the mother of Vietnam Vet Ron Kovic in "Born on the Fourth of July"

CAROLINE ◆Princess Caroline — daughter of Princess Grace and Prince Rainier of Monaco ◆ Caroline Ingalls — mother of

Laura Ingalls on the drama series "Little House on the Prairie" ◆
Caroline Kennedy — daughter of Jackie Onassis

CAROLYN ◆Carolyn Jones — actress whose roles included
Morticia on TV's "The Addams Family" ◆Carolyn McCormick —
actress whose roles included Elizabeth Olivet on TV's "Law and
Order"

CAROLYNE ◆Carolyne Roehm — founder of the Carolyne
Roehm fashion design house

CAROLYNNE ◆Carolynne Snowden — portrayed the African-
American dancer in John Gilbert's "The Merry Widow"

CARRIE ◆Carrie Fisher — Princess Leia in "Star Wars,"
desperate bachelorette in "When Harry Met Sally" ◆ Carrie
Hamilton — actress who played Reggie Higgins on TV's "Fame,"
daughter of Carol Burnett ◆ Carrie Ingalls — youngest sister of
Laura Ingalls on the series "Little House on the Prairie" ◆Carrie
Snodgress — actress whose roles included Tina Balser in "Diary
of a Mad Housewife"

CARROLL ◆Carroll Baker — Oscar nominee for "Baby Doll"

CARRY ◆Carry Nation — she financed the destruction of saloons
by selling souvenir hatchets

CARYL ◆Caryl Churchill — Obie winner for plays "Cloud Nine"
and "Top Girls"

CARYN ◆Caryn Johnson — real name of actress/comedian
Whoopi Goldberg ◆ Caryn Richman — actress whose roles
included Gidget on the sitcom "The New Gidget"

CASS ◆Cass Elliot — round rocker of the group "The Mamas and
the Papas"

CASSANDRA ◆Cassandra Cooper — Missy Francis' role on the
drama series "Little House on the Prairie" ◆ Cassandra Peterson
— real name of Elvira, Mistress of the Dark

CASSIE ◆Cassie Yates — portrayed Diane Wyman on CBS's
"Detective in the House"

CATARINA ◆Catarina Cellino — actress who played Maria on
the Gabe Kaplan sitcom "Welcome Back, Kotter"

CATERINA ◆Caterina Valente — singer whose hits include gold
record "The Breeze and I"

CATHALENE ◆Cydney Cathalene Chase — daughter of comedy
film star Chevy Chase

CATHERINE ◆Catherine Bach — actress whose roles included Daisy Duke on TV's "The Dukes of Hazzard" ◆ Catherine Deneuve — gorgeous French movie star nominated as Best Actress for "Indochine" ◆ Catherine Oxenberg — actress who played Amanda Carrington on "Dynasty," cousin of Prince Charles ◆ Catherine the Great — German born Russian empress who greatly expanded her country

CATHIE ◆Cathie Shirriff — actress who played Zoya Antonova on the Leslie Nielsen sitcom "Shaping Up"

CATHRYN ◆Cathryn Damon — actress whose roles included Mary Campbell on the soap spoof "Soap"

CATHY ◆Cathy Guisewite — created comic strip "Cathy" ◆Cathy Moriarty — actress in "Raging Bull" and "Neighbors" ◆ Cathy O'Donnell — played opposite Oscar winner Harold Russell in "The Best Years of Our Lives" ◆Cathy Rigby — Olympic gymnast who peddled feminine protection products

CATHY LEE ◆Cathy Lee Crosby — host of TV's "That's Incredible!"

CATTE ◆Catte Adams — regular on the music series "You Write the Songs"

CEC ◆Cec Verrell — played Lt.Cdr. Ruth Rutkowski on the navy drama series "Supercarrier"

CECELIA ◆Cecelia Beaux — nineteenth century portrait artist

CECIL ◆Cecil Hoffman — played assistant D. A. Zoey Clemmons on the legal drama series "L.A. Law"

CECILE ◆Cecile Aubry — second to play the luxury-craving whore Manon Lescaut on the screen ◆ Cecile Dionne — one of the Dionne Quintuplets, the first surviving quints

CECILIA ◆Cecilia Parker — actress whose roles included Mickey Rooney's sister in the "Andy Hardy" series

CEIL ◆Ceil Chapman — designer of seductive evening gowns

CELESTE ◆Tennessee Celeste Claflin — early advocate of equal rights for women ◆ Celeste Holm — Oscar winning actress for "Gentleman's Agreement"

CELIA ◆Celia Thaxter — poet whose volumes include "Driftwood"

CHAD ◆Chad Redding — actress whose roles included Sgt. Alice Shepherd on TV's "The Equalizer"

CHAKA ◆Chaka Khan — soul singer, hits include "Tell Me Something Good" and "Once You Get Started"

CHARITA ◆Charita Bauer — played Bert Bauer, longest running character on the soap "Guiding Light"

CHARLENE ◆Charlene Tilton — portrayed rich spoiled brat Lucy Ewing on TV's "Dallas"

CHARLOTTE ◆Charlotte Bronte — English author of "Jane Eyre" ◆Charlotte Rose Jones — daughter of celebrity Rickie Lee Jones ◆Charlotte Rae — starred on TV's "Diff'rent Strokes" and "The Facts of Life" ◆ Charlotte Rampling — gaunt actress betraying Paul Newman in "The Verdict"

CHARLY ◆Charly McClain — country western crossover singer, hits include "Who's Cheatin' Who"

CHARMAINE ◆Charmaine "Shultzy" Schultz (c) — Ann B. Davis' role on the sitcom "The Bob Cummings Show" ◆ Charmaine Sylver — member of the group The Sylvers, soul hits "Boogie Fever" and "Hot Line"

CHARMIAN ◆Charmian Carr — portrayed Liesl von Trapp in Julie Andrews' "The Sound of Music"

CHARNELE ◆Charnele Brown — portrayed Kim Reese on TV's "A Different World"

CHARO ◆Charo — Spanish actress best known for guest appearances on TV's "The Love Boat"

CHASTITY ◆Chastity Bono — daughter of Sonny and Cher who appeared on their TV show as a toddler

CHEERIO ◆Cheerio Meredith — actress who played Lovey Hackett on the Dick Sargent sitcom "One Happy Family"

CHELSEA ◆Chelsea Clinton — First Kid, only child of President and Hillary Clinton ◆ Chelsea Noble — actress whose roles included Kate MacDonald on TV's "Growing Pains"

CHER ◆Cher — poster child of plastic surgery, from "Sonny and Cher" to an Oscar for "Moonstruck"

CHERIE ◆Cherie Johnson — actress who appeared in the sitcom "Punky Brewster" ◆ Cherie Lunghi — actress whose roles included Carlotta in Robert De Niro's "The Mission"

CHERILYN ◆Cherilyn Lalier — real name of singer and Oscar winning actress Cher

CHERYL ◆Cheryl Ladd — played Kris, one of "Charlie's Angels," TV's aerobicized female detectives of the 70's ◆ Cheryl Tiegs — highest paid model of the 1970's

CHEVI ◆Chevi Colton — actress whose roles included Gigi Magagnoli on the soap "The Edge of Night"

CHILI ◆Chili Bouchier — British leading lady in films of the 30's and 40's

CHINA ◆China Muchado — top international high-fashion model during the 1950's

CHITA ◆Chita Rivera — created the role of Anita in the Broadway version of "West Side Story"

CHLOE ◆Chloe Rose — daughter of singing superstar Olivia Newton-John ◆ Chloe Malle — daughter of "Murphy Brown" actress Candice Bergen and Louis Malle ◆Chloe Webb — actress who played USO entertainer Laurette Barber on TV's "China Beach"

CHRIS ◆Chris Evert — professional tennis player

CHRISSIE ◆Chrissie Hynde — founder of The Pretenders, debut hit record "Brass in Pocket"

CHRISSY ◆Chrissy Snow (c) — Suzanne Somers role on the hit sitcom "Three's Company"

CHRISTA ◆Christa McAuliffe — first teacher in space, died in Challenger space shuttle explosion ◆Christa Shields — real name of actress Brooke Shields

CHRISTIAN ◆Alicia Christian Foster — real name of actress/director Jodie Foster

CHRISTIE ◆Christie Brinkley — model and actress, wife of singer Billy Joel ◆ Christie Hefner — daughter of Hugh Hefner, runs his Playboy empire

CHRISTINA ◆Christina Applegate — played Kelly Bundy on the dysfunctional family sitcom "Married . . . With Children" ◆ Christina Crawford — abused daughter of Joan Crawford, book and biopic "Mommie Dearest" ◆ Christina Ferrare — magazine model, film actress, and former wife of John DeLorean

CHRISTINE ◆Christine Ebersole — actress who played the role of Katerina Cavalieri in the film "Amadeus" ◆ Christine Jorgensen — soldier who became the first to get a public sex-change operation

CHRISTOPHER ◆Christopher Norris — actress who played nurse Gloria Brancusi on the TV series "Trapper John, M.D."

CHRISTY ◆Christy Turlington — 1990's supermodel

CHRYSTAL ◆Chrystal Herne — starred in the Pulitzer Prize winning play "Craig's Wife"

CHYNNA ◆Chynna Phillips — singer with the trio "Wilson Phillips," daughter of Michelle and John Phillips

CIARAN ◆Ciaran Madden — played Robin's girlfriend Maid Marian in "Wolfshead: The Legend of Robin Hood"

CICELY ◆Cicely Tyson — star of the miniseries "The Autobiography of Miss Jane Pittman"

CICERO ◆Cicero — code name for Albanian spy Elyesa Bazna during WW II, biopic "Five Fingers"

CINDY ◆Cindy Brady (c) — youngest daughter on ABC's "The Brady Bunch," played by Susan Olsen ◆ Cindy Crawford — supermodel wife of Richard Gere, Prince named his song "Cindy C." after her ◆ Cindy Williams — played the peppy and perfect Shirley Feeney on TV's "Laverne and Shirley"

CIS ◆Cis Rundle — actress whose roles included Chris on the detective series "Matt Houston"

CISSIE ◆Cissie Loftus — actress best known for impersonations

CISSY ◆Cissy Colpitts — actress whose roles included Graziella on the sitcom "The Ted Knight Show" ◆Cissy Houston — first to record "Midnight Train to Georgia," mother of Whitney Houston

CLAIR ◆Clair Barnes — hostage in Iran ◆ Clair Huxtable (c) — Bill Cosby's wife on TV's long running "The Cosby Show"

CLAIRE ◆Claire Bloom — in Chaplin's "Limelight," former wife of Rod Steiger ◆ Claire McCardell — fashion designer of casual, popular-priced fashions ◆ Claire Trevor — received Oscar for "Key Largo" with Bogie

CLARA ◆Clara Barton — founder of the American Red Cross ◆ Clara Bow — "It" girl, movie star of the Twenties who symbolized the Flapper Age ◆ Clara Peller — actress known for saying "Where's the beef?" for Wendy's hamburgers

CLARE ◆Clare Carey — actress whose roles included Hayden Fox's daughter Kelley on the sitcom "Coach" ◆Clare Sheridan — sculpted bronze busts of heads of state, wrote memoirs "To the Fair Winds"

CLARETTA ◆Claretta Petacci — mistress of Italian dictator Mussolini, who was executed with him by partisans

CLARICE ◆Clarice Blackburn — actress whose roles included Mary Lou Northcote on the soap "The Secret Storm" ◆ Clarice Taylor — actress whose roles included Anna Huxtable on the hit sitcom "The Cosby Show"

CLAUDE ◆Claude Merelle — played the vengeful Milady de Winter in Berger's "The Three Musketeers"

CLAUDETTE ◆Claudette Colbert — French actress who won an Oscar for "It Happened One Night" ◆Claudette Robinson — one of Smokey Robinson's "Miracles," hits include "I Second That Emotion"

CLAUDIA ◆Claudia Cardinale — Italian actress whose films include "The Pink Panther" ◆Claudia Schiffer — 1990's German supermodel who looks like Brigitte Bardot ◆ Claudia Wells — played Jennifer Parker in the time paradox movie "Back to the Future"

CLEMENTINE ◆Clementine Paddleford — syndicated food editor known for her vivid descriptions of food

CLEMMIE ◆Clemmie Churchill — wife of English Prime Minister Sir Winston Churchill

CLEO ◆Cleo Staples — member of The Staple Singers, debut hit "Why? (Am I Treated So Bad)"

CLEOPATRA ◆Cleopatra — Queen of the Nile who ruled ancient Egypt during the Roman Empire

CLEOTHA ◆Cleotha Staple — member of The Staple Singers, soul hits include "Let's Do It Again"

CLORIS ◆Cloris Leachman — actress who played the same character on TV's "Mary Tyler Moore" and "Phyllis"

COBINA ◆Cobina Wright — opera singer who was also a columnist for Hearst Newspapers

COCO ◆Coco Chanel — created Chanel #5, Broadway biomusical "Coco," biopic "Chanel Solitaire"

COLETTE ◆Colette — French writer, usually on sex themes, whose works include "Gigi"

COLLEEN ◆Colleen Dewhurst — actress who played Candice Bergen's mother Avery Brown on TV's "Murphy Brown" ◆ Colleen McCullough — author of "The Thorn Birds," which became a miniseries ◆Colleen Moore — leading lady of the silent screen, autobiography is "Silent Star"

COLLETT ◆Lorraine Collett Peterson — model for the Sun-Maid raisin logo which is still used today ◆Glenna Collett Vare — legendary golfer, namesake for Vare Trophy for woman golfers

COMFORT ◆Pearl Comfort Sydenstricker — real name of author Pearl Buck

CONCETTA ◆Concetta Ingolia — real name of actress Connie Stevens ◆ Concetta Tomei — actress who played Dominique on the science fiction series "Max Headroom"

CONCHATA ◆Conchata Ferrell — actress whose films included "Heartland"

CONCHITA ◆Maria Conchita Alonso — actress whose roles included Louisa Gomez in Robert Duvall's gang film "Colors"

CONDOLA ◆Condola Phylea Rashad (c) — daughter of "Cosby Show" Phylicia Rashad and Ahmad Rashad

CONI ◆Coni Hudak — actress whose roles included Kate in the film "David and Lisa"

CONNEE ◆Connee Boswell — member of the singing trio The Boswell Sisters

CONNIE ◆Connie Chung — TV news personality married to Maury Povich ◆ Connie Francis — pop singer, appeared in "Where the Boys Are," "Follow the Boys" ◆Connie Sellecca — dark haired beauty who starred in TV's "The Greatest American Hero" and "Hotel" ◆ Connie Stevens — tousle-haired blond actress Cricket Blake on TV's "Hawaiian Eye"

CONSTANCE ◆Constance Bennett — actress daughter of Richard Bennett, films include "Topper" ◆Constance Cummings — actress who won a Tony award for "Wings" ◆Constance Ford — actress who played Ada Hobson for 25 years on the soap "Another World" ◆ Constance Talmadge — silent heroine and comedienne, films include "Intolerance"

CONSUELO ◆Clare Consuelo Sheridan — sculpted bronze busts of heads of state, wrote memoirs "To the Fair Winds"

CORA ◆Cora Witherspoon — actress whose roles included Carrie Spottswood in Bette Davis' "Dark Victory"

CORA SUE ◆Cora Sue Collins — actress who played Christina as a child in Greta Garbo's "Queen Christina"

CORAL ◆Coral Browne — Australian comedy actress whose films included "Auntie Mame"

CORDELIA ◆Cordelia Howard — played Little Eva in the original stage version of "Uncle Tom's Cabin"

CORETTA ◆Coretta Scott King — widow of Martin Luther King, Jr.

CORINNA ◆Corinna Mura — actress who played the singer in the classic Oscar winning film "Casablanca"

CORINNE ◆Corinne Calvet — French actress, films include "What Price Glory?" and "Flight to Tangiers" ◆ Corinne Griffith — played Emma Hamilton, the mistress of Lord Nelson, biopic "The Divine Lady"

CORITA ◆Corita Kent — designer of the "Love" postage stamp

CORKY ◆Corky Sherwood (c) — character on TV's "Murphy Brown," when married became Corky Sherwood-Forest

CORNELIA ◆Cornelia Guest — self-styled "Deb of the Decade"

CORNELL ◆Cornell Borchers — German leading actress in international films

CORRIE ◆Corrie Ten Boom — author of "The Hiding Place" which was filmed with Julie Harris

CORRINE ◆Corrine Bayley — Roman Catholic nun, founder of the Center for Bioethics

COSIMA ◆Cosima Wagner — daughter of Franz Liszt who married Wagner and founded the Bayreuth Festival

COURTENEY ◆Courteney Cox — actress whose roles included Lauren Miller on TV's "Family Ties"

COURTNEY ◆Courtney Peldon — played Darcy Payne on the Sasquatch sitcom "Harry and the Hendersons" ◆ Courtney Pledger — actress who played Deputy Joan Litton on the drama series "Walking Tall"

CREE ◆Cree Summer — actress whose roles included Freddie Brooks on TV's "A Different World"

CRISTINA ◆Cristina Raines — actress whose roles included Lane Ballou on TV's "Flamingo Road"

CRYSTAL ◆Crystal Bernard — regular on TV's "It's a Living," "Wings" ◆ Crystal Gayle — country singer whose repertoire includes "Don't It Make My Brown Eyes Blue"

CUSI ◆Cusi Cram — actress who played Cassie Howard Callison on the soap "One Life to Live"

CYB ◆Cyb Barnstable — actress whose roles included Betty II in the outer space sitcom "Quark"

CYBILL ◆Cybill Shepherd — played feisty Maddy Hayes, partner of David Addison on TV's "Moonlighting"

CYD ◆Cyd Charisse — balletic actress, danced with Fred Astaire and Gene Kelly in many MGM musicals

CYDNEY ◆Cydney Cathalene Chase — daughter of comedy film star Chevy Chase ◆ Cydney Crampton — actress whose roles included Rose Lobo Perkins on the police comedy "Lobo"

CYNDA ◆Cynda Williams — actress who played Clarke Bentancourt in Spike Lee's "Mo' Better Blues"

CYNDI ◆Cyndi Lauper — rock singer, hits include "Girls Just Want to Have Fun" ◆ Cyndi Wood — actress in the Marlon Brando anti-war film "Apocalypse Now"

CYNTHIA ◆Cynthia Geary — actress whose roles included Shelly on TV's "Northern Exposure" ◆ Cynthia Lynn — curvy and sexy secretary to Col. Klink on the sitcom "Hogan's Heroes"

DAGMAR ◆Dagmar — star of her own variety show "Dagmar's Canteen"

DAGNE ◆Dagne Crane — actress who played Sandra McGuire Tompson on the soap "As the World Turns"

DAKOTA ◆Dakota Mayi Brinkman — daughter of actress Melissa Gilbert of "Little House on the Prairie"

DALE ◆Dale Evans — singing cowgirl and wife of co-star cowboy Roy Rogers ◆ Dale Messick — created comic strip "Brenda Starr," filmed with Brooke Shields

DALIAH ◆Daliah Lavi — Israeli leading lady whose films include Peter O'Tooles' "Lord Jim"

DALLAS ◆Dallas Frazier — country singer, hits include "Elvira" and "Fourteen Carat Mind"

DALLIA ◆Dallia Penn — played Annette Lamotte Forsyte on the British soap import "The Forsyte Saga"

DAMITA ◆Damita Jo Freeman — played Pvt. Jackie Sims on the sitcom version of the film "Private Benjamin" ◆ Janet Damita

Jackson — youngest sister of Michael Jackson, Grammy for "Rhythm Nation"

DANA ◆Dana Delany — actress who played the conscientious nurse McMurphy on TV's "China Beach" ◆Dana Plato — actress whose roles included Kimberly Drummond on TV's "Diff'rent Strokes"

DANDELION ◆Dandelion Richard — daughter of Rolling Stone Keith Richards

DANDY ◆Dandy Nichols — her role on "Till Death Do Us Part" became Edith Bunker on "All in the Family"

DANI ◆Dani Crayne — actress who played the beautiful Helen of Troy in "The Story of Mankind"

DANICA ◆Danica McKellar — actress whose roles included Winnie Cooper on the sitcom "The Wonder Years"

DANIELA ◆Daniela Bianchi — Italian leading lady, heroine of "From Russia With Love"

DANIELE ◆Daniele Gaubert — actress who portrayed the notorious courtesan Camille

DANIELLE ◆Danielle Brisebois — perky child star of TV's "Archie Bunker's Place" ◆ Danielle Spencer — actress whose roles included Dee Thomas on the hit sitcom "What's Happening!" ◆ Danielle Steel — author of many popular mainstream novels

DANITRA ◆Danitra Vance — member of the Not Ready for Prime Time Players on "Saturday Night Live"

DANUTA ◆Danuta Soderman — co-host of "The 700 Club" of the Christian Broadcasting Company

DANY ◆Dany Robin — French leading lady whose films include "The Waltz of the Toreadors"

DAPHNE ◆Daphne Ashbrook — played Kathy "Speed" Davenport on Carl Weathers' TV show "Fortune Dane" ◆ Daphne DuMaurier — author of "Rebecca" and "Jamaica Inn" ◆ Daphne Zuniga — actress in "The Sure Thing," "Gross Anatomy" and TV's "Melrose Place"

DARCI ◆Darci Kistler — star and principal dancer with the NYC Ballet

DARIA ◆Daria Massey — actress who played Naja on the flying adventure series "The Islanders"

DARIAN ◆Darian Mathias — actress whose roles included Rita Zefferelli in the sitcom "Hanging In"

DARLA ◆Darla Jean Hood — one of Hal Roach's collection of child actors known as "Our Gang"

DARLANNE ◆Darlanne Fluegel — actress who played officer Joanne Molenski on the popular police drama "Hunter"

DARLEEN ◆Darleen Carr — actress who played lead Susan Winslow in the sitcom "Miss Winslow and Son"

DARYL ◆Daryl Hannah — actress who played the naive nympho-mermaid with Tom Hanks in "Splash"

DAWN ◆Rae Dawn Chong — actress whose films include "Commando" and "The Color Purple," father is Tommy Chong ◆ Dawn Wells — actress whose roles included Mary Ann on the classic sitcom "Gilligan's Island"

DAWNN ◆Dawnn Lewis — actress whose roles included Jaleesa Vinson on TV's "A Different World"

DAY ◆Lynda Day George — member of the action team on TV's "Mission Impossible" ◆ Sandra Day O'Connor — first woman Supreme Court justice

DAYLE ◆Dayle Haddon — actress who played heroine Pearl Prophet in Jean-Claude Van Damme's "Cyborg"

DEANNA ◆Deanna Durbin — along with Micky Rooney received a special Oscar as "spirit of youth" ◆ Deanna Lund — actress whose roles included Peggy Lowell on the soap "General Hospital"

DEANNE ◆Kathleen Deanne Battle — Grammy winning opera singer, coloratura soprano with the NY Metropolitan Opera

DEBBI ◆Debbi Fields — founder of Mrs. Fields Cookies ◆Debbi Morgan — actress whose roles included Angie Baxter on the soap "All My Children" ◆ Debbi Peterson — member of The Bangles, debut hit single "Manic Monday"

DEBBIE ◆Debbie Allen — dancer on TV's "Fame" ◆ Debbie Gibson — teen singer, hit album "Out of the Blue" ◆ Debbie Harry — rock singer with group Blondie, hits include "Call Me" ◆ Debbie Reynolds — dancer/actress who performed in "How the West Was Won," "Singin' in the Rain"

DEBBY ◆Debby Boone — daughter of Pat Boone, hit single "You Light Up My Life"

DEBI ◆Debi Richter — played Angela Morelli on the drama series "The Innocent and the Damned" ◆ Debi Thomas — first African-American figure skater to win the world championship

DEBORAH ◆Deborah Allen — country singer whose hits included "Baby I Lied" ◆ Deborah Kerr — played Anna in the musical feature "The King and I," but her voice was dubbed ◆ Deborah Anne Norville — Jane Pauley's replacement on "The Today Show"

DEBRA ◆Debra Paget — actress whose roles included the lead in "Cleopatra's Daughter" ◆ Debra Winger — starred in "Black Widow," "Terms of Endearment" and "Urban Cowboy"

DEBRAH ◆Debrah Farentino — actress whose roles included Julie Janovich on TV's "Equal Justice"

DEBRALEE ◆Debralee Scott — actress whose roles included Hotsie Totsie on TV's "Welcome Back, Kotter"

DEE ◆Dee Wallace Stone — mother in "E.T. The Extra-Terrestrial"

DEE DEE ◆Dee Dee Bridgewater — singer and actress ◆ Dee Dee Sperling — member of Dick and Dee Dee, hits include the gold record "The Mountain's High"

DEEDY ◆Deedy Peters — actress whose roles included Mrs. Phipps on Wayne Rogers' sitcom "House Calls"

DEENA ◆Deena Freeman — actress who played April Rush on the Ted Knight sitcom "Too Close for Comfort"

DEIDRE ◆Deidre Hall — played Marlena Evans on the soap "Days of Our Lives" for almost twenty years

DEIRDRE ◆Deirdre Berthrong — actress who played Kathy Hunter on Lance Kerwin's drama series "James at 15" ◆ Deirdre Lenihan — actress who played Wendy Nelson on Norman Fell's sitcom "Needles and Pins"

DEKA ◆Deka Beaudine — played Asheley Brooks on the law student drama series "The Paper Chase"

DELIA ◆Delia Bacon — developed the theory that Shakespeare was written by Francis Bacon

DELILAH ◆Delilah — in the Bible, Samson's love who cut his hair and betrayed him to the Philistines

DELISA ◆Delisa Davis — member of the rock group Shalamar, hits include "A Night to Remember"

DELLA ◆Della Reese — actress who played Judge Caroline Philips on the sitcom "It Takes Two"

DELOISE ◆Marva Deloise Collins — started Chicago's one-room school Westside Preparatory

DELORIS ◆Deloris van Cartier (c) — Whoopi Goldberg's lounge-singer on the lam in her megahit "Sister Act"

DELPHI ◆Delphi Harrington — actress whose roles included Lettie Jean on the soap "All My Children" ◆Delphi Lawrence — Anglo-Hungarian actress in British films

DELTA ◆Delta Burke — actress whose roles included Suzanne Sugarbaker on CBS's "Designing Women"

DEMETRIA ◆Demetria Gene Buynes — real name of actress Demi Moore

DEMI ◆Demi Moore — she cried all the way through "Ghost," then accepted an "Indecent Proposal"

DENA ◆Dena Dietrich — actress whose roles included Dena Madison on the Karen Valentine sitcom "Karen"

DENIECE ◆Deniece Williams — soul singer, hits include "Too Much, Too Little, Too Late"

DENISE ◆Denise Alexander — actress whose roles included Dr. Leslie Weber on TV's soap "General Hospital" ◆ Linda Denise Blair — actress whose roles included the possessed girl in "The Exorcist" ◆ Denise Nicholas — actress in TV series "Room 222"

DESIREE ◆Lucie Desiree Arnaz — actress daughter of Desi Arnaz and Lucille Ball

DEVON ◆Devon Ericson — actress whose roles included Fran on the Harry Hamlin drama "Studs Lonigan" ◆ Devon Odessa — actress who played Debbie Barnhill on the little robot sitcom "Small Wonder"

DEWEY ◆Laura Dewey Bridgman — first blind, deaf-mute to be successfully taught, in 1837

DIAHANN ◆Diahann Carroll — portrayed Dominique Devreaux on TV's "Dynasty"

DIAHN ◆Diahn Williams — actress whose roles included one of the girls on the sitcom "Harry's Girls"

DIAHNNE ◆Diahnne Abbott — actress whose films include De Niro's "Taxi Driver"

DIAMOND ◆Diamond Nicole Strawberry — daughter of baseball player Darryl Strawberry

DIAN ◆Dian Fossey — scientist, Sigourney Weaver biopic "Gorillas in the Mist"

DIANA ◆Diana Canova — actress on TV's prime time comedy "Soap" and the star of "Throb" ◆Diana Muldaur — actress in TV series "McCloud" and "Born Free" ◆Diana Rigg — actress whose roles included secret agent Emma Peel on TV's "The Avengers" ◆ Diana Ross — lead singer with The Supremes, won a special Tony for "The Wiz" ◆ Diana Spencer — Princess of Wales and wife of Prince Charles, well-loved by the tabloids

DIANE ◆Diane Keaton — won Academy Award for "Annie Hall" and started a fashion craze ◆ Diane Ladd — nominated for an Oscar for "Alice Doesn't Live Here Anymore" and "Ramblin' Rose" ◆Diane Sawyer — first female anchor on the network news magazine "60 Minutes" ◆ Diane von Furstenberg — fashion designer

DIANNE ◆Dianne Feinstein — mayor of San Francisco and US senator from California ◆ Dianne Kay — actress whose roles included Nancy Bradford on TV's "Eight Is Enough"

DIDI ◆Didi Conn — actress whose roles included Frenchie in the John Travolta musical "Grease"

DIEDRE ◆Diedre Hall — daytime soap star on "Days of Our Lives"

DILYS ◆Dilys Davis — actress whose films include Rosalind Russell's "The Citadel"

DIMITRA ◆Dimitra Arliss — played Marie Falconetti on the miniseries "Rich Man, Poor Man — Book II"

DINA ◆Dina Merrill — actress, daughter of E. F. Hutton and Marjorie Merriweather Post ◆Dina Ousley — actress who played Ellen Bronkov on the detective drama series "Bronk"

DINAH ◆Dinah Manoff — comic on sitcoms "Soap" and "Empty Nest" ◆ Dinah Shore — singer who has won ten Emmys with her TV shows

DIONNE ◆Dionne Warwick — singer whose hits include "Alfie," "Do You Know the Way to San Jose"

DIONY ◆Diony Jarvis (c) — wife of Daniel Boone in Elizabeth Madox Robert's novel "The Great Meadow"

DITA ◆Dita Parlo — German actress active in the 1930's who later became a character actor

DIVA ◆Diva Gray — member of The Harlettes in Bette Midler's "Divine Madness" ◆ Diva Zappa — daughter of rock musician Frank Zappa

DIXIE ◆Dixie Carter — actress whose roles included Julia Sugarbaker in CBS's "Designing Women" ◆ Dixie Lee — actress who married Bing Crosby ◆ Dixie Whatley — regular host on "Entertainment Tonight"

DIXY ◆Dixy Lee Ray — governor of Washington who received the United Nations Peace Medal

DODIE ◆Dodie Smith — author of "One Hundred and One Dalmations," later filmed by Walt Disney ◆ Dodie Stevens — hit the charts with the gold record "Pink Shoelaces"

DODY ◆Dody Goodman — actress whose roles included Althea Franklin on the soap "Search for Tomorrow"

DOE ◆Doe Avedon — actress in "The High and the Mighty" and "Deep in My Heart"

DOLLEY ◆Dolley Madison — First Lady to James Madison, saved treasures when British burned the White House

DOLLY ◆Dolly Parton — country singer with big hair and big assets turned movie star in "Nine to Five"

DOLORES ◆Dolores Del Rio — actress who played the beautiful Luana opposite Joe McCrea in "Bird of Paradise" ◆Dolores Hart — played Merritt Andrews in the Fort Lauderdale romp "Where the Boys Are"

DOMENICA ◆Domenica Barbaja — Italian opera singer

DOMINIQUE ◆Dominique Dunne — actress in "Poltergeist" who was allegedly strangled by her boyfriend

DONA ◆Dona Drake — Mexican singer, dancer, and general livewire, band vocalist as Rita Rio

DONNA ◆Donna Fargo — country western singer, hits include "The Happiest Girl in the Whole USA" ◆Donna Mills — actress who played self-serving schemer Abby Ewing on TV's "Knot's Landing" ◆ Donna Reed — starred as the happy homemaker of the TV classic "The Donna Reed Show" ◆ Donna Summer — singer, disco hits include "Hot Stuff," "Last Dance," and "Dinner with Gershwin"

DONNIE ◆Arizona Donnie Barker — nickname "Ma Barker," held up banks with her sons during the Depression

DORAN ◆Doran Clark — actress whose roles included Jillian on the drama series "King's Crossing"

DORCAS ◆Dorcas — raised from the dead by Peter in the Bible

DORIS ◆Doris Abrahams — Tony winning producer for "Equus" and "Travesties" ◆ Doris Day — singer/actress/perky good girl in "The Pajama Game" and "Pillow Talk" ◆Doris Lilly — author of "How to Marry a Millionaire" which was filmed with Marilyn Monroe

DORO ◆Doro Merando — actress in Marilyn Monroe's "The Seven Year Itch"

DOROTHEA ◆Dorothea Dix — social reformer who worked for the humane treatment of the insane ◆ Felicia Dorothea Hemans — poet, wrote "The Boy Stood on the Burning Deck" and "England's Dead"

DOROTHEE ◆Dorothee Berryman — actress who played Francine Primeau on the adventure series "Urban Angel"

DOROTHI ◆Dorothi Fox — actress whose films include "Come Back, Charleston Blue"

DOROTHY ◆Dorothy Dandridge — beautiful, sultry actress who starred in the film "Carmen Jones" ◆ Dorothy Gish — silent film actress of the early 1900's and sister of Lillian Gish ◆ Dorothy Lamour — love interest of Bing Crosby and Bob Hope in their "Road" movies

DORRIE ◆Dorrie Kavanaugh — actress whose films include "Hester Street"

DORY ◆Dory Previn — singer and composer of sad pop songs

DOTTIE ◆Dottie West — country music singer, hits include "Till I Can Make It on My Own"

DREE ◆Dree Louise Crisinan — daughter of Mariel Hemingway

DREW ◆Drew Barrymore — child star whose films include "E.T. The Extra-Terrestrial" and "Firestarter"

DULCIE ◆Dulcie Gray — gentle-mannered British leading leady, married to Michael Denison

DUSTIN ◆Dustin Ferrer — one of the twin daughters of "You Light Up My Life" singing star Debby Boone

DUSTY ◆Dusty Springfield — singer whose big hit song was "I Only Want to Be With You"

DWAN ◆Dwan Smith — played Jolene Jackson on Lloyd Bridges' police drama series "Joe Forrester"

DYAN ◆Dyan Cannon — actress whose film credits included "Bob and Carol and Ted and Alice"

DYANA ◆Dyana Ortelli — actress who played the role of Lupe on the very rich sitcom "Marblehead Manor"

DYLAN ◆Dylan Allen — daughter of actress Mia Farrow, and granddaughter of actress Maureen O'Sullivan

EARTHA ◆Eartha Kitt — singer with acting role in "Boomerang"

EBONIE ◆Ebonie Smith — actress whose roles included Jessica Jefferson on the sitcom "The Jeffersons"

EDA ◆Eda Merin — actress whose films include "Hester Street"

EDDI-RUE ◆Eddi-Rue McClanahan — real name of the Emmy winning actress from "The Golden Girls" and "Maude"

EDDRA ◆Eddra Gale — actress who played Anna Fassbender in Woody Allen's "What's New, Pussycat?"

EDEN ◆Eden Phillpotts — author of more than 250 works on rural life in west England

EDIE ◆Edie Adams — singer and actress, wife of comedian Ernie Kovacs ◆ Edie McClurg — actress who played Bonnie Brindle on the little robot sitcom "Small Wonder"

EDITH ◆Edith Head — Hollywood fashion designer of 1,000 films, nominated for 34 Oscars, won eight ◆ Edith Wilson — wife of President Woodrow Wilson, who actually ran the country when he was ill

EDMONIA ◆Edmonia Lewis — first African-American woman sculptor whose works include "Death of Cleopatra"

EDNA ◆Edna Woolman Chase — editor-in-chief of "Vogue," organized first US fashion show ◆ Edna Ferber — Pulitzer Prize winning author, filmed novels include "Show Boat" and "Giant" ◆ Edna St. Vincent Millay — Pulitzer Prize winning author for "The Ballad of the Harp Weaver"

EDWIGE ◆Edwige Fenech — played the tragic Emma Bovary in the fourth version of "Madame Bovary" ◆ Edwige Feuillere — actress who played the infamous Lucrezia in the French "Lucrezia Borgia"

EDWINA ◆Edwina Booth — leading lady who appeared in "Trader Horn" ◆ Edwina Carroll — actress in Kubrick's science fiction classic "2001 A Space Odyssey"

EDYE ◆Edye Byrde — actress whose roles included Ione Redlon on the soap "Another Life"

EDYTH ◆Edyth Walker — mezzo-soprano noted for Wagner, first American opera singer accepted in Europe

EDYTHE ◆Edythe Marrener — real name of actress Susan Hayward

EILEEN ◆Eileen Brennan — starred in both the movie and TV versions of "Private Benjamin" ◆ Eileen Ford — founder of the Ford model agency

EILY ◆Eily Malyon — actress who played Mrs. Cruncher in Ronald Colman's "A Tale of Two Cities"

ELAINE ◆Elaine Irwin — 1990's teen hearthrob, top fashion model and wife of John Cougar Mellencamp ◆Elaine Kaufman — founder of the famous Elaine's Restaurant in New York City

ELAYNE ◆Elayne Heilveil — actress whose roles included daughter Nancy Lawrence on TV's "Family"

ELDA ◆Elda Anderson — physicist who studied radiation protection ◆ Elda Furry — real name of Hedda Hopper

ELDRA ◆Eldra De Barge — member of the rock group De Barge, debut hit single "I Like It"

ELEANOR ◆Eleanor Roosevelt — humanitarian wife of FDR, and niece of Teddy Roosevelt ◆Eleanor of Aquitaine — mother of Richard the Lion-Hearted, biopic "The Lion in Winter"

ELEANORA ◆Eleanora Brown — actress who played Rosetta, the violated daughter of Sophia Loren in "Two Women" ◆ Eleanora Fagan — real name of Billie Holiday

ELENA ◆Elena Verdugo — played Millie Bronson on TV's "Meet Millie," Consuelo Lopez on "Marcus Welby MD"

ELENI ◆Eleni Anousaki — actress whose roles included Lola in Anthony Quinn's classic "Zorba the Greek"

ELENORE ◆Rita Elenore Gam — actress, films include "Klute" and "Night People"

ELEONORA ◆Eleonora Duse — eminent Italian tragedienne whose one film appearance was in "Cenere" ◆ Eleonora Sears — first woman squash champion, broke through into many men's sports

ELETTRA ◆Elettra — daughter of actress Isabella Rossellini, granddaughter of Ingrid Bergman

ELIE ◆Elie Kedourie — noted authority on the Middle East, author "Politics in the Middle East"

ELINOR ◆Elinor Donahue — teenage actress on TV's "Father Knows Best," played mother on "Get a Life"

ELISE ◆Hope Elise Lange — Oscar nominee for "Peyton Place," star of TV's "Ghost and Mrs. Muir" ◆ Joan Elise Lunden — interviewer with TV's "Good Morning, America"

ELISSA ◆Elissa Landi — aristocratic Austrian leading lady, films include "The Count of Monte Cristo" ◆Elissa Leeds — originated role of Brooke Cudahy on the soap "All My Children"

ELIZA ◆Frances Eliza Burnett — author of "Little Lord Fauntleroy" and "The Little Princess," both filmed ◆ Eliza Susan Pitts — real name of actress ZaSu Pitts

ELIZABETH ◆Elizabeth Ashley — plays Marilu Henner's aunt on TV's "Evening Shade" ◆Elizabeth Barrett Browning — when Robert Browning heard her poems, he immediately married her ◆ Elizabeth Montgomery — actress whose roles included the good witch Samantha on TV's "Bewitched" ◆Elizabeth Shue — star of "Adventures in Babysitting" and "Cocktail," "Karate Kid's" girlfriend ◆ Elizabeth Taylor — actress in "National Velvet," "Cleopatra," "Cat on a Hot Tin Roof"

ELKE ◆Elke Sommer — star of the Pink Panther film "A Shot in the Dark,"

ELLA ◆Ella Fitzgerald — jazz singer who has won eight Grammys ◆ Ella Geisman — real name of actress June Allyson ◆ Ella Wilcox — poet who wrote "Laugh, and the world laughs with you, weep, and you weep alone"

ELLA MAE ◆Ella Mae Morse — jazz vocalist, hits include "The Blacksmith Blues"

ELLALINE ◆Ellaline Terriss — British stage actress and the widow of Sir Seymour Hicks

ELLE ◆Elle Macpherson — model known for appearing on the covers of "Sports Illustrated" swimsuit issues

ELLEN ◆Ellen Barkin — her films include "Tender Mercies" ◆ Ellen Burstyn — her Oscar winning role was "Alice Doesn't Live Here Anymore" ◆ Ellen Cleghorne — regular "Saturday Night Live" cast member who plays Queen Shenequa

ELLENE ◆Ellene Bowers — actress who appeared in Victor Mature's "Violent Saturday"

ELLICE ◆Tula Ellice Finklea — real name of actress/dancer Cyd Charisse

ELLIN ◆Ellin Berlin — wife of Irving Berlin, writer for the "New Yorker" and "Saturday Evening Post"

ELLY ◆Elly Ameling — Dutch opera singer

ELLYN ◆Ellyn (c) — Polly Draper's role on the comedy/drama series "thirtysomething"

ELMA ◆Elma Lewis — founder of the Elma Lewis School of Fine Arts

ELNA ◆Elna Hubbell — actress who played Kathy Jo Elliott on the rural sitcom "Petticoat Junction"

ELOISE ◆Eloise Engle — author of "Dawn Mission" and "The Winter War" ◆ Dorothy Eloise Maloney — real name of actress Dorothy Malone

ELOYSE ◆Monetta Eloyse Darnell — real name of actress Linda Darnell

ELSA ◆Elsa Lanchester — wife of Charles Laughton whose roles included the Bride of Frankenstein ◆ Elsa Martinelli — actress discovered by Kirk Douglas, starred with him in "The Indian Fighter" ◆ Elsa Peretti — fashion model and jewelry designer

ELSBETH ◆Elsbeth Sigmund — did a more realistic job on the screen than Shirley Temple with "Heidi"

ELSIE ◆Elsie Ferguson — silent screen star whose films include "A Doll's House" ◆ Elsie Janis — first American to entertain troops in World War I

ELSPET ◆Elspet Gray — actress whose films include Meg Tilly's "Girl in a Swing"

ELSPETH ◆Elspeth Dudgeon — actress who appeared in Irene Dunne's classic film musical "Show Boat" ◆ Elspeth Huxley — author of "Man From Nowhere," "Scott of the Antarctic"

ELVERA ◆Elvera Roussel — actress who played Hope Bauer Spaulding on the soap "The Guiding Light"

ELVI ◆Elvi Hale — played Anne of Cleves in the historical drama "The Six Wives of Henry VIII"

ELVIA ◆Elvia Allman — actress who played Selma Plout on the rural sitcom "Petticoat Junction"

ELVIRA ◆Elvira — creator of character Elvira, Mistress of the Dark, host of "Movie Macabre" ◆ Elvira Madigan — love of a young Swedish Army officer, biopic "Elvira Madigan"

ELYA ◆Elya Baskin — actress whose roles included Yuri on the police drama series "True Blue"

ELYSE ◆Elyse Keaton (c) — mother played by Meredith Baxter-Birney on TV's "Family Ties"

ELYSSA ◆Elyssa Davalos — actress who played Nikki Carpenter on the action adventure series "MacGyver"

EMILIA ◆Emilia Maurer — dancer, choreographer, and director of Radio City Music Hall's Rockettes

EMILIE ◆Emilie Dionne — one of the Dionne Quintuplets, the first surviving quints ◆ Emilie Trampusch — Barbara Ferris' role on the romantic drama series "The Strauss Family"

EMILY ◆Emily Bronte — author of the brooding romance "Wuthering Heights" ◆ Emily Chase — daughter of actor Chevy Chase ◆ Emily Dickinson — she wrote 1,700 poems, only 7 of which were published during her lifetime ◆ Emily Post — wrote the definitive work on proper social behavior, "Etiquette"

EMMA ◆Emma Samms — actress whose roles included filthy rich Fallon Carrington on TV's "Dynasty" ◆Emma Thompson — won best actress Oscar for "Howard's End" ◆ Emma Willard — founder of the Emma Willard School

EMMALINE ◆Emmaline Henry — played Amanda Bellows on the popular genie sitcom "I Dream of Jeannie"

EMMANUELLE ◆Emmanuelle Bataille — actress who appeared in Dirk Bogarde's film "Daddy Nostalgia"

EMMUSKA ◆Baroness Emmuska Orczy — creator of the Scarlet Pimpernel brought to the screen by Leslie Howard

EMMYLOU ◆Emmylou Harris — country western singer, hits include "If I Could Only Win Your Love"

ENID ◆Enid Bagnold — wrote "National Velvet" ◆Enid Markey — actress who played the first Jane in the first "Tarzan" film with Elmo Lincoln

ENNI ◆Enni Buttykay — played the fiery man-eater Katharina in Shakespeare's "The Taming of the Shrew"

ENYA ◆Enya — vocalist whose album is "Shepherd Moons"

ERICA ◆Erica Gimpel — actress whose roles included Coco Hernandez on TV's "Fame" ◆ Erica Jong — author of "Fear of Flying"

ERIKA ◆Erika Eleniak — actress who played Shauni McLain on the bodywatch adventure series "Baywatch" ◆ Erika Slezak — actress who played Victoria Lord Buchanan on the soap "One Life to Live"

ERIN ◆Erin Gray — actress in TV's "Buck Rogers in the 25th Century" and "Silver Spoons" ◆ Erin Moran — actress who played younger sister Joanie Cunningham on TV's "Happy Days"

ERMA ◆Erma Bombeck — humorous syndicated columnist who concentrates on household tips

ERNA ◆Erna Morena — one of many actresses to portray the notorious 19th century courtesan Camille

ERNESTINE ◆Ernestine Carter — journalist with the London Times whose books include "Flash in the Pan"

ESMERALDA ◆Esmeralda Ruspoli — actress whose roles included Mary, Queen of Scots in "Seven Seas to Calais"

ESMERELDA ◆Esmerelda (c) — Maureen O'Hara character saved by the hunchback in "The Hunchback of Notre Dame"

ESPHYR ◆Esphyr Slobodkina — self-illustrated children's books include "Long Island Ducklings"

ESTEE ◆Estee Lauder — cosmetics magnate who founded the company bearing her name

ESTELITA ◆Estelita Rodriguez — portrayed Consuela in John Wayne's "Rio Bravo"

ESTELLE ◆Estelle Getty — actress who played Sophia Petrillo on TV's old-age sitcom "The Golden Girls" ◆ Estelle Parsons — actress who played Blanche Barrow in Warren Beatty's classic

"Bonnie and Clyde" ◆ Estelle Winwood — played the dirty old lady in Mel Brooks comedy classic "The Producers"

ESTER ◆Maria Ester Bueno — won the women's singles title at Wimbledon and Forest Hills

ESTHER ◆Esther Rolle — actress whose roles included lead Florida Evans on TV's hit sitcom "Good Times" ◆ Esther Williams — made a lot of her films in the pool, including "Million Dollar Mermaid"

ETHEL ◆Ethel Barrymore — mainly a theatrical actress, but like her brothers, appeared in some films ◆ Ethel Merman — Broadway singer whose best known song is "Everything's Coming Up Roses" ◆Ethel Waters — Oscar nominee for "Pinky," active in Billy Graham's crusade

ETTA ◆Etta James — soul singer, hits include "At Last," "Pushover," "Stop the Wedding" ◆ Etta Place — schoolteacher girlfriend of outlaw Butch Cassidy ◆Etta Plum — Leslie Landon's role on the drama series "Little House on the Prairie"

EUDORA ◆Eudora Welty — Pulitzer Prize winning author for "The Optimist's Daughter"

EUGENIA ◆Eugenia Sheppard — fashion editor who wrote the column "Inside Fashion"

EUGENIE ◆Eugenie Francis — real name of Genie Francis, played Laura on the soap "General Hospital" ◆ Eugenie Ross Leming — writer/creator of "Mary Hartman, Mary Hartman" and "Fernwood 2-night"

EUNICE ◆Eunice Kennedy — sister of President John F. Kennedy ◆ Eunice Quedens — real name of actress Eve Arden ◆ Katherine Eunice Schwarzenegger — daughter of Maria Shriver and Arnold Schwarzenegger

EVA ◆Little Eva — singer, hits include "The Loco-Motion" ◆Eva Fay Anderson — daughter of comedy actor Harry Anderson of TV's "Night Court" ◆Eva Gabor — actress whose roles included city girl Mrs. Douglas on TV's "Green Acres"

EVA MARIE ◆Eva Marie Saint — in Alfred Hitchcock's "North by Northwest," you don't know if she's the enemy

EVALINA ◆Evalina Fernandez — actress whose roles included Juanita Herrera on the hit sitcom "Roseanne"

EVALYN ◆Evalyn McLean — Washington hostess who owned the Hope Diamond

EVANGELINE ◆Ellen Evangeline Hovick — real name of actress June Havoc

EVE ◆Eve Arden — actress whose roles included "Our Miss Brooks" on early TV ◆ Eve Plumb — actress who portrayed Jan Brady on ABC's "The Brady Bunch"

EVELINE ◆Eveline Burns — designer of the Social Security Act

EVELYN ◆Evelyn Ankers — queen of the horror movies, played in "The Wolf Man" and "The Ghost of Frankenstein" ◆ Evelyn Keyes — actress who played Suellen O'Hara in Vivien Leigh's "Gone With the Wind" ◆Evelyn King — singer, disco hits include "Shame"

EVIE ◆Evie — singer who records her gospel music with country backups

EVITA ◆Evita Peron — co-ruler of Argentina with her husband Juan, bioplay "Evita"

EVONNE ◆Evonne Goolagong — Wimbledon winner in 1971 and 1980

EWA ◆Ewa Aulin — star of the James Coburn/Marlon Brando/Ringo Starr/Walter Matthau film "Candy" ◆ Ewa Mataya — top woman's pool player in the world

EYDIE ◆Eydie Gorme — singer married to Steve Lawrence

FABIA ◆Fabia Drake — British actress who usually plays battleaxes

FAITH ◆Faith Baldwin — popular romantic novelist whose works include "American Family" ◆ Faith Popcorn — analyst who predicted that "New Coke" would fail ◆ Faith Prince — Tony award winner for Miss Adelaide in "Guys and Dolls"

FALCONETTI ◆Falconetti — French actress unforgettable in her only film "The Passion of Jeanne d'Arc"

FANIA ◆Fania Fenelon — her memoirs, "Playing for Time," were filmed with Vanessa Redgrave

FANNIE ◆Fannie Farmer — American cookery expert ◆ Fannie Flagg — actress whose roles included Stoney in Jack Nicholson's "Five Easy Pieces"

FANNY ◆Fanny Brice — original "Funny Girl" on whom the Barbra Streisand film is based

FARRAH ◆Farrah Fawcett — actress who graduated from "Charlie's Angels" to "The Burning Bed"

FAWN ◆Fawn Brodie — biographer of Richard Burton, Thomas Jefferson, and Joseph Smith ◆ Fawn Hall — assistant to Contra scandal defendant Oliver North

FAWNE ◆Fawne Harriman — actress whose roles included Honey on the sitcom "The Ted Knight Show"

FAY ◆Fay Bainter — Oscar winner for "Jezebel" ◆ Fay Cheyney — played the scheming Lady Raffles who traveled in British high society ◆ Fay Holden — actress whose roles included Mickey Rooney's mother in the "Andy Hardy" films ◆Fay Wray — starred as the object of an ape's affection in the classic "King Kong"

FAYE ◆Tammy Faye Bakker — ex-wife of notorious evangelist Jim Bakker, always wore too much makeup ◆ Faye Dunaway — actress in "Bonnie and Clyde," "The Three Musketeers," Oscar for "Network" ◆ Faye Grant — actress who played the leading role of Dr. Julie Parrish on the miniseries "V"

FAYETTE ◆Fayette Pinkney — member of The Three Degrees, debut hit record "Gee Baby"

FELIA ◆Felia Doubrovska — dancer who later taught at the School of American Ballet

FELICE ◆Felice Bryant — songwriter, songs include "Wake Up Little Susie" and "Bye Bye Love" ◆ Felice Schacter — actress whose roles included Nancy Olson on TV's "The Facts of Life"

FELICIA ◆Felicia (c) — Kristina Malandro's role on the soap "General Hospital" ◆ Felicia Farr — actress married to Jack Lemmon, films include "3:10 to Yuma"

FELICITY ◆Felicity Kendal — Shakespearean actress, in film "Henry VIII" ◆ Felicity LaFortune — actress whose roles included Leigh Marshall on the soap "Ryan's Hope"

FENELLA ◆Fenella Fielding — Anglo-Rumanian actress, usually in outrageously exaggerated roles on TV

FERN ◆Fern Fitzgerald — actress whose roles included Marilee Stone on TV's "Dallas" ◆Fern Kinney — rock singer, had number one hit in England with "Together We Are Beautiful"

FERNANDE ◆Fernande Giroux — actress whose roles included Monique Wingate on the soap "Moment of Truth" ◆ Danielle Fernande Steel — best selling author, works include "The Promise" and "Jewels"

FIFI ◆Fifi D'Orsay — vivacious Canadian leading lady, trademark "Ello beeg boy!" ◆ Fifi Trixiebelle Geldof — daughter of singer/actor Bob Geldof who started Live Aid

FINN ◆Finn Carter — actress on the soap "As the World Turns," female lead in the film "Tremors"

FINOLA ◆Finola Hughes — actress in John Travolta's disco dancing sequel "Staying Alive"

FIONA ◆Fiona Fullerton — actress whose roles included Alice in "Alice's Adventures in Wonderland"

FIONNULA ◆Fionnula Flanagan — portrayed Kathleen Meacham on the TV adventure series "H.E.L.P."

FLANNERY ◆Flannery O'Connor — author whose works include "A Good Man Is Hard to Find"

FLEUR ◆Fleur Fenton — illustrator who wrote "The Case of Salvador Dali"

FLORA ◆Flora Robson — actress who played the ruthless Queen Elizabeth in "Fire Over England"

FLORENCE ◆Florence Ballard — grew up with Diana Ross, original member of The Supremes ◆ Florence Graham — real name of Elizabeth Arden, pioneer in the advertising of beauty aids ◆Florence Henderson — actress who played mama Brady on the classic TV show "The Brady Bunch" ◆ Florence Nightingale — put nursing on a professional level during the Crimean War

FLORIDA ◆Florida Friebus — played Dobie Gillis' mother and was a patient on "The Bob Newhart Show"

FLORINDA ◆Florinda Bolkan — actress who played adventuress and dancer Lola Montes in "Royal Flash"

FLORRIE ◆Florrie Dugger — actress whose roles included Blousey in the child gangster film "Bugsy Malone"

FLORYNCE ◆Florynce Kennedy — founder of the American Feminist Party

FLOY ◆Floy Dean — actress whose roles included Eve Blake on the soap "Morning Star"

FRAN ◆Fran Allison — star and host of children's TV show "Kukla, Fran, and Ollie" ◆ Fran Carlon — actress whose roles included Ada on the drama series "The Hamptons"

FRANCE ◆France Nuyen — actress who appeared in the film "South Pacific" and TV's "St. Elsewhere"

FRANCES ◆Frances Bavier — actress whose roles included Aunt Bee on the sitcom "The Andy Griffith Show" ◆Frances Cabrini — first American saint, canonized in 1946 ◆ Frances Farmer — Hollywood leading lady who went insane, biopic "Frances"

FRANCESCA ◆Francesca Annis — English actress portrayed Lillie Langtry on TV's "Lillie" ◆Francesca Roberts — played Pvt. Harriet Dorsey on the sitcom version of the film "Private Benjamin"

FRANCINE ◆Francine Barker — Peaches in Peaches and Herb, debut hit record "Let's Fall in Love" ◆Francine Tacker — actress whose roles included Amelia Ladipus on TV's "Empire"

FRANCOISE ◆Francoise Dorleac — actress sister of Catherine Deneuve ◆Francoise Gilot — Picasso's companion and mother of two of his children, author "Life with Picasso"

FRANELLE ◆Franelle Silver — Emmy winning writer for TV's "The Carol Burnett Show"

FRANKI ◆Franki Horner — actress who played widow James Kincaid on the police drama "Houston Knights"

FREDA ◆Freda Payne — rock singer, hit debut gold record "Band of Gold"

FREDERICA ◆Sophie Frederica Alohilani — daughter of actress and singer Bette Midler

FREDERIQUE ◆Frederique Jamet — actress who played Juliette in Francois Truffaut's "The Man Who Loved Women"

FREDI ◆Fredi Washington — actress who played Peola in the Claudette Colbert melodrama "Imitation of Life"

FREE ◆Free Carradine — daughter of actor David Carradine and actress Barbara Hershey

FREYA ◆Freya Littledale — children's author whose books include "The Elves and the Shoemaker"

FRIDA ◆Frida Kahlo — painter whose biography is "Frida"

FRIEDA ◆Frieda Inescort — actress in the Montgomery Clift film "A Place in the Sun"

FRITZI ◆Fritzi Burr — portrayed Mulwray's secretary in Jack Nicholson's thriller "Chinatown"

GABRIEL ◆Tara Gabriel Getty — daughter of oil tycoon J. P. Getty II

GABRIELA ◆Gabriela Mistral — diplomat and Nobel Prize winning poet

GABRIELLA ◆Gabriella Licudi — Italian leading lady whose films include "Casino Royale"

GABRIELLE ◆Gabrielle Ferrer — daughter of "You Light Up My Life" singer Debby Boone ◆ Gabrielle Beaumont — director of "Death of a Centerfold" with Jamie Lee Curtis ◆ Gabrielle Carteris — 1990's teen idol, played Andrea on TV's "Beverly Hills 90210"

GABY ◆Gaby Hoffman — actress who played Karin Kinsella in Kevin Costner's "Field of Dreams" ◆ Gaby Morlay — actress whose roles included English Queen Victoria in "Entente Cordiale"

GAIL ◆Gail Edwards — actress whose roles included waitress Dot Higgin on the sitcom "It's a Living" ◆ Gail Fisher — actress whose roles included Peggy Fair on the drama series "Mannix" ◆ Bonnie Gail Franklin — star of TV's "One Day at a Time"

GALA ◆Gala Dali — model who was the inspiration for her husband Salvador Dali

GALAXY ◆Galaxy Gramaphone Getty — daughter of oil tycoon J.P. Getty II

GALE ◆Peggy Gale Fleming — three-time world champion figure skater ◆Gale Sondergaard — Oscar winning actress for "Anthony Adverse" ◆Gale Storm — actress who played Margie Albright on the hit sitcom "My Little Margie"

GARN ◆Garn Stephens — actress who played Harriet Hastings on Cloris Leachman's sitcom "Phyllis"

GARRY ◆Kate Garry Hudson — daughter of actress Goldie Hawn and singer Bill Hudson

GATES ◆Gates McFadden — played Dr. Beverly Crusher on the series "Star Trek: The Next Generation"

GAY ◆Gay Hamilton — played Robin Hood's girlfriend Maid Marian in "A Challenge for Robin Hood"

GAYL ◆Gayl Jones — author whose works include the novel "Corregidora"

GAYLE ◆Gayle Hunnicut — actress whose roles included Vanessa Beaumont on TV's "Dallas"

GEENA ◆Geena Davis — Oscar winning actress who wielded a gun in "Thelma and Louise"

GELSEY ◆Gelsey Kirkland — dancer with the American Ballet Theatre

GEMMA ◆Gemma Craven — actress who played fairy tale princess Cinderella in "The Slipper and the Rose"

GENA ◆Gena Rowlands — Oscar nominated actress for "Gloria"

GENE ◆Demetria Gene Buynes — real name of actress Demi Moore ◆ Karen Gene Grassle — actress who played Caroline Ingalls on TV's "Little House on the Prairie" ◆ Gene Tierney — beautiful actress in many 40's classic films, including "Laura"

GENEVA ◆Geneva Smitherman — linguist, author "Black Language and Culture"

GENEVIEVE ◆Genevieve Bujold — French Canadian actress who costarred with Clint Eastwood in "Tightrope"

GENIE ◆Genie Francis — portrayed Laura of "Luke and Laura" on TV's daytime soap "General Hospital"

GENNIFER ◆Gennifer Flowers — singer whose 12-year affair with Bill Clinton almost ruined his campaign

GEORGANN ◆Georgann Johnson — actress whose roles included Eugenia Robard on the soap "All My Children"

GEORGE ◆George Sand — pseudonym of Amandine-Aurore-Lucile Dudevant, nee Dupin, nineteenth century French writer notorious for her scandalous love affairs

GEORGEANNA ◆Georgeanna Tillman — member of The Marvelettes, debut number one gold hit "Please Mr. Postman"

GEORGIA ◆Georgia Engel — played the scatterbrained Georgette on the classic sitcom "The Mary Tyler Moore Show" ◆ Georgia Gibbs — hits include "If I Knew You Were Comin' I'd've Baked You a Cake" ◆ Georgia O'Keeffe — artist who was one of the founders of Modernism

GEORGIANA ◆Georgiana Barrymore — actress mother of John, Ethel, and Lionel Barrymore ◆ Georgiana Randolph — author, mystery novels include "The Corpse Steps Out"

GEORGIANNA ◆Gladys Georgianna Greene — real name of comic actress Jean Arthur

GERALDINE ◆Geraldine Chaplin — daughter of Charlie Chaplin, played her own grandmother in "Chaplin" ◆ Geraldine Ferraro — first woman to run for Vice President of the United States ◆ Geraldine Page — well known actress in "The Trip to Bountiful" for which she won an Oscar

GERDA ◆Gerda Holmes — actress whose roles included Robin's girlfriend Maid Marian in the silent era

GERI ◆Geri Jewell — actress whose roles included Geri Warner on TV's "The Facts of Life"

GERTRUDE ◆Gertrude Berg — starred in "The Goldbergs" on both radio and TV ◆ Gertrude Stein — godmother of American expatriates in Paris during the 20s

GERTY ◆Gerty Cori — first woman to win a Nobel Prize for medicine

GHENA ◆Ghena Dimitrova — soprano who made her US debut in "Ernani"

GIA ◆Gia Scala — Italian leading lady best known for "The Guns of Navarone"

GIANNA ◆Gianna Canale — actress whose roles included the Czarina in the film "The Nights of Rasputin"

GIDGET ◆Gidget Lawrence(c) — Sandra Dee created this surf babe in the "Gidget" series of films

GIGI ◆Gigi Perreau — played Katherine Richards on the Hawaii-based TV show "Follow the Sun"

GILA ◆Gila Golan — actress in "Ship of Fools" and "Our Man Flint"

GILDA ◆Gilda Mundson — alluring torch singer who gyrated "down South America way" ◆ Gilda Radner — original cast member of "Saturday Night Live" and wife of Gene Wilder

GILLIAN ◆Gillian Catherine Shaw — daughter of hostage Patty Hearst, descendant of publisher William Randolph Hearst ◆ Gillian Anderson — actress whose roles included the FBI agent on the Fox drama series "The X-Files" ◆ Gillian Dobb — actress who played Agatha Chumley on the hit detective series "Magnum, P.I."

GINA ◆Gina Lollobrigida — sex-bomb who starred with Rock Hudson in the romantic comedy "Come September" ◆ Gina Nemo — actress who played Dorothy on the hit teen police series "21 Jump Street" ◆ Gina Schock — member of The Go-Go's, debut hit single "Our Lips Are Sealed"

GINETTE ◆Ginette Leclerc — French stage and screen actress

GINGER ◆Ginger Grant (c) — Tina Louise's role as the movie star on TV's "Gilligan's Island" ◆ Ginger Rogers — film actress who deserted dancing partner Fred Astaire for an Oscar for "Kitty Foyle"

GIOIA ◆Gioia Bruno — member of group Expose, hit album "Exposure" includes single "Come Go With Me"

GIOVANNA ◆Giovanna Ralli — actress whose roles included the ultimate femme fatale Carmen

GISELE ◆Gisele MacKenzie — Canadian born songstress and star of "Your Hit Parade"

GIULETTA ◆Giuletta Masina — gamin-like actress married to director Federico Fellini

GIULIANA ◆Giuliana Santini — actress who played Gina Sloan on the post WW II era drama series "Homefront"

GLADYS ◆Gladys Cooper — distinguished British actress with a warm, aristocratic personality ◆Gladys Knight — she and the Pips were Motown music chart toppers ◆Gladys Smith — real name of America's sweetheart Mary Pickford

GLENDA ◆Glenda Farrell — won an Emmy for her work on TV's "Ben Casey" ◆Glenda Jackson — dual Oscar winner for "Women in Love," "A Touch of Class"

GLENN ◆Glenn Close — heiress turned actress in "Dangerous Liaisons" and "Fatal Attraction" ◆ Rumer Glenn Willis — daughter of action star Bruce Willis and actress Demi Moore

GLENNA ◆Glenna Sergent — actress whose roles included Nancy in Donald Sutherland's "Alex in Wonderland" ◆ Glenna Vare — legendary golfer, namesake for Vare Trophy for woman golfers

GLENNE ◆Glenne Headly — actress who played the girlfriend Tess Trueheart in Warren Beatty's "Dick Tracy"

GLINDA ◆Glinda (c) — Good Witch of the North, played by Billie Burke in "The Wizard of Oz"

GLORIA ◆Gloria Estefan — member of The Miami Sound Machine, debut hit single "Conga" ◆ Gloria Grahame — Oscar winning actress for "The Bad and the Beautiful" ◆Gloria Steinem — co-founder of "Ms." magazine ◆ Gloria Swanson — her most famous role was one of her last, the aging actress in "Sunset Boulevard" ◆Gloria Vanderbilt — fashion jean designer and heir to the Vanderbilt fortune

GLYNIS ◆Glynis Johns — star of her own sitcom "Glynis" on CBS, played the mother in "Mary Poppins"

GLYNNIS ◆Glynnis O'Connor — actress whose roles included Dee Stewart Dixon on the soap "As the World Turns"

GODIVA ◆Lady Godiva — rode naked through Coventry to lower taxes for the people

GOGI ◆Gogi Grant — hit the charts with a number one gold record "The Wayward Wind"

GOLDA ◆Golda Meir — prime minister of Israel, biopic "A Woman Called Golda"

GOLDIE ◆Goldie Hawn — actress who went from TV's "Laugh-In" to the film "Private Benjamin" ◆Goldie Hill — country music singer, hits "I Let the Stars Get in My Eyes," "Say Big Boy"

GOOGIE ◆Googie Withers — British lady of stage and screen, married to John McCallum

GRACE ◆Grace Jones — dangerous vixen of James Bond's "A View to a Kill" and "Vamp" ◆Grace Kelly — beautiful movie star who became the Princess of Monaco ◆Grace Slick — lead singer of the rock group "Jefferson Airplane"

GRACIE ◆Gracie Allen — funny side of "Burns and Allen," when George was the straight man ◆ Gracie Fields — beloved British nightclub entertainer, sang "Biggest Aspidistra in the World"

GRAMAPHONE ◆Galaxy Gramaphone Getty — daughter of oil tycoon J.P. Getty II

GRAYSON ◆Grayson Hall — actress whose roles included Euphemia Ralston on the soap "One Life to Live"

GREER ◆Greer Garson — actress who received an Oscar for "Mrs. Miniver"

GRETA ◆Greta Garbo — actress famous for the line "I vant to be alone" ◆Greta Scacchi — actress in "The Player" and "Presumed Innocent"

GRETCHEN ◆Gretchen Wyler — stage actress in "Silk Stockings" and "Damn Yankees" ◆Gretchen Young — real name of actress Loretta Young

GRETE ◆Grete Waitz — seven-time winner of the New York City Marathon

GRETL ◆Gretl von Trapp (c) — one of the singing children portrayed in Julie Andrews' classic "The Sound of Music"

GUINEVERE ◆Guinevere — King Arthur's beautiful wife who fell in love with Sir Lancelot

GUNILLA ◆Gunilla Hutton — series regular on the long running hayseed variety show "Hee Haw"

GUYLAINE ◆Guylaine St. Onge — actress who played Joan on the Wings Hauser adventure series "Lightning Force"

GWEN ◆Gwen Farrell — actress whose roles included one of the nurses on the hit sitcom "M*A*S*H"

GWENDOLYN ◆Gwendolyn Brooks — first African-American woman to win a Pulitzer for poetry, for "Annie Allen" ◆ Gwendolyn Oliver — member of The Ritchie Family, disco hit with "Brazil"

GWETHALYN ◆Gwethalyn Graham — author whose novels include "Earth and High Heaven" and "Swiss Sonata"

GWYDA ◆Gwyda DonHowe — actress whose roles included Astrid Rutledge on TV's "Executive Suite"

GWYN ◆Gwyn Gilliss — actress whose roles included Anne Tyler Martin on the soap "All My Children"

GWYNETH ◆Gwyneth Thomas — one of the triplets of actor Richard Thomas

HADDA ◆Hadda Brooks — actress whose films include Humphrey Bogart's "In a Lonely Place"

HAILA ◆Haila Stoddard — actress who played Pauline Harris Rysdale on the soap "The Secret Storm"

HAINI ◆Haini Wolfgramm — member of The Jets, debut hit single "Crush on You"

HALLE ◆Halle Berry — actress whose roles included Emily Franklin on the sitcom "Living Dolls"

HALLIE ◆Hallie Todd — actress who played Kate Griffin on the short-lived sitcom "Going Places"

HAMLIN ◆Hamlin Garland — Pulitzer Prize winning author for autobiography "A Daughter of the Middle Border"

HANA ◆Hana Mandlikova — defeated Chris Evert to win the US Open

HANNA ◆Hanna Waag — actress whose roles included English Queen Victoria in "Waltz Time in Vienna"

HANNAH ◆Hannah Miller (c) — Jamie Lee Curtis' lead role on her hit sitcom "Anything But Love" ◆ Hannah Troy — fashion designer who created the petite size for women ◆ Hannah Van Buren — died eighteen years before her husband became President

HANYA ◆Hanya Holm — choreographer whose musicals include "Kiss Me Kate"

HAPPY ◆Happy Rockefeller — widow of Vice President Nelson Rockefeller

HARIETTE ◆Hariette Lake — real name of the star of TV's "The Ann Sothern Show"

HARLEAN ◆Harlean Carpentier — real name of blond bombshell actress Jean Harlow

HARLEM ◆Gro Harlem Brundtland — prime minister of Norway, youngest woman to run a modern government

HARLEY ◆Harley Kozak — actress who played the wife of the bright young doctor in "Arachnophobia"

HARMONY ◆Harmony — daughter of actress Susan St. James

HARRIET ◆Harriet Nelson — singer in Ozzie Nelson's band, then his co-star on their TV show ◆Harriet Oleson — villain and owner of the store on the series "Little House on the Prairie" ◆ Harriet Beecher Stowe — author of "Uncle Tom's Cabin," the book which helped start the Civil War ◆ Harriet Tubman — former slave who helped slaves escape, biopic "A Woman Called Moses"

HARRIETTE ◆Harriette Arnow — author of novels about Appalachian life, film "The Dollmaker" with Jane Fonda

HARRIOT ◆Harriot Blatch — leader in the women's suffrage movement

HATTIE ◆Hattie Carnegie — designed first international American fashion collection ◆ Hattie McDaniel — received an Oscar for her portrayal of Mammy in "Gone With the Wind"

HAYA ◆Haya Hayareet — portrayed Esther, love interest of Charlton Heston, in the classic "Ben-Hur"

HAYLEY ◆Hayley Rose Bridges — daughter of actor Jeff Bridges, granddaughter of actor Lloyd Bridges ◆ Hayley Mills — child actress in "The Parent Trap," "Pollyanna," "Trouble With Angels"

HAZEL ◆Hazel Bishop — chemist who invented the first non-smear, long-lasting lipstick

HEATHER ◆Heather Locklear — beautiful actress in TV's "Dynasty" and "T.J. Hooker" ◆ Heather Menzies — actress who played Louisa von Trapp in Julie Andrews' "The Sound of Music" ◆ Heather Thomas — well curved asset on TV's "Fall Guy" with Lee Majors

HEDDA ◆Hedda Hopper — gossip columnist who hounded Hollywood stars in the 1940's

HEDWIG ◆Hedwig Kiesler — real name of actress Hedy Lamarr

HEDY ◆Hedy Lamarr — actress who became notorious for her 10-minute nude scene in 1933's "Ecstasy"

HEIDI ◆Heidi (c) — Johanna Spyri's Swiss orphan girl taken from her grandfather's mountain home ◆ Heidi Bohay — actress whose roles included Megan Kendal on TV's "Hotel" ◆ Heidi Zeigler — actress whose roles include a daughter on TV's "Just the Ten of Us"

HELAINE ◆Helaine Lembeck — actress who played Judy Borden on the Gabe Kaplan sitcom "Welcome Back, Kotter"

HELEN ◆Helen Gurley Brown — editor of "Cosmopolitan," author of best selling "Sex and the Single Girl" ◆Helen Hayes — legendary actress long on Broadway, won her second Oscar for "Airport" ◆Helen Hunt — actress, TV series "Mad About You" ◆ Helen Keller — blind educator who was the inspiration for "The Miracle Worker" ◆Helen Reddy — Australian singer, hits include "I Am Woman"

HELENA ◆Helena Bonham Carter — actress who played Lucy Honeychurch in Maggie Smith's "A Room with a View" ◆Helena Rubinstein — founder of Helena Rubinstein cosmetics

HELENE ◆Helene (c) — Genevieve Fontanel's role in Francois Truffaut's "The Man Who Loved Women" ◆ Helene Madison — Olympic three-time gold medal swimmer ◆Helene Vita — actress who appeared in the film "Cabaret" as Fraulein Kost

HELGA ◆Helga Sandburg — author of children's books including "Gingerbread," daughter of Carl Sandburg

HELOISE ◆Heloise — French religious figure best known for love affair with Pierre Abelard ◆ Heloise Evans — writes the nationally syndicated column "Hints from Heloise"

HELVETIA ◆Helvetia Boswell — member of the singing trio The Boswell Sisters

HENRIETTA ◆Joan Henrietta Collins — actress who played Alexis Carrington Colby on the prime time soap "Dynasty"

HENRIETTE ◆Henriette Wyeth — artist who specialized in portraits and murals

HEPHZIBAH ◆Hephzibah Menuhin — pianist who played sonata recitals with brother Yehudi

HERMINE ◆Hermine Sterler — actress whose roles included Czarina Feodorovna in the film "Rasputin"

HERMIONE ◆Hermione Baddeley — Oscar nominee for "Room at the Top," the maid on TV's "Maude" ◆ Hermione Gingold — actress who played one of Gigi's not very helpful relatives in the film "Gigi"

HERSHA ◆Hersha Parady — actress who played Alice Garvey on the drama series "Little House on the Prairie"

HESBA ◆Hesba Brinsmead — Australian author

HETTY ◆Hetty Green — called "The Witch of Wall Street," the richest woman in the US in 1900

HILARY ◆Hilary Thompson — played Lizabeth Barrett on the detective drama series "The Manhunter"

HILDA ◆Hilda Vaughn — actress who played Tina, Kitty's maid in John Barrymore's "Dinner at Eight"

HILDEGARD ◆Hildegard Neil — actress who played Egyptian Queen Cleopatra in "Antony and Cleopatra"

HILDEGARDE ◆Hildegarde Neff — actress whose roles included the empress in "Catherine of Russia"

HILDY ◆Hildy Parks — regular on the TV quiz show "Down You Go"

HILLARY ◆Hillary Brooke — actress whose roles included bad girls in films of the 1940's ◆ Hillary Clinton — wife of President Bill Clinton

HILLIARD ◆Hilliard Nelson — Harriet on TV's long running family sitcom "The Adventures of Ozzie and Harriet"

HOLLAND ◆Holland Taylor — played cranky boss Ruth Dunbar on the cross-dressing sitcom "Bosom Buddies"

HOLLIS ◆Hollis Irving — actress whose roles included Aunt Phoebe on the sitcom "Margie" ◆ Hollis Stacy — US Women's Open winner in 1977, 1978, and 1984

HOLLY ◆Holly Dunn — country music singer, hit single "Daddy's Hands" ◆ Holly Hunter — southern actress in "Broadcast News" and "Raising Arizona" ◆ Holly Palance — co-hosted with her father Jack Palance on TV's "Ripley's Believe It or Not"

HONOR ◆Honor Blackman — actress whose roles included Pussy Galore in James Bond film "Goldfinger"

HOPE ◆Laura Hope Crews — actress whose roles included Aunt Pittypat in "Gone With the Wind" ◆Hope Holiday — actress who played Margie MacDougall in the Oscar winning "The Apartment" ◆ Hope Lange — nominated for an Oscar for "Peyton Place," on TV's "The Ghost and Mrs. Muir"

HORATIA ◆Julianna Horatia Ewing — children's book author who wrote the classic "Jackanapes"

HYPATIA ◆Hypatia — beautiful woman ordered murdered by St. Cyril of Alexander in ancient times

IDA ◆Ida Lupino — actress who teamed up with Humphrey Bogart in "High Sierra" ◆Ida McKinley — First Lady, developed epilepsy after the tragic death of her two children

IGGIE ◆Iggie Wolfington — Tony nominee for "The Music Man"

ILA ◆Ila Rhodes — actress in Bette Davis' great melodrama "Dark Victory"

ILEANA ◆Ileana Cotrubas — Romanian soprano with the New York Metropolitan Opera

ILENE ◆Ilene Kristen — actress whose roles included Delia Ryan Coleridge on the soap "Ryan's Hope"

ILIE ◆Ilie Nastase — winner of the US Open and Wimbledon

ILKA ◆Ilka Chase — regular on TV's interview show "Glamour-Go-Round" ◆ Ilka Gruning — actress who played Mrs. Leuchtag in the classic Oscar winning film "Casablanca"

ILONA ◆Ilona Massey — star of the musical TV series "The Ilona Massey Show" ◆Ilona Staller — porno actress who was elected to the Italian Parliament

ILSA ◆Ilsa Lund (c) — Ingrid Bergman's role in the classic Oscar winning "Casablanca"

ILSE ◆Ilse von Glatz — actress who appeared on the science fiction series "War of the Worlds"

IMAN ◆Iman — wife of David Bowie and cover model for major international magazines

IMELDA ◆Imelda Marcos — wife of the late president of the Philippines, she bought a lot of shoes

IMOGEN ◆Imogen Claire — actress who played the scandalous female writer George Sand in "Lisztomania"

IMOGENE ◆Imogene Coca — comedy cohort to Sid Caesar on TV's "Your Show of Shows"

IMPERIO ◆Imperio Agentina — actress whose roles included the ultimate femme fatale Carmen in film

INA ◆Ina Balin — TV film "Children of An-Lac" detailed her own story of leaving Vietnam ◆Ina Claire — portrayed witty, chic sophisticates on the screen ◆Ina Ray Hutton — leader of Her All-Girl Band on her variety show "The Ina Ray Hutton Show"

INDIA ◆India Adams — singer who provided the voice for a number of non-singing Hollywood actresses ◆ India Edwards — Treasurer of the United States, signed the money

INDIRA ◆Indira Gandhi — prime minister of India, daughter of Nehru

INDUS ◆Indus Arthur — actress who played Brooke Bentley Clinton on the soap "General Hospital"

INES ◆Ines Palange — actress in the crazy Marx Brothers comedy "A Night at the Opera"

INEZ ◆Inez Gomez — actress whose roles included Sebastiana in Greta Garbo's "The Temptress"

INGA ◆Inga Swenson — actress whose roles included Gretchen Kraus on TV's "Benson"

INGEBORG ◆Ingeborg Theek — actress whose roles included Lisa Schumacher on the soap "The Egg and I"

INGER ◆Inger Stevens — blond love interest to Clint Eastwood in "Hang 'em High"

INGRI ◆Ingri d'Aulaire — children's author and illustrator

INGRID ◆Ingrid Bergman — won three Oscars, but is best remembered as Bogart's love in "Casablanca" ◆ Ingrid Newkirk — founder of People for the Ethical Treatment of Animals

IONE ◆Ione Skye — actress in "Say Anything" and "River's Edge," daughter of Donovan

IRENE ◆Irene Castle — dancer who started bobbed hair fad, biopic "The Story of Vernon and Irene Castle" ◆Irene Dunne — actress who played the lead Magnolia Hawks in the classic musical "Show Boat" ◆Irene Ryan — portrayed the cantankerous Granny in "The Beverly Hillbillies"

IRINA ◆Irina Demich — sexy girl on a bicycle in the World War II epic "The Longest Day"

IRLENE ◆Irlene Mandrell — regular on the long running hayseed series "Hee Haw"

IRMA ◆Irma Rombauer — author of "The Joy of Cooking" ◆ Irma Seigel — actress whose roles included Aunt Edity on TV's "Fernwood 2-Night"

IRMENGARDE ◆Irmengarde Eberle — author whose books include "Mustang on the Prairie" and "Moose Live Here"

IRNA ◆Irna Phillips — creator of six soaps, including "The Guiding Light" and "As The World Turns"

ISA ◆Isa Miranda — actress whose roles included Czarina Feodorovna in the film "Rasputin"

ISAK ◆Isak Dinesen — author of the novel and the film "Out of Africa"

ISABEL ◆Isabel Jewell — actress whose roles included western outlaw Belle Starr in "Badman's Territory" ◆ Isabel Sanford — played long suffering wife Louise Jefferson on TV's "The Jeffersons"

ISABELLA ◆Isabella — Queen of Spain, she financed Christopher Columbus' discovery of America ◆Isabella Alden — author of over 80 popular religious books for young people ◆ Isabella Rossellini — actress daughter of Ingrid Bergman who appeared in "Cousins"

ISABELLE ◆Isabelle Adjani — nominated for an Oscar for "The Story of Adele H." ◆ Isabelle Bridges — daughter of actor Jeff Bridges, granddaughter of actor Lloyd Bridges

ISADORA ◆Isadora Duncan — great innovator in modern dance, biopic "Isadora"

ISELA ◆Isela Vega — actress who played Elita in Peckinpah's "Bring Me the Head of Alfredo Garcia"

ISHBEL ◆Ishbel Ross — biographer of famous women

ISOBEL ◆Isobel Elsom — British character actress in Hollywood whose films include "My Fair Lady"

ISSEY ◆Issey Miyake — fashion designer who blends western and oriental styles

IVANA ◆Ivana Trump — former model ex-wife of billionaire Donald Trump

IVIE ◆Ivie Anderson — singer with Duke Ellington, hits include "I Got It Bad"

IVY ◆Ivy Bethune — actress whose roles included Miss Tuttle on TV's "Father Murphy" ◆ Ivy Baker Priest — US treasurer under Dwight Eisenhower

IVYANN ◆Ivyann Schwan — played Patty Merrick on the sitcom version of the hit film "Parenthood"

IYMME ◆Iymme Shore — actress whose roles included Joyce Kendall on TV's "Father Knows Best"

JA'NET ◆Ja'net DuBois — actress who played next door neighbor Willona Woods on the sitcom "Good Times"

JACKEE ◆Jackee — Emmy winning actress for her role of Sandra Clark on TV's "227" ◆ Jackee Harry — actress whose roles included Lily Mason on the soap "Another World"

JACKIE ◆Jackie Collins — Joan's literary sister, author of "Hollywood Wives" ◆ Jackie DeShannon — writer of over 600 songs, hits include "What the World Needs Now" ◆Jackie Joyner-Kersey — Olympic gold medalist in track ◆ Jackie "Moms" Mabley — comedienne known for her "dirty old lady" routine, starred in "Amazing Grace"

JACKLYN ◆Jacklyn Zeman — actress whose roles included Lana McClain on the soap "One Life to Live"

JACKY ◆Jacky Gillott — early British newscaster, author of "Salvage"

JACLYN ◆Jaclyn Smith — dark-haired, skimpily clad bombshell on TV's "Charlie's Angels"

JACQUELINE ◆Jacqueline Bisset — English actress whose movies include "The Deep" and "Rich and Famous" ◆Jacqueline Onassis — second wife of President Kennedy, married Aristotle Onassis ◆ Jacqueline Susann — author who wrote trashy novels like "Valley of the Dolls"

JACQUELYN ◆Jacquelyn Hyde — actress who played Miss Blaire in Woody Allen's "Take the Money and Run"

JADA ◆Jada Pinkett — portrayed Lena James on TV's "A Different World" ◆Jada Rowland — actress whose roles included Penny Drake on the drama series "The Hamptons"

JADE ◆Jade Jagger — daughter of rock superstar Mick Jagger and his wife Bianca

JAIMEE ◆Jaimee Foxworth — actress whose roles included Judy Winslow on Urkel's TV show "Family Matters"

JAIN ◆Jain Wilimovsky — starred as Lady Macbeth in the film version of Shakespeare's play

JAMI ◆Jami Fields — actress whose roles included Penny Davis Dancy on the soap "The Doctors" ◆ Jami Gertz — actress who played preppie Muffy Tepperman on TV's sitcom "Square Pegs"

JAMIE ◆Jamie Lee Curtis — actress who starred in "A Fish Called Wanda" and "Trading Places"

JAMILLA ◆Jamilla Perry — actress whose roles included Tracy Patterson on the Melba Moore sitcom "Melba"

JAN ◆Jan Brady (c) — Eve Plumb's role as the middle daughter on ABC's "The Brady Bunch" ◆Jan Hooks — actress whose roles included Carlene Frazier Dobber on TV's "Designing Women" ◆ Jan Smithers — actress whose roles included Bailey on the sitcom "WKRP in Cincinnati"

JANE ◆Jane Curtin — she went from "Saturday Night Live" to her own TV series "Kate and Allie" ◆ Jane Fonda — political activist turned actress, Oscars for "Klute" and "Coming Home" ◆ Jane Russell — Howard Hughes showed off her best assets in the poster for "The Outlaw" ◆Jane Seymour — English actress who stars in miniseries and TV's "Doctor Quinn, Medicine Woman" ◆ Jane Wyatt — actress who played Spock's Earth mother, with emotions, on TV's "Star Trek" ◆ Jane Wyman — actress who played the stern matriarch of the winery on TV's "Falcon Crest"

JANELLE ◆Janelle Allen — actress whose roles included Carol in the film "Come Back, Charleston Blue"

JANET ◆Janet Gaynor — winner of the first Oscar ◆ Janet Jackson — singing sister in the musical Jackson family ◆ Janet Leigh — she played the woman stabbed to death in the shower scene in "Psycho"

JANETTE ◆Janette Davis — husky-voiced entertainer with Arthur Godfrey's radio show ◆Janette Woolsey — author of "It's Time for Thanksgiving" and "It's Time for Easter"

JANICE ◆Janice Rule — actress whose roles included Mrs. Sommers in Kevin Costner's "American Flyers"

JANIE ◆Janie Fricke — country western singer, hits include "Please Help Me, I'm Falling"

JANINA ◆Janina Faye — portrayed Tania in Christopher Lee's "Horror of Dracula"

JANINE ◆Janine Turner — played Maggie O'Connell on the Emmy winning drama series "Northern Exposure"

JANIS ◆Janis Ian — Grammy winner for "At Seventeen" ◆Janis Joplin — died from drugs, sang "Me and Bobby McGee," Bette Midler fictional biopic "The Rose" ◆Janis Paige — actress whose roles included Nettie McCoy on the sitcom "Gun Shy"

JANNA ◆Janna Leigh — actress whose roles included Julia Shearer on the soap "Another World"

JARMA ◆Jarma Lewis — actress who played the beautiful Queen Guinevere in "The Black Knight"

JASMINE ◆Jasmine Guy — played the spoiled rich kid Whitley on the sitcom "A Different World"

JAWN ◆Jawn McKinley — actress who played Helen Upshaw in Liza Minnelli's "The Sterile Cuckoo"

JAYE ◆Jaye P. Morgan — regular panelist on TV's bizarre talent search "The Gong Show"

JAYNE ◆Jayne Kennedy — host of CBS's "NFL Today," first African-American woman with network sports ◆ Jayne Mansfield — well endowed actress in "Will Success Spoil Rock Hunter?" ◆ Jayne Meadows — actress wife of Steve Allen, on TV's "I've Got a Secret" and "Medical Center"

JAZMIN ◆Jazmin — daughter of basketball player Julius "Dr. J" Irving

JEAN ◆Jean Arthur — vivacious actress whose credits include "Mr. Smith Goes to Washington" ◆ Jean Harlow — platinum blond bombshell in the films "Bombshell," "Platinum Blonde" ◆ Jean Simmons — willowy actress who starred in "Elmer Gantry" and "Spartacus" ◆ Jean Smart — portrayed Charlene Frazier Stillfield on TV's "Designing Women" ◆Jean Stapleton — actress who played the dingbat Edith Bunker on TV's "All in the Family"

JEAN-CELESTE ◆Jean-Celeste Ahern — actress who played Simone Vauvin on the soap "The Young and the Restless"

JEANETTE ◆Jeanette MacDonald — singer in films with Nelson Eddy whose big song was "Indian Love Song" ◆Jeanette Rankin — first woman to serve in Congress

JEANINE ◆Jeanine Cashell — actress who played Alma Jean Dobson on the college sitcom "It's a Man's World" ◆ Jeanine Deckers — singer, hit single "Dominique," biopic "The Singing Nun"

JEANNA ◆Jeanna Michaels — actress whose roles included Constance Townley on the soap "General Hospital"

JEANNE ◆Jeanne Lanvin — founder of the French fashion house of Lanvin ◆ Jeanne Moreau — sexy French bombshell who predated Brigitte Bardot ◆ Jeanne Pruett — country western singer, hits include "Hold On to My Unchanging Love"

JEANNETTA ◆Jeannetta Arnette — played Bernadette Meara on the very successful sitcom "Head of the Class"

JEANNETTE ◆Jeannette Nolan — married to John McIntire, actress on the drama series "The Virginian"

JEANNIE ◆Jeannie C. Riley — country singer, hits include "Harper Valley P.T.A."

JEANNINE ◆Jeannine Riley — actress who played Billie Jo Bradley on the sitcom "Petticoat Junction"

JEHANE ◆Jehane Benoit — star of radio and TV cooking programs, author of over 25 books on cooking

JENILEE ◆Jenilee Harrison — blond actress who replaced Suzanne Sommers on TV's "Three's Company"

JENN ◆Jenn Thompson — played daughter Dee Johnson on Barbara Eden's sitcom "Harper Valley P.T.A."

JENNA ◆Jenna Von Oy — actress whose roles included Blossom's best friend Six on TV's "Blossom"

JENNIE ◆Jennie Brownscombe — painter of American historical scenes ◆ Jennie Garth — plays Kelly Taylor on "Beverly Hills 90210" ◆ Jennie Jerome — American mother of English Prime Minister Sir Winston Churhill

JENNIFER ◆Jennifer Beals — starred in "Flashdance" ◆Jennifer Grey — actress, films "Ferris Bueller's Day Off," "Dirty Dancing" ◆ Jennifer Jones — Oscar winning actress for "The Song of Bernadette" ◆ Jennifer Jason Leigh — actress in "Fast Times at Ridgemont High," "Single White Female" ◆ Jennifer O'Neill — actress in "The Summer of '42"

JENNY ◆Jenny Lind — P.T. Barnum's "Swedish Nightingale" who had triumphant US Tour

JERI LOU ◆Jeri Lou James — actress whose roles included Josie Stewart on the sitcom "It's Always Jan"

JERILYN ◆Jerilyn Britz — winner of the US Women's Open

JERRIANNE ◆Jerrianne Raphael — actress whose roles included Helene Suker on the soap "As the World Turns"

JERRIE ◆Jerrie Cobb — first woman chosen for the astronaut program

JERRY ◆Jerry Hall — top fashion model married to Mick Jagger

JESS ◆Jess Walton — soap star of "Capitol" and "The Young and the Restless"

JESSAMYN ◆Jessamyn West — author of the novel "The Massacre at Fall Creek"

JESSE ◆Jesse Paris — daughter of singer Patti Smith, hit single "Because the Night"

JESSICA ◆Jessica Lange — blond actress who received a Best Supporting Actress Oscar for "Tootsie" ◆ Jessica Tandy — long lived actress who played the annoying Daisy in "Driving Miss Daisy" ◆Jessica Walter — actress who played the crazy lady after Clint Eastwood in "Play Misty for Me"

JESSIE ◆Jessie Ames — reformer who founded the Association of Southern Women for Prevention of Lynching ◆ Jessie Shambaugh — founder of the 4-H clubs, the national junior farm organization

JESSLYN♦Jesslyn Fax — actress who played Angela on the popular Eve Arden sitcom "Our Miss Brooks"

JESSY ♦Sally Jessy Raphael — syndicated talk show host whose trademark is red glasses

JESSYE♦Jessye Norman — Grammy winning Metropolitan Opera singer

JETTA ♦Jetta Goudal — leading lady whose credits include "Business and Pleasure"

JEWEL ♦Jewel Cobb — biologist chosen as the president of Cal State Fullerton

JEZEBEL♦Jezebel — in the Bible, evil queen trampled to death by Israelite chariots

JILL ♦Jill Clayburgh — actress who played high-spirited movie star Carole Lombard in "Gable and Lombard" ♦ Jill Eikenberry — high-powered lawyer married to Michael Tucker on TV's "L.A. Law" and in real life ♦ Jill Ireland — actress wife of Charles Bronson, films include "Breakheart Pass" ♦Jill St. John — actress in "The Concrete Jungle"

JINNY♦Jinny Osborn — member of The Chordettes, debut number one gold record "Mr. Sandman"

JINX ♦Jinx Falkenburg — tall, good-looking model, made a few light comedies and musicals in the 1940's ♦ Jinx Mallory (c) — Kate Capshaw's role on the soap "The Edge of Night"

JO ♦Jo Van Fleet — won as Oscar as James Dean's mother in "East of Eden"

JO ANN♦Jo Ann Castle — ragtime piano player on the music series "The Lawrence Welk Show" ♦Jo Ann Pflug — actress who played the sexy Lieutenant Dish in the military comedy "M*A*S*H"

JO ANNE♦Jo Anne Worley — comedienne with a high, shrill voice on TV's "Laugh-In"

JO MARIE♦Jo Marie Payton-France — Hariette Winslow on both TV's Urkel show "Family Matters" and "Perfect Strangers"

JOANN♦JoAnn Willette — actress who played Connie Lubbock on the family sitcom "Just the Ten of Us"

JOBETH♦JoBeth Williams — played Karen in the ensemble piece "The Big Chill," on soap "The Guiding Light"

JOAN ◆Joan Baez — protest singer, whose songs include "The Night They Drove Old Dixie Down" ◆Joan Collins — actress who played Alexis Colby on TV's nighttime soap opera "Dynasty" ◆ Joan Crawford — her films include "Mildred Pierce," "What Ever Happened to Baby Jane?" ◆ Joan Cusack — policewoman and girlfriend of Rick Moranis in "My Blue Heaven" ◆Joan Lunden — interviewer with TV's "Good Morning, America" ◆ Joan Rivers — comedienne known for guest hosting "The Tonight Show"

JOANNA ◆Joanna Cassidy — actress whose roles included Elizabeth Nichols on TV's "The Family Tree" ◆Joanna Kerns — actress whose roles included the working mother on TV's "Growing Pains"

JOANNE ◆Joanne Dru — actress in "Red River" and "She Wore a Yellow Ribbon" ◆Joanne Woodward — actress in "A Big Hand for the Little Lady," "Rachel, Rachel," "The Long Hot Summer"

JOBYNA ◆Jobyna Howland — actress who played Poker Annie in Edward G. Robinson's "Silver Dollar" ◆ Jobyna Ralston — leading lady of the 20's, especially with Harold Lloyd, played Sylvia in "Wings"

JOCELYN ◆Jocelyn Brando — actress sister of Marlon Brando ◆ Jocelyn Howard — one of the twin daughters of director Ron Howard

JOCELYNE ◆Jocelyne Zucco — actress who played Martine Beaudoin on the adventure series "Urban Angel"

JODEAN ◆Jodean Russo — actress who played Regina Henderson on the soap "The Young and the Restless"

JODI ◆Jodi Thelen — actress whose roles included the wacky sister Jane Kelley on TV's "Duet"

JODIE ◆Jodie Foster — Oscar winning actress for both "The Accused" and "The Silence of the Lambs" ◆ Jodie Sweetin — plays Stephanie Tanner on the sitcom "Full House"

JODY ◆Jody Powell — press secretary for Jimmy Carter ◆ Jody Watley — Grammy winner for best new artist, hits include "Looking for a New Love"

JOELY ◆Joely Richardson — actress who played the studio executive in Nick Nolte's "I'll Do Anything"

JOEY ◆Joey Heatherton — spokesperson for the bed industry's "Perfect Sleeper"

JOHANNA ◆Johanna Gadski — soprano with the New York Metropolitan Opera ◆ Johanna Spyri — author of "Heidi," remade many times, especially with Shirley Temple

JOHNNIE MAE ◆Johnnie Mae Gibson — first African-American woman FBI agent, biopic "Johnnie Mae Gibson: FBI"

JOI ◆Joi Lansing — actress on TV's long running sitcom "Love That Bob"

JOIE ◆Joie Lee — played Indigo Downes, girlfriend to Denzel Washington in "Mo' Better Blues"

JOLEEN ◆Joleen Lutz — actress whose roles included Lisette Hocheiser on the sitcom "Night Court"

JOLENE ◆Jolene Brand — actress whose roles included Indian Pink Cloud on the sitcom "Guestward Ho!"

JOLIE ◆Jolie Gabor — mother of the glamorous Eva, Zsa Zsa, and Magda Gabor

JONE ◆Jone Allison — actress who played Meta Roberts Banning on the soap "The Guiding Light"

JONELLE ◆Jonelle Allen — actress who played Bessie Freeman on Alex Haley's drama series "Palmerstown"

JONI ◆Joni James — rock singer went gold and to number one in 1952 with "Why Don't You Believe Me" ◆ Joni Mitchell — rock singer, hit debut single "Big Yellow Taxi" ◆ Joni Sledge — member of the rock group Sister Sledge, hits include "We Are Family"

JORDAN ◆Elizabeth Jordan Carr — first American test tube baby

JORDANA ◆Jordana Capra — played Monique on the Mario Van Peebles detective drama series "Sonny Spoon" ◆ Jordana "Bink" Shapiro — actress who played Brittany Weston on the comedy/drama series "thirtysomething"

JOSCELINE ◆Elspeth Josceline Huxley — author of "Man From Nowhere" and "Scott of the Antarctic"

JOSEPHINE ◆Josephine — great love of Emperor Napoleon Bonaparte of France ◆ Josephine Baker — Lynn Whitfield's starring role in the biopic "The Josephine Baker Story" ◆ Josephine Cottle — real name of actress Gale Storm ◆Josephine Hull — Oscar winner for "Harvey," one of the murderous aunts in "Arsenic and Old Lace"

JOSETTE ◆Josette Day — French leading lady whose films include "Four Days Leave"

JOSIE ◆Josie Adams — daughter of Brooke Adams whose credits include "Invasion of the Body Snatchers" ◆Josie Bissett — actress who played Cara on the family sitcom with two moms "The Hogan Family"

JOY ◆Joy Adamson — Kenyan game warden who raised a wild lion cub, biopic "Born Free" ◆ Joy Page — actress who played Annina Brandel in the classic Oscar winning film "Casablanca"

JOYCE ◆Joyce Brothers — doctor of love, regular panelist on TV's bizarre "Gong Show" ◆Joyce DeWitt — John Ritter's dark-haired roomate on TV's "Three's Company"

JOYCELYN ◆Joycelyn Elders — surgeon general who advocates distributing contraceptives in school

JUANIN ◆Juanin Clay — actress who played Raven Alexander Whitney on the soap "The Edge of Night"

JUANITA ◆Juanita Hall — actress whose roles on Broadway included Bloody Mary in "South Pacific"

JUDE ◆Jude Alderson — portrayed Ma Vicious, mother of Sid, in the biopic "Sid and Nancy"

JUDI ◆Judi Bowker — actress who played Andromeda in the Harry Hamlin film "Clash of the Titans" ◆ Judi Meredith — she played herself on the sitcom "The George Burns Show"

JUDIANNE ◆Judianne Densen-Gerber — founder of the drug treatment center Odyssey House

JUDIE ◆Judie Brown — founding president of the anti-abortion American Life League

JUDITH ◆Judith Ivey — actress whose roles included B.J. on TV's "Designing Women" ◆ Judith Krantz — author, books include "Scruples," "Princess Daisy" and "Mistral's Daughter" ◆ Judith Light — played Angela Bower on TV's "Who's the Boss," mother on TV's "Phenom"

JUDITH-MARIE ◆Judith-Marie Bergan — actress whose roles included Candy Crane on TV's "Domestic Life"

JUDY ◆Judy Canova — comedienne whose hillbilly yodeling brightened a number of films ◆ Judy Collins — singer whose hits include "Both Sides Now" and "Send in the Clowns" ◆ Judy Garland — child actress launched to fame in "The Wizard of Oz"

◆ Judy Holliday — Oscar winning actress whose classic dumb blond role was "Born Yesterday"

JUICE ◆Juice Newton — country pop singer whose hits include "Bette Davis Eyes"

JULANNE ◆Julanne Johnson — played the princess in Douglas Fairbanks silent classic "The Thief of Bagdad"

JULE ◆Jule Benedic — star of the Harlem Globetrotters' biopic "Go, Man, Go!"

JULIA ◆Julia Duffy — actress who played Stephanie Vander Kellan Harris on the sitcom "Newhart" ◆ Julia Louis-Dreyfus — actress whose roles included Elaine on the sitcom "Seinfeld" ◆ Julia Phillips — author of expose "You'll Never Eat Lunch in This Town Again" ◆ Julia Roberts — perky actress who became a superstar with "Pretty Woman"

JULIANA ◆Juliana Tyson — daughter of actress Shelley Long

JULIANNA ◆Julianna Ewing — children's book author who wrote the classic "Jackanapes"

JULIANNE ◆Julianne Phillips — actress whose roles included Frankie Reed on NBC's "Sisters"

JULIE ◆Julie Andrews — singer/dancer/actress best remembered for "The Sound of Music" and "Mary Poppins" ◆Julie Christie — blond actress in "McCabe and Mrs. Miller" and "Dr. Zhivago" ◆ Julie Kavner — played Brenda Morgenstern on TV's "Rhoda," voice of Marge on "The Simpsons" ◆Julie Walters — nominated for an Oscar for role of Rita in "Educating Rita"

JULIET ◆Juliet Capulet (c) — immortal star-crossed lover of Shakespeare's "Romeo and Juliet" ◆ Juliet Mills — daughter of actor John Mills, starred in TV's "Nanny and the Professor" ◆ Juliet Prowse — actress and dancer famous for her extraordinary Las Vegas shows

JULIETTE ◆Juliette Adam — late nineteenth century author and editor of "Nouvelle Revue" ◆Juliette Lewis — actress in "Cape Fear" and "Husband and Wives" ◆Juliette Low — founder of the Girl Scouts

JUNE ◆June Allyson — best known today as Mrs. Miller in the film "The Glenn Miller Story" ◆ June Carter — country music singer, wife of Johnny Cash ◆June Lockhart — played the mother on TV's "Lassie," and also the mother on "Lost in Space" ◆June Taylor — leader of the June Taylor Dancers

JUNIE ◆Junie Ellis — actress who appeared in Carol Lynley's "Blue Denim" ◆ Junie Morrison — member of the rock/funk group Parliament, hit "One Nation Under a Groove"

JUSTICE ◆Justice Mellencamp — daughter of singing superstar John Cougar Mellencamp

JUSTINE ◆Justine Bateman — played the not-so-bright clothes horse Mallory Keaton on TV's "Family Ties"

KALEENA ◆Kaleena Kiff — actress who played Patti Morgan on Tony Randall's sitcom "Love, Sidney"

KAMI ◆Kami Cotler — actress who played Elizabeth Walton on the popular drama series "The Waltons"

KAREN ◆Karen Allen — actress in "Animal House" and "Raiders of the Lost Ark" ◆ Karen Black — actress who played Rayette Dipesto in Jack Nicholson's "Five Easy Pieces" ◆ Karen Carpenter — female half of the singing group The Carpenters ◆ Karen Valentine — actress whose roles included the bubbly and innocent teacher on TV's "Room 222"

KARI ◆Kari Lizer — actress who played Cassie Phillips on Andy Griffith's series "Matlock" ◆ Kari Michaelson — actress who played daughter Katie Kanisky on the sitcom "Gimme a Break" ◆ Kari Sylwan — actress whose roles included Anna in Ingmar Bergman's "Cries and Whispers"

KARIN ◆Karin Enke — winner of Olympic gold medals in speed skating ◆ Karin Gustafson — actress who made her film debut in "Taps"

KARLA ◆Karla Bonoff — composer of Linda Ronstadt's "Someone to Lay Down Beside Me"

KAROLA ◆Karola Siegel — real name of sex doctor Ruth Westheimer

KARRON ◆Karron Graves — actress whose roles included Katie Larson on TV's "Dolphin Cove"

KARYN ◆Karyn Kupcinet — actress whose roles included Carol on TV's "The Gertrude Berg Show" ◆ Karyn Parsons — actress who played stuck-up Hilary Banks on TV's "Fresh Prince of Bel Air"

KASEY ◆Kasey Rogers — played Julie Anderson, Betty's mother on the nighttime soap "Peyton Place"

KASI ◆Kasi Lemmons — actress whose roles included Alex Robbins in the espionage series "Under Cover"

KATE ◆Kate Capshaw — starred in "Indiana Jones and the Temple of Doom" ◆ Kate Jackson — actress who played one of TV's "Charlie's Angels" and a wife on "The Rookies" ◆ Kate Moss — 1990's supermodel, well known for her Calvin Klein ads ◆ Kate Mulgrew — played amateur detective Mrs. Columbo in the TV series of the same name ◆ Kate Smith — was often found singing "God Bless America"

KATERI ◆Saint Kateri Tekakwitha — first American Indian saint

KATEY ◆Katey Segal — actress whose roles included Peg Bundy on the sitcom "Married . . . With Children"

KATHARINE ◆Katharine Jane Flynn — daughter of actress Jane Seymour, star of "Dr. Quinn, Medicine Woman" ◆ Katharine Hepburn — legendary actress in "The African Queen," "Guess Who's Coming to Dinner," four Oscars ◆ Katharine Ross — starred in "The Graduate" and "Butch Cassidy and the Sundance Kid"

KATHERINE ◆Katherine Bates — composer of the patriotic hymn "America the Beautiful" ◆ Katherine Helmond — starred as Jessica Tate on TV's "Soap," also on "Who's the Boss"

KATHI ◆Kathi Wolfgramm — member of The Jets, debut hit single "Crush On You"

KATHIE ◆Kathie Browne — actress whose roles included Angie Dow on the western series "Hondo"

KATHIE LEE ◆Kathie Lee Gifford — singer and television star of daytime's "Regis and Kathie Lee"

KATHLEEN ◆Kathleen Quinlan — actress whose films included "I Never Promised You a Rose Garden" ◆ Kathleen Sullivan — anchor for "ABC World News This Morning" ◆ Kathleen Turner — sexy actress in "Body Heat," "Romancing the Stone," "Peggy Sue Got Married"

KATHRYN ◆Kathryn Crosby — wife of Bing Crosby, appeared on his TV Christmas specials ◆Kathryn Grayson — actress in "Show Boat," "Kiss Me Kate," and "The Vagabond King" ◆Kathryn Witt — actress whose roles include a sexy young stewardess on TV's "Flying High"

KATHY ◆Kathy Bates — Oscar winning actress for playing psychopath Annie Wilkes in "Misery" ◆ Kathy Garver — actress whose roles included Cissy on Brian Keith's sitcom "Family Affair" ◆ Kathy Ireland — known for modeling swimsuits in "Sports Illustrated" ◆ Kathy Mattea — throaty-voiced country singer, hits include "Eighteen Wheels and a Dozen Roses"

KATIE ◆Katie Lucas — daughter of director, producer, and creator of "Star Wars," George Lucas

KATINA ◆Katina Paxinou — Oscar winner for her role in "For Whom the Bell Tolls"

KATRINE ◆Katrine Boorman — actress whose roles included Jessie Lipscomb in the film "Camille Claudel"

KATY ◆Katy Jurado — Hollywood Mexican actress whose films include "High Noon"

KAY ◆Kay Francis — glamorous star of the 30's, films include "The White Angel" ◆Kay Medford — nominated for an Oscar for "Funny Girl" ◆ Kay Starr — blues, country, and swing singer, hit single "Wheel of Fortune" ◆ Kay Summersby — romantically linked wartime driver for General Eisenhower

KAYE ◆Kaye Ballard — starred in TV's "The Mothers-in-Law" ◆ Linda Kaye Henning — actress whose roles included Betty Joe Bradley on TV's "Petticoat Junction"

KAYLA ◆Kayla Brady — actress who played Catherine Mary Stewart on the soap "Days of Our Lives"

KEELEY ◆Keeley Gallagher — actress whose roles included Sara Tobin on TV's "Family Man"

KEELY ◆Keely Smith — pop vocalist with her husband Louis Prima

KEITA ◆Keita Wonder — daughter of music artist Stevie Wonder

KELLE ◆Kelle Kerr — actress whose roles included Rochelle in the James Woods film "The Boost"

KELLI ◆Kelli Maroney — actress whose roles included Kimberly Harris Beaulac on the soap "Ryan's Hope" ◆ Kelli McCarty — Miss USA for 1991 ◆ Kelli Williams — actress whose roles included Mattie Walker on TV's "Elvis"

KELLIE ◆Kellie Flanagan — actress who played daughter Candice Muir on the sitcom "The Ghost and Mrs. Muir" ◆Kellie Martin — actress whose roles included Becca Thacher on TV's "Life Goes On" ◆Kellie Williams — actress whose roles included Laura Winslow on Urkel's TV show "Family Matters"

KELLY ◆ Kelly Coffield — regular cast member on the comedy TV show "In Living Color" ◆ Kelly LeBrock — "Don't hate me because I'm beautiful" hair model ◆ Kelly McGillis — starred in "Top Gun" and "The Accused"

KELLYE ◆ Kellye Nakahara — actress whose roles included one of the nurses on the hit sitcom "M*A*S*H"

KELSEY ◆ Kelsey Scott — actress who played Pamela Sawyer on the sitcom "The Robert Guillaume Show" ◆ Kelsey Dohring — as a twin, alternated the role of Chrissy Seaver on TV's "Growing Pains"

KENDRA ◆ Kendra King — host of the daredevil series "Stuntmaster"

KENNY ◆ Sister Kenny — nun who fought infantile paralysis, Rosalind Russell biopic "Sister Kenny"

KEREN ◆ Keren Woodward — member of Bananarama, debut hit single "Shy Boy"

KERRI ◆ Kerri Green — actress whose roles included Maggie in the teenage awakening film "Lucas"

KERRIE ◆ Kerrie Keane — actress who played lead Kate Wyler on the "Fugitive" TV ripoff "Hot Pursuit"

KERSTIN ◆ Kerstin Thorborg — considered the greatest Wagnerian mezzo-soprano of all time

KESHIA ◆ Keshia Knight Pulliam — actress who played the youngest daughter Rudy on TV's "The Cosby Show"

KETTI ◆ Ketti Frings — screenwriter whose credits include "Come Back, Little Sheba" and "Foxfire"

KETTY ◆ Ketty Lester — actress whose roles included Helen Grant on the soap "Days of Our Lives"

KHRYSTYNE ◆ Khrystyne Haje — played brainy kid Simone on the successful sitcom "Head of the Class"

KIA ◆ Kia Goodwin — actress who played Tiffany Holloway on the Marla Gibbs hit sitcom "227"

KIKI ◆ Kiki Dee — rock singer who has teamed with Elton John on songs ◆ Kiki Shepard — regular on the musical variety show "It's Showtime at the Apollo"

KIM ◆ Kim Alexis — supermodel who signed exclusive contract for Revlon's Ultima II ◆ Kim Basinger — actress in films

"Batman," "The Marrying Man," and "My Stepmother Is an Alien" ◆ Kim Carnes — singer with a Grammy for "Bette Davis Eyes" ◆ Kim Darby — little girl in the big John Wayne movie "True Grit" ◆Kim Hunter — underneath a lot of ape makeup, she had a career in "Planet of the Apes" movies ◆ Kim Novak — sultry blond actress in "Vertigo," "Bell, Book, and Candle"

KIMBERLEA ◆Kimberlea Jones — wife of actor Tommy Lee Jones

KIMETHA ◆Kimetha Laurie — actress whose roles included Debbie Whipple on the soap "As the World Turns"

KIMMY ◆Kimmy Robertson — actress who played Lucy Moran on David Lynch's drama series "Twin Peaks"

KIRSTIE ◆Kirstie Alley — replaced Shelley Long on "Cheers" with her own character of Rebecca Howe

KITTY ◆Kitty Carlisle — widow of playwright Moss Hart, one of the panelists on "To Tell the Truth" ◆ Kitty Dukakis — wife of Democratic presidential candidate Michael Dukakis ◆ Kitty Kelley — wrote tell-all bios on Jackie Kennedy, Nancy Reagan, and Frank Sinatra ◆Kitty Wells — the queen of country music for more than 30 years

KIZZY ◆Kizzy — Leslie Uggams played this Alex Haley ancestor in the epic miniseries "Roots"

KOO ◆Koo Stark — actress involved in a highly publicized romance with Prince Andrew

KORNELIA ◆Kornelia Ender — four-time Olympic gold medalist who is considered the greatest woman swimmer

KRISTA ◆Krista Errickson — actress who played Diane Alder on McLean Stevenson's sitcom "Hello, Larry" ◆ Krista Murphy — actress whose roles included Carla Healy on the hit sitcom "The Wonder Years"

KRISTAN ◆Kristan Carl — actress who played Suzi Martin Carter on the soap "Search for Tomorrow"

KRISTEN ◆Kristen Dohring — as a twin, alternated the role of Chrissy Seaver on TV's "Growing Pains" ◆ Kristen Meadows — actress whose roles included Mimi King on the soap "One Life to Live"

KRISTI ◆Kristi Yamaguchi — Olympic gold medalist for singles ice skating for the US

KRISTIAN ◆Kristian Alfonso — actress whose roles included Hope Williams on the soap "Days of Our Lives"

KRISTIN ◆Kristin Dattilo — actress who played D.J. Serkin on the musical drama series "Hull High" ◆ Kristin Griffith — portrayed the lead role of Flyn in Woody Allen's "Interiors"

KRISTINA ◆Kristina Kennedy — actress who played the cute little baby dropped on Diane Keaton in "Baby Boom" ◆ Kristina Malandro — actress whose roles included Felicia on the soap "General Hospital"

KRISTINE ◆Kristine Holdereid — first woman valedictorian at the US Naval Academy ◆ Kristine Sutherland — actress who played Mae Thompson in Rick Moranis' "Honey, I Shrunk the Kids"

KRISTY ◆Kristy McNichol — TV actress who played the daughter on "Family," later on "Empty Nest"

KRYSTLE ◆Krystle Carrington (c) — Linda Evans' goody-goody character on TV's "Dynasty"

KYLE ◆Kyle MacDonnell — pretty singing star of Broadway's "Make Mine Manhattan"

KYM ◆Kym Karath — actress who played Gretl von Trapp in Julie Andrews' "The Sound of Music"

KYME ◆Kyme — portrayed Rachel Meadows in Spike Lee's "School Daze"

KYNDRA ◆Kyndra Casper — actress whose roles included Molly Marshall on the sitcom "Working It Out"

KYRA ◆Kyra Schon — actress who played Karen Cooper in the horror classic "Night of the Living Dead" ◆ Kyra Sedgwick-Bacon — wife of Kevin Bacon, featured in "Born on the Fourth of July"

LA TOYA ◆La Toya Jackson — sister of Michael Jackson who has a successful singing career of her own

LADONNA ◆LaDonna Gaines — real name of singer Donna Summer

LARUE ◆Florence LaRue Gordon — member of The Fifth Dimension, hits include "Up, Up, and Away" and "Aquarius" ◆ Scout LaRue Willis — daughter of actor Bruce Willis and actress Demi Moore

LAVERN ◆LaVern Baker — hit the charts with the song "Jim Dandy Got Married"

LAVERNE ◆LaVerne Andrews — member of The Andrews Sisters

LAWANDA ◆LaWanda Page — played Lamont's Aunt Esther, and Fred's nemesis, on TV's "Sanford and Son"

LACEY ◆Lacey Craven — actress who played Janet Steadman on the comedy/drama series "thirtysomething"

LACY ◆Lacy Dalton — country western singer, hits include "Hard Times"

LAILA ◆Laila Robbins — played the wife of James Earl Jones on the drama series "Gabriel's Fire"

LAINIE ◆Lainie Kazan — actress whose roles included Leona Bloom in Bette Midler's "Beaches"

LALA ◆LaLa Brooks — with The Crystals, hit debut single "There's No Other (Like My Baby)"

LALLA ◆Lalla Ward — actress who played the ruthless Queen Elizabeth in "The Prince and the Pauper"

LANA ◆Lana Turner — "Sweater Girl" discovered drinking a soda at Schwab's Drugstore ◆Lana Wood — actress whose roles included Sandy Webber on the nighttime soap "Peyton Place"

LANE ◆Lane Bryant — founder of the Lane Bryant clothing stores

LANGLEY ◆Langley Fox Crisinan— daughter of actress Mariel Hemingway, granddaughter of Ernest Hemingway

LANI ◆Lani Hall — member of Sergio Mendes and Brasil '66, debut hit "Mas Que Nada" ◆Lani Miyazaki — actress whose roles included Michiko Kita on the soap "One Life to Live" ◆ Lani O'Grady — actress whose roles included Mary Bradford on TV's "Eight Is Enough"

LAR ◆Lar Park-Lincoln — actress who played Linda Fairgate on the nighttime soap "Knots Landing"

LARAINE ◆Laraine Day — regular on the popular quiz show "I've Got a Secret" ◆ Laraine Stephens — actress whose roles included Claire Kronski on the TV version of "Matt Helm"

LARK ◆Lark Song Previn — child of actress Mia Farrow and composer/conductor Andre Previn

LARRAINE ◆Larraine Newman — original cast member of "Saturday Night Live"

LARYSSA ◆Laryssa Lauret — actress whose roles included Simone Kincaid on the soap "The Guiding Light"

LATIFAH ◆Queen Latifah — rap star, album "All Hail the Queen"

LAURA ◆Laura Branigan — singer, hits "Gloria," "Solitaire," "Self Control" ◆ Laura Dern — actress daughter of Bruce Dern whose films include "Mask" and "Jurassic Park" ◆ Laura Ingalls — creator of the "Little House on the Prairie" books which became a TV series

LAUREL ◆Laurel Masse — member of Grammy winning group Manhattan Transfer, hits "Vocalese" and "Brasil"

LAUREN ◆Lauren Bacall — acted in "The Big Sleep" and "Key Largo" with hubby Humphrey Bogart ◆ Lauren Tewes — perky cruise director on TV's "The Love Boat"

LAUREN-MARIE ◆Lauren-Marie Taylor — actress whose roles included Stacey Donovan on the soap "Loving"

LAURETTE ◆Laurette Spang — played Cassiopeia on the science fiction series "Battlestar Galactica" ◆ Laurette Taylor — actress, starred in the plays "Peg o' My Heart" and "Glass Menagerie"

LAURI ◆Lauri Hendler — actress who played daughter Julie Kanisky on the sitcom "Gimme a Break"

LAURIE ◆Laurie Metcalf — actress whose roles included the sister Jackie on the hit sitcom "Roseanne"

LAURINDA ◆Laurinda Barrett — actress whose roles included Molly Sherwood on the soap "The Edge of Night"

LAVEEN ◆Aline Laveen MacMahon — Oscar nominee for "Dragon Seed"

LAVERNE ◆Laverne Defazio (c) — ever-optimistic Penny Marshall on TV's "Laverne and Shirley"

LAVINIA ◆Caroline Lavinia Harrison — first wife of President Benjamin Harrison

LEA ◆Rosie Lea Daltrey — daughter of English singer Roger Daltrey ◆ Lea Thompson — actress in "Casual Sex" and all three of the "Back to the Future" movies

LEAH ◆Leah Ayres — actress whose roles included Valerie Bryson on the soap "The Edge of Night" ◆Leah Remini — actress whose roles included Charlie Brisco on the sitcom "Living Dolls"

LEANN ◆Leann Hunley — actress whose roles included Anna Brady DiMera on the soap "Days of Our Lives"

LEATRICE ◆Leatrice Joy — star of Cecil B. DeMille's silents who popularized bobbed hair

LECY ◆Lecy Goranson — actress whose roles included Becky Conner on the smash hit sitcom "Roseanne"

LEE ◆Lee Grant — Emmy winning actress for "Peyton Place," Oscar winner for "Shampoo" ◆Lee Meriwether — Miss America who played Betty Jones, assistant to TV's "Barnaby Jones" ◆Lee Remick — actress in "Telefon," "The Omen," Oscar nominee for "Days of Wine and Roses"

LEEZA ◆Leeza Gibbons — regular host on TV's "Entertainment Tonight"

LEIA ◆Princess Leia (c) — Carrie Fisher as the princess in trouble in Harrison Ford's "Star Wars"

LEIGH ◆Erin Leigh Peck — actress who played Jennifer Abbott on the "Big Chill" TV ripoff "Hometown" ◆ Dorothy Leigh Sayers — creator of the sleuth Lord Peter Wimsey ◆Leigh Taylor Young — actress in "The Adventurers"

LEILA ◆Leila Hyams — actress who played Nell Kenner in Charles Laughton's "Ruggles of Red Gap" ◆ Leila Mourad — portrayed Shakespeare's star-crossed lover in "Romeo and Juliet"

LEINAALA ◆Leinaala Heine — played Mrs Kalikini on the adventure series "The Mackenzies of Paradise Cove"

LELA ◆Lela Brooks — Canadian figure skater ◆ Lela Ivey — actress whose roles included Mitzi Martin on the soap "The Edge of Night"

LELIA ◆Lelia Goldoni — actress in "Shadows" and "Hysteria"

LENA ◆Lena Horne — female vocalist whose big song and film was "Stormy Weather" ◆ Lena Malena — actress whose roles included Gretchen in Jean Harlow's classic "Hell's Angels" ◆ Lena Olin — Oscar nominee for "Enemies: A Love Story"

LENI ◆Farrah Leni Fawcett — starred on TV's "Charlie's Angels," TV movie "The Burning Bed" ◆Leni Lynn — girl singer in "Babes in Arms" who went to England

LENKA ◆Lenka Peterson — actress who played Isabel Kitteridge Moore on the soap "Search for Tomorrow"

LENORE ◆Lenore Hershey — former editor-in-chief of the "Ladies Home Journal" ◆ Helen Lenore Van Slyke — author of best sellers "A Necessary Woman" and "No Love Lost"

LEONA ◆Leona Helmsley — multimillionaire landlord convicted of income tax evasion

LEONIE ◆Leonie Adams — metaphysical romantic whose verse includes "This Measure" ◆ Leonie Norton — actress whose roles included Cindy Clark Matthews on the soap "Another World"

LEONOR ◆Leonor Fini — theatrical designer and book illustrator

LEONORA ◆Leonora Barry — organized women workers into The Knights of Labor in the 1880's

LEONORE ◆Leonore Longergan — regular on TV's musical variety show "Holiday Hotel"

LEONTINE ◆Leontine Kelly — first African-American woman bishop of a major denomination

LEONTYNE ◆Leontyne Price — soprano star of "Porgy and Bess"

LEORA ◆Leora Dana — portrayed Agnes Hirsh in Frank Sinatra's "Some Came Running"

LEOTA ◆Leota Lorraine — played Mrs. Belknap-Johnson in Charles Laughton's "Ruggles of Red Gap"

LESLEY ◆Lesley Gore — singer of the teen classic "It's My Party" ◆ Lesley Stahl — journalist on CBS News and "60 Minutes," coined "The Peggy Principle" ◆Lesley Ann Warren — starred in Mel Brooks' look at the homeless, "Life Stinks"

LESLEY-ANNE ◆Lesley-Anne Down — actress in PBS series "Upstairs, Downstairs," in miniseries "North and South"

LESLIE ◆Leslie Caron — French actress and singer who captured 19th century French life with "Gigi" ◆Leslie Uggams — actress whose roles included Kizzy in the epic TV miniseries "Roots"

LETHA ◆Mary Letha Elting — children's book author, works include "Wheels and Noises" and "The Answer Book"

LETITIA ◆Letitia Baldrige — Kennedy's White House social secretary ◆ Letitia Tyler — first First Lady to die in the White House

LETIZIA ◆Letizia Bonaparte — mother of French Emperor Napoleon

LEZLIE ◆Lezlie Dalton — actress who played Elizabeth Spaulding Marler on the soap "The Guiding Light"

LIA ◆Lia Jackson — played Juanita Priscilla Harris on the family drama "Harris and Company"

LIBBIE ◆Libbie Hyman — specialist in invertebrate zoology whose works include "The Invertebrates"

LIBBY ◆Libby Holman — actress and torch singer whose hits include "Body and Soul" ◆Libby Thatcher — Patti LuPone's role on the drama series "Life Goes On"

LIBERTY ◆Liberty Kasem — daughter of television personality Casey Kasem

LIBRA ◆Libra Astro Max — daughter of artist and designer Peter Max

LICIA ◆Licia Albanese — Italian opera singer in the title role of "Madame Butterfly"

LIESL ◆Liesl von Trapp — one of the singing von Trapp children, portrayed by Charmian Carr in "The Sound of Music"

LIEUX ◆Lieux Dressler — actress whose roles included Alice Grant on the soap "General Hospital"

LIHANN ◆Lihann Jones — actress whose roles included Jessica on the little robot sitcom "Small Wonder"

LIL ◆Lil Armstrong — pianist, arranger, vocalist, composer, and ex-wife of Louis Armstrong

LILA ◆Lila Kent — actress whose roles included Laverne on TV's "The Dukes of Hazzard" ◆Lila Lee — starred with Valentino in "Blood and Sand"

LILI ◆Lili Taylor — actress whose roles included Jojo Barboza in Julia Roberts' "Mystic Pizza"

LILIA ◆Lilia — Debra Paget played her in DeMille's biblical epic "The Ten Commandments" ◆Lilia Skala — actress whose roles included Hanna Long in Jennifer Beals' "Flashdance"

LILIBET ◆Lilibet Stern — played Patty Williams Abbott on the soap "The Young and the Restless"

LILITH ◆Lilith Sternin (c) — Frasier Crane's neurotic wife on TV's long running "Cheers"

LILLA ◆Lilla Pescatori — played Zola's prostitute character in the silent film version of "Nana"

LILLI ◆Lilli Palmer — actress whose roles included Lady Raffles in "Frau Cheyney's Ende"

LILLIAN ◆Lillian Carter — First Mom to President Jimmy Carter ◆Lillian Gish — silent film star in films like "The Birth of a Nation," "Way Down East" ◆ Lillian Hellman — playwright who wrote on lesbianism, author "The Little Foxes" ◆Lillian Roth — singer, Broadway performer, autobiography "I'll Cry Tomorrow"

LILLIE ◆Lillie Collins — daughter of superstar songster Phil Collins ◆ Lillie Langtry — singer and idol of Texas Judge Roy Bean, mistress of King Edward VII

LILO ◆Lilo Pulver — Swiss/German leading lady whose films include "A Global Affair"

LILY ◆Lily Costner — daughter of Kevin Costner, actor from "Dances with Wolves" ◆Lily Pons — soprano and reigning diva at the NY Metropolitan ◆Lily Tomlin — she went from "Laugh-In" to comedy films like "All of Me" and "Big Business"

LILYAN ◆Lilyan Chauvin — actress who played Marianne Rolland in the soap "The Young and the Restless" ◆ Lilyan Tashman — silent screen sophisticate, films include "No, No, Nanette"

LIN ◆Lin Pierson — actress whose roles included Alice Holden on the soap "The Guiding Light"

LINA ◆Lina Montes — one of the many actresses to portray notorious courtesan Camille in films

LINDA ◆Linda Blair — actress whose roles included the possessed girl in "The Exorcist" ◆ Linda Darnell — smoldering actress who played opposite Tyrone Power in "The Mark of Zorro" ◆Linda Evans — actress who played the only daughter of Barbara Stanwyck on TV's "The Big Valley" ◆Linda Hamilton — played Sarah Connor, mother of the savior of humanity in "The Terminator" ◆Linda Kozlowski — she was the major love interest for "Crocodile Dundee" ◆ Linda Ronstadt — popular singer, dated California Governor Jerry Brown

LINDEN ◆Linden Travers — English actress whose credits include Hitchcock's "The Lady Vanishes"

LINDSAY ◆Lindsay Crystal — daughter of comedian Billy Crystal ◆ Lindsay Greenbush — played Carrie Ingalls with her sister

Sidney on "Little House on the Prairie" ◆ Lindsay Wagner — actress who played the title role of a superhuman agent on TV's "The Bionic Woman"

LINE ◆Line Noro — played Emile Zola's tragic heroine Gervaise in the film "L'Assommoir"

LIONA ◆Liona Boyd — Canadian first lady of classical guitar

LISA ◆Lisa Bonet — played the irresponsible Huxtable daughter on TV's "The Cosby Show" ◆Lisa Hartman — actress who played grown-up baby witch "Tabitha" in the TV sequel to "Bewitched" ◆ Lisa Simpson (c) — Yeardley Smith's role on the hit prime time cartoon sitcom "The Simpsons"

LISA JANE ◆Lisa Jane Persky — actress who played Dottie Dworski on the detective series "Private Eye"

LISA MARIE ◆Lisa Marie Presley — only child of Elvis Presley

LISABETH ◆Lisabeth Shean — actress whose roles included Catherine Shaw on the soap "The Doctors"

LISANNE ◆Lisanne Falk — actress whose roles included one of the Heathers in the film "Heathers"

LISELOTT ◆Liselott Neuman — winner of the 1988 US Women's Open

LITA ◆Lita Ford — heavy metal guitarist whose hits include the platinum "Lita"

LIV ◆Liv Ullmann — Norwegian star of Ingmar Bergman films

LIVIA ◆Eva Maria Livia Robbins — actress Susan Sarandon's daughter Livia Ginise — actress whose roles included Mitzi Matuso on the soap "Days of Our Lives"

LIZ ◆Liz Claiborne — fashion designer and founder of "Liz Claiborne" ◆ Liz Sagal — actress whose roles included one of the twins on TV's "Double Trouble" ◆ Liz Taylor — actress best known for "National Velvet" and "Cleopatra"

LIZA ◆Liza Minnelli — following mother Judy, she sang in musicals "Cabaret," "New York, New York"

LIZABETH ◆Lizabeth Scott — played tough, shiftless blonds in films, appeared in "Bad for Each Other"

LIZZIE ◆Lizzie Borden — she killed her mom with forty whacks, and gave her father forty-one, and was acquitted

LOANNE ◆Loanne Bishop — actress whose roles included Rose Kelly on the soap "General Hospital"

LOIE ◆Loie Fuller — burlesque performer who invented the "serpentine dance"

LOIS ◆Lois Gibbs — woman who stood up to toxic wastes, biopic "Lois Gibbs and the Love Canal" ◆ Lois Lane (c) — works with Clark Kent on the Daily Planet, always being rescued by Superman ◆Lois Nettleton — film actress, won Clarence Derwent for her stage role in "God and Kate Murphy"

LOLA ◆Lola Falana — dancer whose roles included Charity Blake on the soap "Capitol" ◆ Lola Montez — 19th century adventuress, dancer, and mistress of Liszt and King Ludwig of Bavaria

LOLEATTA ◆Loleatta Holloway — soul singer, hits include "Cry to Me" and "Hit and Run"

LOLITA ◆Lolita Davidovich — she played Blaze in the film "Blaze" with Paul Newman

LOLLY ◆Lolly Esterman — actress in Robert De Niro and Robin Williams' film "Awakenings"

LONA ◆Lona Andrea — southern belle in Gary Cooper's adventure film "The Plainsman"

LONETTE ◆Lonette McKee — actress who played Lila Rose Oliver in Richard Gere's "The Cotton Club"

LONI ◆Loni Anderson — Jennifer Marlow, the sexy secretary on TV's "WKRP in Cincinnati"

LORE ◆Lore Segal — children's author whose works include "Lucinella" and "Tell Me a Trudy"

LORENA ◆Lorena Hickok — reporter who covered FDR, wrote children's book on Eleanor and Franklin

LORENE ◆Lorene Cary — author of "Black Ice" ◆ Lorene Yarnell — mime in duo Shields and Yarnell, had own TV show

LORET ◆Loret Ruppe — director of the Peace Corps and ambassador to Norway

LORETTA ◆Loretta Lynn — country western singer, Sissy Spacek biopic "Coal Miner's Daughter" ◆ Loretta Swit — actress who played sexy nurse Hot Lips Hoolihan in the TV version of "M*A*S*H" ◆Loretta Young — Oscar winner for "The Farmer's Daughter," own series "The Loretta Young Show"

LORI ◆Lori Loughlin — actress whose roles included Becky on the TV sitcom "Full House" ◆ Lori Saunders — actress who played Bobbi Jo on the hayseed sitcom "Petticoat Junction" ◆Lori Singer — actress who played Ariel in the dancing, singing teenage film "Footloose"

LORI-NAN ◆Lori-Nan Engler — actress whose roles included Greta Powers Aldrich on the soap "The Doctors"

LORIANN ◆Loriann Ruger — actress who played Marianne Randolph Halloway on the soap "Another World"

LORNA ◆Lorna Luft — Judy Garland's other daughter ◆ Lorna Patterson — actress who played bumbling Private Benjamin in the TV series of the same name

LORRAINE ◆Lorraine Bracco — credits as an actress include "Goodfellas" and "Medicine Man" ◆ Lorraine Nicholson — daughter of actor Jack Nicholson

LORRIE ◆Lorrie Morgan — country singer with a melancholy style, hits include the number one "Watch Me"

LORY ◆Lory Patrick — actress whose roles included Tina on the western series "Tales of Wells Fargo" ◆ Lory Walsh — played Bridget Mackenzie on the series "The Mackenzies of Paradise Cove"

LOTA ◆Freya Lota Littledale — children's author whose books include "The Elves and the Shoemaker"

LOTTE ◆Lotte Lenya — Tony winner for "The Threepenny Opera" ◆Lotte Reiniger — German animator well known for her silhouette cartoons

LOU ◆Benjamine Lou Abruzzo — one of the first to make a trans-Atlantic balloon flight

LOUANNE ◆Louanne — actress who played the little girl Tracy in George Burns' "Oh, God! Book II"

LOUELLA ◆Louella Parsons — powerful gossip columnist during Hollywood's "golden age"

LOUISA ◆Louisa May Alcott — author of the autobiographical "Little Women" in 1868 ◆Louisa von Trapp — one of the singing von Trapp children, portrayed by Heather Menzies in "The Sound of Music"

LOUISE ◆Louise Beavers — one of Hollywood's most frequently employed actress, in "Imitation of Life" ◆ Louise Fletcher — she won an Oscar for her nurse role in "One Flew Over the Cuckoo's Nest" ◆ Louise Lasser — actress whose roles included Mary Hartman on TV's "Mary Hartman, Mary Hartman"

LOYITA ◆Loyita Chapel — actress whose roles included Mrs. Kramer on the sitcom "Punky Brewster"

LU ◆Lu Leonard — actress who played Gertrude on the legal drama series "Jake and the Fatman"

LUANA ◆Luana Anders — actress who played Lisa in the Dennis Hopper cult classic "Easy Rider"

LUCI ◆Luci Baines Johnson — younger daughter of President Lyndon Johnson

LUCIA ◆Lucia Bose — former Italian beauty queen and leading lady in films

LUCIANA ◆Luciana Paluzzi — actress whose roles included Simone Genet on TV's "Five Fingers"

LUCIE ◆Lucie Arnaz — actress daughter of Desi Arnaz and Lucille Ball ◆ Lucie DeVito — daughter of "Taxi" comedians Danny DeVito and Rhea Perlman

LUCIEN ◆Lucien Littlefield — actress who played the Kentucky Rose in William S. Hart's "Tumbleweeds"

LUCILE ◆Lucile — fashion designer who introduced fashion parades to England ◆ Lucile Langhanke — real name of actress Mary Astor

LUCILLE ◆Lucille Ball — carrot-topped comic genius who created "I Love Lucy"

LUCINDA ◆Lucinda Dickey — actress whose roles included Kelly in "Breakin' 2: Electric Boogaloo"

LUCINE ◆Lucine Amara — opera singer

LUCRETIA ◆Lucretia Garfield — First Lady to President Garfield ◆ Lucretia Mott — co-founder of the women's rights movement in the United States

LUCREZIA ◆Lucrezia Borgia — incest and poisonings make her the perfect subject of numerous biopics

LUCY ◆Lucy Hayes — Lemonade Lucy, First Lady who refused to serve liquor in the White House ◆ Lucy Ricardo (c) — nutsy redhead always getting into trouble on TV's "I Love Lucy" ◆Lucy

Van Pelt (c) — arch-enemy of comic strip character Charlie Brown

LUDI ◆Ludi Claire — actress whose roles included Elizabeth McGrath on the soap "The Edge of Night"

LUELLA ◆Luella Gear — actress whose roles included Mrs. Spooner on the sitcom "Joe and Mabel" ◆ Pearl Luella Kendrick — developed the shot for diphtheria, whooping cough, and tetanus

LUGENE ◆Lugene Sanders — played Babs Riley Marshall on the William Bendix sitcom "The Life of Riley"

LUISA ◆Luisa Tetrazzini — soprano whose operas include "Rigoletto" and "Lakme"

LUISE ◆Luise King — one of the singing King Sisters, musical variety series "The King Family Show" ◆ Luise Rainer — Oscar winner for "The Great Ziegfeld" and "The Good Earth"

LULAMAE ◆Lulamae Golightly (c) — Audrey Hepburn's role in Truman Capote's filmed novel "Breakfast at Tiffany's"

LULU ◆Lulu — singer whose biggest hit was "To Sir With Love" in the movie of the same name ◆Lulu Roman — series regular on the long running hayseed variety show "Hee Haw"

LULUBELLE ◆Lulubelle — half of the country music group Lulubelle and Scotty

LUPE ◆Lupe Ontiveros — actress whose roles included Grandma Gomez on the adventure series "Grand Slam" ◆ Lupe Velez — actress whose roles included Zola's prostitute in the film "Nana"

LURENE ◆Lurene Tuttle — actress who played Doris Dunston on TV's "Father of the Bride," also in "Psycho"

LURLEEN ◆Lurleen Wallace — first woman governor of Alabama

LYDIA ◆Lydia Maria Shaw — daughter of hostage/terrorist Patty Hearst, descendant of William Randolph Hearst ◆ Lydia Cornell — played wife Sarah Rush on Ted Knight's sitcom "Too Close for Comfort"

LYDIE ◆Lydie Denier — actress whose roles included Jane on the Wolf Larsen version of TV's "Tarzan"

LYN ◆Daphne Lyn Jones — actress whose roles included Lisa on the school based sitcom "Homeroom" ◆ Lyn St. James — first woman auto racer to be named rookie of the year at the Indianapolis 500

LYNDA ◆Lynda Carter — went from being a beauty queen to TV's comic book hero "Wonder Woman" ◆Lynda Day George — member of the action team on TV's "Mission: Impossible" ◆ Lynda Goodfriend — actress who played Richie Cunningham's girlfriend on the sitcom "Happy Days"

LYNDALL ◆Lyndall Hobbs — director of the updated beach party movie "Back to the Beach"

LYNETTE ◆Lynette Fromme — nicknamed Squeaky, convicted of attempting to assassinate Gerald Ford ◆ Lynette Winter — actress whose roles included Larue on Sally Field's sitcom "Gidget" ◆ Lynette Woodard — first female member of the Harlem Globetrotters

LYNN ◆Lynn Anderson — country singer whose hits include "Rose Garden" ◆Lynn Bari — husky-voiced siren who played the "other woman" in B films ◆ Lynn Redgrave — star of the film "Georgy Girl," part of the Redgrave acting dynasty

LYNN-HOLLY ◆Lynn-Holly Johnson — Ice Capades performer who starred in the film "Ice Castles"

LYNNE ◆Lynne Moody — actress who played nurse Julie Williams on Elliot Gould's TV show "E/R" ◆ Lynne Thigpen — actress whose roles included Nancy on the Tony Randall sitcom "Love, Sidney"

LYNSEY ◆Lynsey Baxter — actress who played Ernestina in Meryl Streep's "The French Lieutenant's Woman"

LYOVA ◆Lyova Rosenthal — real name of actress Lee Grant

LYRIC ◆Lyric Benson — daughter of actor Robby Benson and Karla De Vito

MABEL ◆Mabel Mercer — cabaret performer after whom the annual Stereo Review awards are named ◆ Mabel Normand — silent screen comedienne, a leading player at Keystone and Chaplin co-star

MABLE ◆Mable Ellen — daughter of comedian Tracey Ullman

MACKENZIE ◆MacKenzie Phillips — from the film "American Graffiti" she migrated to TV's "One Day at a Time"

MACHIKO ◆Machiko Kyo — Japanese actress whose films include "The Teahouse of the August Moon"

MADALYN ◆Madalyn O'Hair — founder of the American Atheists who stopped prayer in public schools

MADDIE ◆Maddie Corman — played Zuzu Petals in Andrew Dice Clay's "The Adventures of Ford Fairlane"

MADELEINE ◆Madeleine Carroll — drop-dead beautiful blond of 1930's films ◆ Madeleine Stowe — actress who is the object of Richard Dreyfuss' attention in "Stakeout" ◆ Madeleine Vionnet — fashion designer who invented the revolutionary bias cut for women's fashion

MADELINE ◆Madeline Harris — daughter of "thirty-something's" Mel Harris ◆ Madeline Kahn — Mel Brooks' comedienne in "Blazing Saddles," "High Anxiety," "Young Frankenstein" ◆Madeline LeBeau — actress who played Yvonne in the classic Oscar winning film "Casablanca"

MADGE ◆Madge Kennedy — one of Sam Goldwyn's glamorous leading ladies ◆Madge Sinclair — three-time Emmy nominee for her role on TV's "Trapper John, M.D."

MADLYN ◆Madlyn Rhue — actress whose roles included Hilary Madison on TV's "Executive Suite"

MADOLYN ◆Madolyn Smith — actress whose roles included Peggy in Steve Martin's comedy hit "All of Me"

MADONNA ◆Madonna Ciccione — controversial "Material Girl" turned actress in "A League of Their Own"

MADY ◆Mady Christians — actress whose roles included Mama in the play "I Remember Mama" ◆Mady Kaplan — played Axel's girl in Robert De Niro's classic anti-war film "The Deer Hunter"

MAE ◆Mae Clark — actress whom Cagney mashed in the face with a grapefruit in "The Public Enemy" ◆Edna Mae Gillooly — real name of Ellen Burstyn, Oscar for "Alice Doesn't Live Here Anymore" ◆ Mae West — created the idea of a sex goddess, "Goodness had nothing to do with it"

MAEVE ◆Maeve Kinkead — actress whose roles included Angie Perrini Frame on the soap "Another World" ◆Maeve McGuire — actress whose roles included Elena de Poulignac on the soap "Another World"

MAG ◆Mag Bodard — one of the first woman film producers

MAGALI ◆Magali Noel — French lead character Gradisca in Fellini's "Amarcord"

MAGDA ◆Magda Gabor — elder sister of Zsa Zsa and Eva Gabor ◆Magda Sonja — dancer/spy in the silent "Mata Hari: The Red Dancer"

MAGDALENA ◆Anna Magdalena Bach — wife of Johann Sebastian Bach, biopic "The Chronicle of Anna Magdalena Bach"

MAGGI ◆Maggi Parker — played McGarrett's secretary May on the popular police drama "Hawaii Five-O"

MAGGIE ◆Maggie Smith — caustic actress who won an Oscar for the film "The Prime of Miss Jean Brodie"

MAHALIA ◆Mahalia Jackson — gospel singer, hits include "He's Got the Whole World in His Hands"

MAIA ◆Maia Brewton — actress who played Holly Bankston on Mitchum's TV show "A Family for Joe"

MAJEL ◆Majel Barrett — played Nurse Christine Chapel on the science fiction series "Star Trek" ◆ Majel Coleman — actress whose roles included the wife of Pilate in the silent "The King of Kings"

MALA ◆Mala Powers — actress whose roles included Mona Williams on the successful sitcom "Hazel"

MALLORY ◆Mallory Keaton (c) — dumb daughter played by Justine Bateman on TV's "Family Ties"

MALVINA ◆Malvina Hoffman — sculptor known for 101 life-size bronze statutes at the Field Museum in Chicago

MAME ◆Mame Dennis (c) — flamboyant heiress with unorthodox ideas and lifestyle in "Auntie Mame"

MAMIE ◆Mamie Eisenhower — First Lady to President Eisenhower ◆ Mamie Van Doren — sexy blond bombshell who appeared in a lot of B movies

MANDY ◆Mandy Ingber — actress whose roles included Deborah Wyman on TV's "Detective in the House"

MANON ◆Manon Theaume — first woman to play in a National Hockey League game

MARA ◆Mara Corday — leading lady of the 1950's whose credits include "Man Without a Star"

MARABEL ◆Marabel Morgan — militant anti-feminist who advocates total submission to husbands

MARCELITE ◆Marcelite Harris — first African-American woman air force general

MARCELLA ◆Marcella Martin — actress whose roles included Flo Murray on the soap "Another World" ◆ Marcella Thum — Edgar award winning author of "Mystery at Crane's Landing" and "Margarite"

MARCHETTE ◆Marchette Chute — award winning writer of children's stories

MARCIA ◆Marcia Brady (c) — Maureen McCormick's role on ABC's "The Brady Bunch" ◆ Marcia Carsey — producer of "The Cosby Show" and "Roseanne" ◆ Marcia Strassman — actress whose roles included Julie Kotter on the sitcom "Welcome Back, Kotter"

MARDI ◆Mardi Bryant — regular on the music series "The Ted Steele Show"

MARE ◆Mare Winningham — actress who appeared in "St. Elmo's Fire" and "Turner and Hooch"

MAREN ◆Maren Jensen — actress who played Athena on the science fiction series "Battlestar Galactica"

MARG ◆Marg Helgenberger — actress who played Natalie Thayer on the Margot Kidder sitcom "Shell Game"

MARGARET ◆Margaret Dumont — straight lady and comic foil for the Marx Brothers in their movies ◆ Margaret Hamilton — went down in history as the Wicked Witch of the West in "The Wizard of Oz" ◆ Margaret Mitchell — won a Pulitzer Prize with her only novel "Gone With the Wind" ◆Margaret Sullivan — pert actress, first wife of Henry Fonda ◆ Margaret Thatcher — prime minister of Great Britain known as the "Iron Lady"

MARGARETHE ◆Maria Margarethe Schell — actress whose films include "The Brothers Karamazov"

MARGARITA ◆Margarita Sierra — actress who played Cha Cha O'Brien on the detective drama series "Surfside Six"

MARGAUX ◆Margaux Hemingway — actress granddaughter of Ernest Hemingway, films include "Lipstick"

MARGE ◆Marge Ganser — member of the Shangri-Las, debut hit "Remember (Walkin' In the Sand)" ◆ Marge Redmond — played Mrs. Florence Kimball on TV's "The Double Life of Henry Phyfe" ◆ Marge Simpson (c) — Julie Kavner's role on the prime time hit cartoon sitcom "The Simpsons"

MARGERY ◆Margery Allingham — English author who created the detective Albert Champion

MARGHERITA ◆Margherita Wallmann — internationally known producer of opera, film, TV, and stage

MARGO ◆Margo Castillo — actress known for her role as the rapidly aging refugee from Shangri-La in "Lost Horizon"

MARGOT ◆Margot Kidder — actress whose roles included reporter Lois Lane in the feature film "Superman"

MARGUERITA ◆Maya Marguerita Angelou — author of "I Know Why the Caged Bird Sings"

MARGUERITE ◆Marguerite Chapman — dependable heroine of many 40's features ◆Marguerite Clark — top silent screen actress, best known for "Uncle Tom's Cabin"

MARI ◆Mari Blanchard — actress whose roles included Kathy O'Hara on the adventure series "Klondike" ◆ Mari Gorman — played Vivian Washburn on Barbara Eden's sitcom "Harper Valley P.T.A."

MARIA ◆Maria Montez — hot-blooded Spanish actress in "Arabian Nights," "Cobra Woman" ◆Maria Shriver — television personality, President Kennedy's niece, wife of Arnold Schwarzenegger ◆ Maria von Trapp — governess who taught her charges to sing, biopic "The Sound of Music"

MARIAH ◆Mariah Carey — Grammys for best new artist and best pop female vocalist

MARIAN ◆Marian — maid of Sherwood, played best by Olivia de Havilland as Robin's girlfriend ◆ Marian Jordan — actress whose roles included Molly on radio's "Fibber McGee and Molly" ◆ Marian Mercer — actress who played slavedriver Nancy Beebe on the sitcom "It's a Living"

MARIANA ◆Mariana Hill — actress whose roles included Ruth in the film "Medium Cool"

MARIANN ◆Mariann Aalda — actress whose roles included Didi Bannister on the soap "The Edge of Night"

MARIANNE ◆Marianne Faithful — pop singer, hits include "As Tears Go By" ◆ Marianne Rogers — series regular on the long running hayseed variety series "Hee Haw"

MARICLARE ◆Mariclare Costello — actress whose roles included Julia Bailey on Brenda Vaccaro's western "Sara"

MARIE ◆Marie Dressler — Oscar winning actress for "Min and Bill" with Wallace Berry ◆ Marie Osmond — pop singer who partnered with her brother for the TV series "Donny and Marie"

MARIE-ALISE ◆Marie-Alise Recasner — portrayed Millie on TV's "A Different World"

MARIEL ◆Mariel Hemingway — star of TV's "Civil Wars," movies include "Star 80," "Lipstick"

MARIETTA ◆Marietta Tree — US representative to the Human Rights Committee of the United Nations

MARIETTE ◆Mariette Hartley — actress best known for her Polaroid commercials with James Garner

MARILU ◆Marilu Henner — actress who played cabbie Elaine Nardo on TV's "Taxi," then appeared on "Evening Shade"

MARILYN ◆Marilyn McCoo — original member of The Fifth Dimension, hit "Aquarius," went solo ◆ Marilyn Monroe — sexy superstar who played the innocent dumb blonde to the hilt ◆ Marilyn vos Savant — no idiot savant, she has the highest IQ ever recorded

MARINA ◆Marina Sirtis — played Counselor Deanna Troi on the series "Star Trek: The Next Generation"

MARINE ◆Marine Jahan — danced for Jennifer Beals in "Flashdance" without screen credit

MARION ◆Marion Davies — girlfriend of newspaper tycoon William Randolph Hearst ◆ Marion Ross — played Marion, the mother to the Cunningham clan on TV's "Happy Days"

MARISA ◆Marisa Berenson — model and actress who starred in "Barry Lyndon" ◆ Marisa Pavan — actress who played Maria in Gregory Peck's "The Man in the Gray Flannel Suit" ◆ Marisa Tomei — Oscar winning automotive expert in the film "My Cousin Vinnie"

MARISKA ◆Mariska Hargitay — actress who played Jesse Smith on TV's "Downtown," daughter of Jayne Mansfield

MARJ ◆Marj Dusay — actress whose roles included Myrna Clegg on the soap "Capitol"

MARJIE ◆Marjie Millar — actress whose roles included Susan on the sitcom "The Ray Bolger Show"

MARJORIE ◆Marjorie Lord — actress whose roles included the mother on TV's "The Danny Thomas Show" ◆ Marjorie Main —

actress whose roles included Ma in the nine "Ma and Pa Kettle" films ◆ Marjorie Merriweather Post — Post cereal heiress, wife of E.F. Hutton, mother of Dina Merrill ◆ Marjorie Rawlings — author of the twice-filmed book "The Yearling"

MARKETA ◆Marketa Kimbrell — actress whose roles included Tessie in Rod Steiger's "The Pawnbroker"

MARKIE ◆Markie Post — a regular on TV's "Fall Guy" and "Night Court"

MARLA ◆Marla Gibbs — actress who played the maid Florence Johnston on the sitcom "The Jeffersons" ◆ Marla Maples — former model and wife of real estate tycoon Donald Trump

MARLEE ◆Marlee Matlin — deaf Oscar winning actress

MARLENA ◆Marlena Davis — member of The Orlons, gold record "The Wah Watusi" ◆ Marlena MacGuire — actress whose roles included Twinky in Jack Nicholson's "Five Easy Pieces"

MARLENE ◆Marlene Dietrich — German actress in "Morocco," "Shanghai Express," "Destry Rides Again" ◆Marlene Warfield — actress whose roles included Victoria Butterfield on the sitcom "Maude"

MARLO ◆Marlo Thomas — starred in the sitcom "That Girl," the daughter of Danny Thomas

MARLYN ◆Marlyn Mason — actress whose roles included Nikki Bell on the detective series "Longstreet"

MARNI ◆Marni Nixon — actress who played Sister Sophia in Julie Andrews' "The Sound of Music"

MARSHA ◆Marsha Mason — actress who played Janice Morrison in Bette Midler's melodrama "Stella" ◆ Marsha Warfield — actress whose roles included bailiff Roz Russell on the sitcom "Night Court"

MARTA ◆Marta Heflin — played Edna in "Come Back to the Five and Dime, Jimmy Dean, Jimmy Dean" ◆ Marta Kristin — played Maureen Robinson on the science fiction series "Lost in Space" ◆ Marta von Trapp — one of the singing von Trapp children whose lives were portrayed in "The Sound of Music"

MARTHA ◆Martha Mitchell — called reporters in the middle of the night with White House gossip ◆ Martha Plimpton — actress who is really a Carradine, from the acting Carradine clan ◆ Martha Quinn — video DJ for MTV for ten years ◆ Martha Raye — "Big Mouth" of the denture cleaner TV ads ◆ Martha Reeves

— leader of Martha and the Vandellas, hits include "Dancing in the Street"

MARTHE ◆Marthe Keller — actress in "Marathon Man," "Bobby Deerfield" and "Fedora"

MARTIKA ◆Martika — actress who played Dahlia Mendez on the hit police drama series "Wiseguy"

MARTINA ◆Martina Arroyo — leading soprano at the Metropolitan Opera in the 1970's ◆ Martina Navratilova — winner of the US Open and Wimbledon ◆ Martina Weymouth — member of The Talking Heads, debut hit single "Psycho Killer"

MARTINE ◆Martine Beswick — actress whose roles included the female killer in "Dr. Jekyll and Sister Hyde" ◆ Martine Carol — actress and French sex symbol of the 1950's

MARTITA ◆Martita Hunt — portrayed the spiteful Estella in Dickens' "Great Expectations"

MARVA ◆Marva Collins — founder of Chicago's Westside Preparatory

MARY ◆Mary Astor — actress who played Brigid O'Shaughnessy in Bogart's "The Maltese Falcon" ◆ Mary MacGregor — rock singer, debut number one gold record "Torn Between Two Lovers" ◆ Mary Martin — stage and TV star in the role of Peter Pan; mother of Larry Hagman ◆ Mary Tyler Moore — star of her own television series as well as "The Dick Van Dyke Show" ◆ Mary Pickford — "world's sweetheart" in silent films, co-founder of United Artists ◆ Mary Poppins (c) — Julie Andrews in the Oscar winning title role of Disney's "Mary Poppins"

MARY ANN ◆Mary Ann Mobley — Miss America turned actress, films include "Smokey and the Bandit II" ◆ Mary Ann Summers (c) — Dawn Wells role as the sweet, naive country girl on "Gilligan's Island"

MARY KAY ◆Mary Kay Ash — founder of Mary Kay Cosmetics ◆ Mary Kay Place — Emmy winner for "Mary Hartman, Mary Hartman"

MARY LOU ◆Mary Lou Retton — gymnast, first American woman to win an individual medal in the Olympics ◆ Mary Lou Williams — queen of jazz, wrote for Benny Goodman and Duke Ellington

MARY-CHAPIN ◆Mary-Chapin Carpenter — country singer, hits include "Quittin' Time" and "You Never Had It So Good"

MARYA ◆Marya Small — played Candy in the Academy award winning "One Flew Over the Cuckoo's Nest"

MARYAM ◆Maryam d'Abo — actress who played Kara Milovy in the James Bond film "The Living Daylights"

MARYEDITH ◆Maryedith Burrell — regular on the comedy variety show "Fridays"

MARYLYN ◆Marylyn Monk — actress whose roles included Jane Edwards on the soap "The Secret Storm"

MATHILDE ◆Mathilde Carre — Mata Hari of World War II caught by the Allies

MATILDA ◆Matilda Brown — daughter of actress Rachel Ward and actor Bryan Brown ◆ Anna Matilda Whistler — James Whistler painted her in the famous "Whistler's Mother"

MATINA ◆Matina Horner — former president of Radcliffe College

MATOAKA ◆Matoaka — real name of the Indian princess Pocahontas

MATTIA ◆Mattia Battistini — Italian opera singer for over fifty years

MAUD ◆Maud Adams — starred in the James Bond films "The Man With the Golden Gun" and "Octopussy" ◆ Lucy Maud Montgomery — author of popular girl's stories such as "Anne of Green Gables"

MAUDE ◆Annie Maude Starke — child of "Fatal Attraction" actress Glenn Close ◆ Maude Adams — actress whose roles included more than 1,500 performances as Peter Pan

MAUREEN ◆Maureen McCormick — actress whose roles included Marcia on the classic sitcom "The Brady Bunch" ◆ Maureen McGovern — sang "The Poseidon Adventure's" "The Morning After," "Superman's" "Can You Read My Mind?" ◆ Maureen O'Hara — hot-tempered, flame-haired Irish actress and frequent co-star of John Wayne ◆ Maureen O'Sullivan — actress who played Jane to Johnny Weissmuller's Tarzan; mother of Mia Farrow ◆Maureen Stapleton — Oscar winning actress for "Reds"

MAURINE ◆Maurine Trainor — actress who played Betsy Stewart Montgomery on the soap "As the World Turns"

MAVIS ◆Mavis Staples — member of The Staple Singers, debut hit "Why? (Am I Treated So Bad)"

MAXINE ◆Maxine Andrews — member of The Andrews Sisters singing group ◆ Maxine Brown — member of The Browns, number one debut gold record "The Three Bells" ◆Maxine Jones — with the group En Vogue, smash single "My Lovin' (You're Never Gonna Get It)"

MAY ◆Louisa May Alcott — author of the autobiographical "Little Women" in 1868 ◆ May Britt — Swedish actress in "The Blue Angel," wife of Sammy Davis, Jr. ◆ May Pang — secretary and mistress of Beatle John Lennon

MAYA ◆Maya Angelou — actress whose roles included Nyo Boto on the Alex Haley miniseries "Roots" ◆Maya Deren — producer of avant-garde films ◆Maya Ying Lin — designer of the Vietnam War Memorial in Washington, D.C.

MAYBELLE ◆Maybelle Carter — member of the groundbreaking country western group The Carter Family

MAYI ◆Dakota Mayi Brinkman — daughter of TV's "Little House on the Prairie" actress Melissa Gilbert

MAYIM ◆Mayim Bialik — comedic star of NBC's hit series "Blossom"

MAYME ◆Mayme Kelso — actress who played Susan Ambie in Theda Bara's "The Unchastened Woman"

MCKEE ◆McKee Anderson — actress whose roles included Helen in the remake of "Night of the Living Dead"

MEG ◆Meg Ryan — Sally in "When Harry Met Sally," sleepless in "Sleepless in Seattle" ◆Meg Tilly — actress in "Agnes of God," "The Big Chill"

MEGAN ◆Megan Gallagher — actress who played the hooker and heroin addict on TV's "China Beach" ◆ Megan Mullally — actress whose roles included Susan on the drama series "My Life and Times"

MEGS ◆Megs Jenkins — British actress in kindly or motherly roles whose films include "Oliver!"

MEIER ◆Meier Tzelniker — British character actor whose films include "A Night to Remember"

MEL ◆Mel Harris — star of TV's "thirtysomething"

MELANIE ◆Melanie — rock singer, hit debut single "Lay Down (Candles in the Rain)" ◆ Melanie Chartoff — played principal Grace Musso on the hit sitcom "Parker Lewis Can't Lose" ◆

Melanie Griffith — showed that a "Working Girl" can get ahead ◆
Melanie Mayron — red-haired actress on TV's "thirtysomething"

MELBA ◆Melba — Australian singer who inspired peach melba
and melba toast ◆ Melba Montgomery — country singer,
sometimes paired with George Jones ◆Melba Moore — provided
the voice of Whippet Angel in "All Dogs Go to Heaven"

MELINA ◆Melina Mercouri — actress whose roles included the
good natured prostitute in "Never on Sunday"

MELINDA ◆Melinda Dillon — Oscar nominee for "Close
Encounters of the Third Kind" ◆Melinda Naud — actress whose
roles included Maggie Ferguson on ABC's "Detective School"

MELISSA ◆Melissa Gilbert — actress who played author Laura
Ingalls on TV's "Little House on the Prairie" ◆ Melissa
Manchester — rock singer, debut hit single "Midnight Blue" ◆
Melissa Mathison — Oscar nominated screenwriter for "E.T. The
Extra-Terrestrial"

MELISSA SUE ◆Melissa Sue Anderson — actress whose roles
included Mary Ingalls on TV's "Little House on the Prairie"

MELODY ◆Melody Anderson — played Brooke McKenzie on
TV's "Manimal," and Dale, girlfriend of "Flash Gordon" ◆
Melody Fox — award winning comedy writer ◆Melody Patterson
— actress whose roles included Wrangler Jane in a tight shirt on
TV's "F Troop"

MELONIE ◆Melonie Haller — played Angie Globagoski on the
Gabe Kaplan sitcom "Welcome Back, Kotter"

MELORA ◆Melora Hardin — actress whose roles included
Frances Kellerman on TV's "Dirty Dancing"

MERCEDES ◆Mercedes McCambridge — Oscar winner for "All
the King's Men" ◆ Mercedes Porsche — daughter of Ferdinand
Porsche, after whom he named the car ◆ Mercedes Ruehl —
actress who played Dr. Elizabeth Baylor in Dudley Moore's
"Crazy People"

MERCY ◆Mercy Otis Warren — author of political satires on the
Loyalists and the Revolution

MEREDITH ◆Meredith Baxter-Birney — actress whose roles
included the mother on TV's long running "Family Ties" ◆
Meredith MacRae — starred in TV's hayseed sitcom "Petticoat
Junction"

MERETE ◆Merete Van Kamp — actress whose roles included Daisy in the TV movie "Princess Daisy"

MERI ◆Meri Welles — played the Hollywood starlet in Peter Sellers' brilliant "The Pink Panther"

MERIANN ◆Meriann Aaida — actress who played Elizabeth on the Redd Foxx sitcom "The Royal Family"

MERIE ◆Merie Earle — actress who played Maude Gormsley on the popular drama series "The Waltons"

MERIEL ◆Meriel Forbes — British stage actress and wife of Sir Ralph Richardson

MERLE ◆Merle Norman — founder of a chain of cosmetics stores ◆ Merle Oberon — exotic looking actress in "Divorce of Lady X," "Wuthering Heights"

MERRIE ◆Merrie Ross — actress whose roles included Emma Lutz on the soap "General Hospital"

MERRILL ◆Merrill Ashley — star of Balanchine's NYC Ballet

MERRY ◆Merry Anders — actress who co-starred on TV's "How to Marry a Millionaire" ◆ Merry Clayton — played Verna Dee Jordan on the hit police drama series "Cagney and Lacey"

MERYL ◆Meryl Streep — double Oscar winner, films include "Silkwood," "Out of Africa," "Julia," "Sophie's Choice"

MIA ◆Mia Farrow — actress in "The Great Gatsby," "Broadway Danny Rose," and "Rosemary's Baby" ◆ Mia Sara — played Sloane, the girlfriend to Matthew Broderick in "Ferris Bueller's Day Off"

MICHAEL ◆Brigitte Michael Sumner — daughter of rock singer Sting ◆ Michael Learned — actress whose roles included mother Olivia on TV's "The Waltons" ◆Michael Steele — member of The Bangles, hits include "Walk Like an Egyptian" and "Manic Monday"

MICHELE ◆Michele Lee — actress who played Karen Fairgate MacKenzie on the nighttime soap "Knots Landing" ◆ Michele Matheson — actress whose roles included Rona Lieberman on the drama series "Life Goes On" ◆ Michele Tobin — actress whose roles included Maureen Fitzpatrick on TV's "The Fitzpatricks"

MICHELETTE ◆Michelette Burani — actress in the Claudette Colbert/Fred MacMurrays' film "The Gilded Lily"

MICHELINE ◆Micheline Lanctot — played Yvette in Richard Dreyfuss' "The Apprenticeship of Duddy Kravitz" ◆ Micheline Presle — one of the many actresses to portray Camille in films

MICHELLE ◆Michelle Pfeiffer — actress in "Batman Returns," "Dangerous Liaisons," "Married to the Mob" ◆Michelle Phillips — member of The Mamas and the Papas, debut gold record "California Dreamin'"

MICKI ◆Micki Free — member of the group Shalamar, hits include "A Night to Remember" ◆ Micki Grant — portrayed Peggy Nolan on the soap "Another World"

MIDGE ◆Midge Decter — author whose books include "Liberal Parents, Radical Children"

MIE ◆Mie Hunt — actress whose roles included Jane Funakubo on TV's "Domestic Life"

MIEP ◆Miep Gies — hid Anne Frank from the Nazis, found her diary, and published it as a book

MIGNON ◆Mignon Dunn — opera singer with the New York Metropolitan ◆ Mignon Eberhart — author who created sleuth nurse Sarah Keate

MILDRED ◆Mildred Dunnock — Oscar nominee for "Death of a Salesman" ◆Mildred Natwick — actress who played Ethel Banks in the Redford/Fonda film "Barefoot in the Park"

MILES ◆Miles Franklin — published her autobiography "My Brilliant Career" at age 16

MILIZA ◆Miliza Korjus — opera singer in composer Johann Strauss' MGM biopic "The Great Waltz"

MILLA ◆Milla Jovovich — actress whose credits include "Return to the Blue Lagoon" and "Chaplin"

MILLEE ◆Millee Taggart — actress who played Gerry McGrath Pollock on the soap "The Edge of Night"

MILLETTE ◆Millette Alexander — actress whose roles included Sylvia Hill Suker on the soap "As the World Turns"

MILLICENT ◆Millicent Fenwick — congresswoman who is the inspiration for "Doonesbury" comic strip's Lacey Davenport ◆ Millicent Martin — actress whose roles included Harriet Conover on TV's "Downtown"

MILLIE ◆Millie Perkins — actress whose films include "The Diary of Anne Frank"

MILLY ◆Milly Vitale — actress whose films include "The Juggler" and "War and Peace"

MIMI ◆Mimi Rogers — actress who played Blair Harper-Fenton on the drama series "Paper Dolls"

MINA ◆Mina Kolb — actress whose roles included Peggy Briggs on the sitcom "Pete and Gladys"

MINDI ◆Mindi Miller — actress who played Revel on Robert Wagner's detective drama series "Switch"

MINDY ◆Mindy Carson — singer, hits include "Wake the Town and Tell the People" ◆ Mindy Cohn — actress whose roles included Natalie on the sitcom "The Facts of Life"

MINERVA ◆Minerva Pious — actress whose roles included Mrs. Nussbaum on the radio show "Allen's Alley" ◆Minerva Urecal — actress who played "Mother" on the detective drama series "Peter Gunn"

MINNA ◆Minna Everleigh — ran the most expensive bordello in Chicago with her sister ◆ Minna Gombell — actress who played Mimi Wynant in the original William Powell "Thin Man" film

MINNIE ◆Minnie Pearl — Grand Ole Opry country western comedienne who wears a price tag on her hat

MIRA ◆Mira McKinney — actress in Charlie Chaplin's industrial classic "Modern Times"

MIREILLE ◆Mireille Balin — French leading lady of the 1933 version of "Don Quixote" ◆Mireille Darc — French leading lady, credits include "Weekend" and "Galia"

MIRELLA ◆Mirella Freni — soprano who sang Mimi in La Scala's film version of "La Boheme"

MIRIAM ◆Miriam Hopkins — sophisticated blond whose films include "Design for Living," "Becky Sharp"

MISHA ◆Misha McK — actress whose roles included Gerri Kilgore on the sitcom "Me and Mrs. C."

MISKA ◆Miska Petersham — children's author who wrote the "Story Book of" series

MISSY ◆Missy Francis — played Cassandra Cooper on the drama series "Little House on the Prairie"

MISTY ◆Misty Morgan — with her husband Jack Blanchard, part of the 1970's Nashville Sound dominance ◆ Misty Rowe — well endowed cast regular on TV's "Hee Haw"

MITZI ◆Mitzi Gaynor — in "South Pacific" she had to "wash that man right out of her hair" ◆ Mitzi Kapture — actress who played Sgt. Rita Lance on the police drama "Silk Stalkings"

MOANA ◆Moana Wolfgramm — member of The Jets, debut hit single "Crush On You"

MOINA ◆Moina Michael — originated Poppy Day to raise money for war veterans

MOIRA ◆Moira Kelly — actress whose roles included Charlie Chaplin's wife Oona O'Neill in "Chaplin" ◆ Moira Shearer — ballet dancer with the lead role in "The Red Shoes"

MOLISSA ◆Molissa Fenley — choreographer who founded an experimental dance company

MOLL ◆Moll Cutpurse — in the seventeenth century, became the first professional female criminal

MOLLA ◆Molla Mallory — nine-time US National tennis champion

MOLLIE ◆Mollie Birney — twin daughter of Meredith Baxter-Birney and David Birney

MOLLY ◆Molly Pitcher — heroine of the American Revolution who carried water at the Battle of Monmouth ◆ Molly Ringwald — red-haired actress in "Betsy's Wedding," "Sixteen Candles," "Pretty in Pink"

MONA ◆Mona Barrie — films include "Never Give a Sucker an Even Break" ◆ Mona Ray — actress who played Mammy Yokum in the Dogpatch extravaganza "Li'l Abner" ◆ Mona Van Buyn — US poet laureate, Pulitzer Prize winner

MONA LISA ◆Mona Lisa — most famous of the clients of artist Leonardo Da Vinci

MONETTA ◆Monetta Darnell — real name of actress Linda Darnell

MONICA ◆Monica Blumenthal — psychiatrist who won an Emmy for "What Shall We Do About Mother?"

MONIQUE ◆Monique Lanier — actress whose roles included Paige Thatcher on the series "Life Goes On" ◆ Monique Van de VenCor — actress who played Truus Coster in the 1987 Academy

Award winner "The Assault" ◆ Monique Van Vooren — actress who appeared in the film "Damn Yankees," author of "Night Sanctuary"

MONTY ◆Monty Margetts — actress who played Una Fields on the Walter Brennan sitcom "The Tycoon"

MOON ◆Soleil Moon Frye — child star of the sitcom "Punky Brewster"

MOON UNIT ◆Moon Unit Zappa — her hit song was "Valley Girl," inherited musical talent from father Frank Zappa

MORGAN ◆Morgan Brittany — Vivien Leigh look-alike actress ◆ Morgan Fairchild — actress who played the girlfriend of Sandra Bernhard on ABC's "Roseanne" ◆ Morgan le Fay (c) — ruthless sister of King Arthur in "A Connecticut Yankee in King Arthur's Court"

MORGANNA ◆Morganna King — played Mama Corleone in the Academy Award winning film "The Godfather"

MORNA ◆Morna Anne Murray — Grammy winning singer, gold record "Snowbird," hits include "You Needed Me"

MOVITA ◆Movita Castenada — actress whose roles included Ana on the nightime soap "Knots Landing"

MOYRA ◆Moyra Fraser — Australian comedienne whose films include "Prudence and the Pill"

MURIAL ◆Murial Williams — actress whose roles included Helen Moore on the soap "Another World"

MURIEL ◆Muriel Myers — first actress to play Beth March in the film versions of "Little Women" ◆Muriel Spark — author of "The Prime of Miss Jean Brodie," made into a play and a film

MURPHY ◆Murphy Brown (c) — hard edged network news reporter on the TV show of the same name ◆ Murphy Cross — actress whose roles included the lead Phyl in the sitcom "Phyl and Mikhy"

MUSETTA ◆Musetta Vander — played Zander Tyler on the science fiction police series "Super Force"

MYA ◆Mya Akerling — played Marilyn Elliot on the Ann Jillian sitcom "Jennifer Slept Here"

MYLENE ◆Mylene Demengeot — actress who played the vengeful Milady de Winter in "The Three Musketeers"

MYRA ◆Myra Gale Lewis — underage wife of Jerry Lee Lewis ruined his career, biopic "Great Balls of Fire"

MYRIAM ◆Myriam Bru — third to play the luxury-craving whore in "The Loves of Manon Lescaut"

MYRNA ◆Myrna Loy — actress who played wisecracking Nora Charles in the "Thin Man" movie series

MYRTLE ◆Myrtle Reed — author whose works include the best-selling "Lavender and Old Lace"

NADENE ◆Nadene Ashdown — actress in William Holden's anti-war film "The Bridges at Toko Ri"

NADIA ◆Nadia Comaneci — Olympic gold medalist in gymnastics, biopic "Nadia"

NADJA ◆Nadja Tiller — actress who played the infamous Frankfurt call girl in "The Girl Rosemarie"

NAN ◆Nan Agle — co-writer of the children's series "Three Boys"

NANA ◆Nana Bryant — actress who played Mrs. Nestor on the popular Eve Arden sitcom "Our Miss Brooks" ◆Nana Tucker — actress who played Svetlana on the Russian based sitcom "Ivan the Terrible"

NANCI ◆Nanci Griffith — storytelling folksinger whose hit albums include "Lone Star State of Mind"

NANCY ◆Nancy Kerrigan — won silver medal for ice skating in 1994 Winter Olympics ◆ Nancy Kulp — played Miss Jane, Mr. Drysdale's competent secretary on "The Beverly Hillbillies" ◆ Nancy McKeon — actress whose roles included Jo on the sitcom "The Facts of Life" ◆Nancy Reagan — first an actress, then the wife of President Ronald Reagan ◆ Nancy Sinatra — Frank's daughter, went to the top ten with "These Boots Are Made for Walkin' " ◆Nancy Walker — actress who played the wisecracking maid to TV detectives "McMillan and Wife"

NANDU ◆Nandu Hinds — actress whose roles included Sophie in Jack Nicholson's thriller "Psych-Out"

NANETTE ◆Nanette Fabray — Emmy and Tony winning actress ◆ Nanette Newman — British leading lady whose films include "The Wrong Box"

NAOMI ◆Naomi Campbell — model whose roles included Julia on the sitcom "The Cosby Show" ◆ Ellen Naomi Cohen — real name of singer Cass Elliot of The Mamas and the Papas ◆ Naomi Judd — elder half of the mother-daughter country western group "The Judds" ◆ Naomi Sims — model, founder of Naomi Sims Beauty Products

NARDA ◆ Narda Onyx — played Frankenstein's granddaughter in "Jesse James Meets Frankenstein's Daughter"

NASTASSJA ◆ Nastassja Kinski — acted in "Tess" and the cult film "Cat People"

NATALIE ◆ Natalie Cole — Grammy winning vocalist, hits include "Killing Me Softly" ◆ Natalie Schafer — actress whose roles included Lovey Howell on the sitcom "Gilligan's Island" ◆ Natalie Talmadge — silent film star who retired to marry Buster Keaton ◆ Natalie Wood — actress in "Miracle on 34th Street," "West Side Story," "Rebel Without a Cause"

NATASHA ◆ Natasha Gurdin — real name of actress Natalie Wood

NATHALIE ◆ Nathalie Baye — played Martine Desdoits in Francois Truffaut's "The Man Who Loved Women"

NATIVIDAD ◆ Natividad Abascal — actress whose roles included Yolanda in the Woody Allen comedy "Bananas"

NATJA ◆ Natja Brunkhorst — actress who played the lead role of the teenage prostitute in "Christiane F."

NAYA ◆ Naya Rivera — actress whose roles included Hillary on the Redd Foxx sitcom "The Royal Family"

NEDENIA ◆ Nedenia Hutton — real name of actress Dina Merrill

NEDRA ◆ Nedra Talley — member of The Ronettes, hits include "Be My Baby" and "Walking in the Rain" ◆ Nedra Volz — actress whose roles included Miz Emma Tisdale on TV's "The Dukes of Hazzard"

NEFERTIRI ◆ Nefertiri — Anne Baxter played the Egyptian ruler in DeMille's "The Ten Commandments"

NELL ◆ Nell Brinkley — artist, pen-and-ink drawings of boys and girls were syndicated throughout US ◆ Nell Carter — actress whose roles included Nellie Harper on the sitcom "Gimme a Break"

NELLA ◆ Nella Barnier — actress who played Liliane in Francois Truffaut's "The Man Who Loved Women"

NELLE ◆Nelle Nugent — producer whose stage productions include "The Dresser" and "Mass Appeal"

NELLIE ◆Nellie Bly — muckraking journalist, Linda Purl biopic "The Adventures of Nellie Bly" ◆Nellie Oleson — bad girl of the long-running drama series "Little House on the Prairie"

NENEH ◆Neneh Cherry — singer who combines rap and pop, hit singles include "Buffalo Stance"

NESTA ◆Mary Nesta Keane — author of the novel "Good Behaviour," later filmed

NETTIE ◆Nettie Rosenstein — designer of the classic "little black dress"

NEVA ◆Neva Patterson — regular on TV's "Doc Elliot," "The Governor and J.J." ◆Neva White — one of the first two women inducted into the Basketball Hall of Fame

NIA ◆Nia Peeples — actress whose roles included Nicole Chapman on TV's "Fame"

NICHELLE ◆Nichelle Nichols — played communications officer Uhura in films and on TV's "Star Trek"

NICOLA ◆Nicola Cowper — actress who appeared in Coral Browne's film "Dreamchild" ◆ Nicola Pagett — actress who played in TV shows "Upstairs, Downstairs" and "Anna Karenina"

NICOLE ◆Diamond Nicole Strawberry — daughter of baseball player Darryl Strawberry ◆Nicole Kidman — actress who played in "Dead Calm" and "Far and Away," married to Tom Cruise

NICOLETTE ◆Nicolette Goulet — actress whose roles included Mary Ryan Fenelli on the soap "Ryan's Hope" ◆Nicolette Larson — singer, hit single "I Only Want to Be With You"

NICOLLETTE ◆Nicollette Sheridan — actress who played Paige Mathison on the nighttime soap "Knot's Landing"

NIKA ◆Nika Hazelton — author of the world famous "International Cookbook"

NIKI ◆Niki Taylor — 1990's supermodel and teen heartthrob

NILE ◆Nile Lanning — actress who played Melissa Sandler on the sitcom "The Marshall Chronicles"

NINA ◆Nina Bawden — English author, wrote "Familiar Passions" ◆Nina Foch — nominated for an Oscar for "Executive Suite"

NINETTE ◆Ninette DeValois — British choreographer who toured with the Russian Ballet

NITA ◆Nita Naldi — temptress opposite Valentino in "Blood and Sand" ◆ Nita Talbot — actress who played Judy Evans on Larry Hagman's sitcom "Here We Go Again"

NITANJU ◆Nitanju Bolade — Sweet Honey in the Rock, hit "B'lieve I'll Rin On See, What the Ends Gonna Be"

NOBLETTE ◆Irene Noblette Ryan — played Granny Clampett on the classic sitcom "The Beverly Hillbillies"

NOEL ◆Noël Francis — played Mrs. Eden in the Claudette Colbert tearjerker "Imitation of Life"

NOELLE ◆Noelle Bou-Sliman — actress whose roles included Belinda on the comedy/drama series "Jack and Mike"

NONNY ◆Nonny Hogrogian — award-winning children's illustrator for "Always Room for One More"

NORA ◆Nora Dunn — cast member of "Saturday Night Live," actress in film "Passion Fish" ◆ Nora Efron — screenwriter of "Sleepless in Seattle"

NORADA ◆Norada Walden — member of the music group Weather Report, instrumental hits include "Birdland"

NORAH ◆Norah Lofts — writer of historical romances, biographies including "Anne Boleyn"

NORMA ◆Norma Jean — Porter Wagoner's first female singing partner on his syndicated TV show ◆ Norma Shearer — Oscar winning actress for "The Divorcee," married to Irving Thalberg ◆ Norma Talmadge — silent screen star whose films include "Camille" and "Forbidden City"

NORMA JEAN ◆Norma Jean Baker — real-life name of screen legend Marilyn Monroe

NOVA ◆Nova Pilbeam — British teenage star of the 30's, films include "The Man Who Knew Too Much"

NTOZAKE ◆Ntozake Shange — author of "For Colored Girls Who Have Considered Suicide/When the Rainbow is Enuf"

NUALA ◆Nuala Fitzgerald — actress whose roles included Nurse Wynn on TV's "Dr. Simon Locke"

NYDIA ◆Nydia Westman — actress whose roles included Mrs. Featherstone on the TV series "Going My Way"

NYREE ◆Nyree Porter — played Irene Heron Forsyte on the British soap import "The Forsyte Saga"

OCTAVIA ◆Frances Octavia Smith — real name of cowgirl Dale Evans, the wife of Roy Rogers

ODA ◆Oda Alstrup — one of the actresses to play the notorious nineteenth century courtesan Camille

ODESSA ◆Odessa Cleveland — actress whose roles included Lt. Ginger Ballis on the hit sitcom "M*A*S*H"

ODETTA ◆Odetta — folksinger who appeared in TV's "The Autobiography of Miss Jane Pittman"

ODETTE ◆Odette Laure — actress who appeared in Dirk Bogarde's film "Daddy Nostalgia" ◆ Odette Sansom — undercover agent tortured by the Nazis, biopic "Odette" with Anna Neagle

ODILE ◆Odile Versois — French leading lady whose credits include "A Day to Remember"

OLA ◆Ola Winslow — Pulitzer Prize winning author whose works include "Jonathan Edwards"

OLAVE ◆Olave Baden-Powell — founder of the Girl Scouts

OLETA ◆Oleta Adams — Grammy nominee for "Get Here"

OLGA ◆Olga Bellin — actress who appeared in Robert Duvall's film "Tomorrow" as Sarah Eubanks ◆ Olga Korbut — phenomenal Olympic gold medal gymnast from the former Soviet Union

OLINKA ◆Olinka Berova — actress whose roles included the infamous Lucrezia Borgia in "Lucrezia"

OLIVE ◆Olive Higgins Prooty — author of "Now, Voyager"

OLIVIA ◆Olivia De Havilland — actress who played the sweet and forgiving Melanie in "Gone With the Wind" ◆Olivia Hussey — played a very young Juliet in the film version of "Romeo and Juliet" ◆ Olivia Newton-John — singing star and actress, film credits include "Grease" with John Travolta

OLYMPE ◆Olympe Bradna — former circus bareback rider turned film leading lady

OLYMPIA ◆Olympia Dukakis — actress who is also the cousin of the 1984 Democratic candidate

OLYMPIA-ANN ◆Olympia-Ann Sylvers — member of The Sylvers, debut hit single "A Fool's Paradise"

ONA ◆Ona Munson — played the gold-hearted prostitute Belle Watling in "Gone With the Wind"

OONA ◆Oona O'Neill — daughter of Eugene O'Neill, wife of Charlie Chaplin, mother of Geraldine Chaplin

OPRAH ◆Oprah Winfrey — queen of the daytime TV talk shows, Oscar nominee for "The Color Purple"

ORANE ◆Orane Demazis — actress whose roles included the title role in the film "Fanny"

ORESTE ◆Oreste Kirkop — operatic tenor who appeared in "The Vagabond King"

OSA ◆Osa Johnson — explorer who accompanied husband on expeditions, author of "Safari" ◆ Osa Massen — Danish-born actress in Hollywood from the late 1930's

OVETA ◆Oveta Hobby — publisher of the Houston Post and first secretary of HEW

PAGE ◆Page Hannah — actress whose roles included Kate Riley on TV's "Fame" ◆ Mary Page Keller — actress whose roles included lovebird Laura Kelley on TV's "Duet"

PAIGE ◆Paige Howard — twin daughter of actor/director Ron Howard

PALLAS ◆Pallas Dorris — daughter of Louise Erdich and Michael Dorris

PALOMA ◆Paloma Estevez — daughter of actor Emilio Estevez ◆ Paloma Picasso — designer, daughter of artist Pablo Picasso

PAM ◆Pam Dawber — played the patient Mindy who put up with the outrageous antics of Mork from Ork

PAMELA ◆Pamela Anderson — played the sexy Lisa, assistant to tool man Taylor, on TV's "Home Improvement" ◆ Pamela Grier — actress, films include "On The Edge," "Something Wicked This Way Comes" ◆Pamela Hensley — actress whose roles included CJ on TV's "Matt Houston"

PAMELA SUE ◆Pamela Sue Martin — actress who played teenage detective Nancy Drew on TV's "The Hardy Boys"

PAOLA ◆Paola Tedesco — actress whose roles included the seductive biblical Salome in "King of Kings"

PARIS ◆Jesse Paris — daughter of "Because the Night" singer Patti Smith

PARK ◆Park Overall — actress whose roles included nurse LaVerne Todd on TV's "Empty Nest"

PASCALE ◆Pascale Petit — French leading lady whose films include "The Witches of Salem"

PAT ◆Pat Benatar — rock singer, hits include "Love is a Battlefield" ◆ Pat Nixon — wife of US President "Tricky Dick"

PATRICE ◆Patrice Ledoux — producer of the 1984 musical film "Carmen" ◆ Patrice Munsel — portrayed the Australian soprano singer in "Melba" ◆Patrice Rushen — child prodigy pianist, jazzy dance hits include "Feels So Real"

PATRICIA ◆Patricia Neal — love interest for John Wayne "In Harm's Way," Oscar winner for "Hud" ◆ Patricia Richardson — actress who played the wife on TV's popular tool sitcom "Home Improvement" ◆ Patricia Wettig — actress whose roles included Nancy Weston on TV's "thirtysomething"

PATRIKA ◆Patrika Darbo — played Penny on the Patrick Duffy/ Suzanne Somers sitcom "Step by Step"

PATSEY ◆Patsey Tahn — actress who played Dr. Monica Webber Quartermaine on the soap "General Hospital"

PATSY ◆Patsy Cline — country singer killed in a plane crash, hits include "Crazy" ◆ Patsy Montana — queen of country music, composed over 200 songs

PATTI ◆Patti Andrews — member of The Andrews Sisters singing group ◆Patti Austin — singer with hit single "Baby Come to Me," love theme for "General Hospital" ◆Patti LaBelle — pop singer whose hits include "New Attitude" and "On My Own" ◆ Patti LuPone — Tony winner for "Evita," starred on TV's "Life Goes On" ◆ Patti Page — sang the popular tune "How Much Is That Doggie in the Window?" ◆ Patti Smith — singer, hit single "Because the Night"

PATTY ◆Patty Duke — energetic star of TV's "The Patty Duke Show," autobiography is "Call Me Anna" ◆ Patty Hearst — granddaughter of William Randolph Hearst, victim of sensational kidnapping ◆ Patty Loveless — country singer, albums include "Patty Loveless"

PAULA ◆Paula Abdul — pop singer of the 90's whose hits include "Opposites Attract" ◆Paula Poundstone — stand-up comedienne, often seen on cable comedy shows ◆ Paula Prentiss — actress wife of Richard Benjamin, starred in "What's New, Pussycat?"

PAULETTE ◆ Paulette Goddard — actress married to Charlie Chaplin, starred in his "Modern Times"

PAULI ◆ Pauli Murray — founder of the National Organization of Women

PAULINA ◆ Paulina Gretzky — daughter of actress Janet Jones and professional hockey player Wayne Gretzky ◆ Paulina Porizkova — supermodel, acted with Tom Selleck in "Her Alibi"

PAULINE ◆ Pauline (c) — Pearl White, queen of silent movie series, biopic is "The Perils of Pauline" ◆ Pauline Collins — actress whose roles included the lead in the film "Shirley Valentine"

PAULYN ◆ Paulyn Garner — played Mrs. Ramsey in the Claudette Colbert tearjerker "Imitation of Life"

PAXTON ◆ Paxton Quigley — film firearms expert who trains celebrities

PEACHES ◆ Peaches Bartkowicz — professional tennis player ◆ Peaches Geldof — daughter of singer Bob Geldof

PEARL ◆ Pearl Bailey — best known for singing in the musical "Hello Dolly" on Broadway ◆ Pearl Buck — Pulitzer Prize winning author for her novel "The Good Earth" ◆ Pearl White — silent movie queen of cliffhangers, biopic "The Perils of Pauline"

PEGGIE ◆ Peggie Castle — actress whose films include "I, the Jury"

PEGGY ◆ Peggy Fleming — Olympic ice skater ◆ Peggy Lee — singer/composer whose voice was heard in "Lady and the Tramp" ◆ Peggy Lipton — portrayed the long-haired hippie cop in a miniskirt on TV's "The Mod Squad"

PENELOPE ◆ Penelope Milford — actress whose roles included Vi Munson in Jane Fonda's "Coming Home" ◆ Penelope Ann Miller — actress in "Kindergarten Cop" and "The Gun in Betty Lou's Handbag"

PENNEY ◆ Penney Parker — actress who played daughter Terry Williams on TV's "The Danny Thomas Show"

PENNY ◆ Penny Marshall — was Laverne DeFazio on "Laverne and Shirley," also the director of "Big" ◆ Penny Singleton —

actress who played comic strip character Blondie in films of the same name

PERI ◆Peri Gilpin — actress whose roles included Irene on TV's "Flesh 'N' Blood"

PERNILLA ◆Pernilla Allwin — actress whose roles included Fanny in the film "Fanny and Alexander"

PERRI ◆Perri Klass — doctor, author, and winner of four O. Henry awards

PERSIA ◆Persia Dorris — daughter of Louise Erdich and Michael Dorris

PERSIS ◆Persis Khambatta — starred in "Star Trek—The Motion Picture" and "Nighthawks"

PERT ◆Pert Kelton — comedienne whose films include "The Music Man"

PETRONIA ◆Petronia Paley — actress whose roles included Quinn Harding on the soap "Another World"

PETULA ◆Petula Clark — international pop singer, starred with Fred Astaire in "Finian's Rainbow"

PHILECE ◆Philece Sampler — actress who played Renee Dumonde Banning on the soap "Days Of Our Lives"

PHILLIPPA ◆Phillippa Scott — real name of actress Pippa Scott, who appeared in "Auntie Mame"

PHOEBE ◆Phoebe Cates — actress whose roles included Kate in Steven Spielberg's "Gremlins" ◆ Phoebe Omlie — first woman to make a parachute jump ◆ Phoebe Snow — singer, albums include "Never Letting Go" and "Rock Away"

PHYLEA ◆Condola Phylea Rashad — daughter of "Cosby Show" Phylicia Rashad and Ahmad Rashad

PHYLICIA ◆Phylicia Ayers-Allen — actress whose roles included Courtney Wright on the soap "One Life to Live" ◆ Phylicia Rashad — actress whose roles included Cliff's wife on "The Cosby Show"

PHYLLIS ◆Phyllis Diller — rubber-faced comedienne, does a lot of TV, a few movies ◆ Phyllis Schlafly — ultra-conservative opponent of equal rights for women

PIA ◆Pia Lindstrom — New York based entertainment reporter for NBC, daughter of Ingrid Bergman ◆ Pia Zadora — actress whose roles include the tawdry fifteen year old in "Butterfly"

PIER ◆Pier Angeli — Italian actress, twin sister of Marisa Pavan

PILAR ◆Pilar Thomas — triplet daughter of actor Richard Thomas

PIPER ◆Piper Laurie — nominated for an Oscar for playing the mother in the film "Carrie"

PIPPA ◆Pippa Scott — actress whose roles included May in Julie Christie's film "Petulia"

PIPPI ◆Pippi Longstocking (c) — Tami Erin's title role in "The New Adventures of Pippi Longstocking"

PIXIE ◆Pixie Geldof — daughter of singer/actor Bob Geldof

PLEASANT ◆Pleasant Rowland — founder of Pleasant Co., makes American Girl and New Baby doll collections

POCAHONTAS ◆Pocahontas — Indian maiden of Virginia who saved Captain John Smith from certain death

POLA ◆Pola Negri — actress who played in the second of four films entitled "Madame Bovary"

POLDI ◆Poldi Vogelhuber — long suffering wife of composer Johann Strauss, biopic "The Great Waltz"

POLLY ◆Polly Adams — notorious madam of the 1920's, biopic "A House is Not a Home" ◆ Polly Bergen — radio singer turned actress, played Rhoda Henry on the miniseries "Winds of War"

POLLYANNA ◆Pollyanna (c) — books by Eleanor Porter, portrayed in the film by Hayley Mills

POPPY ◆Poppy Cannon — magazine food editor and author of "The Fast Gourmet Cookbook"

PRESLEY ◆Presley Tanita — daughter of country western singer Tanya Tucker

PRISCILLA ◆Priscilla Barnes — actress whose roles included Terri Alden on the hit sitcom "Three's Company" ◆ Priscilla Mullins — caught in the middle of the love triangle on board the Mayflower ◆ Priscilla Presley — wife of Elvis Presley, went on to do the "Naked Gun" film series

QUEENIE ◆Queenie Smith — actress in Irene Dunne's classic musical "Show Boat"

QUINN ◆Quinn Cummings — as a child actress, was nominated for an Oscar for "The Goodbye Girl"

RACHEL ◆Rachel Carson — author of environmental book "Silent Spring" ◆ Rachel Trudeau — twin daughter of newscaster Jane Pauley and cartoonist Garry Trudeau ◆ Rachel Ward — star of the TV miniseries "The Thorn Birds"

RACHELE ◆Rachele Mussolini — widow of dictator Benito Mussolini, autobiography "My Life with Mussolini"

RAE ◆Rae Dawn Chong — actress whose films include "Commando" and "The Color Purple," daughter of Tommy Chong ◆Edna Rae Gilooly — real name of actress Ellen Burstyn

RAFAELA ◆Rafaela Ottiano — actress whose roles included Russian Rita in Mae West's "She Done Him Wrong"

RAFFAELLA ◆Raffaella de Laurentiis — producer of Arnold Schwarzenegger's "Conan the Destroyer"

RAIN ◆Rain Pryor — cast member of TV's "Head of the Class," daughter of Richard Pryor

RAINBOW ◆Rainbow Harvest — actress who played the incredibly sexy computer repairperson on TV's "FM" ◆ Rainbow Phoenix — actress sister of River Phoenix

RALNA ◆Ralna Hovis — vocalist on the music series "The Lawrence Welk Show"

RAMONA ◆Ramona Castle Demme — daughter of "Silence of the Lambs," director Jonathan Demme

RAMSAY ◆Ramsay Ames — leading lady of the early 40's whose films include "The Mummy's Tomb"

RANDA ◆Randa Haines — director of "The Doctor" and "Children of a Lesser God"

RANDEE ◆Randee Heller — actress who played Rita DeLatorre on the sitcom "Husbands, Wives, and Lovers"

RANDI ◆Randi Brooks — actress whose roles included Joanie in James Woods' film "Cop" ◆ Randi Brough — played twin Geri Garrison with her sister Candi on the series "B.J. and the Bear" ◆ Randi Kiger — played Celia Mackenzie on the series "The Mackenzies of Paradise Cove"

RANDY ◆Randy Stuart — actress who played the long-suffering wife of "The Incredible Shrinking Man"

RAQUEL ◆Raquel Welch — voluptuous actress in "The Three Musketeers," "Mother, Jugs, and Speed"

RAVEN-SYMONE ◆Raven-Symone — cute little actress whose roles included Olivia on TV's "The Cosby Show"

RAY ◆Alexa Ray Joel — child of model Christie Brinkley and rock star Billy Joel

REBA ◆Reba McEntire — award winning country and western singer, "You Lie," "For My Broken Heart"

REBECCA ◆Rebecca DeMornay — actress in "Risky Business" and "The Hand That Rocks the Cradle"

REBECCAH ◆Rebeccah Bush — actress whose roles included Jill on the Valerie Bertinelli sitcom "Sydney"

REBEKAH ◆Rebekah Harkness — founder of The Harkness Ballet

REBIE ◆Rebie Jackson — another of Michael Jackson's sisters

REGINA ◆Regina Bell — rhythm and blues singer, albums "All by Myself" and "Stay with Me" ◆ Eileen Regina Brennan — starred in both the movie and TV versions of "Private Benjamin" ◆ Regina King — actress whose roles included Brenda Jenkins on the Marla Gibbs hit sitcom "227"

REGINE ◆Regine — owner of nightclubs bearing her name in New York and Paris

REINA ◆Tai Reina Babilonia — failed to win an Olympic medal when her partner Randy Gardner was injured ◆ Reina King — actress whose roles included Carolyn on the hit sitcom "What's Happening!"

REIZL ◆Reizl Bozyk — actress whose roles included Bubbie Kantor in Amy Irving's "Crossing Delancey"

RENA ◆Rena Briand — Canadian journalist and author

RENATE ◆Renate Muller — German leading lady best known abroad for "Sunshine Susie"

RENE ◆Rene Russo — actress toting guns "In the Line of Fire" and "Lethal Weapon 3"

RENEE ◆Renee Adoree — French circus dancer who appeared in films in the 1920's ◆ Renee Taylor — actress who played Eva Braun in the Mel Brooks comedy classic "The Producers"

RENIE ◆Renie Conley — Oscar winning designer for "Cleopatra," designed Disneyland's costumes ◆ Renie Riano — actress who appeared in the Randolph Scott film "The Road to Reno"

RENNE ◆Renne Jarrett — actress who played Phoebe Smith Jamison on the soap "The Edge of Night"

RETA ◆Reta Shaw — played Martha Grant on the long running sitcom "The Ghost and Mrs. Muir"

RHEA ◆Rhea Perlman — actress whose roles included the caustic waitress Carla on TV's "Cheers" ◆ Rhea Seddon — one of the first five women astronauts

RHETA ◆Rheta Door — journalist who wrote "Inside the Russian Revolution"

RHONDA ◆Rhonda Fleming — titian-haired actress in films like "Pony Express"

RICKI ◆Ricki Lake — actress turned daytime talk show host

RICKIE ◆Rickie Lee Jones — won 1980 Grammy as best new artist, hits include "Chuck E's in Love"

RIPLEY ◆Ripley (c) — Sigourney Weaver's alien fighting woman in "Alien" and "Aliens"

RISE ◆Rise Stevens — attractive mezzo-soprano with the Metropolitan, films include "Going My Way"

RITA ◆Rita Coolidge — ex-wife of Kris Kristofferson◆ platinum album "Anytime, Anywhere" ◆ Rita Hayworth — Latina actress who starred in "Gilda," married Orson Welles ◆ Rita Moreno — received an Academy Award for "West Side Story" ◆Rita Rudner — stand-up comedian, co-host of TV's "Funny People"

ROBERTA ◆Roberta Flack — Grammy winner for "The First Time Ever I Saw Your Face" and "Killing Me Softly" ◆ Roberta Maxwell — actress whose roles included Barbara Weaver on the soap "Another World" ◆Roberta Streeter — real name of singer Bobbie Gentry

ROBIN ◆Robin Cousins — won gold medal in figure skating at the Olympics ◆ Robin Givens — actress on TV's "Head of the Class," divorced boxer Mike Tyson

ROBYN ◆Robyn Douglass — actress who played Katherine in the bicycle racing film "Breaking Away" ◆ Robyn Miller — actress whose roles included Roz on the sitcom "The Patty Duke Show" ◆

Robyn Peterson — played ranger Jackie Hawkes on Robert Conrad's series "High Mountain Rangers"

ROCHELLE ◆Rochelle Hudson — actress whose roles included Sally Glynn in Mae West's "She Done Him Wrong" ◆ Rochelle Owens — dramatist, writings include "The String Game"

ROLANDA ◆Rolanda Mendels — actress whose roles included Molly Ordway Randolph on the soap "Another World"

ROMA ◆Roma Downey — actress whose roles included Danielle St. Clair on TV's "Black Jack Savage"

ROMY ◆Romy Schneider — actress who played the 19th century English monarch in "The Young Victoria"

RONA ◆Rona Anderson — Scottish actress who made film debut in "Sleeping Car to Trieste" ◆ Rona Barrett — Hollywood gossip columnist ◆ Rona Jaffe — author of "The Last Chance" and "Class Reunion"

RONEE ◆Ronee Blakeley — singer, Oscar nominee for screen debut in "Nashville"

RONNE ◆Ronne Troup — actress whose roles included Barbara on the nighttime soap "Knots Landing"

RONNIE ◆Ronnie Edwards — actress who played Corabeth Godsey on the popular drama series "The Waltons" ◆ Ronnie Spector — lead singer of The Ronettes, hits include "Be My Baby"

RORI ◆Rori King — actress who played Becky Cassidy on the Danny Thomas sitcom "I'm a Big Girl Now"

ROSA ◆Rosa Hawkins — member of The Dixie Cups, hits include number one gold record "Chapel of Love"

ROSALIE ◆Rosalie Allen — "queen of the yodelers" in country music during the 1940's and 50's

ROSALIND ◆Rosalind Ashford — member of Martha and the Vandellas, hits include "Dancing in the Street" ◆Rosalind Russell — comic actress in "Auntie Mame," "His Girl Friday," and "The Trouble With Angels"

ROSALINDA ◆Rosalinda Guerra — actress whose roles included Ramona Gonzalez on the soap "Ryan's Hope"

ROSALYN ◆Rosalyn Drexler — Obie winner for "The Writer's Opera" ◆Rosalyn Yalow — second woman to win the Nobel Prize in medicine

ROSALYNN ◆Rosalynn Carter — First Lady to President Jimmy Carter

ROSAMOND ◆Rosamond Lehmann — author whose novels include "The Ballad and the Source" and "The Sea-Grape Tree"

ROSAMUND ◆Rosamund John — gentle-mannered British leading lady

ROSANA ◆Rosana DeSoto — played Elaine in the Sean Connery/Dustin Hoffman film "Family Business"

ROSANNA ◆Rosanna Arquette — actress whose first big break was in "Desperately Seeking Susan"

ROSE ◆Rose Wilder Lane — daughter of Laura Ingalls Wilder, became Vietnam war correspondent

ROSE-MARIE ◆Rose-Marie — actress who played Sally Rogers on the sitcom "The Dick Van Dyke Show"

ROSEANNE ◆Roseanne Arnold — sitcom superstar comic of ABC's "Roseanne" ◆ Roseanne Cash — country singer and daughter of Johnny Cash

ROSELLA ◆Rosella Hightower — ballerina noted for enormous repertoire

ROSELYNE ◆Roselyne Puyo — actress who played Nicole in Francois Truffaut's "The Man Who Loved Women"

ROSEMARY ◆Rosemary Clooney — popular top ten singer from the 1950's, hits "Hey There," "This Ole House"

ROSEMOND ◆Elizabeth Rosemond Taylor — Oscar winner for "Butterfield 8" and "Who's Afraid of Virginia Woolf?"

ROSENDA ◆Rosenda Monteros — actress who played Petra in the classic western film "The Magnificent Seven"

ROSETTA ◆Rosetta Hightower — singer with The Orlons, hits include "The Wah-Watusi" ◆ Rosetta Jacobs — real name of actress Piper Laurie ◆ Rosetta LeNoire — actress who played Grandma Winslow on Urkel's TV show "Family Matters"

ROSI ◆Rosi Mittermaier — Olympic gold medal skier

ROSIE ◆Rosie Brown — daughter of actress Rachel Ward and Bryan Brown ◆ Rosie Perez — hot 1990's comedienne, starred in the film "Fearless"

ROSINA ◆Rosina Lawrence — played tiny blond musical comedy star Marilyn Miller in "The Great Ziegfeld"

ROSINE ◆Rosine Bernard — real name of legendary actress Sarah Bernhardt

ROSLYN ◆Roslyn Kind — vocalist and Barbra Streisand's younger sister

ROSSANA ◆Rossana Podesta — actress who played the most beautiful woman in the world in "Helen of Troy"

ROSSIE ◆Rossie Harris — actress who played Dylan Chapin on the Beau Bridges sitcom "United States"

ROXANA ◆Roxana Zal — Emmy winning actress for "Something About Amelia"

ROXANN ◆Roxann Biggs — played Yolanda Elena Peunte on the medical drama series "Nightingales"

ROXANNE ◆Roxanne (c) — Cyrano de Bergerac's love, also played for laughs by Steve Martin in "Roxanne" ◆ Roxanne Pulitzer — went through headline-making divorce from publishing heir Peter Pulitzer

ROXIE ◆Roxie Roker — played next door neighbor Helen Willis on the sitcom "The Jeffersons"

ROYANA ◆Royana Black — actress who played the lead role of Miranda in the sitcom "Raising Miranda"

ROYCE ◆Jessie Royce Landis — character actress in mother roles, films include "North by Northwest"

ROZ ◆Roz Ryan — actress whose roles included Amerlia Hetebrink on the hit sitcom "Amen"

RUBY ◆Ruby Dee — actress in "A Raisin in the Sun," wife of Ossie Davis ◆Ruby Keeler — star of Busby Berkeley musicals like "42nd Street"

RUDY ◆Rudy Huxtable (c) — youngest daughter on TV's "The Cosby Show"

RUE ◆Rue McClanahan — saucy senior citizen of TV's "The Golden Girls"

RUGGERO ◆Ruggero Raimondi — actress whose roles included Escamillo in the musical "Carmen"

RULA ◆Rula Lenska — Rita Hayworth look-alike, noted for 1980's TV commercials

RUMER ◆Rumer Glenn Willis — daughter of action star Bruce Willis and actress Demi Moore

RUTANYA ◆Rutanya Alda — portrayed Angela in Robert De Niro's anti-war film "The Deer Hunter"

RUTH ◆Ruth Buzzi — regular on "Rowan and Martin's Laugh-In" ◆ Ruth Gordon — starred in "Harold and Maude," and with Clint Eastwood in his orangutan movies ◆ Dr. Ruth Westheimer — sexual psychiatrist on radio and television

SABINE ◆Sabine Glaser — played Bernadette in Francois Truffaut's film "The Man Who Loved Women"

SABRINA ◆Sabrina Le Beauf — actress whose roles included Sondra on TV's "The Cosby Show" ◆ Sabrina Scharf — actress whose roles included Sarah in Dennis Hopper's cult classic "Easy Rider"

SACAJAWEA ◆Sacajawea — Shoshone Indian guide to Lewis and Clark, Donna Reed played her in "Far Horizons"

SADA ◆Sada Thompson — actress whose roles included mother Kate Lawrence on TV's "Family"

SADIE ◆Sadie Frost — played Dominique in the Jimmy Smits/Cheech Marin TNT movie "The Cisco Kid"

SAGAN ◆Sagan Lewis — actress who played Dr. Jaqueline Wade on the medical series "St. Elsewhere"

SALLI ◆Salli Flynn — vocalist on the music series "The Lawrence Welk Show" ◆ Salli Sachse — actress whose roles included Glenn in Peter Fonda's counterculture "The Trip"

SALLIE ◆Sallie Brophy — actress whose roles included Julie Fielding on the soap "Follow Your Heart" ◆ Sallie Shockley — actress whose roles included Valerie on the George Kennedy drama series "Sarge"

SALLY ◆Sally Field — double Oscar winner, went from "The Flying Nun" to "Smokey and the Bandit" ◆ Sally Kellerman — actress whose roles included Hot Lips in the feature film version of "M*A*S*H" ◆Sally K. Ride — first woman astronaut in space, aboard the space shuttle ◆ Sally Struthers — portrayed Archie Bunker's daughter Gloria Stivik on TV's "All in the Family"

SALOME ◆Salome — slipped off seven veils, and in return was given the head of John the Baptist ◆ Salome Jens — actress who played Mrs. Kipfer on TV's film ripoff "From Here to Eternity"

SAMANTHA ◆Samantha Eggar — Cannes Film Festival award winner for "The Collector" ◆ Samantha Fox — pop singer, hits "Naughty Girls" and "I Wanna Have Some Fun"

SAMILE ◆Samile Diane Friesen — real name of actress Dyan Cannon

SAMMI ◆Sammi Davis-Voss — actress who played Caroline Hailey on the post WW II era drama series "Homefront" ◆Sammi Smith — country western singer, "Help Me Make It Through the Night"

SAMUELLE ◆Samuelle Prater — member of Club Nouveau, hits include "Lean on Me" which sold six million copies

SANDAHL ◆Sandahl Bergman — actress who played Valeria in Arnold Schwarzenegger's "Conan the Barbarian"

SANDI ◆Sandi Patti — Christian singer whose albums include "Morning Like This"

SANDRA ◆Sandra Bernhard — comedienne who made her film debut in "The King of Comedy" ◆Sandra Dee — perky virgin in such films as "Gidget" and "Tammy and the Doctor" ◆ Sandra Day O'Connor — first woman Supreme Court Justice

SANDS ◆Sands Hall — actress whose roles included Maya Waterman on the soap "The Guiding Light"

SANDY ◆Sandy Dennis — quirky star of "The Out-of-Towners" and "Up the Down Staircase" ◆Sandy Duncan — actress in TV's "The Sandy Duncan Show," "Roots," and "The Hogan Family"

SANDYE ◆Sandye Wilson — actress in director Charles Lane's 1989 black and white silent "Sidewalk Stories"

SARA ◆Sara Gilbert — played the obnoxious daughter Darlene on TV's smash sitcom "Roseanne"

SARAH ◆Sarah Bernhardt — renowned French actress of the late nineteenth century, "The Divine Sarah" ◆ Sarah Ferguson — Duchess of York, "Fergie," separated from her husband Prince Andrew ◆Sarah Purcell — co-host of TV's "Real People"

SARAH JESSICA ◆Sarah Jessica Parker — went from star of TV's "Square Pegs" to features like "Honeymoon in Vegas"

SARITA ◆Sarita Montiel — one of the many actresses to portray Camille in films ◆ Sarita Wooton — actress in Merle Oberon's version of the classic novel "Wuthering Heights"

SASHA ◆Sasha — child of actress Jessica Lange and Mikhail Barishnykov

SAUNDRA ◆Saundra Santiago — played Detective Gina Calabrese on the police drama series "Miami Vice" ◆ Saundra

Sharp — actress who played nurse Peggy Shotwell on the medical series "St. Elsewhere"

SCARLETT ◆Elizabeth Scarlett Jagger — daughter of rock star Mick Jagger and Jerry Hall ◆ Scarlett O'Hara (c) — heroine of "Gone With the Wind"

SCHUYLER ◆Schuyler Elizabeth — daughter of actress Sissy Spacek

SCOTTISH ◆Scottish Rogers — daughter of western stars Roy Rogers and Dale Evans

SCOUT ◆Scout Willis — daughter of actress Demi Moore and action star Bruce Willis

SEAN ◆Sean Young — seductress in the back seat of the limo in the film "No Way Out"

SEASON ◆Season Hubley — once wed to Kurt Russell, played Salina Magee on TV's "Family"

SEBIE ◆Sebie Hendricks — played Claudette Colbert's daughter in the tearjerker "Imitation of Life"

SEENA ◆Seena Owen — silent screen star whose films include "Intolerance"

SELA ◆Sela Ward — actress whose roles included Teddy Reed on TV's "Sisters"

SELENA ◆Selena Royle — actress in the John Garfield/Shelley Winters film "He Ran All the Way"

SELMA ◆Selma Diamond — gravel-voiced security guard on TV's "Night Court"

SENTA ◆Senta Berger — actress in the films "Major Dundee," "The Glory Guys" and "The Quiller Memorandum"

SEVEN ◆Seven McDonald — actress whose roles included Jennie Brown on TV's "Eddie Capra Mysteries"

SHALANE ◆Shalane McCall — actress whose roles included Charlie Wade on TV's "Dallas"

SHANA ◆Shana Alexander — commentator on CBS's "60 Minutes"

SHANE ◆Shane Gould — first woman to win three Olympic medals in world record times

SHANI ◆Shani Wallis — actress whose films include "Terror in the Wax Museum"

SHANNA ◆Shanna Reed — actress whose roles included the wife and mother on the hit sitcom "Major Dad"

SHANNEN ◆Shannen Doherty — well publicized bad girl who stars on TV's "Beverly Hills 90210"

SHANNON ◆Shannon Tweed — Playmate of the Year turned soap star

SHANYGNE ◆Kellie Shanygne Williams — played Urkel's love interest Laura Winslow on the sitcom "Family Matters"

SHARI ◆Shari Belafonte — actress who played Julie in TV's "Hotel" and daughter of Harry Belafonte ◆Shari Lewis — starred in TV's "The Shari Lewis Show" with her hand-puppet Lambchop ◆ Shari Sabo — actress whose roles included a nurse on the hit sitcom "M*A*S*H"

SHARON ◆Sharon Gless — won two Emmys as Cagney on the drama series "Cagney and Lacey" ◆Sharon Stone — femme fatale in "Basic Instinct" ◆ Sharon Tate — actress wife of Roman Polanski, murdered by Charles Manson family

SHARY ◆Shary Marshall — actress whose roles included Katy Elliott on the soap "Morning Star"

SHARYN ◆Sharyn Moffett — child actress in Cary Grant's "Mr. Blandings Builds His Dream House"

SHAWN ◆Shawn Weatherly — actress whose roles included Jill Riley on the adventure series "Baywatch"

SHEBA ◆Sheba — in the Bible, the wealthy queen who visited King Solomon

SHEENA ◆Sheena Easton — rock singer, debut number one gold record "Morning Train"

SHEILA ◆Sheila E. — singer who has worked with Prince, solo single "The Glamorous Life"

SHEILAH ◆Sheilah Graham — Hollywood columnist who had an affair with F. Scott Fitzgerald

SHELAGH ◆Shelagh Delaney — English dramatist whose works include "A Taste of Honey"

SHELBY ◆Shelby Hiatt — actress whose roles included Jane Harland Dawson on the soap "General Hospital" ◆Shelby Lynne — country torch singer, albums include "Tough All Over"

SHELIA ◆Shelia MacRae — played Alice Kramden for one year on the early TV sitcom "The Honeymooners"

SHELL ◆Shell Kepler — actress whose roles included Amy Vining on the soap "General Hospital"

SHELLEY ◆Shelley Duvall — actress in "Popeye," "The Shining," produced "Faerie Tale Theatre" on cable ◆ Shelley Fabares — actress whose roles included daughter Mary Stone on TV's "The Donna Reed Show" ◆Shelley Hack — played Tiffany Welles on TV's bikini detective show "Charlie's Angels" ◆Shelley Long — portrayed the over-educated self-important Diane Chambers on TV's "Cheers" ◆Shelley Winters — actress in "The Poseidon Adventure," "Lolita," "Winchester '73," "The Scalphunters"

SHELLIE ◆Shellie Clark — with The Honey Cone, debut hit single "While You're Out Looking for Sugar"

SHERE ◆Shere Hite — author whose controversial works on sexuality are known as "Hite Reports"

SHEREE ◆Sheree North — played Edie McKendrick on the Danny Thomas sitcom "I'm a Big Girl Now" ◆Sheree Wilson — actress whose roles included April Stevens on TV's "Dynasty"

SHERILYN ◆Sherilyn Fenn — actress in "Boxing Helena," "Two Moon Junction" and TV's "Twin Peaks"

SHERL ◆Sherl Stern — regular panelist on TV's quiz show "Down You Go"

SHERRIL ◆Sherril Rettino — actress whose roles included Jackie Dugan on TV's "Dallas"

SHERRY ◆Sherry Lansing — first woman to head a major film studio, Twentieth Century-Fox ◆ Sherry Miles — regular on the long running hayseed variety series "Hee Haw"

SHERYL ◆Sheryl Lee — played murdered Laura Palmer on David Lynch's drama series "Twin Peaks"

SHERYL LEE ◆Sheryl Lee Ralph — actress who played waitress Ginger St. James on the sitcom "It's a Living"

SHIRI ◆Shiri Appleby — actress whose roles included Amy Escobar on the sitcom "Knight and Daye"

SHIRL ◆Shirl Conway — Emmy nominated actress for "Nurses"

SHIRLEY ◆Shirley Bassey — Welsh singer of the title song from "Goldfinger" ◆ Shirley Booth — won an Emmy for her portrayal of Hazel on the TV series of the same name ◆ Shirley Jones — singer whose roles included mom Partridge on the "Partridge Family" sitcom ◆ Shirley MacLaine — author, dancer/actress in "Sweet Charity," Oscar for "Terms of Endearment" ◆ Shirley Temple — pint-sized actress who was the top moneymaker for Fox in the 1930's

SHUKO ◆Shuko Akune — actress whose roles included Maria Amardo on Elliot Gould's TV show "E/R"

SIAN ◆Sian Phillips — actress who played Gwendolen in the Richard Burton version of "Becket"

SIBYL ◆Sibyl Hathaway — author whose works include "Maid of Sark"

SIDNEY ◆Sidney Greenbush — played Carrie Ingalls with her sister Lindsay on "Little House on the Prairie"

SIGNE ◆Signe Hasso — Swedish leading lady in US films like "Picture Mommy Dead"

SIGOURNEY ◆Sigourney Weaver — starred in "Alien," "Working Girl" and "Gorillas in the Mist"

SIGRID ◆Sigrid Valdis — sexy and curvy secretary to Col. Klink on the sitcom "Hogan's Heroes" ◆ Sigrid von Richthofen — actress who appeared in the film "Cabaret" as Fraulein Mayr

SILVANA ◆Silvana Mangano — Italian actress and model, wife of producer Dino de Laurentiis ◆ Silvana Pampanini — actress whose roles included Poppaea, the royal mistress in "O.K., Nero!"

SILVIA ◆Silvia Tennenbaum — author whose works include "Rachel, the Rabbi's Wife"

SIMKA ◆Simka Gravas (c) — Carol Kane's role as Andy Kaufman's girlfriend on the hit sitcom "Taxi"

SIMONE ◆Simone Signoret — French actress who was an Oscar winner for "Room at the Top" ◆ Simone Simon — French actress in the original "Cat People"

SIMONETTA ◆Simonetta — Rome's leading designer who established the first "haute boutique" ◆ Simonetta Stefanelli — actress who played Apollonia in the Academy Award winning film "The Godfather"

SINEAD ◆Sinead O'Connor — bald controversial pop singer, hits include "Nothing Compares 2 U"

SIOBHAN ◆Siobhan Fallon — member of The Not Ready for Prime Time Players on "Saturday Night Live" ◆Siobhan Finneran — star of the sex comedy "Rita, Sue and Bob Too" ◆ Siobhan McKenna — fiery Irish lass who played Anna in Omar Sharif's Russian epic "Doctor Zhivago"

SIPPIE ◆Sippie Wallace — Grammy nominated blues singer for "Sippie"

SIRRY ◆Sirry Steffen — actress who played the maid on the hit sitcom "The Beverly Hillbillies"

SISSY ◆Sissy Spacek — dramatic actress known for "Carrie," Oscar winner for "Coal Miner's Daughter"

SKEETER ◆Skeeter Davis — country western singer, hits "Set Him Free" and "The End of the World"

SMYLLA ◆Smylla Brind — real name of actress Vanessa Brown, films include "The Ghost and Mrs. Muir"

SOLEIL ◆Soleil Moon Frye — child star of the sitcom "Punky Brewster"

SONDRA ◆Sondra Locke — girlfriend and co-star to Clint Eastwood in a number of his films

SONG ◆Lark Song Previn — child of actress Mia Farrow and composer/conductor Andre Previn ◆ Summer Song Previn — daughter of conductor Andre Previn and actress Mia Farrow

SONIA ◆Sonia Braga — actress whose roles included the spider woman in "Kiss of the Spider Woman" ◆Sonia Goring — member of The Chantels, debut hit "He's Gone" ◆Sonia Rykiel — fashion designer whose designs include tight knits and clinging dresses

SONJA ◆Sonja Henie — Olympic gold medal skater turned movie actress

SONORA ◆Sonora Smart — founder of Father's Day

SONYA ◆Sonya Levien — Oscar nominated screenwriter for "State Fair"

SOPHIA ◆Sophia Loren — actress in "El Cid," "Fall of the Roman Empire;" Oscar winner for "Two Women" ◆Sophia Smith — founder of Smith College

SOPHIE ◆Sophie Lyons — bank robber who became America's first society columnist ◆ Sophie Tucker — vaudeville singer called the last of the red-hot mamas

SOPHONISBA ◆Sophonisba Breckinridge — first woman admitted to the bar in Kentucky

SOSIE ◆Sosie Bacon — daughter of actor Kevin Bacon and actress Kyra Sedgwick

SPANKY ◆Spanky McFarlane — real name Elaine, leader of Spanky and Our Gang, hit "Sunday Will Never Be the Same"

SPENCER ◆Spencer Margaret Richmond — daughter of actress Jaclyn Smith

SPRING ◆Spring Byington — fluttery star of the TV series "December Bride"

STACI ◆Staci Keanan — actress who played Nicole Bradford, who didn't know her father on "My Two Dads"

STACY ◆Stacy Lattisaw — rock singer whose hits include the worldwide smash "Jump to the Beat"

STAR-SHEMAH ◆Star-Shemah Bobatoon — actress who played Dian Freeman on Alex Haley's drama series "Palmerstown"

STARLETTA ◆Starletta Dupois — portrayed Robert Townsend's mother in his debut film "Hollywood Shuffle"

STARLITE ◆Starlite Melody Golub — daughter of actress Marisa Berenson

STEFANIE ◆Stefanie Powers — star of TV's "Hart to Hart," and was also "The Girl from U.N.C.L.E."

STELLA ◆Stella Adler — acting teacher at her Conservatory of Acting ◆ Stella Stevens — "The Poseidon Adventure" provided ample scenes in which to remove her clothes

STEPFANIE ◆Stepfanie Kramer — played the "brass cupcake," detective Dee Dee McCall on TV's "Hunter"

STEPHANE ◆Stephane Audran — sophisticated French film beauty

STEPHANIE ◆Princess Stephanie — daughter of Grace Kelly and Prince Rainier of Monaco ◆ Stephanie Mills — rock singer, debut hit single "What Cha Gonna Do With My Lovin'" ◆ Stephanie Zimbalist — starred as detective Laura Holt on TV's "Remington Steele"

STEFFI ◆Steffi Duna — Hungarian dancer turned actress, appeared in "Waterloo Bridge" ◆ Steffi Graf — winner of US Open, Indoor and Wimbledon titles

STEVIE ◆Stevie Nicks — singer from Fleetwood Mac, solo album "Bella Donna" ◆ Stevie Smith — depressive British poet devoted to her aunt, Glenda Jackson biopic "Stevie"

STOCKARD ◆Stockard Channing — actress who played Jane Applegate, animal in human form, in "The Applegates"

STUART ◆Dorothy Stuart Hamill — gold medal Olympic figure skater ◆ Mary Stuart Masterson — actress whose roles included Terry in Sean Penn's "At Close Range"

SU ◆Su Tissue — actress who played Peggy Dillman in the wild and crazy film "Something Wild"

SUDIE ◆Sudie Bond — actress whose roles included Flo on TV's "Alice"

SUE ◆Sue Randall — actress whose roles included Miss Landers on the sitcom "Leave It to Beaver"

SUMMER ◆Summer Song Previn — daughter of conductor Andre Previn and actress Mia Farrow ◆ Summer Sanders — double gold medal Olympic swimmer

SUNNIE ◆Sunnie O'Dea — actress in Irene Dunne's classic film musical "Show Boat"

SUNSHINE ◆Sunshine Lucas — daughter of actress Susan St. James ◆ Sunshine Phoenix — actress sister of River Phoenix

SUSAN ◆Susan B. Anthony — suffragette immortalized on the US silver dollar ◆Susan Anton — actress and singer, films include "Golden Girl" ◆ Susan Dey — played Laurie Partridge on TV's "The Partridge Family," then starred on "L.A. Law" ◆ Susan Hayward — tempestuous actress who received an Oscar for "I Want to Live" ◆ Susan Sarandon — actress whose roles included the gun-toting Louise in "Thelma and Louise" ◆Susan St. James — played the wife in TV's "McMillan and Wife," starred on "Kate and Allie"

SUSANNA ◆Susanna Foster — actress best known for "Phantom of the Opera" ◆Susanna Hoffs — singer, hits include "Walk Like an Egyptian"

SUSANNAH ◆Susannah York — actress nominated for an Oscar for "They Shoot Horses, Don't They?"

SUSIE ◆Susie Tompkins — founder of Esprit Clothing

SUZAN ◆Suzan Ball — leading lady of the fifties whose films include "City Beneath the Sea"

SUZANNA ◆Suzanna Leigh — British leading lady, films include "Boeing Boeing" and "Paradise Hawaiian Style"

SUZANNE ◆Suzanne Pleshette — actress who played Emily Hartley, Bob's wife on TV's "Bob Newhart Show" ◆ Suzanne Somers — first dumb blonde on ABC's "Three's Company"

SUZETTE ◆Suzette Charles — Miss America, succeeded Vanessa Williams when she was disqualified ◆ Pamela Suzette Grier — actress, films include "On The Edge," "Something Wicked This Way Comes"

SUZI ◆Suzi Dean — played Scarlett Taylor on Barbara Eden's sitcom "Harper Valley P.T.A." ◆ Suzi Quatro — rock singer, debut hit single "All Shook Up"

SUZY ◆Suzy Amis — actress whose roles included Maggie Donaldson in Matt Dillon's "The Big Town" ◆ Suzy Gilstrap — paraplegic star of TV movies "Skyward" and "Skyward Christmas" ◆ Suzy Parker — highest-paid fashion model of the 1950's

SVETLANA ◆Svetlana Stalin — daughter of Joseph Stalin who defected to the West

SWOOSIE ◆Swoosie Kurtz — Broadway actress who landed on TV's "Sisters"

SYBIL ◆Sybil Danning — sexy European blond bombshell who played primarily in B movies ◆ Sybil Leek — astrologer who predicted assassination of Kennedy, election of Nixon ◆ Sybil Thorndike — actress best known for her lead role in "Saint Joan"

SYBILLE ◆Sybille Bedford — author whose works include "A Legacy" and "A Compass Error"

SYDNEY ◆Sydney Penny — actress who played Danni Collins, Gidget's niece, on the sitcom "The New Gidget" ◆Sydney Brooke Simpson — daughter of athlete O.J. Simpson

SYLVIA ◆Sylvia Ashton-Warner — teacher of Maori children in New Zealand, biopic "Sylvia" ◆Sylvia B. Chase — Emmy winning correspondent on ABC News' "20/20" ◆ Sylvia Kristel — actress whose roles included the softcore heroine in the film "Emmanuelle" ◆ Sylvia Miles — Oscar nominee for "Midnight Cowboy"

SYNDA ◆Synda Scott — actress whose roles included Helen Davis on TV's syndicated "Foreign Intrigue"

SYRETTA ◆Syretta Wright — singer, ex-wife of Stevie Wonder, hits include "With You I'm Born Again"

TABATHA ◆Tabatha Foster — longest survivor of a five-organ transplant operation

TABITHA ◆Tabitha Soren — MTV news correspondent

TAHNEE ◆Tahnee Welch — daughter of Raquel Welch, played Kitty in "Cocoon"

TAI ◆Tai Reina Babilonia — failed to win an Olympic medal when her partner Randy Gardner was injured

TAINA ◆Taina Elg — Finnish leading lady whose films include "The 39 Steps"

TALA ◆Tala Birell — leading lady whose films include "Crime and Punishment"

TALIA ◆Talia Balsam — actress whose roles included Judy in the Patrick Dempsey film "In the Mood" ◆ Talia Shire — actress in "The Godfather" and "Rocky," sister of director Francis Ford Coppola

TALISA ◆Talisa Soto — played Lupe Lamora in the Timothy Dalton James Bond film "Licence to Kill"

TALLULAH ◆Tallulah Bankhead — popular actress of the 30's and 40's, in Alfred Hitchcock's "Lifeboat" ◆ Tallulah Belle Willis — daughter of actress Demi Moore and actor Bruce Willis

TAMA ◆Tama Janowitz — author whose works include the best selling "Slaves of New York"

TAMARA ◆Tamara Desni — British leading lady, credits include "Fire Over England" ◆ Tamara Dobson — actress whose roles included the lead in the film "Cleopatra Jones" ◆Tamara Geva — choreographer whose dance roles include "On Your Toes"

TAMERLAINE ◆Tamerlaine Phillips — child of John Phillips and Genevieve Waite

TAMI ◆Tami Conner — actress who appeared as Margie in Lana Turner's "Peyton Place" ◆ Tami Erin — actress who played the title role in "The New Adventures of Pippi Longstocking"

TAMLYN ◆Tamlyn Tomita — actress whose roles included Lily in Dennis Quaid's "Come See the Paradise"

TAMMI ◆Tammi Terrell — soul singer, hits include "Ain't No Mountain High Enough"

TAMMY ◆Tammy Faye Bakker — ex-wife of notorious evangelist Jim Bakker, always wore too much makeup ◆ Tammy Grimes — star of the sitcom "The Tammy Grimes Show" ◆ Tammy Wynette — country singer best known for "Stand By Your Man"

TANIA ◆Tania Mallett — actress who played Tilly Masterson in the James Bond adventure "Goldfinger"

TANITA ◆Presley Tanita — daughter of country western singer Tanya Tucker ◆ Tanita Tikaram — folk rock performer, debut album "Ancient Heart"

TANNIS ◆Tannis Vallely — played brainy kid Janice in the successful sitcom "Head of the Class"

TANYA ◆Tanya Roberts — played "Sheena, Queen of the Jungle," and one of many Charlie's Angels ◆ Tanya Tucker — country singer, debut hit single "Delta Dawn" ◆ Tanya Welk — vocalist on the music series "The Lawrence Welk Show"

TARA ◆Tara Buckman — actress whose roles included Brandy on the police comedy series "Lobo" ◆Tara Gabriel Getty — daughter of oil tycoon J.P. Getty II

TARO ◆Taro Meyer — actress whose roles included Melissa Needham on TV's "Another World"

TARYN ◆Taryn Haegy — member of the group Kid Creole and the Coconuts, hit album "Tropical Gangsters"

TASIA ◆Tasia Talenza — played Yeoman Rosie Henriques on the series "Supercarrier"

TATA ◆Tata Vega — rock singer whose hits included "Give It Up for Love"

TATIANA ◆Tatiana Samoilova — portrayed Tolstoy's tragic heroine in "Anna Karenina" ◆ Tatiana Celia Schlossberg — daughter of Caroline Kennedy and Ed Schlossberg

TATJANA ◆Tatjana Patitz — blond beauty who died memorably in Sean Connery's "Rising Sun"

TATUM ◆Tatum O'Neal — youngest actress ever to win an Oscar for her role in "Paper Moon"

TATYANA ◆Tatyana Ali — played youngest daughter Ashley Banks on TV's "Fresh Prince of Bel Air"

TAWNEY ◆Tawney Little — Los Angeles area newscaster and former Miss America

TAWNY ◆Tawny Kitaen — actress who played Debbie in Tom Hanks' early film romp "Bachelor Party"

TAYLOR ◆Barbara Taylor Bradford — popular author, of "A Woman of Substance" and "Hold the Dream" ◆ Taylor Caldwell — English author, novels include "The Captains and the Kings" ◆ Taylor Fry — actress who played Amy Potter on Chris Elliot's quirky sitcom "Get a Life"

TEAL ◆Teal Ames — actress whose roles included Sara Lane Karr on the soap "The Edge of Night"

TEDDI JO ◆Teddi Jo Mellencamp — daughter of singer John Cougar Mellencamp

TEENA ◆Teena Marie — rock singer, hits include "I'm Just a Sucker for Your Love"

TELMA ◆Telma Hopkins — singer with Tony Orlando and Dawn, also an actress

TEMPE ◆Tempe Pigott — actress who played Mrs. Hawkins in Fredric March's "Dr. Jekyll and Mr. Hyde"

TEMPESTT ◆Tempestt Kenieth Bledsoe — actress who played the boy crazy daughter Vanessa on TV's "The Cosby Show"

TENLEY ◆Tenley Albright — Olympic gold medal figure skater

TENNESSEE ◆Tennessee Claflin — early advocate of equal rights for women

TERESA ◆Mother Teresa — Nobel Peace Prize winning Catholic nun, documentary "Mother Teresa" ◆ Teresa Brewer — singer, pop hits include "Music! Music! Music!" ◆Teresa Wright — Oscar winner for "Mrs. Miniver," nominated for "Pride of the Yankees"

TERI ◆Teri Copley — maid, and also the star of the sitcom "We Got it Made" ◆ Teri Garr — comic actress in "Oh, God!" and "Tootsie," also good on TV's "McCloud" ◆Teri Murphy — host of the tabloid news series "Hard Copy"

TERRI ◆Terri Garber — actress whose roles included Leslie Carrington on TV's "Dynasty" ◆ Terri Gibbs — blind country singer, hit single "Somebody's Knockin'" ◆ Terri Treas — actress in "All That Jazz" and "The Best Little Whorehouse in Texas"

TERRY ◆Terry Moore — actress who, after a long legal battle, was recognized as the widow of Howard Hughes

TESS ◆Tess Lynch — daughter of actress Jane Curtin, star of TV's "Kate and Allie"

TESSA ◆Tessa Ferrer — daughter of rock singer Debby Boone, granddaughter of singer Pat Boone

TESSIE ◆Tessie O'Shea — played Alice Foss in "The Russians Are Coming, The Russians Are Coming"

TEVAITE ◆Tevaite Vernette — played Mauatua, Fletcher Christian's Tahitian love on "The Bounty"

TEXAS ◆Texas Guinan — speakeasy owner known for saying "Hello, Sucker!" biopic "Incendiary Blonde"

THAN ◆Than Wyenn — actress who played George Lupo on the drama series "Pete Kelly's Blues"

THEA ◆Thea Vidale — star of her own TV series "Thea"

THEDA ◆Theda Bara — film "A Fool There Was" shot her to success in the early 1900's

THELMA ◆Thelma McQueen — real name of actress Butterfly McQueen ◆ Thelma Ritter — supporting actress in films like "Rear Window" and "Pillow Talk" ◆ Thelma Todd — actress, biopic "White Hot: The Mysterious Murder of Thelma Todd"

THEODORA ◆Theodora Dupree Richards — daughter of musician Keith Richards and Patti Hanson

THEODOSIA ◆Theodosia Alston — daughter of Aaron Burr who stood by him in his troubles, drowned at sea ◆ Theodosia Goodman — real name of actress Theda Bara

THERESA ◆Theresa Conover — actress who played Mrs. Hamlin in Edward G. Robinson's "Silver Dollar" ◆ Theresa Russell — actress whose films include "Black Widow" and "Whore"

THERESE ◆Jane Therese Curtin — went from "Saturday Night Live" to playing Allie on "Kate and Allie" ◆Therese Graham — portrayed Marlene Ivy in Jessica Lange's "Country" ◆ Maureen Therese McGovern — singer, hits "The Morning After" and "We May Never Love Like This Again"

THORA ◆Thora Hird — British character comedienne from a theatrical family

THYRA ◆Uta Thyra Hagen — won Tonys for "The Country Girl" and "Who's Afraid of Virginia Woolf?"

TI-GRACE ◆Ti-Grace Atkinson — feminist who helped pass the New York State abortion law

TIA ◆Tia Carrere — actress whose roles included Cassandra, the singer in the film "Wayne's World"

TIANA ◆Tiana Lemnitz — leading soprano during the 1950's

TIBERIA ◆Tiberia Mitri — actress who played Marianne Randolph Halloway on the soap "Another World"

TICHI ◆Tichi Wilkerson — publisher of the "Hollywood Reporter"

TIFFANY ◆Tiffany — teenage pop singer, sang "Electric Youth," was a loser on "Star Search" ◆ Tiffany Brissette — actress who played the little robot Vicki on the sitcom "Small Wonder"

TILLERY ◆Tillery Banks — actress who played Angie Adams on the family drama series "Harris and Company"

TIMI ◆Timi Yuro — rock singer, debut hit single "Hurt"

TINA ◆Tina Louise — actress who played Ginger Grant on the classic sitcom "Gilligan's Island" ◆ Tina Sinatra — Hollywood producer and daughter of Frank ◆ Tina Turner — singer/actress whose bio pic is "What's Love Got to Do with It" ◆Tina Yothers — actress whose roles included daughter Jennifer Keaton on TV's "Family Ties"

TIPPER ◆Tipper Gore — wife of Vice President of the United States Al Gore

TIPPI ◆Tippi Hedren — star of "The Birds," mother of Melanie Griffith

TIRRELL ◆Tirrell Barbery — actress whose roles included Carol Raven on the soap "Love of Life"

TISCH ◆Tisch Raye — actress who played Christine on the network-based drama series "W.E.B."

TISHA ◆Tisha Campbell — actress whose roles included Jane Toussaint in Spike Lee's "School Daze"

TITA ◆Tita Bell — actress whose roles included Trudy on the long running sitcom "Happy Days" ◆ Tita Colorado — actress who played the rancher's wife in the cult classic "Easy Rider"

TOINETTE ◆Kay Toinette Oslin — Grammy winning country singer, gold debut album "80's Ladies"

TONI ◆Toni Basil — actress whose roles included Mary in the cult classic "Easy Rider" ◆ Toni Morrison — Pulitzer Prize winning author, works "Song of Solomon" and "Tar Baby" ◆Toni Tennille — "Love Will Keep Us Together" is the theme song for TV's "The Captain and Tennille"

TONJA ◆Tonja Walker — actress whose roles included Lisbeth Bachman on the soap "Capitol"

TONY ◆Tony Perry — actress after whom the Tony award is named

TONYA ◆Tonya Crowe — actress who played Olivia Cunningham Dyer on the nighttime soap "Knots Landing"

TORA ◆Tora Teje — actress who portrayed the notorious nineteenth century courtesan Camille

TORI ◆Tori Spelling — star of TV's "Beverly Hills 90210," daughter of producer Aaron Spelling

TOTIE ◆Totie Fields — nightclub entertainer known for self-deprecating humor

TOUKIE ◆Toukie Smith — actress whose roles included Eva Rawley on the Marla Gibbs hit sitcom "227"

TOVAH ◆Tovah Feldshuh — actress in TV's "Amazing Howard Hughes," "Holocaust," "Beggarman-Thief"

TRACEY ◆Tracey Gold — played super-smart daughter Carol Seaver on the sitcom "Growing Pains" ◆Tracey Ullman — star of TV's "The Tracey Ullman Show"

TRACI ◆Traci Lords — porno film star turned regular actress in films and on TV

TRACY ◆Tracy Austin — youngest tennis player to break the million dollar prize barrier ◆ Tracy Chapman — singer, Grammy winning single "Fast Car" ◆ Tracy Nelson — daughter of Ricky Nelson, starred in TV's "Father Dowling Mysteries"

TRESA ◆Tresa Hughes — actress who appeared in the kids-turned-performers film "Fame"

TRICIA ◆Tricia Barnstable — actress whose roles included Betty I in the outer space sitcom "Quark" ◆Tricia Nixon — daughter of President Nixon

TRINI ◆Trini Alvarado — actress whose roles included Jenny Claire in Bette Midler's version of "Stella"

TRIOLA ◆Michelle Triola Marvin — live-in friend of Lee Marvin, first palimony case in California

TRISH ◆Trish Hawkins — actress whose roles included Mimi Haines Frame on the soap "Another World" ◆ Trish Van Devere — actress wife of George C. Scott, with whom she starred in "Day of the Dolphin"

TRISHA ◆Trisha Yearwood — country music artist compared to Linda Ronstadt

TRIXIE ◆Trixie Friganza — actress, credits include "Gentlemen Prefer Blondes"

TRIXIEBELLE ◆Fifi Trixiebelle Geldof — daughter of singer/actor Bob Geldof

TRUDI ◆Trudi Morrison — first African-American woman appointed deputy sergeant-at-arms of the US Senate

TRUDY ◆Trudy Marshall — leading lady of films of the 1940's

TRULA ◆Trula Hossier — actress in director Charles Lane's black and white 1989 silent film "Sidewalk Stories"

TRULY ◆Truly Shattuck — actress whose roles included Mrs. Garrison in Marion Davies' "Beauty's Worth"

TUDI ◆Tudi Wiggins — actress whose roles included Karen Martin on the soap "The Guiding Light"

TUESDAY ◆Tuesday Weld — played Thalia Menninger on TV's "Dobie Gillis," went on to make movies

TULA ◆Tula Ellice Finklea — real name of dancer and actress Cyd Charisse

TWIGGY ◆Twiggy Lawson — 1960's English super-thin megamodel turned actress

TWYLA ◆Twyla Tharp — choreographer dancer, she wrote "Push Comes to Shove"

TYLER ◆Mary Tyler Moore — star of her own television series as well as "The Dick Van Dyke Show"

TYNE ◆Tyne Daly — star of TV's "Cagney and Lacey," film credits include "The Enforcer"

TYREN ◆Tyren Perry — actress whose roles included Trish Reagan on the sitcom "Bustin' Loose"

TYSON ◆Tyson McVey — daughter of celebrity Neneh Cherry

ULA ◆ Ula Hedwig — played one of The Harlettes in Bette Midler's "Divine Madness"

ULLA ◆ Ulla Jacobsson — Swedish leading lady, credits include "Zulu" and "The Heroes of Telemark" ◆ Ulla Stromstedt — actress whose roles included Ulla Norstrand on TV's underwater "Flipper"

ULTRA ◆ Ultra Violet — actress in Dustin Hoffman's classic film "Midnight Cowboy"

UMA ◆ Uma Thurman — puffy-lipped ingenue in "Dangerous Liaisons" and "Final Analysis"

UNA ◆ Una Merkel — started as Lillian Gish's double, still making films in the 1960's ◆ Una O'Connor — actress in Boris Karloff's sequel "The Bride of Frankenstein"

URSULA ◆ Ursula Andress — sexy Swiss actress whose films include "What's New, Pussycat?" and "The Blue Max" ◆ Ursula Bloom — author of more than 500 novels, including "Secret Lover" ◆ Ursula Thiess — beautiful 40's actress who abandoned her career to wed Robert Taylor

UTA ◆ Uta Hagen — won Tonys for "The Country Girl" and "Who's Afraid of Virginia Woolf?" ◆ Uta Levka — one of the actresses who played the ultimate femme fatale Carmen in film

VALENTINA ◆ Valentina — fashion designer known for soft, flowing, bias-cut clothing ◆ Valentina Cortesa — Italian romantic actress, US credits include "The Barefoot Contessa"

VALERIE ◆ Valerie Bertinelli — queen of the "made for television" movie ◆ Valerie Harper — played Rhoda on TV's "The Mary Tyler Moore Show," later, had her own series "Valerie" ◆ Valerie Perrine — Gene Hackman's girlfriend in "Superman," Oscar nominee for "Lenny"

VALESKA ◆ Valeska Suratt — actress whose roles included the 2,000 year old sorceress in the silent "She"

VANA ◆ Vana Tribbey — actress whose roles included Alice Frame on the soap "Another World"

VANDA ◆ Vanda Godsell — British character actress, usually in blowsy roles

VANESSA ◆ Vanessa Huxtable (c) — another of the many daughters on TV's "The Cosby Show" ◆ Vanessa Redgrave — Oscar winning actress for "Julia" ◆ Vanessa Williams — Miss America who lost her crown in scandal and became an actress

VANETTA ◆ Vanetta Rogers — regular on "Pat Paulsen's Half a Comedy Hour"

VANITY ◆ Vanity — singer and actress who appeared with Carl Weathers in "Action Jackson"

VANNA ◆ Vanna White — she turns the letters on "Wheel of Fortune," and dresses elegantly for the job

VARINIA ◆ Varinia — wife of slave rebel leader Spartacus, played by Jean Simmons in the biopic

VASHTI ◆ Vashti — ancient Persian queen beheaded for refusing to flaunt her beauty

VEANNE ◆ Veanne Cox — actress whose roles included Tessy Mahoney in Holly Hunter's "Miss Firecracker"

VEDA ◆ Veda Borg — actress who reliably played good-hearted tarts and gangster's molls

VELEKA ◆ Veleka Gray — actress whose roles included Lyle Montgomery on the soap "As the World Turns"

VELMA ◆ Velma Barfield — executed in 1984, the first woman executed in the United States since 1962

VELVET ◆ Velvet Brown (c) — Elizabeth Taylor's starring role in the film "National Velvet"

VERA ◆ Vera — designer who founded the Vera Company ◆ Vera Miles — actress in "The Searchers" and "Psycho" (but not the dead one) ◆ Vera Ralston — Republic Pictures leading lady who married studio boss Herbert Yates

VERA-ELLEN ◆ Vera-Ellen — played Jessie Brown Kalmar in the Fred Astaire musical "Three Little Words"

VEREE ◆ Veree Teasdale — comedy actress, played Empress Agrippa in Eddie Cantor's comedy "Roman Scandals"

VERNA ◆ Verna Aardema — author of African folk tales for children ◆ Verna Bloom — actress whose roles included Eileen in the film "Medium Cool" ◆ Verna Felton — actress who appeared on the TV series "December Bride"

VERNEE ◆ Vernee Johnson — actress whose roles included Denise on the sitcom "Foley Square"

VERONICA ◆ Veronica Cartwright — films include "The Birds" and "The Right Stuff," sister of Angela Cartwright ◆ Veronica Hamel — actress whose roles included the public defender on

NBC's "Hill Street Blues" ◆ Veronica Lake — blond actress famous for her "peek-a-boo" bangs

VERONIQUE◆Veronique Vendell — actress who played the pretty French girl in Richard Burton's "Becket"

VERUSCHKA◆Veruschka — model and actress whose films include "Blow Up"

VET◆Vet Boswell — member of the singing trio The Boswell Sisters

VICKI◆Vicki Lawrence — actress who played Mama on TV's "The Carol Burnett Show," own show "Vicki!" ◆Vicki Morgan — mistress of Alfred Bloomingdale who sued his estate for ten million dollars

VICKILYN◆Vickilyn Reynolds — co-star of the situation comedy "Sugar and Spice"

VICTORIA◆Victoria Jackson — member of The Not Ready for Prime Time Players on "Saturday Night Live" ◆Victoria Principal — actress whose roles included the outsider Pamela Barnes Ewing on TV's "Dallas" ◆ Victoria Tennant — Steve Martin's love interest in real life and in the film "L.A. Story"

VIDA◆Vida Hope — British character actress, usually in comic proletarian roles

VIKKI◆Vikki Carr — pop singer whose hits include "It Must Be Him"

VILMA◆Vilma Banky — actress who starred with Rudolph Valentino in "The Eagle"

VINA◆Vina Delmar — author whose novels include "The Laughing Stranger"

VINNETTE◆Vinnette Carroll — producer of musicals, works include "Your Arms Too Short to Box with God"

VINNIE◆Vinnie Day — ditzy wife of Clarence Day in the book, film, and TV "Life With Father"

VIOLA◆Viola Allen — actress best known for Shakespearean roles ◆ Viola Liuzzo — civil rights leader killed while driving marchers from one town to another ◆Viola Spolin — actress who played the mother in Donald Sutherland's "Alex in Wonderland"

VIOLET◆Violet Bonham-Carter — English public official, Baroness Asquith, grandmother of Helena Bonham-Carter

VIOLETTE ◆Violette Szabo — secret service agent executed by the Nazis, biopic "Carve Her Name With Pride"

VIRGILIA ◆Virgilia Peterson — moderator for radio's "The Author Meets the Critic"

VIRGINIA ◆Virginia Davis — real name of Oscar winning motion picture star Geena Davis ◆ Virginia Mayo — glamorous actress of the 1940's; films include "The Secret Life of Walter Mitty" ◆ Virginia Woolf — British novelist who wrote in a stream of consciousness style

VIRNA ◆Virna Lisi — voluptuous leading lady in Jack Lemmon's "How to Murder Your Wife"

VITTORIA ◆Vittoria Lepanto — actress who portrayed the notorious nineteenth century courtesan Camille

VITYA ◆Vitya Vronsky — pianist who performed two-piano concerts with her husband Victor

VIVA ◆Viva Birkett — actress who played George du Maurier's tragic heroine Trilby in "Svengali"

VIVECA ◆Viveca Lindfors — actress whose roles included Catherine the Great in the film "Tempest"

VIVEKA ◆Viveka Davis — actress whose roles included Cak on the Dana Delany sitcom "Sweet Surrender"

VIVI ◆Vivi Jannis — actress whose roles included Myrtle Davis on TV's "Father Knows Best"

VIVIAN ◆Vivian Blaine — actress in stage and film version of "Guys and Dolls" ◆ Vivian Vance — actress who played Ethel Mertz, the next door neighbor on TV's "I Love Lucy"

VIVIANE ◆Viviane Tomance — actress whose roles included the ultimate femme fatale Carmen in film

VIVIEN ◆Vivien Leigh — role of feisty Scarlett O'Hara in "Gone With the Wind" launched her career

VIVIENNE ◆Vivienne Segal — Broadway star whose plays include "Desert Song" and "Pal Joey"

VONETTA ◆Vonetta McGee — actress whose roles included Sister Indigo on the TV drama "Hell Town"

WALLIS ◆Wallis Simpson — divorcee for whom Edward VIII abdicated the throne of England

WANDA ◆ Wanda Jackson — rockabilly artist, hits include "There's a Party Goin' On"

WENDIE JO ◆ Wendie Jo Sperber — actress in TV's "Bosom Buddies" and Spielberg's comedy film "1941"

WENDY ◆ Wendy Schaal — actress who played waitress Cassie Cranston on the sitcom "It's a Living" ◆ Wendy Thomas — namesake of Wendy's hamburger chain, founded by her father ◆ Wendy Wilson — singer with rock group "Wilson Phillips," daughter of Beach Boy Brian Wilson

WHITNEY ◆ Whitney Blake — actress whose roles included Dennis' mother on TV's "Dennis the Menace" ◆ Whitney Houston — chart-topping pop singer, niece of Dionne Warwick, turned actress in "Bodyguard"

WHITTNI ◆ Whittni Wright — precocious child actor playing a child actor in Nick Nolte's "I'll Do Anything"

WHOOPI ◆ Whoopi Goldberg — stand up comic turned box office star in "Sister Act"

WILHELMINA ◆ Queen Wilhelmina — Dutch ruler who became the symbol of Dutch resistance during World War II ◆ Wilhelmina Cooper — founded Wilhelmina Models

WILLA ◆ Mary Willa Gummer — daughter of actress Meryl Streep ◆ Willa Cather — Pulitzer Prize winning author for "One of Ours" ◆ Willa Mamet — daughter of Lindsay Crouse and David Mamet

WILLI ◆ Willi Burke — actress whose roles included Fran Gordon on the soap "One Life to Live" ◆ Willi Smith — fashion designer, founder of Willi Wear

WILLIE MAE ◆ Willie Mae — hit the charts with her hit song "Hound Dog"

WILLOW ◆ Willow Amber Daltrey — daughter of English singer Roger Daltrey

WILMA ◆ Wilma Deering (c) — Buck Rogers' young, pretty, constant companion in comics, TV, and movies ◆ Wilma Flintstone (c) — wife of Fred on TV's animated stone-age classic "The Flintstones" ◆ Wilma Rudolph — triple Olympic gold medal winner, biopic "Wilma"

WINIFRED ◆ Winifred Black — one of the first woman reporters

WINONA ◆Winona Ryder — actress who became a big hit in "Beetlejuice," her real name is Winona Horowitz

WISA ◆Wisa D'Orso — Wisa D'Orso Dancers were regulars on the funny "Jonathan Winters Show"

WYN ◆Wyn Cahoon — actress in the Cary Grant comedy "The Awful Truth"

WYNETTE ◆Wynette Pugh — real name of country western singer Tammy Wynette

WYNNE ◆Wynne Gibson — leading lady of film in the 1940's who worked her way up from the chorus

WYNONNA ◆Wynonna Judd — younger half of the mother-daughter country music act "The Judds"

WYOMIA ◆Wyomia Tyus — first woman Olympic double gold medal winner in the 100 meter sprint

XAVIERA ◆Xaviera Hollander — madam of one of the most famous bordellos in New York, film "The Happy Hooker"

XERNONA ◆Xernona Clayton — creator of "Moments in History" for Black History Month on TNT

YAHEE ◆Yahee — actress whose roles included Star Wilson Stoner on the soap "The Edge of Night"

YANA ◆Yana Nirvana — actress who played Sgt. Martha Haggerty on the sitcom "The Last Precinct"

YASMEEN ◆Yasmeen Ghauri — 1990's top fashion model

YASMIN ◆Yasmin Aga Khan — princess who is the daughter of Rita Hayworth and Prince Aly Khan

YASMINE ◆Yasmine Bleeth — actress whose roles included Lee Ann Demarest on the soap "One Life to Live"

YEARDLEY ◆Yeardley Smith — actress who played Louise on "Herman's Head," also the voice of Lisa Simpson

YOCHABEL ◆Yochabel — Martha Scott played her in DeMille's biblical epic "The Ten Commandments"

YOKO ◆Yoko Ono — longtime wife and collaborator of Beatle John Lennon ◆ Yoko Tani — Japanese actress, films include "Marco Polo"

YOLANDA ◆Yolanda King — actress daughter of Martin Luther King, Jr.

YOLANDE ◆ Yolande Donlan — American successful on the British stage as the dumb blond in "Born Yesterday" ◆ Susannah Yolande Fletcher — real name of actress Susannah York

YSAYE ◆ Ysaye Barnwell — Sweet Honey in the Rock, hit "B'lieve I'll Rin On See, What the Ends Gonna See"

YVETTE ◆ Yvette Mimieux — actress in "Death Takes a Holiday," "The Black Hole," "The Time Machine" ◆ Yvette Wilson — a supporting cast member on TV's "Thea"

YVONNE ◆ Yvonne DeCarlo — actress who played Lily Munster, the monster mother on TV's "The Munsters" ◆ Yvonne Elliman — rock singer, debut hit single "I Don't Know How to Love Him"

ZAIDA ◆ Zaida Coles — actress whose roles included Anna Ford on the soap "The Doctors"

ZANDRA ◆ Zandra Rhodes — revolutionary dress designer

ZARA ◆ Zara Cully — played obnoxious mother Olivia Jefferson on the sitcom "The Jeffersons"

ZARAH ◆ Zarah Leander — actress whose roles included Mary Queen of Scots in "Heart of a Queen"

ZASU ◆ ZaSu Pitts — actress whose roles included Gale Storm's sidekick on TV's "The Gale Storm Show"

ZEFFIE ◆ Zeffie Tilbury — actress whose credits include "Tobacco Road" and "Maid of Salem"

ZELDA ◆ Zelda Fitzgerald — author wife of F. Scott Fitzgerald, wrote "Save Me the Waltz"

ZELMA ◆ Zelma Hedrick — real name of actress Kathryn Grayson

ZEME ◆ Zeme North — actress who played Judy Kimball on TV's "The Double Life of Henry Phyfe"

ZENA ◆ Zena Marshall — British actress of French ancestry, appeared in "Dr. No" ◆ Zena Walker — Tony winner for "A Day in the Death of Joe Egg"

ZERNA ◆ Zerna Sharp — teacher who created the "Dick and Jane" series of books

ZINA ◆ Zina Bethune — actress who played Robin Lang Fletcher on the soap "The Guiding Light" ◆ Zina Garrison — Olympic gold medal tennis player

ZITA ◆Zita Moulton — actress in Cary Grant's comedy "The Awful Truth"

ZIZI ◆Zizi Jeanmaire — French ballerina and sometime Hollywood film star

ZOE ◆Zoe Kravitz — daughter of actress Lisa Bonet from "The Cosby Show" ◆Zoe Akins — Pulitzer Prize winner for "The Old Maid" ◆Zoe Emily Winkler — daughter of actor Henry Winkler — the Fonz on TV's "Happy Days"

ZOHRA ◆Zohra Alton — actress whose roles included Greta Powers on the soap "A Time to Live" ◆Zohra Lampert — star of TV series "The Girl with Something Extra"

ZOLA ◆Zola Taylor — member of The Platters, debut hit single "Tell the World"

ZONA ◆Zona Gale — novelist of small-town midwestern life, Pulitzer for "Miss Lulu Bett"

ZORA ◆Zora Neale Hurston — author whose works include "Mules and Men" and "Their Eyes Were Watching God"

ZSA ZSA ◆Zsa Zsa Gabor — famous Hollywood actress who has resurrected her acting career

EXPERT CHILD-CARE ADVICE AND HELP—

from St. Martin's Paperbacks

FAMILY RULES
Kenneth Kaye, Ph.D.
Here's how to custom-design a straightforward set of rules on discipline that will fit *your* family.
_____ 95220-1 $5.99 U.S./$6.99 Can.

THE FIRST FIVE YEARS
Virginia E. Pomeranz, M.D., with Dodi Schultz
The classic guide to baby and child care, including answers to the 33 most-asked questions.
_____ 90921-7 $3.99 U.S./$4.99 Can.

BABY SIGNALS
Diane Lynch-Fraser, Ed.D., and Ellenmorris Tiegerman, Ph.D.
There are four distinct styles which infants communicate with—and this book tells you what they are and how to respond.
_____ 92456-9 $3.99 U.S./$4.99 Can.